D1109239

UNIVERSITY OF WINNIPEG
PORTAGE & BALMORAL
WINNIPEG 2, MAN. CANADA

DISCARDED

CHILDREN IN THE POLITICAL SYSTEM: Origins of Political Legitimacy

McGRAW-HILL SERIES IN POLITICAL SCIENCE

JA
76
·E3
1969

CHiLDreN in the POLitiCAL SYstem

ORIGINS OF POLITICAL LEGITIMACY

DAVID EASTON
Professor of Political Science
University of Chicago

JACK DENNIS
Associate Professor of Political Science
University of Wisconsin

with the assistance of **Sylvia Easton**

McGraw-Hill Book Company
New York St. Louis San Francisco London Sydney Toronto Mexico Panama

Children in the Political System:
Origins of Political Legitimacy

Copyright © 1969 by McGraw-Hill, Inc. All rights reserved. Printed in the United States of America. No part of this publication may be reproduced, stored in a retrieval system, or transmitted, in any form or by any means, electronic, mechanical, photocopying, recording, or otherwise, without the prior written permission of the publisher.

Library of Congress Catalog Card Number 68-58506

18844

1234567890 MAMM 7654321069

Drawings by School Children in Madison, Wisconsin.

Politician: **Mark Dennis, 6**
Policeman: **Judy Yelk, 10**
Capitol: **Peter Thalbofer, 9**
Riot: **Louis Colescott, 10**
Campaign Headquarters: **Margaret Zahn, 11**

For Steve E.
and for Brent, Mark, and Joseph D.
Our frequent and favorite subjects

PREFACE

The reader has two options as he approaches this book. He may read it from a general interest in what children learn about politics. In this event we hope he will find much to inform him, especially about the way in which children make their first connections with the political system and about the kinds of sentiments this relationship stimulates. Children, our evidence argues, are not the political innocents they were once thought to be.

If the reader chooses broader perspectives, however, he will find that this book is not merely a description of the political attitudes and knowledge of children. It represents an effort to draw together in a new and meaningful way empirical political theory and data about children in the political system.

In all the disciplines in which empirical theory has acquired some momentum of its own, the complaint has in due course arisen that theory becomes estranged from fact. This has certainly been as true of physics as it has been, say, of econometrics or psychology. As empirical theory has taken the first tentative steps toward autonomous development in political science, this criticism has already begun to raise its head here as well.

It is questionable whether the accumulation of data and the elaboration of theory can ever avoid a certain degree of independent development in which each follows a path divergent from the other. Partial separation for varying lengths of time may even be an essential condition for the discovery of new knowledge. Each kind of enterprise — factual research and theorizing — has a logic of its own which, if not carried to its implicit conclusions, may defeat the pursuit of reliable explanation and understanding.

For example, to deliver on its full potential and utility, empirical theorizing requires maximum freedom, uninhibited by what is presumed to be known, to pursue the logical implications of its premises and theorems. Whereas the rules of empirical research exhort the investigator to keep his inferences close to the data — overinterpretation is a frequent charge — it is only through temporary release from bondage to the facts that the theorist can usefully ply his trade. In physics, mathematics has helped to emancipate the imagination from this indenture to data. In political science, however, only the first groping and uncertain steps to secure this release through mathematics have as yet been taken.

Our description may seem to violate the approved canons of science, by which theory and empirical research are to go hand in hand in intimate and fruitful partnership. By ideal standards, data collection and analysis are to be ordered by theory; theorizing is to hew close to the known facts. But the history of science is never as neat and orderly as its ex post facto rationalization. The scientific imagination will not be curbed by so neat and simple a rule.

What appears in fact is a cyclical pattern. Theory and data may survive for long periods in comparative isolation. Historically, one may be emphasized, indeed exaggerated out of proportion, at the expense of the other. Severe dissatisfaction of each with the other arises. The tensions finally reach a point that inspires efforts at their reduction. Attempts are then made to reformulate theory so that it becomes more relevant to ongoing empirical research; data collection and analysis in turn may be pointed more directly to the validation of theory. In the resultant realignment of sights, both theorizing and empirical research may be set going in new directions until once again some distance between them arises and efforts are again needed to bridge the newly created chasms. To this cyclical evolution there can be no end in the search for more certain knowledge and understanding.

This book is one effort to bring theory and research into closer accord. We seek to stretch a slender footbridge between systems (or persistence) theory, as it has been developing within the terms of its own logic, and behavior in the political system. General theorizing has dictated the major hypothesis that the persistence of any kind of political system at all depends on the input of diffuse support to a number of political objects, among them the structure of political authority. As a case study, we wished to know when and how this support for political authority arises in the American political system. Our speculations had led us to believe that it has its origins at a very improbable age, childhood, and further that this early source has profound consequences for the functioning of political systems.

Our research, therefore, examines aspects of the socialization of children in the area of politics. Our theoretical interest in political socialization began early in the 1950s, and it took empirical form as early as 1955. Six years and about fifteen pilot studies later, the final instrument that has provided the bulk of the data analyzed in this book had been designed and administered under a project of which David Easton and Robert Hess were the principal investigators. Our methods and procedures are described in the Appendix.

In the first phase of our research — the construction of the questionnaire, its administration in the field, and the initial compilation of the data —we had the expert and dedicated assistance of David Jackson as project director with major support from Jack

Dennis and Judith Torney. Jack Dennis then joined David Easton in analyzing the data for their relevance to the functioning of political systems. Robert Hess and Judy Torney assumed responsibility for a separate analysis of the specific implications of the data for the psychology of child development. In various periods of our project we were able to rely on the enthusiastic and insightful participation of a number of graduate students, most of whom have since that time become actively engaged in teaching and research of their own: Reginald Bartholomew, Keith Billingsley, William Fisher, John Fitzgerald, Charles Hamilton, Ronald Inglehart, Daniel Leatherman, Kenneth McRoberts, Roger Masters, Tadao Okamura, Albert Robles, Margaret Tropp, and Elliott White.

The research analyzed in this book has been supported by the Bureau of Research of the Office of Education, U.S. Department of Health, Education, and Welfare. Aside from providing this support, the Office of Education played no part in and bears no responsibility for the delineation of the research, the selection of specific topics, the development of the questionnaire, the determination of the sample, the interpretation of the data, or the conclusions derived therefrom. Supplementary financial aid was provided by the Social Science Research Committee of the Division of the Social Sciences at the University of Chicago and by the Research Committee of the Graduate School at the University of Wisconsin.

To Necia Gamm we are grateful for skilled and arduous labor in piloting the manuscript through the important details involved in its typing. Barbara Dennis aided our efforts in preparing many of the original typescripts and in providing useful editorial criticisms.

The substance of chapters 2 and 6 has appeared previously in D. Easton, "The Theoretical Relevance of Political Socialization," *Canadian Journal of Political Science,* 1, pp. 124-146, 1968; and D. Easton and J. Dennis, "The Child's Image of Government." *The Annals of the American Academy of Political and Social Science,* 361, pp. 40-57, 1965. We wish to acknowledge permission to reprint these articles in revised form.

David Easton
Jack Dennis

CONTENTS

TABLES

FIGURES

CHILDREN IN THE POLITICAL SYSTEM: Origins of Political Legitimacy

A POLITICAL
THEORY OF
POLITICAL SOCIALIZATION

SOCIALIZATION
AND
THE POLITICAL SYSTEM

Child. *"There's somewhere."*
Father. *"I can't park there."*
Child. *"Why?"*
Father. *"It's not allowed."*
Child. *"Who say so?"*
Father. *"I'll get a ticket."*
Child. *"Uh."*
Father. *"A policeman will stop me."*
Child. *"Oh."*

When a three-and-a-half-year-old child, safely seated in the backseat of his father's car, helpfully sought to point out a parking space and entered into this laconic conversation, he learned if not his first political lesson at least the beginning of an important one. He was being introduced to the notion that his father is not omnipotent, that there is a power external to the family to which even his father has to submit, and that somehow the policeman represents this power.

This episode symbolizes the very tender age, even earlier than primary school, at which political learning begins. As political theorists from classical days to the present have repeatedly proclaimed, the kind of power called "authority" and the willingness of people to accept it within specifiable limits are central phenomena of political life. It would seem to be an appropriate confirmation of this insight for the child to begin his understanding of his political role in society by sensing the significance of political authority for even the humdrum routines of daily existence.

THE SOCIALIZATION OF SUPPORT

Even though we begin by talking about children and will extensively analyze data about them, this book is really about political systems. It addresses itself to one major condition—socialization—that contributes to the capacity of a political system to persist in a world either of stability or of change.

A political system is that system of behavior through which society is able to make decisions that most people accept as authoritative or binding most of the time. From the perspective of a systems analysis of political life[1] one of the critical features of a political system is that it is open to disturbances from its environment. Through these it is subject to various kinds of stress. One of the conditions that make it possible for an open system of this kind to persist even in the face of stress is the level of commitment or support that members are prepared and able to extend to it. Our central purpose will be to investigate how this kind of support is marshaled through the early socialization of those new to the system by virtue of their birth in it. Our starting point therefore will be political theory, and we shall end on the same note. But the connecting link between beginning and end will be an analysis of a considerable body of data about childhood political orientations.

Through a systems analysis of politics we are led to the hypothesis that every system utilizes a multitude of typical devices for attempting to build up support and sustain it at some minimal level, even though not all systems are equally successful.[2] A system may carefully match its outputs to demands in the hope of keeping its members more contented. It may persistently nourish a set of beliefs conducive to winning the confidence and trust of its adult members. It may even as a last resort compel by force those who refuse to commit themselves spontaneously. But among mechanisms such as these it may also seek to win the members by shaping their orientations and behavior patterns at the earliest feasible moment after birth into the system.

Theoretically childhood would seem to be an appropriate starting point for the absorption of political orientations. From Plato through Bodin and Rousseau, classical philosophers have argued on behalf of an early start for political education. What is learned during the first few years, it has been assumed from time immemorial, is less easily dislodged later in life. But what is theoretically imaginable is not always empirically feasible. At what stage can a system in fact begin to expose its youngest members to political orientations relevant to support or for that matter to any other major aspect of a system, with any hope of meaningful impact? By orientation we imply all the perceptions (cognitions, knowledge), affect (feelings and attitudes), and evaluations (values and norms) through which a person relates himself to social objects. We can arrive at a tentative answer to this question if we locate the age at which systems do in fact first manage to evoke political orientations, favorable or hostile, from their maturing members. We can reformulate the question therefore and ask: Where do the earliest roots of political perceptions, sentiments, and values lie? Specifically, is there any evidence at all that either negative or positive orientations toward a system have their source in childhood experiences?

It is our theoretical interest in the origins of support as a major mechanism in the persistence of political systems that leads us directly to children. Notwithstanding preconceptions, until recently very prevalent, about the political innocence of children, we shall show that by the time children leave elementary school they have assembled a formidable array of basic political orientations. Among them are relatively well-defined sentiments about the system, and not all of them necessarily favorable or supportive. But our inquiry will ineluctably lead us to the hypothesis that the persistence of some kind of system may in part be dependent upon the success of a society in producing children most of whom acquire positive feelings about it.

In its main objective, therefore, this book is an inquiry about the input of support, a problem dictated by general theory. But because we search for the early sources of this support, we are forced to concentrate on childhood, a period of life when basic political orientations first take shape. Derivatively therefore we become concerned with political socialization during childhood.

Our data are based on a purposively selected sample of white urban children ages seven through thirteen or fourteen, in elementary schools selected from four large and four small metropolitan regions in the United States. These are located in four major geographical regions, the Northeast, Southeast, Midwest, and Far West.[3] From our data about these children we have sought to identify some of the major dimensions in political socialization that contribute to the level of support put into the American system, as a test case. This single study about children and their basic political orientations should help to extend our knowledge about the conditions surrounding the persistence of political systems as a class of phenomena.

But before we can proceed to an analysis of our data, certain theoretical issues need to be raised. First, what do we mean by socialization? There are many ways of describing the processes to which the word is presumed to refer, and each description helps to predetermine the kinds of data examined, the modes of analysis applied to them, and even their final interpretation.

Second, what part does socialization play in helping us to understand the functioning of political systems? Although there has been too little theorizing on this score to clarify the central significance of political socialization, at least two theoretical perspectives appear implicit in the literature. By examining these we shall put ourselves in a favorable position to assess the alternatives opened up by our own systems-analytic approach.

Finally, although we shall begin by assuming that childhood socialization, as contrasted with socialization during infancy, adolescence, and adulthood, has vital consequences for the persistence of political systems, we shall have to pause at the outset to examine this presupposition. Is it even plausible to say that political socialization does originate in childhood? Affirmation is not a foregone conclusion. Some theorists would seem to argue against it; others who would acknowledge its occurrence at this early phase in the life cycle would contend that whatever is learned has little bearing on subsequent political behavior.

In Parts 1 and 2 of this book we address ourselves to these three types of questions. Then in Part 3 we shall turn to a description of our research and an analysis of our data as they bear on our major theoretical problems. We shall seek to penetrate the obscuring screen of childhood to observe the ways in which children, in one political system, that of the United States, begin to perceive critical elements in political life and to learn to put in or withhold support. In Part 4 we shall look at group differences in an effort to explain some of the orientations of the children. And in Part 5 we shall draw together the fundamental implications of the analysis for a theory of political systems.

THE MEANING OF POLITICAL SOCIALIZATION

What is the theoretical relevance of socialization for an understanding of the way in which political systems operate? This question will engage our attention throughout Part 1.

Although we have already hinted at our own theoretical perspectives, we shall now approach the issue more systematically. To do so, we need to deal with several problems. What do we mean when we refer to the study of political socialization? How have others interpreted the theoretical import of research in this area? For what purposes are these other modes of conceptualization useful? After these questions are answered, we shall be in a position to propose an alternative theoretical perspective, one that informs the body of our research. In this chapter we shall explore the possible meanings of socialization, leaving the other questions to the next two chapters.

Definition of socialization

We shall define *political socialization* restrictively as *those developmental processes through which persons acquire political orientations and patterns of behavior.* Simple as it is, the implications of this conceptualization for theory and research are both numerous and consequential.

Socialization identifies a developmental process, one that takes place over time. It is in this reference to the development of orientations that the study of socialization differs most strikingly from the usual attitude and opinion polls. The latter are primarily cross-sectional in character; they describe the orientations persons hold at a moment in time. Normally research about political attitudes turns to existing or immediately preceding conditions to explain a person's views or his actions. The emphasis is on current attitudes and behavior explained by reference to current experiences. But insofar as opinion-survey research deals with changes in attitudes, it verges on research about socializing phenomena and contributes to our understanding of them.

Omitted from this preoccupation of attitude and opinion surveys with current determinants, however, is a concentrated effort to discover the extent to which orientations and behavior are molded by circumstances and events from the past. In contrast, the idea of socialization alerts us precisely to the need to take into account those past processes through which orientations have been acquired. The past acquisition process itself becomes a determinant with a possible independent influence upon subsequent orientations. It thereby should help to explain the nature of the current and future knowledge, values, and feelings of the persons involved. In this meaning of socialization, a cross-sectional study of a set of orientations, with no historical depth, contributes in itself very little to an understanding of the function of prior experiences. It lacks an etiological perspective that might enable us to explain some portion of the present in terms of past events.

But the past itself is not an undifferentiated bloc of time. It represents a process through which persons may (or may not) change as time runs on. Each present moment has as a possible determinant all preceding moments. In this lies the source of an emerging pattern of change for a person or for an aggregate of persons. We often refer to this process by suggesting that a person has "developed" in a certain way. By this we mean that he has been exposed to a particular sequence of events that can be expected to produce a particular or a characteristic outcome.

Identification of time as a determinant therefore inevitably leads to a developmental perspective. We look not at a given moment in the past but at a sequence of time periods so as to be able to appreciate the extent to which current behavior or orientations are the outcome of a characteristic pattern of development. The study of socialization goes therefore beyond simple etiology, a search for origins. It includes a search for developmental patterns during the originating phases.

Socialization research accordingly directs our attention to questions such as the following: Where do patterns of behavior and orientations come from? How do they begin, and how do they change as a person matures biologically? To what extent can orientations or behavior at any moment of time be explained by what has occurred through a sequence of earlier time periods?

Where we begin the etiological inquiry will depend upon where our insight informs us that continuing effects over time have had their origins. Although it is common to think of childhood as the major formative period for later behavior, in fact socialization is known to be a continuous process, one that typically continues into old age. An adult immigrant into a society, for example, whatever his age, is in many ways as new to it as a newborn child. But the resocialization of adults suggested in this illustration raises problems that are vastly different from those we meet among children.[4] Thus for an understanding of the way in which new members become integrated in varying degrees into the purposes of, say, an existing business enterprise, an army, a religious organization, or a prison, the desocialization of old practices over time and the resocialization of the persons undergoing the new experiences may be central explanatory variables. Hence experiences during the adult phase of socialization may loom large. But in many areas of inquiry we may nevertheless hold to the theory that what is learned early in life tends to be retained and to shape later attitudes and behavior. Here the search for an adequate explanation may impel us to return to the period of childhood as well.

Whatever the phase in the life cycle on which we concentrate, an interest in socialization indicates the acceptance of the premise that the present cannot always be explained exclusively in its own terms. An important determinant of current orientations and behavior is to be found in what has happened over a span of time in the past. It is this developmental quality that sets research into socialization apart from cross-sectional studies of current attitudes and practices and from a general interest in attitude change.

Omissions from the definition

By perceiving political socialization simply as a developmental process through which orientations and patterns of behavior are acquired, we depart from most earlier kinds of definitions. The latter typically refer to phenomena that we consider too variable to include with confidence in the basic description of political socialization. In the first place, for example, unlike standard prevalent definitions of socialization, ours says nothing about the nature of the acquisition processes. It does not specify who or what the agencies and agents of socialization are. It does not even presume to indicate in advance whether children learn their attitudes and behavior from others or acquire them from autonomous experiences. In the second place, our definition does not even allude to the systemic consequences of socialization, such as whether it serves to perpetuate, stabilize, or destroy a system.

To be sure, the nature of the acquisition process and the effects of socialization on a system are both central subjects for inquiry.

But they are variable phenomena in the socializing processes. Any substantive assertion about them in a definition would be inappropriate if only because it would prematurely foreclose alternative possibilities. Hence we deliberately refrain from identifying any specific aquisition process or systemic consequences. To explicate more fully the implications of our own definition, we shall closely examine these deliberate omissions of characteristics and outcomes that others typically include.

The nature of the acquisition process

Our definition is restrictive not only because it focuses on the time dimension among determinants of behavior but also because it insists on keeping this developmental factor separate from considerations about the nature of the acquisition process itself. To clarify this point let us look at a representative definition of socialization that contrasts with ours. Socialization, it is frequently proposed, is "a process of learning through which an individual is prepared, with varying degrees of success, to meet the requirements laid down by other members of society for his behavior in a variety of situations. These requirements are always attached to one or another of the recognized positions or statuses in this society such as husband, son, employee, and adult male."[5]

In addition to implying that there is some process of acquisition going on through time, a point with which we of course have no argument, this typical definition also suggests something about the way in which persons acquire their orientations. It leads us to believe that it is central to the socializing processes that others should lay down for the child what he is to know or how he is to behave, and the "others" normally turn out to be adults. But whoever the socializers may be, the view is usually explicit that socialization consists exclusively of a transmission process whereby orientations and behaviors are passed from one generation to another.

No one could quarrel about this recognition of a transmission belt along which orientations move. Children undoubtedly do learn from their parents and from other significant adults (as well as peers) in their environment. But does this fully describe the nature of the acquistion process?

What this view leaves out is that socialization may signify more than or even something other than the inculcation of a culture or the absorption of orientations from others. It may, for example, be a product of what we would call autonomous learning and of the projection of inferences from such learning in one sphere to experiences in another. Socialization need not always involve a process through which one person, usually an adult, instills orientations in another person, usually a newcomer in a society, such as a child, or an immigrant, or a new member of a group. There may well be circumstances, for example, in which the orientations a child acquires cannot be attributed to any agent upon whom he models his behavior, with whom he identifies, or by whom he is influenced, as through a pattern of rewards and punishments.

Again, the process of socialization may and normally does involve a transmission belt connecting the younger and older generations. Whatever passes along this belt constitutes the content of socialization. But this describes only one mechanism through which a person may acquire (or fail to acquire) orientations. What is equally pertinent is that a person may just as frequently learn to behave or orient himself in a certain way out of the depths of his own raw intragenerational experiences. It is too constricting to limit the acquisition process to induction or inculcation by others. Such an interpretation precludes independent learning; it disregards the observable variability of the mechanisms of socialization.

Thus a child may learn to approve of the political authorities because he has been taught to do so by his parents or because he has modeled himself on the behavior of his older siblings. But his attitudes toward the authorities may also be formed partly through direct experience, unmediated by transmission from others and interpreted in the light of his inner needs. For example, he may learn to dislike all authorities, including, by projection or transference of affect, the political, because of what he interprets as unjust treatment at the hands of familial authorities. A self-learned orientation such as this may become part of the personality structure of the child, and it may override alternative political orientations that he might otherwise have inadvertently absorbed from the culture or that relevant adults might have deliberately sought to inculcate. But for the possibility of independent learning we could scarcely account for many instances in which new generations adopt political positions and orientations in direct conflict with preceding generations, as in the case of the so-called "protest politics" among young people in the United States during the 1960s.

It would not seem useful therefore to include any conclusions about the specific nature of the acquisition process in the conceptualization of socialization itself. By leaving this matter for research we open the door to an understanding of an important source of change over the generations. The maturing generation may turn out differently from its predecessors not because of "failure" in the transmission belt in some way but because of some unique combination of experiences and personality predispositions on the part of children that leads them to interpret life differently. In this way, through autonomous learning, a new generation may be able to elude the hand of the past, however active this hand may be in trying to guide maturing children toward conformity with tradition or toward some other preconceived goal. What a child becomes or what happens to an adult over time may be in part a product of longitudinal patterns gradually altered through various kinds of autonomous experiences. We need not prejudge the matter especially by incorporating it in our definition of socialization itself.

The systemic consequences of socialization

If the nature of the way in which children acquire orientations and behavior need not be specified in advance, neither need we include any specific kinds of consequences for the system under consideration. Yet the representative definition of socialization that we noted earlier embraces some advance conclusions about the consequences that socialization apparently must have for the system. It predicts that socialization will prepare the individual, "with varying degrees of success, to meet the requirements laid down by other members of society for his behavior." Other definitions typically convey the same type of message. At times it is argued, for example, that through socialization the child will develop "the proper (i.e., adult) kinds of interaction with others"[6] or that he will be subject to a "process of induction into the political culture,"[7] presumably the existing culture. These definitions clearly leave the impression that socialization must lead to conformity with established patterns or at the very least with the standards transmitted by the older generations.

We scarcely need to insist, in a world so marked with generational conflict, that each succeeding generation need not pattern itself on its predecessors exclusively. Innovation is not only possible, it may even be considered desirable by the previous generation.[8] Not that this is usually overlooked in the literature, whatever the limitations on outcome suggested by the definitions. But what is more likely to be neglected is that regardless of the intentions of the socializers, those being socialized may strike out on their own and create substantially new roles.[9] The definitions would seem to exclude or overlook this possibility, a point to which we shall return more fully from a different direction in the next chapter.

Our own definition of socialization, however, leaves the outcome moot. It is not essential for an adequate description of the central characteristics of socialization to specify its consequences for a system. We need not settle in advance whether the process replicates the existing society or ends in innovations unexpected or undesired by the older generations. Indeed, the prevalent tendency of definitions in the literature, toward identifying socialization as a process for perpetuation of the status quo (or of stability, a frequent synonym), has transparent undesirable theoretical implications. We shall return to these in the next section in a somewhat broader context. It is enough here to draw attention to the predictable variability in outcomes of socialization and hence to the unnecessary limitation in defining it in terms of its possible results for a system.

It is therefore useful, in order not to prejudice the identification of problems for research and the interpretation of findings, to eliminate from the definition all references to the nature of the acquisition process and to the consequences of socialization. This frees us to use "socialization" in a neutral way, to refer only to the developmental processes through which orientations and behavior are (or are not) acquired.

DISCIPLINARY PERSPECTIVES ABOUT SOCIALIZATION

The definition of a concept is only a first step toward spelling out its theoretical significance. It indicates to us in general the nature of the processes we will be examining, but it does not point to the kinds of political phenomena with respect to which we ought to examine these processes. We need to probe further into the theoretical relevance that socialization has for an understanding of the political system.

The disconcerting fact is that all political practices and orientations have historical antecedents. We do not inherit our political behavior, attitudes, values, and knowledge through our genes. They must be learned in some way. There is therefore potentially an infinitude of topics that could become the subject of socialization research. We need some theoretical guidance to sort out the political orientations that we will find worth investigating.

Implicitly, by formulating our problem in this way, we have already made a major theoretical commitment. In advocating criteria for establishing theoretical relevance in politics, we are indirectly affirming that in the study of *political* socialization we may have objectives different from inquiry using other disciplinary perspectives. Let us glance very briefly at the relevance of socialization in the other disciplines the better to appreciate the need for an independent focus in political science.

As we might expect, because each social science concentrates on a different if overlapping set of subjects, each has appropriately developed its own perspectives on the significance of socialization. There is as yet little sign of a general theory of socialization on the horizon; it is not even clear what such a theory might begin to look like. For example, psychology, in which the vast bulk of research into socialization has been conducted and in which the main guidelines were initially set, has concentrated on the part that early life experiences and training play in the formation of personality. Child-rearing practices have constituted its universe of research, with attention to the origins and development of such personality traits as aggression, achievement, oral behavior, dependency, fear, trust, intelligence, and moral judgment.[10]

Given the diversity of interests in sociology as a discipline, it is difficult to characterize comprehensively its focuses in the area of socialization. But two major concerns have arisen. For those in sociology concentrating on personality as a major determinant of social behavior, personality is often conceived as structurally determined—i.e., it is interpreted as the sum of the roles a particular person has learned to play. The characteristic motives, attitudes, and values composing an individual's personality are viewed as deriving from the combination of roles a person learns as he moves through various stages of the life cycle.[11] Other sociologists, more directly concerned with accounting for the structure of social systems, have looked upon socialization as a major mechanism in forming that structure. From this point of view socialization helps to assure the fulfillment of various postulated functional requirements of society. Socialization therefore represents a mechanism through which persons learn the skills, motives, knowledge, and evaluations viewed as necessary for the roles they will be called upon to play at various stages in their lives as participants in a specified social structure.[12]

Anthropologists have similarly moved in directions appropriate to the theoretical interests of their own discipline. To the extent that anthropology and sociology have overlapping concerns about social structure, they join hands in viewing socialization as one of the means for providing a society with what is presumed to be role structures required to fulfill its functional needs. But beyond that, research on socialization has represented a means for understanding one of the central sources of cultural continuity and change. It has led to considerable emphasis on child-rearing practices, the part they play in the formation of personality, and the effects of the interaction between the two for culture.[13]

Interest in socialization is so recent in political science—a concomitant of the behavioral revolution of the 1950s and 1960s—that it is not only appropriate but essential to ask whether this discipline has begun to interpret socialization in a way most suitable for its own purposes. This is especially critical since in effect political science has been introduced to the relevance of socialization largely by persons from other disciplines.[14] The progress of social science has typically depended upon this blending of the disciplines at their peripheries. But as is entirely appropriate, an approach to socialization in the political sphere dictated by the theoretical interests of other disciplines need not coincide with the potential concerns of political science. At the very least we cannot assume that a conceptualization of the relevance of socialization adequate for the problems of disciplines not centrally devoted to politics will automatically satisfy the major analytic needs of political science. If there is any rationale behind the division of labor that we call the social sciences, we might even expect that the contrary would be true. It therefore behooves us as students of political life to spell out the nature of our interest in socialization. This we propose to do in the following two chapters. They will guide us toward a possible political theory of socialization out of which our empirical research, analyzed in Part 3, has sprung.

NOTES

1. See D. Easton, *A Framework for Political Analysis* (Englewood Cliffs, N.J.: Prentice-Hall, 1965); and *A Systems Analysis of Political Life* (New York: Wiley, 1965) for a full discussion of a systems analysis of politics or what may alternatively be called a system-persistence theory.
2. Ibid.
3. See Appendix for a description of the study design and methods.

4. For these see S. Wheeler, "The Structure of Formally Organized Socialization Settings," in O. G. Brim, Jr., and S. Wheeler, *Socialization After Childhood: Two Essays* (New York: Wiley, 1966), pp. 51 - 106.

5. O. G. Brim, Jr., "Personality Development as Role-Learning," in I. Iscoe and H. Stevenson (eds.), *Personality Development in Children* (Austin, Tex.: University of Texas Press, 1960), p. 128.

6. R. Sears, E. Maccoby, and H. Levin, *Patterns of Child Rearing* (New York: Harper & Row, 1957), p. 465.

7. G. A. Almond, "Introduction: A Functional Approach to Comparative Politics," in G. A. Almond and J. S. Coleman (eds.), *The Politics of the Developing Areas* (Princeton, N.J.: Princeton, 1960), p. 27.

8. A. Inkeles, "Social Change and Social Character: The Role of Parental Mediation," *Journal of Social Issues*, 11, pp. 12 - 23, 1955.

9. F. A. Pinner, "Student Trade-Unionism in France, Belgium and Holland: Anticipatory Socialization and Role-Seeking," *Sociology of Education*, 37, pp. 177 - 199, 1964.

10. I. L. Child, "Socialization," in G. Lindzey (ed.), *Handbook of Social Psychology*, vol. II (Cambridge, Mass.: Addison-Wesley, 1954), pp. 655 - 692.

11. O. G. Brim, Jr., and S. Wheeler, op. cit.

12. T. Parsons, *The Social System* (Glencoe, Ill.: Free Press, 1951); T. Parsons and R. F. Bales, *Family, Socialization and Interaction Process* (New York: Free Press, 1955); M. J. Levy, Jr., *The Structure of Society* (Princeton, N.J.: Princeton, 1952).

13. D. F. Aberle, "Culture and Socialization," in F. L. K. Hsu (ed.), *Psychological Anthropology: Approaches to Culture and Personality* (Homewood, Ill.: Dorsey, 1961); G. Gorer, *The American People* (New York: Norton, 1948); M. Mead, *Soviet Attitudes Towards Authority* (New York: McGraw-Hill, 1951); R. Benedict, *The Chrysanthemum and the Sword* (Boston: Houghton Mifflin, 1946); A. F. C. Wallace, *Culture and Personality* (New York: Random House, 1961).

14. H. Hyman, *Political Socialization* (New York: Free Press, 1959); and the works of G. Gorer, M. Mead, R. Benedict, E. Fromm and T. W. Adorno, among others.

2

THE THEORETICAL
RELEVANCE OF
POLITICAL SOCIALIZATION

What kinds of special interest might students of politics have in socialization? Clearly we are not particularly concerned with personality formation in and of itself, as are psychologists, or with the way in which developmental patterns contribute to social structure in general or to the perpetuation and change of a culture, as are sociologists and anthropologists respectively. These concerns of general socialization are not beyond the bounds of our interests, but they do not constitute the central focus of political science. They fall within our purview only when it can be shown that knowledge of this kind will somehow help us to understand some specifically political problems better.

But how are we to test the relevance of studies in socialization for political research? To do so, we need some guidance in the form of a theory or conceptual structure, that will serve to identify the major variables about which research might be initiated.

TYPES OF THEORIES OF SOCIALIZATION

Theory about socialization might take one of three forms, even though no one form is completely independent of the others. First, it might be a *general theory of socialization*. Presumably this would be designed to describe and explain at the most general level the way in which socialization occurs, regardless of subject area. Although such a theory may still lie on a very distant horizon, students of political science could use it to good advantage. Concentration on this type of theory, however, would distract them from their central concerns, the explanation of political phenomena.

Second, we might focus on a *theory of political socialization*. From this perspective our objective would be to attempt to understand the way in which socialization occurs in the political sphere. The nature of the subject matter and the salience level of politics in a society might generate socializing processes in this area different from those, say, about sex roles, economic behavior, or religious patterns. Thus there is little question that the family plays a vital part in transmitting various aspects of a society's general culture and in preparing a child for the kinds of occupational or sex roles he may be called upon to play. But in the area of politics, some important differences seem to occur. Only certain kinds of orientations may be the subject of family socialization; others may depend more on agencies outside the family.[1] Childhood may be the period for learning basic orientations and adolescence and young adulthood for acquiring attitudes on issues and on specific candidates for office. We can conceive that in time a specific theory of socialization in the political sphere — a theory of political socialization — may emerge. This, when combined with theories of socialization about culture in general, personality, social structure, and the like, will be a source from which a broad theory of socialization might ultimately be constructed. But a theory of political socialization has still to be contemplated in political science.

There is, however, a third kind of theory from which the most general guidance about the pertinence of research in socialization might be obtained. This is a *political theory of political socialization*. Its objective would be to demonstrate the *relevance* of socializing phenomena for the operations of political systems. Logically it is prior to the other two kinds of theory we have just discussed, for unless we have some idea about why it is important or significant to study socialization processes in the first place, there can be little reason even to begin to talk about socialization in relation to political life. We must therefore begin by inquiring into the part that socialization plays in the workings of political systems. At the theoretical level this means that we need to explore the position which, in a general theory that seeks to encompass the operations of any and all kinds of political systems, we attribute to socializing processes.

It is on a political theory of political socialization that we shall focus in this book. But what we have to say will have implications for both other types of theory.

ALTERNATIVE CRITERIA OF RELEVANCE

To explain the relevance of socialization for political research we can find at least four kinds of alternatives in the literature. These consist of a nontheoretical option and three possible political theories of political socialization — allocative theory, system-maintenance (or stability) analysis, and systems (or systems-persistence) theory. The nontheoretical posture suggests only that we charge directly into unguided exploration of this new terrain, political socialization, a strategy not to be belittled when an area has hitherto been infrequently traversed. Among the three theoretical options, the first would concern topics of socialization that fall within the sphere of what we may call political allocations. These topics would seem to be most relevant to a possible but as yet unformulated allocative theory. The second theoretical alternative—resting on presuppositions closely associated in the past with disciplines other than political science—would lead us to interpret political socialization as a means for helping us to understand integration and system maintenance in the political sphere. The final theoretical option — discussion of which will be postponed to the next chapter — represents our own positive suggestion, at the most general level of analysis, for relating political socialization to the functioning of political systems.

To be able to realize the full implications of the nontheoretical and the first two theoretical options, to which the rest of this chapter will be devoted, requires a very generous rule of interpretation. In the slender writings on socialization, these alternatives appear largely as latent premises and tendencies uncrystallized into deliberate or systematic formulations. Yet if we wish to evaluate the theoretical implications of past research and to appreciate the pressure they exert for some viable theoretical alternative, we must make the most of these options by attributing to them a coherence they have yet to obtain.

THE NONTHEORETICAL OPTION

Unfortunately the major unstated dilemma still confronting students of political socialization lies not in the selection among competing theories but in the decision to work with or without some explicit theoretical design. The easiest way out of this dilemma is to offer no pretense of operating within a definable theoretical context. As we have noted, every political orientation has antecedents of some sort; hence there is no limit to the subjects that may be adopted for research in the area of socialization. We might plunge into a discussion of any subject about children and politics that intuitively appears interesting, especially if we could link it up with adult behavior that has already drawn the continuing attention of students of politics. In this event there need be little theoretical guidance, except for the assumptions that topics of interest for the study of adults may be equally relevant for the study of children and that childhood learning may point forward to adult behavior.

If we take the little existing empirical research at its face value, without probing for latent theoretical perspectives, we might conclude that what has just been said indeed describes its character. Hyman's inventory of research in political socialization reveals that relevant research tends to do little more than to trace back to adolescence or, infrequently, to childhood, attitudes and knowledge already found useful in some way for the understanding of adult behavior.[2] For the research worker this has seemed sufficient justification in itself. Similarly Remmers and Radler have found it cogent to test pre-adults for their attitudes toward a broad range of topical issues related to American democratic practices and to daily political concerns, much as one would survey the opinions and attitudes of adults.[3] The premise would appear to be that since adolescents will soon be adults, it is helpful to try to get what may be a preview of the issue orientations of the upcoming adult generation. The selection of topics of inquiry — such as attitudes toward war, the atom bomb, civil liberties, medical care, and the economic role of government — seems to hinge on what the investigator feels most people would consider interesting and significant topics of the day. In most other studies, even in recent years, it is clear that the main topics of inquiry about political socialization have derived from or have been dependent upon research about adults.[4] Hence we find an intuitive concern in the studies on socialization for matters already made popular in the literature on voting behavior, such as party identification, political interest, political information, and issue orientations or ideology.

A nontheoretical approach such as this might have some justification in the earliest stages of inquiry, when research workers are still trying to get their initial bearings in a subject matter. But if theoretically unfocused research were to continue unabated beyond this initial phase, it could readily lead to an enormous waste of resources. We would have little means except intuition for testing, either in advance or at the conclusion of the research, whether the results were worth the effort. The results themselves would accumulate into a consistent and scientifically useful body of knowledge only by chance.

ALLOCATIVE THEORY FOR DEMOCRATIC SYSTEMS

A more fruitful and at the same time more generous rule of theoretical analysis would dictate that where no theoretical context has been explicated, the one that best fits the data might appropriately be imputed. If we were to abide by this rule, we might propose an alternative interpretation to the one just suggested to account for the content of current research; the subject-matter focus would indicate an interest that is consistent with what we may describe as a possible theory of political allocations in a democracy.[5]

A theory of political allocations would be a partial theory about system behavior in contrast, say, to a more general systems theory. Such an allocative theory about democratic systems would attempt to provide a conceptual structure for understanding how values (valued things) are allocated among members of a democracy. Some efforts in this direction have already appeared in the form of an implicit equilibrium or an explicit group theory of politics, as they were developed between the two world wars.[6] In addition, an allocative orientation is central to numerous theories about power and about decision making.[7]

Not that at the present stage of theoretical development in political science these efforts represent any pervasive, conscious striving toward a partial theory of political allocations. This would be ascribing a kind of awareness about theoretical needs and directions that is extremely difficult to achieve throughout any discipline and is only in process of developing in political science. But even in the existing theoretical literature we can begin to see the dim outline of a partial theory of political allocation in democracies. However unsystematically the ideas may be presented, we have more than a vague idea of the major variables and of their important relationships, through which policies are made and implemented in democratic systems. The scrutiny of any up-to-date introductory text about politics will amply testify to this.

Indeed most research about the American political system is likely to be cast in allocative terms and to be consistent with one or another theoretical interpretation of the way in which values are transformed into policies. Voting research, for instance, characteristically gains its relevance from the understanding it provides about the way in which the public influences policy and policy makers and about the means through which this is achieved. Research about legislative behavior reveals the part that legislators play in the policy-making (allocative) process and unearths the determinants of this behavior, as illustrated in investigations of party alignments, practices affecting recruitment to legislative office, conceptions of legislative roles, and sources of power vis-à-vis other branches of government. Similarly most other institutional or behavioral research about American politics can be shown to be consistent with and contributory to an implicit understanding of politics as a process through which valued things are allocated.

A great deal of the research on socialization that we have referred to before can now be reinterpreted as relevant to a possible allocative theory. For example, Hyman organized his inventory about research on socialization to emphasize its contribution to our understanding of the roots of such adult behavior as political participation (party preferences and political interest) and of ideological predispositions defined along a right-left axis.[8] In dealing with these matters Hyman was inadvertently also focusing on two major sets of determinants of the allocative processes in a democratic system. Others have similarly, even if unwittingly, enriched our understanding of this theoretical area in their explorations of the impact of pre-adult experiences on such matters as perceptions of political offices and recruitment to them,[9] the acquisition of information about political affairs, and the development of orientations to issues, candidates, and parties as a source of political preferences.[10]

Whereas previously we offered a less generous interpretation of topics like these, considering them merely as a follow-up, or, more literally, a follow-back on adult research, we can now view them in a new light—as a way of attacking another major determinant of the allocative process. They seek to isolate and analyze the impact of early experiences and learning on future participation in the struggle over the making and implementing of public policies, that is, on the overall allocative process. In this light, pre-adult socialization constitutes an important set of variables, the influence of which would have to be included in any rounded theory of political allocations.

Whatever the promise of these inarticulate assumptions in the study of political socialization, however, the fact is that no allocative theory has yet been developed with sufficient coherence to provide explicit guidance for research about adult behavior, even in gross terms. It is not surprising therefore that students of political socialization should find few serious constraints on the range of topics that they might select. Typically they have not even considered it necessary to search for an overall theoretical justification. But even if they had, to warrant their research on children they would not have needed to do more than refer to the ongoing research about adults. They might place the full onus, for establishing theoretical relevance, on students of adult behavior, because presumably inquiry in the area of childhood socialization need merely follow up problems already set in the adult field. Yet if adult research itself lacks an explicit theoretical context, this shortcoming cannot help but work its way back to infect the whole area of pre-adult socialization as well. Thus to the extent that research in socialization could enable us to understand how time determinants influence the way a system manages to allocate valued things, the current absence of any sustained and self-conscious theoretical inquiry at the adult level reduces the probability of explicitly theoretical contributions about earlier phases of the life cycle.

The interest in socialization from an allocative perspective joins the nontheoretical option in failing to offer a theoretical justification for socialization research. Both simply assume that the task of the student of socialization is to explore the roots of existing adult behavior and attitudes and to estimate the impact of this early learning on the future adult.

We need to go well beyond these two alternatives, however, if we wish to begin to understand the overall place of socialization in political systems. For one thing, these approaches tend to ignore the possibility that socialization is as significant for political change as it is for current behavior. This we would fail to appreciate if we in fact confined ourselves only to an effort to trace the roots of present adult orientations. We shall return to this point later. Furthermore, socialization may have broader and more profound consequences for political systems than are implied merely in its recent identification as a determinant of adult orientations. It is to the merit of the third option—system stability—to which we now turn that, whatever its other shortcomings, this option does draw attention to the broader implications of socialization for the operation of political systems.

A SYSTEM-MAINTENANCE THEORY OF SOCIALIZATION

Although allocative interests represent the mode of analysis most apparent in research about political socialization, interwoven in this approach we can discover the early beginnings of a more general theory, what we might call a system-maintenance theory. Most research, with a few notable exceptions,[11] unobtrusively assumes that in one way or another socializing processes assure the continuity of a political system in relatively unchanged form. Not that change is ignored, as we shall find, but it becomes a residual rather than a central or expected product of socialization. Allocative analysis is shot through with similar assumptions. They imply that for the most part a maturing generation will participate in political processes in a manner replicative of the adult generation. In this view it would appear that the task and outcome of socialization is to contribute to the stability or maintenance of a political system.

As sparse as theorizing about socialization is in political science, this interpretation has already taken more than a slight, if as yet an unsignalized, hold. If it were to become the dominant mode of analysis, it would ultimately and unfortunately distort our understanding of the multiple and divergent consequences that socialization may have in varying circumstances and for different kinds of systems. It would bias research toward investigating those conditions favoring the perpetuation of stability or the status quo.

The meaning of stability, or system maintenance

Stability is a highly ambiguous term in the social sciences.[12] It conveys two different kinds of meanings, and both may be implied simultaneously in research on socialization. Frequently it is used to describe a system that incorporates whatever the writer considers to be the political virtues. In a broad usage such as this, to say a system is stable is somehow to impute to it the capacity to solve its problems pacifically and with some modicum of equity. It leads us to speak of systems as unstable when what we mean is that they are prone to violence, to sharp reversals of policies and regime, and to unpredictability of behavior. In this sense stability tends to be an evaluative criterion varying somewhat with the predilection of the user.

But the term may also occur in a narrower, technical sense. It may refer simply to the constancy of a state of affairs over a period of time. Rigorously speaking, a system which characteristically employed violence and fluctuated wildly in its behavior could be said to be constantly in a state of violent flux. It would be stable with respect to this quality if in the face of any change in its environment there was a tendency for the system to return to its unpredictable behavior. In this technical meaning, very much in the tradition of its use in economics and the natural sciences, stability need not imply peace, order, or any other substantive state. It describes only the tendency of the given state of the system to continue over time.

At the very least the idea of system maintenance embodies the notion of stability in this second or technical sense. A system maintains itself when it remains constant from one generation to the next. Although we would eliminate much confusion if we could confine stability to this second sense, unfortunately we shall see that in the social sciences outside of economics the word also bears inescapable overtones of cohesion, consensus, peace, and harmony, states of affairs that are at times associated, however improperly, with the absence of forces pushing toward change. Given the prevalence of the broad usage in political science, it would be artificial and probably ineffectual to try to restrict the idea to its narrower, technical meaning. In our discussion we shall nonetheless seek to distinguish clearly each of these two meanings.

Stability and prevalent definitions of socialization

Political science is not alone in attributing stabilizing consequences to the overall processes of socialization. In fact we might suspect that it has borrowed this assumption from other social sciences. Political science has only recently come to express an interest in socialization and has therefore had to lean on the other disciplines to inform itself initially of the major general issues. In doing so, it is understandable that political science might unsuspectingly absorb system-maintaining assumptions prevalent in these other social sciences. If we now look again at some typical descriptions of what others from neighboring disciplines have meant by socialization, we will see that the evidence bears this out.

As we noted earlier, the consequences of socialization are often, and inappropriately in our view, included in the definitions of the term itself.[13] We may now add that most of these definitions seem to point toward social and political stability as the characteristic outcome. The hazards of this kind of theoretical perspective are so serious for future political research that it is worth dwelling for a moment on this point. To expose these hazards we set forth below a number of additional definitions and descriptions from several disciplinary contexts aside from political science. We shall then compare these definitions with a few from political science.

> [Socialization covers] the whole process by which an individual born with behavioral potentialities of enormously wide range is confined within a much narrower range—the range of what is customary and acceptable for him according to the standards of the group.

> Socialization consists of those patterns of action . . . which inculcate in individuals the skills . . . motives, and attitudes necessary for the performance of present and anticipated roles.

> [Socialization describes] the acquisition of dispositions toward behavior that is positively valued by a group, and the elimination of dispositions toward behavior that is disvalued.

> Socialization refers to the process by which persons acquire the knowledge, skills, and dispositions that make them more or less able members of their societies.

> [Socialization is a process] in which the child gradually comes to approximate the prevailing attitudes of the adults in his culture.[14]

These descriptions could be continued indefinitely, so thoroughly have they become a part of the established literature. Various euphemisms take the place of the notion of stability, but they add up to the same thing. Acceptability according to "the standards of the group," becoming "able members of their societies," or approximating "the prevailing attitudes of the adults in his culture" are all formulations which reflect the conviction that more or less successful adaptation to existing social patterns, that is, system maintenance, is a dominant element in the theoretical structure with which socialization is to be approached.

It is understandable that under the pressure from the widespread acceptance of these assumptions in the other disciplines, many who have come to apply themselves to parallel problems in politics should easily fit into the same system-maintaining mold.

The importance of such a formulation [of politics as learned behavior] to understanding the stability of political systems is self-evident — *humans must learn their political behavior early and well and persist in it.* Otherwise there would be no regularity — perhaps even chaos.

Political socialization is the process of induction into the political culture.

Political socialization refers to the learning process by which the political norms and behaviors acceptable to an ongoing political system are transmitted from generation to generation.

[Political socialization refers to] the processes through which values, cognitions, and symbols are learned and "internalized," through which operative social norms regarding politics are implanted, political roles institutionalized, and political consensus created, either effectively or ineffectively.[15]

These quotations leave little doubt that regardless of disciplinary affiliation or perspectives, students of socialization typically understand the process as one that helps to adapt the behavior of the maturing generation to the existing patterns among adults in society. Whatever the terms used in the literature, and they are numerous — inculcation, adequate socialization, customary and acceptable behavior, able member, approximation of prevailing attitudes, effective learning, adaptation, maintenance, consensus, induction into a culture — and however ambiguous each may be, they all share one implication, that somehow an adult generation is able to mold a rising generation into something like its own image. Theoretically, this kind of conceptualization clearly implies that the outcome of socialization is to provide for the continuity of existing forms and actions, that is, to assure the stability, in the sense of both consensus or order (as against chaos) and constancy, of the system over time.

The system-maintaining bias of functional analysis

Functional analysis, as we find it in other social sciences and as in recent years it has haltingly been creeping into political research (particularly into the comparative field), similarly tends to carry inquiry about socialization in a system-maintaining, stability-emphasizing direction. Functionalism assumes that social mechanisms can best be described in terms of their functions. The function of socialization becomes one of assuring the stability of a political system.

Political science has imported a functional approach from adjacent disciplines. Although the fact of being borrowed bears no relationship to its shortcomings as a mode of analysis,[16] that its origins are elsewhere suggests that we might look there to alert ourselves to some of the problems associated with its use.

Functionalism, as it appears in anthropology and sociology, stands on two fundamental tenets. It holds that no society can maintain itself (or remain stable) without meeting certain postulated invariant functional requirements. Derivative from this is the further principle that variable structures and processes in a society serve to fulfill these constant functions. As they appear in functional analysis, system maintenance and stability are usually interchangeable terms. Both not only imply constancy but subtly suggest peace and order as concomitants of the self-maintenance of a system over time.[17]

From this theoretical perspective, socialization stands as one of the basic functions necessary for system maintenance, or stability. Every society must provide for the fulfillment of such functions as the production of goods and services, the biological replacement of its members, the creation of a sense of common purpose, and the like. Although every scholar is free to specify his own list of functions, all scholars agree that various roles need to be filled if the identified functions are to be met. Somehow the members of the system must acquire sufficient motivation, skill, knowledge, and values to induce and enable them to undertake the role activity necessary to these postulated social functions. Otherwise as the existing role occupants died or retired, a society would lack the personnel to meet its functional prerequisites.

The specific function of socialization, in this view, is to assure the continuity of those structures through which the other functional requirements are met. Each generation must learn what is expected of it if the postulated prerequisites of society are to be fulfilled. If socialization were to fail, no society could maintain itself; disorganization, even chaos might ensue.

This is clearly brought out in the following typical description of socialization from the field of sociology.

> By the term *socialization* is meant the inculcation of the structure of action of a society on [*sic*] an individual (or group). Socialization in this sense is a matter of degree. An individual is *adequately socialized* if he has been inculcated with a sufficient portion of the structures of action of his society to permit the effective performance of his roles in the society. There is *adequate socialization* in a society if there is a sufficient number of adequately socialized individuals for the structural requisites of a society to operate.[18]

The function of socialization in the political sphere has been cast in a similar mold by those who lean toward a functional approach.[19] Consistent with this approach, the language of their re-search is couched in terms that assess the contribution of sociali-zation to system maintenance. To the extent that socialization does serve this end, the members of the society are said to be "effectively," "satisfactorily," or "adequately" socialized, depend-ing upon the degree to which they have learned what is deemed necessary to adapt to the prevailing culture or to fulfill the exist-ing roles. Or, elliptically, the literature speaks of a person as becoming or failing to become socialized, meaning thereby that he has or has not been *adequately* socialized. Socialization loses its neutral character as a term referring to a process that may have positive, negative, or indifferent consequences for society, and typically carries a positive connotation for the fulfillment of postu-lated functions.

In effect the functional study of socialization represents an effort to understand the way in which persons learn to fit into a preexisting pattern of roles or culture. It is as though the struc-ture and culture were just waiting to be reproduced on some *tab-ula rasa* of the child. In this sense socialization is essentially a process whereby one generation inculcates its patterns of behavior and attitudes in the next. The transmission may take place not only from adult to child but from adult to adult, as in the recruit-ment of adults to political office. Through this kind of replica-tion of a system, stability in the sense of continuity of the system is implied and indeed is often made explicit, as we have just seen.

Socialization and modes of stability

It is clear therefore that from a strictly functional point of view we would have to assume that socialization has certain func-tions or specifiable tasks to perform in society and in a political system. But in political science and, indeed, in the social sciences as a whole, there is no overwhelming commitment to a functional approach. Most students of politics go only no further than to indicate that socialization has some possible consequences or outcomes for a system; they do not assign it specific functions. But, as we have noted, regardless of whether socialization is in-terpreted as a postulated function or merely in the light of its observed consequences, most research does unobtrusively in-cline toward the conclusion that it leads to the maintenance of a system, to stability.

But we have also observed that the idea of stability is used ambiguously to mean both a substantive state associated with peace and harmony and a formal condition of constancy regardless of the substantive state. In order to demonstrate fully the hazards of fixing on system maintenance (in either the broad or narrow sense) either as a presumed purpose or as an outcome of socialization, we need to probe much more deeply into how socialization is assumed to lead to stability.

Socialization is interpreted as contributing to system-maintenance in two fundamentally different ways: vertically (across the generations) and horizontally (within the generations). The two terms do not exist in the literature as a way of distinguishing these differences but we can usefully adopt them to describe the directions in which discussions of socialization actually move. Furthermore there are two variants of the way in which horizontal stability seems to be attainable: through intragenerational group homogeneity and through subjective congruence in orientations and behavior within the individual himself. We shall now examine what we mean by vertical and horizontal stability.

Vertical (intergenerational) stability

Normally, in speaking of stability as a function or an outcome of socialization, we have in mind continuity or constancy across the generations. As we have observed, functional analysis postulates that if a system is to maintain itself, the existing generation must replicate itself in the maturing one. This is the vertical, or intergenerational, dimension of stability. We need not pursue this aspect of the socializing function further; it is very familiar in the literature, as the quotations have shown.

Horizontal (intragenerational) stability

Stability not only has an intergenerational dimension, it also is frequently linked to conditions that prevail within a single generation. When looking at a dominant generation in a political system we may speak about the similarity of its members' views and behavior, or at least about their compatibility, which contributes to internal harmony for the group. From this intragenerational view, to say that a system is stable is to attribute its stability to the presence of consensus, the absence of deep internal cleavages and conflicts within the dominant generation. There is little that threatens to upset the existing balance of forces or political accommodations. Here stability depends on the lack of horizontal discontinuities, strains, or incompatibilities rather than on cross-generational factors.

In this context stability has the dual meaning previously noted. On the one hand, it describes a substantive state of affairs. The members of the generation have become mutually adjusted and are able to solve their problems in some pacific way. On the other hand, it implies that the members are able to maintain this condition over time. Stability therefore goes further than merely to suggest replication of generations; it depicts a relatively harmonious and continuing condition within one generation.

In this interpretation, the function of socialization would seem to be to work toward this congruence in outlook and behavior within a generation, that is, to bring about *collective homogeneity*. System-stability would falter, strains and conflict might prevail, if socialization did not help to confine a generation within some minimal range of diversity. Since diversity and "intragenerational discontinuities," so-called, are most likely to occur where there are ethnic, regional, economic, occupational, linguistic, or religious differences, socialization is presumed to bring about some congruence along these lines even within a given generation, not only between generations.

In one way or another most studies of political socialization seek to uncover the extent to which different categories of a population socialize their members differently over the generations. A major task of the study of socialization is to ascertain the extent to which discontinuities across subcategories of the members in a system can be discovered and explained. The interest in this subject rests on the latent premise that where different ethnic groups, social classes, regional groups, or even school systems, for example, implant contrasting political concepts and patterns of behavior in children, the rising generation will be more likely to develop diverse and possibly conflicting political points of view. If the socialization process raises children who upon reaching adulthood have among themselves conflicting aspirations, conceptions of the rules of the system, attitudes toward compliance, and feelings about authority, it is assumed that this will probably build social and political cleavages into a system and that instability will result.

To put the matter in a positive way, stability would seem to require some congruence in what the varying components of a maturing generation learn. The implication is that there is a range of acceptable variability in political orientations and behavior within a generation; beyond this range lie conflict and stress. A person is often said to be "well or satisfactorily socialized" or just "socialized" if he fits into the overall pattern in a harmonious way, "poorly or inadequately socialized" or just "not social-ized" if he deviates beyond some unspecified range. So many studies of socialization take this theoretical premise for granted that no special reference to the literature is required.

It is clear, for example, that this approach to the contribu-tion of socialization to system stability imbues the melting-pot assumptions with which most research on one major source of diversity, ethnicity, is conducted in the United States. From the beginning of multi-ethnic immigration, Americans have hoped that somehow over the generations ethnic and linguistic differ-ences would slowly disappear. Educational practice and social policy have been strongly colored by this expectation. Most social pressures have automatically moved in the same direction. Indeed immigrants to the United States have arrived psychologically prepared to blend into the dominant Anglo-Saxon cultural and linguistic environment. The failure to do so, the lingering ethnic differences and intractable resistance to assimilation by some ethnic minorities needs to be accounted for by theories that go beyond the melting-pot preconceptions.[20]

The disappearance of diversity into this melting pot was not sought for its own sake. It was thought that social and politi-cal stability would otherwise be impossible. We shall return to the implications of this operating assumption in a moment. Here it is enough to establish that frequently research has treated so-cialization as a mechanism for promoting stability because so-cialization traditionally has been seen as harmonizing the politi-cal and other predispositions within any generation.

The stability associated with system maintenance at times has also implied something other than intragenerational homo-geneity. Strains within a generation, it is thought, may arise from the failure of the individual himself to achieve some minimal inner consistency in his own orientations and patterns of be-havior. System stability may therefore be associated with *sub-jective homogeneity* or *consistency*.

For example, it might be argued that a democratic system would scarcely be likely to survive if children were brought up under highly authoritarian conditions in the family, school, job, and voluntary associations and then were expected to behave in a democratic manner in the political arena. Conversely if chil-dren grew up with a high degree of involvement and responsi-bility for their own affairs and a significant voice, appropriate to their age, in decisions affecting them in family, school, and so forth, we might question whether an authoritarian political regime could operate without strain as the children attained their political maturity.

With assumptions such as these about a possible source of instability, we might be inclined to interpret socialization as an important device for bridging these discontinuities and for ameliorating or erasing these longitudinal diversities developed during the life cycle of the individual. One might expect the system to display a "strain toward congruence"[21] in order to alleviate subjective discontinuities in experience.

This second variant of horizontal socialization, subjective consistency or homogeneity, therefore emphasizes the effect of discontinuities in the learning of the individual. A good illustration is to be found in the five-nation study by Almond and Verba. There the authors address themselves to the question of whether experiences in the nonpolitical sphere such as family, school, and job are consonant with those in the political sphere.[22] The problem centers on the extent to which discontinuities in the socialization of members in a system may produce conflicting attitudes and expectations within the individual that would ultimately contribute to political instabilities. As the authors themselves put it, they are searching for

> . . . hypotheses about the kinds of personality tendencies and so-cialization practices that are likely to produce *congruent political cultures and stable polities.* Thus in the case of the civic culture, we may say that a pattern of socialization which enables the individual to *manage the inevitable dissonances* among his diffuse primary, his obedient output [compliance], and activist input roles supports a democratic polity. We can then look at socialization patterns and personality tendencies and ask just which of these qualities are crucial, to what extent they must be present, and what kinds of experience are most likely to produce this capacity for *dissonant political role management* [italics added].[23]

On the acknowledged uncertain basis of retrospective evidence[24] they find that, depending upon the specific political system and the generation in question, family and school experiences may lean toward the nonparticipatory side in contrast with the participatory behavior expected in the adult political sphere in democratic systems. The implication is that normally we could expect this "dissonance," as they term it—lack of homogeneity in subjective experiences—to contribute to conflicting expectations among the affected members and therefore to some instability in the political arena.

The authors argue that inner dissonance and any ensuing political instability are avoided for two reasons. In part this is because early life experiences may fail to carry over fully to adult behavior.[25] But in part it may also be owing to the low salience of politics in some systems and the related capacity of the members to handle their internal inconsistencies without strain. In reply to their own query about "whether these inconsistencies cause [the expected] instability in the civic culture,"[26] the authors argue that inconsistency "creates no undue strain within the citizen; for politics, as much of our data suggest and as the data from many other studies confirm, is not the uppermost problem in his mind."[27] Thus by reversing Freud and undervaluing childhood experiences in the political sphere and by relying on low political salience to reduce inner tensions, the authors are able to explain away intragenerational subjective disharmony, a disharmony that might otherwise have been disastrous, presumably, for the stability of a democratic regime.

In the five-nation study the authors in fact had been adducing evidence that seemed to lend weight to somewhat earlier speculations by Eckstein. The latter had addressed himself to the basic issues raised during the 1920s by the Freudian social scientists in Germany about the relationship of attitudes bred in the authoritarian family to the failure of the democratic Weimar constitution to strike deep roots.[28] Eckstein had reconsidered this question by theorizing about the impact, on behavior toward political authority, of attitudes and practices about authority learned in the family, school, and occupational groups. Expanding on the Freudian theme of the significance of primary learning, he hypothesized that a "government will tend to be stable if its authority pattern is congruent with the other authority patterns of the society of which it is part."[29] But for him this does not necessarily imply that stability requires the congruence of experiences in all organizations or social institutions, particularly the primary ones. Some heterogeneity is possible, but only on condition that those structures in which divergent authority patterns may be learned—as the family, church, and schools—are not too close to governmental institutions themselves. In this the theory visibly departs from Freudian presuppositions. It is social distance from the governmental structure that seems to be the decisive factor in enabling a system to tolerate variations in learned responses to patterns of authority.

Thus Eckstein speculates that

> Government will be stable, (1) if social authority patterns are identical with the government patterns, or (2) if they constitute a graduated pattern in a proper segmentation of society, or (3) if a high degree of resemblance exists in patterns adjacent to government [such as parties and civil service] and one finds throughout the more distant segments [such as families and schools] a marked departure from functionally appropriate patterns for the sake of initiating the governmental pattern or extensive imitation of the governmental pattern in ritual practice.[30]

This theory requires the author to modify the intuitive meaning of congruence and to redefine it to suggest that ". . . social authority patterns [will be considered] congruent, either if they are very similar, or if similarity to the governmental pattern increases significantly as one approaches the governmental segment itself."[31] In the face of diversity, distance breeds content.[32] The "further" a structure is from government (the structure of political authority, *we* might say), the less likely are contradictory general authority patterns to impose strains on the individual as he participates in the political sphere.

Regardless of the validity of this theory, its significance for us at the moment is not that early socialization here, as in the five-nation study, is seen as having little meaning for later political behavior. Nor does it matter that the authors of neither study conclude that instability in the political system can be traced to inner inconsistency or conflict associated with early socialization. What does matter is that in the elaboration of their ideas about congruence, these studies do turn to political stability as a means for establishing the theoretical relevance of their speculations. Each considers that but for the presence of certain structural arrangements—the "distance" of early political socialization from the political sphere—the members of a political system might find themselves under conditions of subjective strain, which would in turn make a stable democratic order difficult to sustain. For the authors the key to an understanding of socialization is its consequences, either positive or negative, for the stability of the system.

As we have observed, the literature is not particularly clear about this distinction between vertical and horizontal stability and about the two ways (collective homogeneity and subjective consistency) in which horizontal stability might be impaired. Nonetheless there is little doubt that these are the theoretical modes dominant in the study of socialization. We have a substantive theory with strong functional overtones if we have anything at all. Socialization, it is implied, may produce generations in a political system each of which looks much like the preceding one. Socialization may also contribute to harmonious political behavior within a given generation and may thereby help to reduce internal cleavages. If it fails to do so, the continued stability of a system requires some other kind of explanation. What is clear from all this is that the major focus of research about socialization is on stability and its conditions. It was to demonstrate this that we have looked at these alternative, if latent, conceptualizations as closely as we have. They reveal that the study of socialization has steadily pushed forward in one direction, toward clarifying its place in the production of political stability or system maintenance.

THE LIMITATIONS OF STABILITY AS A THEORETICAL CONTEXT

The major drawback of a theoretical perspective that emphasizes system maintenance is that research inspired by a concern for stability, vertical or horizontal, must overlook a whole range of consequences that socialization has for political diversity, conflict, and change.

Not that change has been completely ignored in present research or that instability has been denied. By the nature of the case, especially in politics, this would be highly unlikely if not impossible. Discontinuities, both vertical and horizontal, in the transmission of existing political patterns are too apparent to be neglected entirely. But the current theoretical premises do convey the impression that the primary task is to explain something other than change—how systems come to reproduce themselves over time and to sustain themselves in an integrated, relatively homogeneous state at any moment of time. This perspective directs our attention to the effectiveness with which socializing processes draw people together toward the creation of a melting pot or of a politically harmonious population.

For much of current research on socialization, whether and how diversity itself may be perpetuated and how change may occur do not appear to be significant or central questions. It is as though system maintenance is the norm from which all else, such as basic change or diversity and cleavage, is deviant. Yet in this age, when most children in the world are growing up in a culture alien to their parents, and when change may be the rule and stability the exception, a theory of socialization that is not broad enough to encompass both change and continuity as equally imperative phenomena immediately reveals its inherent weaknesses.

If we conduct research with the assumption that socialization serves to reinforce stability of systems, we are forced to address ourselves to a limited though significant order of problems. We would wish to know, for example, how new members learn the existing adult political roles. We would assume that what new members acquire is supposed to prepare them to step into roles that are already waiting for them, that in this way a political structure manages to maintain itself even though the personnel changes from generation to generation. We would attribute importance to socialization because it prepares individuals for roles, the prescriptions for which would seem to be known in advance. We are easily led to conclude that to the extent to which a person learns how he is to behave politically, he has been "adequately" socialized. To the extent that he is unable "to take his place" in the system, socialization has "failed." Similarly where, say, a child learns different patterns in varying sectors of his experiences, or where classes of children receive different training, the system fails through "improper" socialization to bring about the degree of homogeneity presumed to be necessary for stability. Other mechanisms may need to be activated to achieve this result.

If we adopt broader theoretical horizons, however, we can begin to appreciate that system-maintenance theory, with its suggestion of stability in both the broad and narrow sense of the term, is far too limiting to reveal the major consequences of political socialization. It elevates one possible major resultant to an exclusive and dominant position.

Socialization is neither inherently conservatizing nor is it for that matter fundamentally destabilizing. It can contribute to disorder just as it can to peace and harmony, depending on the specific circumstances. A useful theory would recognize that the consequences of socialization will depend upon the prior state of the political system (whether it is stable or already in a condition of change), what it is that one generation is transmitting to another one (replicative or otherwise), and what the persons being socialized independently learn from their experiences. If the fact is accepted that an interpretation of the consequences of socialization must be kept widely enough open to incorporate both stability and change as possible central outcomes, the kinds of questions asked and the ways of analyzing data will differ significantly from the approach of students who adopt stability as a primary focus. In particular, childhood socialization will assume a new character, and discontinuities within a group or individual will be differently interpreted.

Replication as an outcome

A major difficulty with the replicative thesis of a system-maintenance perspective is that socialization does not always succeed in recapitulating one generation in the next. It does not always assure stability in the sense of continuity or constancy.

In the first place, the older generation itself may not be interested in perpetuating its patterns in its children. Adults may be only too well aware of the emergence of a new world. In the hope of preparing their children to take advantage of the new benefits and to avoid the deprivations that they might otherwise incur, the adults may deliberately train their children for the acceptance of new political goals, norms, and structures. Inkeles discovered this to be true for a small sample of the prerevolutionary generation in the Soviet Union. In spite of their opposition to the new Soviet order, they were not prepared to subject their children to the hazards of opposition. They consciously sought to avoid replicating their own generation.[33] Indeed if they had reproduced their political behavior in their children, this would undoubtedly have increased the probability of political instability. It would have perpetuated rather than ameliorated the post-revolutionary conflicts.

In the second place, replication may fail to occur if experiences of the rising generation lead them to reject what their elders seek to instill. Where, according to system-maintenance standards, children are socialized "poorly," a different theoretical context enables us to interpret this not as a flaw in the outcome but as an occasion or opportunity for change. It may be that in spite of what their parents and other significant adults would have them learn, as children mature their own experiences teach them to prefer new ways of handling things politically when they move into the more active stages of the life cycle. They may end up by defining new roles for themselves and by searching out new modes of political expression.

From a system-maintenance posture, the student-protest movement of the sixties in Europe and the United States, for example, may be interpreted as a disequilibrating force resulting

UNIVERSITY OF WINNIPEG
PORTAGE & BALMORAL
WINNIPEG 2. MAN.   CANADA

DISCARDED

from "inadequacies" in socialization. This would seem to be an implicit inference from the prevalent judgments, such as the following, in the literature on socialization. "Unfortunately for the best adjustment of the adolescent, cultural change has been so rapid that his parents have grown up in a different world, and thus are ill-equipped to teach him how to behave and adjust in the here and now."[34] In this vein we might be inclined to attribute the "inadequacies" in socializing practices to such factors as the excessive permissiveness of parents who are themselves unable to set firm standards. Alternatively we might see in the "deviations" of young people from past adult political norms something that we could call the "cat's paw" effect, where successful middle-class parents are subconsciously working out their own stifled liberal sentiments through their children.[35]

If we assume that socialization is supposed to replicate previous outlooks, with perhaps tolerable variations, we need to account for the breakdown of socialization, and research into problems such as the above is suggested. But if we broaden our theoretical horizons, we may discover that the protesting students are purposively in search of new roles. The total impact of their experiences with several wars, aimless affluence, and dangerous and difficult political forces in an atomic age may be leading them, regardless of any inadvertent inadequacy or connivance of their parents and even in opposition to them, to seek a way of defining new purposes and inventing new kinds of structures to implement these purposes.[36] The research worker is not called upon to approve or disapprove of these student activities. But as a social scientist he must be prepared to enlarge the scope of his analytic tools so as to see widespread movements — such as the new student activism—not only as deviations, for explainable reasons, from a norm called stability, but as outcomes of socializing experiences that may lead toward innovation and change. Novelty in political behavior and orientations is as "legitimate" or expected an outcome of socialization as is conformity.

Replication of instability

As we have said, the trouble with replicative theory is that socialization may not replicate. But even if it does, it need not always reproduce stability. Here we now interpret stability in the broad sense, to mean not constancy alone but peace and order as well. If a system is in process of change and if socialization tends to reproduce the patterns of the preceding generation, it would be the changing state of affairs that would be continued in the rising generations. Many of the political systems in the modern world exist under conditions of instability; developing nations have been and may well continue in this state for long periods of time. Instability seems to be a better description of the political norm in this age than stability.[37] Under these circumstances it would be surprising if the new generations gaining political power necessarily learned patterns of behavior and political outlooks that contributed more to stability than to its contradictory.

Thus, to cast research about socialization in system-maintenance or stability terms is to interpret change pejoratively, as though it were a product of error or moral failure. In fact it may prove to be a way of life for many societies in certain historical epochs, such as the present. As has been pointed out, "so few individuals may now hope to grow up under conditions of sociocultural [and, we may add, political] stability that we may regard this situation as almost unusual, and its products as in a sense 'deviants'."[38] For long historical intervals political socialization might conceivably contribute more to instability than to peace and order.

The melting pot and the mosaic as outcomes

The emphasis on group congruence or integration as a major function or consequence of socialization similarly draws unnecessarily rigid boundaries around political research. In assuming that socialization somehow tends to level differences, the research worker commits himself to the idea that stability requires the elimination of differences. Assimilation, the melting pot, becomes a precondition of stability.

If, however, one assumes that what counts, even for the stability of social and political systems, is not the presence or absence of diversity but the way in which it is managed or organized,[39] he can immediately appreciate that socialization may well replicate diversity as well as cleavages and that a political system with high diversity could continue even in some stable state. The responsibility for attaining and maintaining congruence, or integration, could then be shifted to some other mechanisms. This approach might lead us to substitute a conception of society as a mosaic of ethnic groups living in cooperative diversity for the current image of the assimilative melting pot.[40] But the latent commitment to cultural homogenization is so deeply ingrained in American thinking, both lay and scholarly, that it is extraordinarily difficult to accept the assertion that enduring nonassimilative patterns are consistent with an orderly political life.

Yet it is clear that members of a political system need not share all or even most political orientations and cultural assumptions in order to support a common regime. Indeed, unless we accept the plausibility of a mosaic hypothesis, it would be difficult to understand how multi-ethnic political systems, as found, say, in Belgium, Switzerland, and Canada—based as they are on a plurality of languages, religions, and cultures—could possibly have continued. Current ethnic discontents and instability in some of these systems may not necessarily or always indicate that they are failing to manage their differences but only that their mode of management is undergoing some fundamental revisions. Change, even if accompanied by turmoil, is itself a process of adaptation to new circumstances. In developing systems where ethnic diversity has seemed to put major barriers in the way of creating a viable political system *de novo*, we may have evidence not of the failure of the mosaic pattern but of the time and ingenuity necessary to discover adequate mechanisms of accommodation. But regardless of the specific impact of diversity on the operations of a political system, it is clear that socialization may be as important for its capacity to retain broad variability as for its creation of pressures toward homogenization of a people.

The tendency to interpret homogeneity as a condition of stability is perhaps linked with the almost instinctive dominance of the melting-pot concept of society in the United States, for well-known reasons.[41] The levelling of linguistic and religiocultural differences has hitherto been accepted almost without question as a preferred state of affairs. A theoretical premise about socialization built on this preconception would naturally tend to equate assimilation and stability. But if the major impulse for research in the field of socialization had come from scholars immersed in multi-ethnic societies, some political systems might have been more congenially interpreted as continuing mosaics of ethnic groups living under conditions of acceptable mutual accommodations of interests. At the very least, with both melting-pot and mosaic patterns as possible polar alternatives, and with many combinations in between, a political theory about socialization needs to be sufficiently broad to embrace them all.

CONCLUSION

Thinking about political socialization is now too well advanced to be able to fall back on the nontheoretical option as a meaningful alternative. Allocative interests do little but follow up on adult behavior and continue to leave us at theoretically loose ends. System-maintenance theory at least has the merit of adumbrating a possible political theory of socialization. Whatever its shortcomings it does seek to determine the relevance of socialization for the operation of a political system as a whole.

But system-maintenance analysis imposes excessively severe limits on the kinds of problems central for research about socialization. Our examination of these drawbacks does, however, help to reinforce further the utility of our own neutral conception of socialization as the acquisition of political orientations and patterns of behavior, without regard initially to its consequences or presumed functions for the system as a whole. But if one defines socialization so as to posit some preexisting structure, for participation in which the individual is being trained, it is necessary to make some instrumental judgments about the adequacy of his preparation for the assumption of existing roles in society. This is the conserving, and therefore the conservative, bias of system maintenance as a theoretical viewpoint.

If, however, one starts in a neutral vein and interprets socialization as just those processes through which an individual learns about interaction with others, it may be that even though his behavior is inappropriate for conforming with the standards of existing generations, or for bringing about political consensus, for his own generation the individual's learning may reflect a search for new patterns of behavior. What may be "inadequate" socialization for maintaining existing political structures may be highly "appropriate" for bringing into being new structures based upon new ideals and new kinds of political accommodations among the members of a system.

In an explanatory science we are not concerned with the appropriateness of the socialized behavior. We simply seek to trace the consequences for the existing system of whatever results from the socializing experiences of its members. It would be hazardous to assume either indirectly or unwittingly that any given political structure is to be preserved intact. Rather we need a more comprehensive conception of the theoretical relevance of socialization for the political system, one in which change is not interpreted as a failure of the system to reproduce itself but is viewed positively. Change needs to be as integral to the conceptualization as stability is today.

A wholesale reconsideration of the way to interpret the theoretical tasks of research into socialization is necessary. We require a context that will encourage us to explore how it is that pre-adult members of a system acquire their political orientations and behavior patterns regardless of whether they conform to adult standards, run into conflict with the existing political structure, or just move laterally in a neutral direction. What is of significance for the adoption of a political theory of political socialization is the impact that the socializing processes have on the political system, and the theory must leave us free of any preconceptions about the consequences socialization should have or the functions it ought to fulfill. We shall turn to systems analysis (or persistence theory) for this kind of uncommitted interpretation of political socialization.

NOTES

1. M. K. Jennings and R. G. Niemi, "The Transmission of Political Values from Parent to Child," *American Political Science Review,* 62, pp. 169-184, 1968. Compare with R. A. LeVine, "The Role of the Family in the Authority Systems," *Behavioral Science,* 5, p. 291, 1960, where the role of family in a segmentary political system appears to be more significant.

2. H. Hyman, *Political Socialization* (New York, Free Press, 1959).

3. H. H. Remmers and D. H. Radler, *The American Teenager* (Indianapolis: Bobbs-Merrill, 1957).

4. J. J. Patrick, "Political Socialization of American Youth: Implications for Secondary School Social Studies," National Council for the Social Studies, Research Bulletin no. 3, 1967; R. E. Dawson, "Political Socialization," in J. A. Robinson (ed.), *Political Science Annual* (Indianapolis: Bobbs-Merrill, 1966), pp. 1-84; J. Dennis, "A Survey and Bibliography of Contemporary Research on Political Learning and Socialization," University of Wisconsin, Research and Development Center for Cognitive Learning, Occasional Paper no. 8, April, 1967; J. Dennis, "Major Problems of Political Socialization Research," *Midwest Journal of Political Science,* 12, pp. 85-114, 1968.

5. For this notion see D. Easton, *A Systems Analysis of Political Life,* (New York: Wiley, 1965), p. 31; and "Political Science," in *New International Encyclopedia of the Social Sciences* (New York: Macmillan, 1968).

6. For the equilibrium approach see D. Easton, *The Political System* (New York: Knopf, 1953), chap. 11; "Limits of the Equilibrium Model in Social Research," *Behavioral Science,* 1, pp. 96-104, 1956; and *A Framework for Political Analysis* (Englewood Cliffs, N.J.: Prentice-Hall, 1965).

7. See, for example, A. Downs, *An Economic Theory of Democracy* (New York: Harper, 1957).

8. Hyman, op. cit.

9. J. Wahlke et al., *The Legislative System* (New York: Wiley, 1962), especially chap. 4; K. Prewitt, "Political Socialization and Leadership Selection," *The Annals of the American Academy of Political and Social Science,* 361, pp. 96-111, 1965; K. Prewitt et al., "Political Socialization and Political Roles," *Public Opinion Quarterly,* 30, pp. 569-581, 1966-1967; A. Kornberg and N. Thomas, "The Political Socialization of National Legislative Elites in the United States and Canada," *Journal of Politics,* 27, pp. 761-774, 1965; J. D. Barber, *The Lawmakers: Recruitment and Adaption to Legislative Life* (New Haven, Conn.: Yale, 1965).

10. See F. Greenstein, *Children and Politics* (New Haven, Conn.: Yale, 1965); Jennings and Niemi, op. cit.; Remmers and Radler, op. cit.; L. A. Froman and J. K. Skipper, "An Approach to the Learning of Party Identification," *Public Opinion Quarterly,* 27, pp. 473-480, 1963.

11. Such as Greenstein, op. cit., especially pp. 158-159; L. W. Pye, *Politics, Personality and Nation Building* (New Haven, Conn.: Yale, 1962); A. Inkeles, "Social Change and Social Character: The Role of Parental Mediation," *Journal of Social Issues,* 11, pp. 12-23, 1955. F. A. Pinner, "Student Trade-Unionism in France, Belgium and Holland: Anticipatory Socialization and Role-Seeking," *Sociology of Education,* 37, pp. 177-199, 1964.

12. Easton, "Limits of the Equilibrium Model in Social Research," op. cit.

13. See pp. 9-10.

14. I. L. Child, "Socialization," in G. Lindzey (ed.), *Handbook of Social Psychology,* vol. II (Cambridge, Mass.: Addison-Wesley, 1954), p. 655; D. F. Aberle, "Culture and Socialization," in F. L. K. Hsu (ed.), *Psychological Anthropology: Approaches to Culture and Personality* (Homewood, Ill.: Dorsey, 1961), p. 387; R. LeVine, "Political Socialization and Culture Image," in C. Geertz (ed.), *Old Societies and New States* (New York: Free Press, 1963), p. 280; O. G. Brim, Jr., and S. Wheeler, *Socialization After Childhood: Two Essays* (New York: Wiley, 1966), p. 3; M. Wolfenstein and G. Kliman (eds.), *Children and the Death of a President* (Garden City, N.Y.: Doubleday, 1965), p. xxi.

15. Hyman, op. cit., p. 17; G. A. Almond, "Introduction: A Functional Approach to Comparative Politics," in G. A. Almond and J. S. Coleman (eds.), *The Politics of Developing Areas* (Princeton, N.J.: Princeton, 1960), p. 27; R. Sigel, "Assumptions about the Learning of Political Values," *The Annals of the American Academy of Political and Social Science,* 361, p. 1, 1965; H. Eckstein, "A Perspective on Comparative Politics, Past and Present," in H. Eckstein

and D. Apter (eds.), *Comparative Politics* (New York: Free Press, 1963), p. 26.

16. See D. Easton (ed.), *Varieties of Political Theory* (Englewood Cliffs, N.J.: Prentice-Hall, 1966), chap. 1, in which the point is made that innovative theory in a discipline frequently results from the migration of ideas from other disciplines.

17. We cannot undertake here a thorough and rounded analysis of other shortcomings of functional theory, as applied to political science. In any event, this is not essential. The journals are filled with numerous, distinguished critiques. For one definitive evaluation of the inherent weaknesses of functional perspectives as a unique mode of analysis and its unavoidability as a simple, expected premise of all scientific research, see K. Davis, "The Myth of Functional Analysis as a Special Method in Sociology and Anthropology," *American Sociological Review,* 24, pp. 757-773, 1959.

18. M. J. Levy, Jr., *The Structure of Society* (Princeton, N.J.: Princeton, 1952), p. 187.

19. In *Comparative Politics: A Developmental Approach* (Boston: Little, Brown, 1966), G. A. Almond and G. B. Powell, Jr., explicitly adopt functionalism for political analysis. But even though they employ the notion of "functions" extensively, it would seem to be used so broadly as to lose most of whatever special systematic analytic significance it might have had. Indeed functionalism gradually seems to be overpowered by the categories of systems analysis (inputs-outputs) with which it becomes intertwined. Functionalism seems to recede to the theoretically unobtrusive position it must normally hold in all scientific social research (see Davis, op. cit.). Hence in their book the authors are able to deal with socialization in a way that permits them to transcend the system-maintaining limitations hitherto implicit in a pristine functional analysis (see pp. 29-30, 121, 163).

20. See N. Glaser and D. P. Moynihan, *Beyond the Melting Pot* (Cambridge, Mass.: M.I.T., 1963).

21. G. A. Almond and S. Verba, *The Civic Culture* (Princeton, N.J.: Princeton, 1963), p. 372. The authors also speak of the "strain toward homogeneity" among the various roles an individual plays (p. 327).

22. Ibid., p. 327.

23. Ibid., pp. 34-35.

24. The suspicion of unreliability has since been strongly reinforced. See R. G. Niemi, "A Methodological Study of Political Socialization in the Family," unpublished doctoral dissertation, University of Michigan, 1967.

25. "Family experiences do play a role in the formation of political attitudes, but the role may not be central; the gap between the family and the polity may be so wide that other social experiences, espe-

cially in social situations closer in time and in structure to the political system, may play a larger role." Almond and Verba, op. cit., p. 373.

26. Ibid., p. 482.

27. Ibid.

28. See the extensive writings of T. W. Adorno, M. Horkheimer, and E. Fromm.

29. H. Eckstein, *Division and Cohesion in Democracy* (Princeton, N.J.: Princeton, 1966), p. 234.

30. Ibid., pp. 240-241.

31. Ibid., p. 239.

32. For a further study of the impact of subjective heterogeneity see J. Stoetzel, *Without the Chrysanthemum and the Sword* (New York: Columbia, 1955). See also S. Verba, "The Comparative Study of Socialization," a paper delivered at the annual meeting of the American Political Science Association, Chicago, 1964.

33. Inkeles, op. cit., p. 22.

34. R. G. Kuhlen, *The Psychology of Adolescent Development* (New York: Harper, 1952).

35. R. Flacks, "The Liberated Generation: An Exploration of the Roots of Student Protest," *Journal of Social Issues,* 23, pp. 52-75, 1967.

36. Pinner, op. cit.

37. A. Zolberg, *Creating Political Order: the Party-States of West Africa* (Chicago: Rand McNally, 1966).

38. Inkeles, op. cit., p. 12, paraphrasing Margaret Mead.

39. A. F. C. Wallace, *Culture and Personality* (New York: Random House, 1961).

40. See J. A. Porter, *Vertical Mosaic* (Toronto, Canada: University of Toronto Press, 1965).

41. See Glaser and Moynihan, op. cit.

3

A POLITICAL
THEORY OF
POLITICAL
SOCIALIZATION

As we have argued in the preceding chapter, system maintenance would seem to be a singularly inappropriate foundation on which to build a political theory of political socialization. Conceptually it is too restrictive for interpreting the overall theoretical significance of socialization in politics. It does not even present a plausible working point of departure, since the unassailable fact is that few systems do maintain themselves intact, however satisfying a perception of stability may be in a world filled with turmoil. We clearly require an approach which not only includes the possibility that socialization contributes to stability but which also recognizes that change itself may be an equally frequent outcome of socialization.

As a means for broadening the range of consequences linked to socialization, we may pose a kind of theoretical question more inclusive than any associated with allocative or system-maintenance perspectives. How do political systems manage to continue as such, that is, as sets of behavior through which valued things are authoritatively allocated? More precisely put, how do they manage to persist regardless of whether their forms remain stable or change? If we can discern the relevance of political socialization to this problem, we shall have taken a major step toward recognizing the variable consequences of socialization for the operation of political systems and the first step toward a comprehensive and specifically political theory of political socialization.

SYSTEMS PERSISTENCE

We have already described a political system in brief as those interactions through which values are authoritatively allocated for a society, that is, through which binding decisions are made and implemented. Concretely a political system is a set of structures and processes through which demands of the "politically relevant members" are converted into binding decisions and related actions.[1] This conversion process becomes feasible as long as some type of system is able to elicit the support of the relevant members. Conceptually therefore it is helpful to interpret a political system as a vast conversion process through which the inputs of demands and support are transformed by various structures and processes into outputs, that is, into authoritative decisions and actions, as depicted in Figure 3-1.[2]

Figure 3-1. A simplified model of a political system.

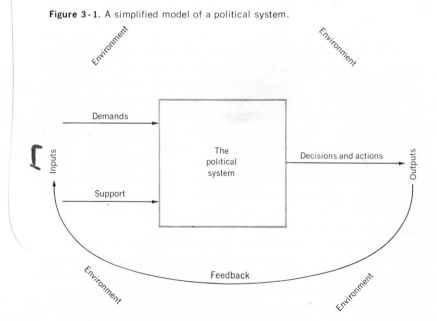

We will say that a political system persists when two conditions prevail: when its members are regularly able to allocate valued things, that is, make decisions; when they are able to get these allocations accepted as authoritative by most members most of the time. We shall designate these two conditions as the *essential variables* of any political system.

In this context it is useful to interpret political systems as open, self-regulating, goal-directed, and self-transforming units of behavior. Briefly, what this means is that they are influenced by what happens in their natural and social environments, that their members can take purposive decisions to change the course of events, and, if necessary or desirable, that these decisions may include modifications or fundamental transformations of the system itself.

Thus in the society called the United States a political system has persisted over the centuries through the very fact that it has been able to change itself, radically, from a relatively decentralized federal system without extensive popular participation at its founding to one with a relatively high degree of political centralization and universal adult suffrage. In the 1960s it is undergoing further changes in the informal patterns of the regime, and these modifications may ultimately permit effective participation by at least one additional ethnic group, the Negro.

Similarly some kind of political system has managed to prevail in France in the face of fundamental transformations in the regime over the ages, oscillating as it has among monarchical, democratic, and authoritarian forms. Indeed, persistence of any kind of political system in France may well have been contingent upon its readiness to respond to environmental and internal changes by regulating itself through such basic political alterations. But for this readiness to accept periodic and radical transformations in the regime, the society we call France might have found itself unable to continue to make and implement authoritative decisions for its members. Not that any particular historical change was necessarily inescapable; many alternative solutions might have existed. But the persistence of a political system of some sort may have hinged upon the ability to adopt important modifications of the status quo.

RELEVANCE OF SOCIALIZATION FOR PERSISTENCE THEORY

Two points stand out from a theoretical approach adopting systems persistence as its central concept. In the first place, system maintenance, or stability, no longer remains the assumed goal or condition. It becomes converted into only one kind of response that may or may not contribute to the capacity of a society to sustain some kind of political system. System change becomes an equally important type of response.

In the second place, in spite of the latent dominance of allocative guidelines for past research on socialization—and in the next chapter we shall have more to say about the differences between allocative and system politics—we need no longer follow this lead as we reach toward a political theory of political socialization. How adults come to acquire left-right orientations in politics, why they vote as they do, where they develop their authoritarian or democratic tendencies, how they come to hold particular views on domestic or foreign issues, the way in which elites arrive and survive in the seat of power, and similar matters are undoubtedly of intense practical importance. They shed considerable light on which political party or faction is likely to win high office, which policies may be acceptable to the members of the system, and why members participate as they do. Certainly in the final details of political analysis we could not be indifferent to allocative matters such as these. Indeed the predispositions of the membership in a system, the competence and fate of its leadership, and the forces that move policy in various directions have important spillover effects for the system as a whole, for they contribute to or alleviate the stress on it.

But for systems-persistence theory, however vital these matters may otherwise be, they are at most derivative. They do not stand at the forefront, forming the initial issues, as they do from the perspectives of a partial theory of political allocations. For our theoretical purposes we need to ask questions pertinent to any and all political systems and having to do with the generic capacity of a society to support some kind of network of relationships through which binding decisions are made and implemented.

To put the matter in a different way, even if we had a fully rounded theory of political allocations—which is scarcely visible on the horizon as yet—it would tell us little about the major dimensions of all political systems, those aspects we need to investigate if we are ever to understand, at the most general level, how and why political systems operate in the way they do. If our objective is to enlarge our theoretical knowledge, then we have to interpret political socialization in relation to such a broader theory.

To work toward such a general theory, we need to analyze the conditions surrounding the persistence of political systems. In this light the question we must pose about socialization is apparent: What part, if any, does socialization play in enabling a political system to persist, even in the face of a variety of stresses and strains on the essential system variables to which most systems are exposed? We need to be able to answer such a question regardless of whether a system remains stable or changes and regardless of the nature of the specific internal processes for allocating valued things.

A full grasp of the implications of this more general theoretical point of view for the study of political socialization is not easily attained. As students of politics we are accustomed to dealing with the immediate issues of the day, partisan politics and its various determinants. These very practical issues direct our attention frequently and insistently to the study of the conditions of stability, especially for democratic regimes. These have become deeply ingrained assumptions for intuitively testing the validity of new directions in research. It becomes understandably difficult to shift intellectual direction, reinterpret what we have been doing in new terms, and isolate the new kinds of problems that new research objectives pose.

Yet to attack the basic problems of how political systems operate, what makes it possible for any political system to hang together in a society, we have no choice but to pursue a distinctively different theoretical course. Unless the reader constantly bears in mind that we are here concerned primarily with political socialization as part of a general political theory, and that this leads to an effort to understand the relationship between political socialization and the conditions underlying the capacity of any society to provide a system for allocating values authoritatively, the significance of our procedures and analysis will be obscured. For other purposes different kinds of data might have been collected about the political system from which our data are drawn—the United States—and certainly the data we have would need to be analyzed very differently.

SYSTEM STRESS

Socialization plays a vital part in enabling some kind of political system to persist. In most general theoretical terms, we may interpret socialization as one of a number of major kinds of response mechanisms through which a political system may seek to cope with stress on its essential variables. The extent to which any system does in fact utilize this kind of response and the consequences it has for the particular system will be empirical questions varying for each system.

The introduction of the notion of stress suggests that there may be forces at work that threaten to undermine the capacity of a society to sustain some kind of system through which values are authoritatively allocated. The persistence of some kind of political system would therefore depend upon the way in which it handles typical stresses.

Clearly if we are to understand the way in which socialization may contribute to the persistence of political systems, we first need to clarify what we mean by stress. As we would expect from our definition of persistence, we can say that stress will occur in any political system when there is a danger that one or both of two conditions may prevail: that the relevant members of the system will be unable to make decisions regularly for the society; or if they are able to do so, that they do not succeed in getting them accepted as authoritative by most members most of the time. When this occurs we may say that the essential variables have been stressed beyond their normal range. As has been said elsewhere,

> One of the important reasons for identifying [the] essential variables is that they give us a way of establishing when and how the disturbances acting upon a system threaten to stress it. Stress will be said to occur when there is a danger that the essential variables will be pushed beyond what we may designate as their *critical range*. . . . That is to say, it is not always a matter as to whether the essential variables are operating or have ceased to do so. It is possible that they may only be displaced to some extent as when the authorities are partially incapacitated from making decisions or from getting them accepted with complete regularity. Under these circumstances the essential variables will remain within some normal range of operations; they may be stressed but not in sufficient degree to displace them beyond a determinable critical point. As long as the system does keep its essential variables operating within what [we] shall call their critical range, some kind of system can be said to persist.[3]

Stress therefore implies something more than just the inability of a particular kind of political system to function in accord with some preconceived idea or ideal about how it should operate. In the latter, more limited sense, we might say that a democracy experiences stress when the people take to the streets to enforce their will or when the representatives act without concern for the wishes of the represented. But for general theory we are only derivatively concerned with such matters. Our primary focus is on those kinds of conditions that might prevent any and all types of political systems from functioning. If circumstances prevented any decisions from being taken or, once taken, from being accepted as binding, no political system, democratic, authoritarian, or otherwise, could endure. It is this possible outcome that becomes the test for determining whether a stressful condition has occurred.

But as we have suggested, we cannot help but be derivatively interested in what happens to a particular type of system. If a given type does suffer stress for one or another reason and this threatens to destroy that type of system, it could conceivably be the first step to undermining the capacity of the given society for sustaining any kind of political system. If, for example, a specific democratic system were threatened in the ways depicted a moment ago, the society might turn to some other type of system, such as a dictatorship, and preserve its capacity for making authoritative decisions. In this sense the change would be interpreted as a response that permitted some kind of political system to endure. A shift toward a dictatorial regime need not, of course, necessarily be the only type of outcome. There might be a whole range of alternatives, each of which might have been equally successful for assuring the persistence of some kind of political system. But when a specific political system does undergo stress, this immediately raises the question of whether the society will be able to take measures to continue behavior patterns through which political decisions can be made and implemented. In this sense, every threat to an existing political system arouses doubts as to whether in its outcome, the stress may undermine the capacity of the society to provide some means for taking political action.[4]

Stress may come from a number of major directions, and there are numerous characteristic structures and procedures that have been invented in systems and that have helped to alleviate (often to aggravate) its causes. Among these we find socialization itself. But if we are to understand something about the way in which socialization may or may not operate on stress, we need to inspect the sources from which stress on systems typically arise.

Although in this book the data will be concerned with only one type of stress, that occasioned by insufficient support, we can put this special interest in better perspective if we glance briefly at the range of types of stress to which socialization itself is relevant. We need to address ourselves therefore to the questions: What are the typical ways through which stress may arise for a political system? How may socialization be interpreted as a response to these kinds of stress?

OUTPUT STRESS

Stress may result from the failure of most of the politically significant members to accept most of the outputs as binding most of the time. *Outputs* are *those decisions and actions taken by the political authorities.* It requires little argument to demonstrate that unless the decisions and actions of those members who bear the responsibility for taking care of the day-to-day problems of the system — the political authorities — are normally accepted as binding or authoritative, a society will quickly be reduced to a state of chaos.

Socialization represents an important mechanism that may help members of a system to internalize a need to comply, or, as we say in legal systems, a need "to obey legally constituted authority." Generally we might assume that in most systems childhood socialization probably contributes significantly to the growth of a belief that it is good and necessary to comply with authoritative outputs.

We cannot however take this for granted. In the first place, however purposively socialization may be used to induce automatic compliance, it need not implant this obligation so deeply that it withstands every strain. As revolutions, riots, tumultuous street demonstrations, and individual deliberate violations of the law reveal, even in presumably stable systems, other pressures may build up sufficient strength to override any sense of a duty to obey. Most systems find it necessary to devise alternative means to compensate for the possible failure of childhood socialization to establish the desired level of compliance. These alternative means act directly on adults, often in the form of threats of coercion, promises of special benefits, or calculated appeals to deep underlying feelings of patriotism.

In the second place, not all members in a system necessarily seek to implant in children the desire to comply with political outputs. On occasion in developed systems, such as the United States, new adult patterns toward political authorities — as among blacks and other ethnic groups — may offer children behavior models that will encourage the rejection of many kinds of political decisions. Similarly, changing ideas of morality, as we find them in the New Left in the United States during the 1960s, have already led significant numbers of pre-adults to search for new political roles in which automatic obedience to the political order does not rank high.

In many developing systems as well, where opposition to the regime may be intense and widespread, it is not clear that children either directly or inadvertently learn to prefer compliance to resistance and change. The experiences of children may lead in opposite directions. For example, in South Vietnam during the early 1960s, children and young adolescents appear to have been used as shock troops in street demonstrations opposing the existing leadership.[5]

Although we might suspect that the autonomous experiences of childhood and the teaching of adults might lead most children to acquire sentiments favoring compliance, there is no guarantee that this will be the outcome in fact or that adults will universally seek to encourage such obedience. Socialization under some circumstances may therefore serve to aggravate rather than ameliorate stress. But regardless of the outcome, one aspect of the theoretical significance of socialization is the consequences it may have for stress due to the reluctance to accept outputs as binding.

DEMAND-INPUT STRESS

Another major source of stress lies in the overload that may result from an excess of demands put into a system. If a system is confronted with too many demands in a given interval of time, the communication and processing structures can become so clogged that the system will be faced with a possible breakdown.

Systems have typical ways of handling this condition in order to preserve some way of processing demands through to outputs. They may modify the structure of the regime so that more channels are opened up. They may speed up the processing of demands through existing channels. They may invent rules for cutting off discussion on any single demand. But among the varied means at the disposal of systems, the development of a sense of self-restraint in the conversion of social wants into political demands represents a major device in every age. The individual member's own sense of what is or is not appropriate to inject into the political process imposes limits on the volume and variety of demands which a system is called upon to process.

The assumption here is that the members of every society possess many wants. Some of these can be satisfied or handled through the autonomous interaction of the members themselves, individually or in groups. Typically the members will not feel it proper to attempt political settlements for all their wants. In only a limited number of areas, depending upon the particular culture, will wants be converted into political demands.

For example, in no two types of systems will the members necessarily agree about the kinds of wants considered appropriate for political negotiations. In small tribal systems it may be that most matters, including those that in larger systems might be considered exclusively family concerns, may be handled by the elders in their councils. But in most large industrialized systems, severe cultural restrictions may be imposed on introducing many matters into the political arena. If many disputes among the members of large-scale systems were not settled autonomously, without invoking the complex machinery of the political processes, it is doubtful whether any kind of political system could operate at all, let alone operate according to any established criteria of efficiency. No two types of political systems therefore need show equal tolerance for the same kinds of political demands or equal capacity for handling the same proportion of wants politically.

Furthermore, no two eras in any single type of system need utilize the same standards for determining the appropriateness of converting wants into political demands. In Western political systems, during the mercantilist period, no detail of commerce was considered too small as a subject for government regulation. But in the succeeding laissez-faire epoch, new standards emerged. In its ideal formulation political regulation was to be countenanced only for the maintenance of law and order. With the modern welfare state, however, a far broader range of subjects is typically accepted for political settlement even in the ideologically most conservative systems. But regardless of the criteria employed, even in one and the same type of system each age produces knowable cultural restraints on the kinds of matters it will entertain for political discussion.

Whatever the nature of the cultural restrictions imposed on political demands, few systems in fact postpone to adulthood all instruction in the kinds of restraints to be expected. At a very early age the members in every system probably begin to acquire some sense of what the members in that particular system consider appropriate matters for political discussion. At the very least they probably learn that they ought not to consider it necessary or desirable to turn to political means in order to satisfy all wants. Beyond this they will be exposed to cues about various specific types of demands that may lie beyond the political pale.

Not that maturing members of a system need abide by the conventions of the past. Indeed it may be that a major source of change in political systems is the way in which a rising generation, from its own experiences, seeks to transform the raw material which forms the subject matter of political contention. Each generation may develop a unique sense of the kinds of matters they ought to inject into the political process and those that ought to remain outside. This may be a major source of intergenerational political conflict, as differences in the youthful radicalism of the Depression years and of the New Left of the 1960s would suggest. But whatever the nature of the process governing the input of demands, socialization may serve as a system response through which each generation learns some degree of self-restraint, if the system is not to suffer from the stress of demand-input overload.

STRESS FROM THE INPUT OF SUPPORT

Stress from outputs and from the input of demands are both subject to possible regulation through the socializing processes in a political system. The way in which this regulation may operate lies beyond our present concern even though for a rounded view of the theoretical relevance of socialization, it has been necessary to touch on these sources of system stress. Our research concentrates rather on the stress that may arise from the inability of a system to keep the input of support at some minimal level.

But even here we need to continue to narrow our focus for purposes of manageable research. We shall not be able to consider the input of support for all political objects. Our attention will be confined in this book to support only for the structure of authority. But to sharpen the specific theoretical focus of our interest in political socialization, we shall examine in some detail the general part that the input of support plays in a political system.

The meaning of support

Support we may define simply as *feelings of trust, confidence, or affection, and their opposites, that persons may direct to some object.* If support is positive, a person favors an object; if support is negative, he withholds or withdraws his favor from the object. Support will vary in degree from absolute hostility to blind loyalty. Typically the notion of support is used in its positive sense. For negative support it is normal to adopt such synonyms as hostility, discontent, dissatisfaction, and distrust.[6] But in our discussion, *unless the context indicates otherwise,* when we speak of support we shall mean both negative and positive support. This convention will spare us the tedium of needlessly repeating that support may move in both directions.

The objects of support

When we speak of support for a political system, it may appear satisfactory to view the system as an undifferentiated whole. But this is probably the least helpful way of approaching the study of support. When positive support declines in a political system, for example, it typically does so only for certain of the basic aspects of the system and not for others. The members may become disaffected from the existing rulers but continue to place confidence in the constitutional order. They may become dissatisfied with the constitutional order but retain a strong identification with those whom they typically see as part of their political system. Support — attachment for a system, confidence and trust in it, and similar kinds of feelings — is thus better understood if we see it as directed to specifiable aspects of a system, not to all its elements without differentiation. By identifying the basic components of a political system that seem relevant to the input of support, we shall obtain a useful tool for analyzing the specific nature of the stress on the system and thereby a way of sorting out the particular part that socialization may play.

For theoretical purposes that go beyond the objectives of the present research, it is helpful to break a political system into three major components or objects: the political community, the regime, and the authorities. These categories are discussed in great detail elsewhere, so here we need only describe their meanings briefly.[7] Major sources of stress are to be found in the decline of support (that is, in the growth of negative support) for any one of these political objects.

The *political community* refers to *that aspect of a political system that we can identify as a collection of persons who share a division of political labor.* Part of what uniquely identifies a member of the French political system, for example, is his belief that there are others with whom he should participate in making and implementing most day-to-day decisions and whom he calls his fellow Frenchmen or countrymen. It does not matter that in fact he is totally uninvolved in politics and cooperates with the other members of the system only to the extent that he complies with political outputs. He shares a political community with others in that he does not expect that these daily political issues will be resolved through a structure that will normally include, say, those in Germany or Great Britain. The mode of resolving differences may change radically in France, from a democracy in the Third and Fourth Republics to a semi-authoritarian system in the Fifth. But the persons with whom he expects to cooperate or to join in making, implementing, and accepting binding decisions — regardless of his own role in the process — may remain relatively constant.

Departure from the political community is possible, and this is the final act of dissatisfaction, or withdrawal of positive support. If a person were sufficiently unhappy with life in France and if he had the resources to execute his desires, he could throw his lot in with members of some other system and, for example, migrate to French Canada. In this event the person would be in process of transferring his identification to a new political community. Aspirations and actions that look toward emigration, separatism, irredentism, and cargo sectarianism usually reflect at least some negative support for the political community. Whatever the specific motivation may be — such as the search for an improved standard of living, increased social tolerance for deviant relations, the pursuit of adventure, or the longing for a release from current frustrations — the consequences for the input of support is for us the politically relevant aspect.

The *regime* describes *that part of the political system that we may call its constitutional order in the very broadest sense of the term.* It refers to the underlying goals that the members of the system pursue, the norms or rules of the game through which they conduct their political business, and the formal and informal structures of authority that arrange who is to do what in the system. Political science has given birth to many different ways of classifying regimes ranging from the classical Aristotelian set — monarchy, aristocracy, and polity, with their corrupted forms — to the extremely variable modern categories of democracy, totalitarianism, authoritarianism, dictatorship, competitive-party regime, one-party regime, and the like. Each type reflects a unique combination of goals, operating norms, and structural arrangements.

The assumption here is that no aggregate of persons would be able to resolve its differences authoritatively unless it had developed some minimal structure of authority, even if represented only in the difference between elders in a tribal group and the rest of the members. Neither could the members hope to continue as a group if they did not share some minimal goals and abide by some kinds of rules for solving their differences in common, at least for those cases where private settlements could not be achieved. In this sense it is difficult to conceive of any kind of society, however small, in which a political regime did not emerge for handling those kinds of differences we would call political, that is, those that require some kind of settlement through the making of binding decisions.[8]

Finally, *the authorities* are *those members of a system in whom the primary responsibility is lodged for taking care of the daily routines of a political system.* In democratic systems we describe them as the elected representatives and other public officials, such as civil servants. In other systems we may identify them as the rulers, governors, or political elite. In our terminology they are the actual occupants of the seats of political authority, excluding the aspirants and contenders for office, who are usually also vital forces in a political system.

It is clear that no system could hope to persist unless it had some members who saw it as their duty or responsibility to conduct the routine business of the system. It is not enough that members identify strongly with their political community and have faith in some regime. Most of the politically relevant (or effective) members must also be prepared to lend their favor to some set of authorities and accept their actions as binding, even if only tentatively, reluctantly, or under coercion. At the very least their support must take the form of acquiescent neutrality, if some kind of political system is to persist.

Stress on the essential variables, therefore, may flow from a condition in which support declines below some determinate level for one or another of these three basic political objects. Below this level of support, one or another of these fundamental components of a system would be inoperative. For some kind of system to persist, a society must be able to assure itself that its members share a division of political labor, that there is a regime acceptable to most politically relevant members, and that some authorities are ready and able to govern. If a society is unable to sustain any one of these three objects (political community, regime, political authorities), we hypothesize that its political system—a network of relationships through which authoritative allocations of valued things occur—will not endure for long.

It should be clear that change in any of the objects need not necessarily destroy the capacity of the society in question to allocate values authoritatively. The form of the regime, the occupants of the authority roles, or the size, composition, and degree of cohesiveness of the political community may vary enormously. Yet the society might still be able to make decisions and get them accepted as binding.

In line with this, our interest is in the conditions for the persistence of all kinds of political systems, and not only those of any special type such as democracy or dictatorship. If we were primarily concerned with democratic systems, for example, we would want to inquire into the conditions for the persistence of that type of system, as a type. We would ask: How do democratic systems manage to avoid stress.of the various sorts already described? But our point is that regardless of type, no system for making and implementing binding decisions can hope to persist unless it can provide for the existence of some kind of political community, regime, and set of authorities.

Types of support

The support that a member extends toward any political object is not always of a uniform kind. In some instances he may be favorably disposed toward one or another object because of the specific benefits or advantages he associates with it; in other instances he may develop some diffuse, generalized sentiments which tie him firmly to the object even though he may at times suffer considerable inconvenience as a result. Each of these two types of support is differently linked to the capacity of a system to persist over time. This suggests the utility of dividing support into two basic types, specific and diffuse. We shall examine each of these briefly.

To some extent members of a system may be willing to praise or blame the authorities for the benefits or deprivations associated with membership in the system. The rewards and disadvantages of membership may be attributed to something that those thought to be responsible for making decisions do or fail to do. The responses of the members are in part a *quid pro quo* for what they see themselves as obtaining from membership in the system. In this sense the support the members extend is *specific*. It will increase or decline depending upon the way in which the members interpret the consequences of the various outputs of the system.

It is clear that if members feel that the existing authorities are not providing them with the kinds of outputs they believe they have a right to expect, one kind of stress on the system may result. If the system could not provide some set of authorities over time that met these expectations, the inability to generate specific support might become critical. In time, discontent with outputs might spill over to the regime. If each succeeding set of authorities proved unable or unwilling to satisfy the demands of the politically relevant members in a system, these members might begin to believe that there was something basically deficient in the regime. Similarly if changes introduced into the regime did little to satisfy the situation or if it were impossible to obtain such changes, the decline of specific support might spread from both the authorities and the regime to the political community itself. The relevant members of the system might begin to feel that there was little point in seeking to share a common division of labor. Groups of persons participating in the system might begin to lose their sense of political solidarity, and they might seek to form new political systems, independent of each other. Alternatively, some significant part of the membership might break away, as in a separatist movement, to link themselves with other systems.

But regardless of the particular outcome for the stability or change of the basic political objects, we can recognize the independent contribution that specific support—both negative and positive—makes to the capacity of a system to persist. Through specific support we are able to isolate those sentiments that are linked to what the members see the authorities as doing or failing to do. Although specific responses may begin as feelings about the authorities, they may ultimately spill over to infect the attitudes toward the regime and political community itself.

Of course stressful negative sentiments need not necessarily destroy a system. The discontented members require the resources and the will to act on their feelings. Also, many compensating mechanisms may be activated to help reduce the stress of increasing dissatisfactions. Yet if the members in a system who count— those whom we may call the politically relevant or significant members—begin to lose confidence in all basic objects of the system, as manifested through the decline of their specific support, the presence of stress is apparent. The persistence of some kind of system would have to be ascribed to other factors, probably to the level of what we call diffuse support.

Diffuse support is a second line of defense, as it were, against stress in a system. By *diffuse support* we mean *the generalized trust and confidence that members invest in the various objects of the system as ends in themselves.*[9] The peculiar quality of this kind of attachment to an object is that it is not contingent on any *quid pro quo;* it is offered unconditionally. In its extreme form it may appear as blind loyalty or unshakable patriotism.

But for the presence of diffuse support it is difficult to understand how a political system would be able to weather the discontent brought on by objectionable policies (outputs) and resultant cleavages in a system. Diffuse support forms a reservoir upon which a system typically draws in times of crises, such as depressions, wars, and internecine conflicts, when perceived benefits may recede to their lowest ebb. A system must also rely on diffuse support on a day-to-day basis, as outputs frequently call upon members to undergo hardships for the system in the form of taxes, hazardous military service, or other sacrifices of time, labor, and even life. An ideally rational member might bring himself to balance present sacrifices and deprivations against specific future benefits. But few members pursue such a calculus. Yet even if everyone did and the calculus were notoriously out of balance on the side of hardships, there might be little question in the minds of most as to whether they ought to continue to extend positive support to the various objects in the system. By adulthood a member may have acquired a deep-rooted attachment to the system that could withstand enormous pressures of dissatisfaction.

The presence of diffuse support helps us to understand why the fabric of a political system is not always rent asunder by cleavage and conflict among its constitutive groups as each seeks to increase its share of the goods and to shift to others a higher part of the costs. Rational self-interest at times might dictate holding out to the bitter end for one's goals. But conciliation and concession may be a response to a learned need and desire, reinforced throughout life, to abide by conditions that will permit the given political system to work. Attachment to the system may override particular needs. But when a society fails to breed such internalized positive sentiments in its members about some kind of political system or when the experiences of the members militate against such feelings, stress is likely to occur.

Withdrawal of diffuse support from a given regime or political community need not mean of course that the society is unable to sustain some other type of regime or community. The decline of diffuse support may only mark the occasion for members to seek important changes in the nature of the regime or the community. If timely and appropriate, these changes may enable *some* kind of political system to persist even though the previous regime or political community may have disappeared.

We do not hypothesize therefore that all members must learn to extend unrequited love for their system or its component objects. Rather we are only suggesting that *for some kind of system to persist over time*—either with the same authorities, regime, or community, or with one or another of these changed—most of the politically relevant members must have learned to put in a minimal level of diffuse support for the various political objects, whatever their form. In this way a system can hedge against breakdown as a result of the absence or the decline of specific support. But when both diffuse and specific support fall to a low level, the system will be in difficulties, and we can say that critical stress has occurred. There is a danger that the society will not be able to provide some structures and processes for handling political differences.

For the persistence of some kind of political system, therefore, support is a theoretically critical dimension in all political systems. The extent to which and the way in which socialization contributes to the input of support emerge as central questions.

STRUCTURAL STRESS

As we have observed, a political system is in effect a vast and complex set of processes through which inputs of support and demands are converted into authoritative outputs. This suggests that even if members should learn behaviors that avoid stressing the essential variables on the input and output sides, breakdown might occur in the structures and processes through which conversion itself takes place.

Every type of system has its own kinds of structures and processes through which demands are collected, reduced in numbers, and organized into some kind of agenda for action.[10] Each system has also to mobilize positive support and move it toward the appropriate basic political objects. In addition, outputs of some kind need to be formulated and put into effect if differences left unregulated through autonomous processes are to be settled authoritatively. All these activities will take different form depending upon the kind of regime under consideration—democratic, dictatorial, tribal, authoritarian, or whatever. In some systems the basic units participating in one way or another in the conversion processes may take the form of interest groups, parties, legislatures, administrative organizations, courts, and aggregated publics. In other systems the structure may consist only of a group of elders who gather in the fields of an evening, supplemented by informal channels and roles through which communication with the ordinary members of the system takes place.

But however well differentiated the political roles and organizations may be, if some kind of system is to be able to persist, processes need to occur within the society whereby some members acquire the knowledge, skills, and motivations to take some active part in political life. If this does not occur, if the system fails to provide the personnel for helping to convert inputs into outputs and for implementing the outputs, stress of a structural nature is the result.

Similar to our remarks about stress from demands, support, and outputs, these about structural sources of stress do not imply that the members of a system necessarily learn how to perform its existing specific roles. Any implication of this kind would impel us toward unacceptable system-maintenance assumptions. It follows logically from our analysis to this point that a system may fail to prepare its members for the particular political roles in the society at a given time. Indeed, as we have noted, the older generations might consciously "unprepare" the young people for the existing way of doing things. Change may be deliberately sought, and thereby new kinds of roles and new goals defined.

What we are suggesting here is that regardless of whether the members of the system seek to perpetuate the given conversion structure in identical form or search for a diametrically opposite way of doing things, the essential variables will not be able to operate unless some kinds of conversion structures are present in the system. One of the important tasks of a political theory of political socialization, therefore, would be to inquire into the way in which a system introduces its members to its structures. Socialization is a mechanism available for a system to help it handle possible structural stress.

SOCIALIZATION, CHANGE, AND STABILITY

We may conclude therefore that a political theory of political socialization need not be restricted to tracing out the roots of adult behavior relevant to the allocative processes of a system or to exploring the childhood origins of political stability. In each of these areas early socialization may well be significant, but socialization may have numerous other possible consequences for a system. In the prevailing implicit theories, these tend to be ignored or to be of peripheral concern. A theoretical design that alerts us to a broader range of outcomes is needed. This is precisely why we cast our understanding of socialization within the framework of systems analysis, or systems-persistence theory.

From this point of view, political socialization is one major kind of response by which a system may seek to avoid stress on its essential variables. It must be able to reduce such stress if it is to continue to operate as a system of behavior through which values in a society may be authoritatively allocated. On the output side, through socialization the system may be able to assure itself of the acceptance of decisions as binding. On the input side, socialization may help to limit the volume and variety of demands and thus prevent the communication networks from becoming overburdened to the point of collapse. Socializing processes may prepare members to undertake those roles relevant for the conversion of inputs to binding outputs. Finally, socialization may also act as a major response by which a system seeks to generate at least a minimal level of positive support for those basic political objects without which no system could operate at all. All these major systemic consequences need to be included in any possible theory about the political relevance of socialization.

It bears repetition that systems analysis does not possess a built-in conservative bias. Our theoretical posture does not allow us to predict in advance whether the particular content and methods of socialization will in fact enable some kind of political system to continue. Indeed, if we include nonliterate or tribal societies in our sample of political systems, more systems have probably disappeared in the past than have endured. In some important instances the socializing processes may have made their small contribution to the destruction of these systems. At least this is a possible source of system failure that needs to be investigated. On the other hand, those societies under stress that have been able to retain some kind of system for making and implementing binding decisions have probably adopted socializing procedures to which part of their success may be attributed. It is clear, therefore, that socialization may have many broad outcomes. In principle it may contribute to the maintenance or replication of a given system, to its transformation, or to its total destruction.

SOCIALIZATION AND DIFFUSE SUPPORT

Our present research interest is guided by the broad perspectives of a political theory of political socialization such as this.

But out of the total range of subjects of dominant theoretical importance to the area of socialization as it bears on systems persistence, our inquiry limits itself to diffuse support. By seeking to unearth the roots of diffuse support, we hope to shed some light on the way in which socialization operates as a response mechanism to potential stress on support. Subsequently we shall impose additional constraints that further narrow our research concerns to the input of diffuse support for the structure of authority.

In this search for an understanding of the way in which socialization acts as a system response, certain major questions present themselves. To begin with, does socialization contribute to the input of support at all, or is this simply a theoretical possibility without empirical reference? And if socializing processes do stimulate support for basic political objects, at what age do members typically begin to learn to extend support? In what ways does it become possible for them to acquire their positive or negative sentiments?

Diffuse support in childhood

We cannot take it for granted that the introduction to supportive sentiment begins in childhood. Indeed it is possible and even plausible that so theoretically and empirically vital a sentiment could be postponed to adolescence or early adulthood. Presuppositions in the little speculation available on this subject suggest starting points as late as these. (We shall examine the validity of these presuppositions in the next chapter.) But whatever the period of the life cycle at which supportive orientations strike root, they are not biologically inherited; they need to be acquired. The extent to which socialization makes a contribution to their presence needs to be explored and understood.

If we assume temporarily that children are able to acquire supportive sentiments about so apparently abstruse a subject as basic political objects, one point is clear. Diffuse rather than specific support is likely to be particularly relevant in the study of childhood socialization. Only under very unusual circumstances could we conceive of children being motivated to extend specific support to any of the political objects. They are seldom aware of the relationship between what happens to them on the one hand and the specific outputs of the authorities on the other. Not that they fail to envisage government as being concerned about them and their families and even as being vigilant and active on their behalf. We shall discuss this in detail in later chapters.

But this perception is not related to specific outputs from which they consider themselves to benefit. At best, if children do have sentiments about the various political objects, these sentiments will probably be diffuse, they will not fluctuate directly with perceivable variations in the outputs of the authorities.

This is not to argue that we should expect children to learn only to feel positively toward political objects, any more than this is a legitimate expectation about adults. If, for example, the children were part of a minority group the adults of which felt oppressed or unjustifiedly deprived, neglected, or rejected, we would expect that the children would be likely to pick up similar kinds of sentiments. In each system we need to determine the degree to which, if children do indeed learn to put in diffuse support, it moves in a negative or positive direction.

We cannot assume, therefore, that socialization of diffusely supportive sentiments will necessarily lead either to stability or to change, to the perpetuation of a given type of system or to its destruction. Even if supportive orientations have their beginning in childhood, the consequences for the system will depend upon the content transmitted or learned and, because not all members need be socialized in the same direction, also upon the nature of the distribution of these attitudes throughout the population of children. This is an additional reason why we need to disassociate ourselves carefully from the prevailing assumptions about socialization that see it as contributing to the maintenance of existing patterns of behavior.

Nevertheless, even if the systemic consequences of socialization will always depend upon the orientations young people acquire, one thing is clear. Unless a society is able to fashion some bond between a member and its political authorities, regime, and political community, no kind of political system could possibly endure. It is from this primary and overarching hypothesis that we are led to investigate the nature of political socialization in childhood in the American political system as it relates to the input of diffuse support for basic political objects.

Diffuse support in the American system

Why do we turn to the American system as the subject of our research? At least two reasons lie behind this choice. For one thing, it is impossible to examine directly the feelings of a person for the basic political objects in the abstract. We need to look at children in the concrete setting of some specific political system.

But more than this is involved. Although the comparative study of a number of systems was an available option, it seemed to be the least productive way of initiating research in this area. When we began our research in the late 1950s, we were still at the earliest stage of inquiry about primary socialization and support. We had no bench marks to guide us in establishing a design for the comparison of political systems. It seemed appropriate therefore to begin with a system in which a rich body of ancillary knowledge, especially about adults, such as we have for the American system, would permit us to make the best use of what we could learn about children.

But we do recognize the ultimate limits this imposes on our findings. Only when a number of different types of systems, in addition to the American, have been explored will it be feasible to propose reliable generalizations about the sources of diffuse support and its connection with the persistence of political systems.

Because we have selected the American system, furthermore, most readers will find in our data and conclusions much of interest about the early forces shaping adult political behavior in democratic systems; or because the American system has been stable over past years, some inferences may be drawn about the conditions of stability. There is little doubt that our analysis will present substantial spin-off benefits of these kinds. We recognize, however, that in this there lurks the danger that our intentions will be misconstrued and our analyses misunderstood. It should be clear by now that these kinds of interpretations will be incidental to our major purposes. Our primary objective is to expand the boundaries of general theory, not to add to a partial or special theory of democracy or of the conditions of political stability. It is only incidentally that we present a case study of that class of systems we call democracies. Our long-range interest is in political systems as such in contrast with other kinds of social systems. It is within this context that our interpretations ultimately need to be evaluated.

NOTES

1. For this concept see D. Easton, *A Systems Analysis of Political Life* (New York: Wiley, 1965), p. 222. Politically relevant "applies only to those members of a system who count, those who share in the effective power of the system. They may be few or many . . ."
2. For a full discussion of this way of describing a political system,

see D. Easton, *The Political System* (New York: Knopf, 1953); and *A Framework for Political Analysis* (Englewood Cliffs, N.J.: Prentice-Hall, 1965).

3. D. Easton, *A Systems Analysis of Political Life,* pp. 24-25. For the full theoretical implications of these concepts, see also D. Easton, *A Framework for Political Analysis.*

4. We do not suggest of course that the experience of political stress by a system is by its very nature, from an ethical point of view, undesirable. Stress is a neutral term. A philosophy of politics may call for radical changes and thereby deliberately seek to undermine the prevailing order. The stress on the persistence of any political system is here incidental to the higher good embodied in the proposed political order. The mere fact that the members of every society must act so as to make it possible to arrive at political settlements, if the society itself is to continue, has nothing to say about the relative merits of one kind of system as against another. The purpose of this analytic formulation is not to pass judgment on efforts to bring about change but to provide a framework for analyzing the consequences of the changes that do or do not take place.

5. The involvement of children in politics is exemplified further in the life of one of the leaders of the guerrillas in Guatemala during the 1960s. Cesar Montes, at age thirteen, was reported to have been "expelled from a Catholic school, due to his fury over the CIA's coup against the leftist Arbenz regime. At 18 he led student demonstrations and saw his fellow students shot dead before his eyes. At 20 he went to the mountains. By 24 he was the leader of one of the most important guerilla movements in Latin America." E. Galeano, "With the Guerrillas in Guatemala," *Ramparts,* 6, p. 57, 1967.

6. For a fuller discussion of this concept in its positive and negative implications see D. Easton, *A Systems Analysis of Political Life.*

7. Ibid.

8. We consider the structure of authority in greater detail in Chapter 5.

9. This kind of support is fully discussed in *A Systems Analysis of Political Life,* pp. 273ff.

10. Ibid.

PRIMARY SOCIALIZATION
OF SUPPORT
FOR
THE STRUCTURE
OF AUTHORITY

PART

2

4

THE BEGINNINGS
OF
POLITICAL
SOCIALIZATION

We have noted the shortcomings of allocative and system-maintenance models for assessing the significance of political socialization and have turned to systems-persistence theory, a mode of analysis that favors neither stability nor change. It looks upon political interaction as a system capable of coping with environmental and internal conditions either by stabilizing or changing one or another of its basic components. Specifically, we have argued that one of the unalterable conditions for the persistence of a political system, whatever its type, is its capacity to evoke a minimum of positive support for these components.

A system may take a number of alternative paths to promote sentiments of this sort. It could, for example, ignore all pre-adults and concentrate on marshalling support only among adults. Or it could hedge against placing all its eggs in the adult basket and seek to nurture supportive sentiments in children. In this chapter we shall examine the plausibility of assuming that this is indeed where support has its roots. We shall seek a preliminary answer to the following question: At what stage of their life do members of a political system first become capable of expressing favorable or unfavorable sentiments toward basic political objects?

When we have some initial sense that childhood is indeed a sensible place to begin looking for one source of basic political commitment or alienation, we shall then be able to pass on to other questions about the specific targets and nature of these sentiments. We will be able to ask: At what points or locations in the system do members during childhood make their initial contacts with the political objects?

To examine how members begin to feel about theoretically significant aspects of politics, however, we need to know what it is that they perceive. What the child reacts to may serve as important linkage points to the system. In addition, the very nature of the perceived political objects may limit or expand the kinds of emotions that the child can express about them. This suggests a final question: What kinds of perceptions and sentiments do the members of the system acquire for the political objects at these various points of contact? We need to lay bare the nature or quality of the support, its negative or positive tendencies.

In effect these three questions sketch out the major paths of our research. We sought to discover whether at an early stage in the life cycle members become capable of relating themselves to important political things, to what on their political horizon they can become attached at that stage, and the kinds of supportive sentiments they entertain about these objects together with the potential consequences for the political system.

In this chapter we open up the first subject. When may we reasonably assume that political learning begins and on what a priori grounds can we support our answer? Later, analysis of our data will of course give us positive evidence for the preliminary theoretical conclusion here that childhood is a period of rapid political learning in certain areas. But it is important, in order to get some sense not only of the novelty of political research about children but also of its sound theoretical underpinnings, to inquire, if only briefly, into how children have happened to be overlooked and why students of politics have almost universally put political learning off until after childhood. In seeking therefore to justify on theoretical grounds our turning to socialization during childhood, we shall find it mandatory to isolate and assess theoretical assumptions that in the past have led to the neglect of this period as one of significant political learning.

EARLY SOCIALIZATION AND ITS SYSTEMIC CONSEQUENCES

Before setting out on this task, however, we need to be completely clear about what we plan to do. We shall not be seeking to *prove* that what is learned early is likely to be more influential than what is learned later and that therefore students of adult behavior have underestimated the impact of childhood socialization on the political system. This may well be true, *at least in certain political areas,* as we shall affirm later. But we would not mislead the reader into thinking that we plan to test this assumption or that we have direct and reliable evidence about its validity. It remains merely a plausible working assumption. In this we are no worse off than the rest of social science. Nowhere has any solid evidence been adduced about the longitudinal impact of early socialization.[1] Surprisingly, even in an era shot through with Freudian preconceptions, the effect of childhood experience on adult behavior is still moot. The answer to it is typically based largely on the overwhelming weight of impressionistic or loose circumstantial evidence. The technical requirements for determining the validity of this assumption are so complex and time consuming that they have hitherto discouraged any reliable testing efforts.

At this point in our discussion, however, we are not as yet concerned with the systemic consequences of early political socialization. We wish only to ascertain how it happens that students of politics, as distinct from those interested in other types of social behavior, have not considered childhood a period in which maturing members of a system are exposed to important kinds of political orientations. Whether children in fact undergo direct political learning seems, for many researchers, to be intertwined almost inextricably with the conviction that even if they do, it has little importance for subsequent behavior—it comes too early in the life cycle not to be washed out by later experiences. Inevitably a presupposition such as this helps to turn research away from childhood. Thus even though we cannot escape paying some attention to the significance of early learning, we shall do so here only to help us understand better why past research about political socialization has uniformly turned its back on children.

THE CASE AGAINST EARLY POLITICAL SOCIALIZATION

At what age would it be reasonable to expect persons to be ready to absorb information and develop feelings about political life? Defining childhood arbitrarily as the years between six and thirteen, can we give any credence to the idea that children of so tender an age, particularly in the early years of this stage, can hold political views and express political feelings? Unless it is theoretically plausible to adjudge children capable of orienting themselves cognitively and emotionally to political things, there can be little point in trying to search out their supportive attitudes, whether negative or positive.

The prevailing trend

From time immemorial, social philosophers have thought that political education *should* have an early start. For Plato and Rousseau there was also little question about the feasibility of such early instruction; to them it was common sense that young children could be educated in fundamental political matters. They felt little need to exert themselves trying to demonstrate this. The only unknown was the nature of what should be taught.

Modern research has seemed to challenge, indirectly and unwittingly, what the classical social philosophers over the ages have assumed. Socialization of many nonpolitical roles and traits is known to begin as early as infancy. Yet for political roles and attitudes, there has been a strange reluctance even to entertain the possibility of the same early origins. Extensive studies have contributed to the belief that oral, aggressive, dependent, delinquent, achieving, sexual, neurotic, affiliative, and other behavior can be traced to infancy[2] and childhood, and even that politically relevant personality dispositions toward authority in general are learned at a very early age.[3] However, few scholars have recognized direct learning of significant political orientations during this period. Until recently the entire weight of evidence, such as it was, pointed firmly toward adolescence and early adulthood as the politically formative stage, although not always for the same reasons.

On what grounds has this apparent judgment been based? We can discern at least three fairly well-defined if latent explanations for believing that political socialization begins only in some period well past childhood. For some, the "personality school," childhood is a period in which only a prepolitical personality takes shape; subsequent reactions to political phenomena are molded by the basic personality. For others, those whom we shall designate as the "proximity theorists," children may in fact learn some things about politics. But the significance of this is seriously diminished because what is learned later in life, being closer to adult political experiences, overshadows any earlier political learning. Finally, still others would claim that past research reveals that children are really not in a "state of readiness," as the argot of professional educationists puts it, for political learning. They are capable of absorbing little by way of political knowledge or attitudes. In addition they show such a slight interest in politics that there is little reason for believing that they would be affected by the political sphere.

On examining each of these positions in turn we shall find that the validity of assigning socialization to postchildhood periods rests essentially on an excessively narrow conception of politics. If we change one of the premises central to these positions—about the meaning to be ascribed to politics—we greatly increase the plausibility of important direct political socialization among children.

Prepolitical personality

Most theorizing about the early socialization of personality removes politics from the sphere of primary (infancy and childhood) socialization and places it at the secondary (adolescence and adulthood) level. As we have noted, childhood is seen primarily as a period of nonpolitical but politically relevant learning.[4] It is a position that has often been tied to widely accepted psychoanalytic presuppositions about the significance of infancy and childhood and the early family milieu for later life.

Peculiarly, the emphasis of this approach is upon primary socialization as the fundamental determinant of later political attitudes. Yet it carefully excludes direct or even inadvertent learning of a specifically political nature. Adult political behavior is interpreted as projective or a derivative of basic personality, modal personality type, or character structure; personality itself is considered to be a product of modes of child rearing typical of a culture. In this kind of personality-in-culture theorizing the acquisition of political attitudes is postponed to secondary phases of the life cycle; politics is largely the acting out of predispositions developed at an earlier stage. At the very least, later political behavior filters through the individual's culturally shaped personality.

Pye, for example, clearly reflects this conception. He postulates that individuals ". . . become members of first the society and then the polity."[5] Indeed he elaborates a three-stage theory according to which, in the first stage, that of basic socialization,

". . . the child is inducted into his particular (general) culture and trained to become a member of his society." In the second stage ". . . comes political socialization, through which the individual develops his awareness of his political world . . . just as he was first socialized to his political culture . . ." Finally, ". . . there is the process of political recruitment, when the individual goes beyond the passive role of citizen and observer to become an active participant. . ."[6]

Although this theory of the socializing sequence is not central to Pye's study, it does help to accent elements important for those who adopt personality-in-culture as a point of departure. It designates infancy and childhood as politically preparatory phases in which direct political learning is either absent or, if present, of so little consequence that it can be ignored. At some later point, the basic personality predispositions so formed express themselves in the political sphere. They may account for the individual's way of reacting to political authority (for example, in authoritarian or democratic patterns), they may influence modes of political participation, and they may even predetermine the particular political roles for which a person is equipped or which he may seek.[7] But whatever the precise influence on later political behavior, little room is left for the independent effect of direct political learning during childhood.

To the extent that the emphasis is on politics as the arena for playing out earlier general personality characteristics or predispositions, we have here a kind of personality determinism. It is as though exclusive explanatory claims were being lodged for the following kind of paradigm: Culture → child-rearing practices → basic modal personality types or predispositions → patterns of adult political behavior and roles. Politics becomes the end product of a sequential chain of determinants that roughly parallels the progression of stages in the life cycle.

This paradigm probably overstates the case somewhat, but it does typify the kind of thinking that underlies a considerable part of the extensive and varied literature on character structure and personality formation as it relates to adult patterns of interaction.[8] As this paradigm suggests, personality-in-culture interpretations ask for a considerable prior commitment to the idea that of all the variables that might affect the adult, personality is the decisive one. It leads almost to a monocausal explanation of behavior.

But the fact is that it is possible to give due weight to personality structure, as formed in the early stages of life, and yet also to accept the possibility of direct political learning during the same period. In other words, we may adopt a customary multi-causal explanation of political behavior, by which the child acquires specific political orientations even while his personality is in formation. Indeed, if we were concerned with expanding not only our knowledge of political socialization but personality theory as well, we might even wish to draw attention to the strong possibility, usually overlooked, that under certain circumstances general predispositions may be permanently shaped by the political context itself. We require a rounded formulation of the relationship, even in childhood, among culture, personality, and politics, a formulation that provides for the independent effects of variables other than personality. Our theoretical assumptions ought to be such as to allow us at least to keep an open mind, until we have more evidence than has hitherto been available, toward the possibility that some of the variance in adult political behavior is accounted for not only by personality but by the direct learning of political orientations.[9]

Our data will show that it is more useful and revealing to assume that in childhood a person is subject to at least two major sets of experiences. They may have independent as well as interactive effects on his later political orientations. The kind of personality an individual acquires will undoubtedly be reflected in the way he handles political matters, both as a child and as an adult. About this we shall have nothing to say empirically, as there are no reliable devices for measuring or delineating the personality of children considered in large aggregates through survey techniques. But in addition to personality influences, we shall claim, the various facets of the child's specifically political learning, as transmitted by adults and as refracted through his own direct experiences, begin to provide him with a repertoire of developing attitudes and responses to meet political situations as he moves through subsequent phases of his life. Since our data will reveal that specifically political learning does begin at a surprisingly early age even within the period of childhood itself, any special reverence for a "staging" theory of political learning which confines childhood to the acquisition of broad general predispositions cannot be easily sustained. But this raises the question of what we mean by politics, and we shall have to return to this matter if we are able to support this last assertion.

The proximity hypothesis

Although personality theory probably presents the strongest argument against the presence of pre-adolescent political learning, there is some suggestion from other kinds of research that points in the same direction, although for very different reasons. The underlying hypothesis here is deceptively simple. That which is nearest to the adult in time is likely to leave the greatest impact on his political behavior. The proximity in time of the experience is the decisive element. This "proximity hypothesis," as we may designate it, stands Freud on his head. What is learned later is likely to be more influential than what is learned earlier in life. Even if children do acquire political orientations, this is of little consequence for them or for the system. We have already encountered this argument in another context in Chapter 2, but here we can analyze it fully for the first time.[10]

Unfortunately all that we have to represent this important opinion are a suggestion or two, and even these have yet to be systematically pursued. However, on purely a priori grounds what seems to lend credence to this position is the past literature on pre-adult socialization. Most of it deals almost exclusively with adolescents and early adulthood as though we can take it for granted that this is where significant political socialization begins. This concentration on postchildhood phases has been so impressively unanimous as to discourage any serious conceptual reflection about children and politics, an effort that might have led students of socialization to reconsider their theoretical premises.

Thus the single major analytic inventory of research on socialization reports only an exceptional investigation or two that push their inquiries below age thirteen.[11] The same study refers to a piece of research in which ". . . adolescence was reported most frequently as the age at which political views were first formed."[12] In an earlier résumé another author found that ". . . it is difficult, if not impossible, to make any reliable estimate, on the basis of empirical evidence, of the age at which politics becomes meaningful to children or youth. Examination of the skimpy research data, plus general agreement by psychologists, anthropologists, and sociologists, lead us, however, to focus on adolescence."[13]

By far the strongest defense of the postponement of direct political socialization to some period beyond childhood comes from the Almond and Verba cross-country survey. As we noted in Chapter 2, the data are retrospective and are acknowledged to be less reliable than desirable. Nonetheless the authors do offer the judgment, based on these data, that there is little consequential political learning among children. The authors are even doubtful about the importance of nonpolitical experiences in childhood for later political behavior. They argue that ". . . there is some evidence that later experiences have a more direct political implication. Early socialization experiences significantly affect an individual's basic personality predispositions and may therefore affect his political behavior, but numerous other factors intervene between these earliest experiences and later political behavior that greatly inhibit the impact of the former on the latter."[14] They conclude that ". . . those institutions closer to the political realm and in which authority patterns become more similar in kind to authority patterns in the political system may be *more crucial* for the formation of political attitudes [italics added]."[15] Since a person does not participate in institutions with notable proximity to the political system until he is himself close to adulthood, earlier learning is apparently of minimal significance.[16]

It is clear therefore that the periods beyond childhood, adolescence and young adulthood, are selected as most salient politically. Not that the authors of the previous quotations are arguing that childhood is devoid of political learning. They reserve judgment on this. But even if the child should absorb some political orientations, the critical modifying words in these quotations—"meaningful" and "more crucial"—indicate that this early learning is thought to have little later significant impact on adult behavior or on the system in general.

By underplaying early life experiences for later political behavior Almond and Verba do of course part company with the personality-in-culture proponents and with strict psychoanalytic theorists. Both these groups impute highest significance to infancy and childhood for later adult political development. But in maintaining that specifically political experiences of significance first come after childhood, this proximity theory joins forces with personality-in-culture and psychoanalytic theories. By different paths each comes to the same conclusion: There is little of importance that children directly learn about political life.

In a moment we shall see that the qualifiers "meaningful," "more crucial," "important," and "significant" are critical words. Some implicit classification of political learning is apparently taking place. What kinds of criteria are being used to determine when political learning is to be considered more or less meaningful or crucial? According to one conception of politics the conclusion may indeed be valid, we shall argue. But if the conception itself is changed—and we shall suggest that it does need to be broadened—it may turn out that early socialization can indeed be described by precisely these adjectives, meaningful and crucial.

The child's "state of readiness" for politics

These prevalent impressions about the absence of specific political socialization during childhood both reflect and reinforce the whole folklore that has inhibited systematic exploration of political orientations in this period of life. Until the 1960s there were few references to the possibility that children may be going through direct political experiences of a kind consequential for the operation of political systems. At most, children were seen as possessing some information about the formal structure of government, the contents of constitutions, the names of occupants of some political offices, and other facts that can readily be committed to memory and as easily forgotten.[17] But this was considered to be prepolitical learning, preparatory to the development of good adult citizens, and citizenship somehow seemed to lie outside the realm of politics.

Indeed adults are likely to consider politics part of their own world. Tolerantly they may share it with adolescents who are, after all, approaching their legal majority. But as for children, adults typically think of politics as beyond their ken and competence. Children are not ready for it intellectually. Further, the strife and turmoil of politics, its image as a somewhat sordid business, a dirty game, probably encourage adults to seek to shield children from it in the same subtle way as their own Victorian parents had carefully sheltered them, the present adults, from the distasteful facts about sex.[18] Children are thought to be too young for knowledge of politics. Nor are they ready for it morally.

If adults tend to see children as not yet prepared to cope with politics, children themselves reinforce this impression. It does not require very intimate knowledge of children to realize that politics stands very low in their hierarchy of concerns, either in its own terms or when compared with other activities, such as play, sports, television, movies, or reading.[19]

If adults in general do not see children as intellectually or morally ready for the business of politics and if children themselves show little inclination toward it, we can readily understand why scholars should reflect this and expect little of a direct political nature to be happening to children. In fact, in the initiation of our research, at a period well before recent publications in political socialization, we ourselves became caught up in this prejudice and we comfortably began our inquiries about political socialization with the high school age group. We assumed with everyone else that it was there we would find significant beginnings for the kind of political orientations in which we were interested. Only when we found to our surprise and puzzlement that for a variety of basic attitudes high school students did not seem to change very much from freshman to senior year were we compelled to reconsider our own presuppositions—and thus those prevalent in the literature—about where political socialization has its beginnings.[20]

When we turned to children and also broadened our conception of politics to include more than political controversy and party politics—the typical subjects about which adolescents are tested—we discovered broad changes occurring over the years.[21] A search for the beginning of at least certain kinds of specifically political orientations finally forced us to consider the elementary school age group. We have since concluded that knowledge about the low political interest of children and a predisposition to view politics as an inappropriate or improbable subject for their tender minds constitute shaky and misleading premises from which to begin an exploration into what children do in fact learn.

THE MEANING OF POLITICS IN PRIMARY SOCIALIZATION

On various a priori grounds, therefore, related to the presumed function of early socialization in the formation of personality, the dominance of proximate political experiences, and the immaturity of children, most previous thinking delayed any significant political socialization to some point beyond childhood. Although we have clearly expressed our doubts about the general validity of this conclusion as it stands, we need not wholly challenge it. In fact, if we are prepared to impose one condition, we might even be able to give this proposition our blessing, at least as a useful working hypothesis. This condition is that we recognize the limited conception of politics on which this hypothesis must rest.

Those who argue that political socialization occurs or is meaningful only after childhood, or when the socialization of the basic personality is complete, usually refer to only one category of political interaction, which we may call *allocative* (or *partisan*) *politics; the controversial, competitive areas of political life.* It is an aspect of the political system with which a person probably becomes familiar only as he grows older. The experiences that come with maturation improve a person's capacity to handle the complexities of this part of life and tend to arouse at least a minimal interest in politics, in some systems and for some of the members. In literate societies, age also usually brings with it formal school instruction in the history and politics of a country, adding to the fund of knowledge upon which a member may draw to interpret surrounding political events.

Thus for the area of a political system which we have been calling the allocative processes, we can expect older rather than younger members, adolescents rather than children, to be better informed and more concerned. But it may be that in order to detect the areas in which children are likely to have the capacity and opportunity for acquiring political orientations we need to distinguish the partisan allocative processes from what is often, although not necessarily always, a less contentious political area, what in a moment we shall describe as system politics. The extent of political socialization discovered during childhood may be an artifact of the area of political behavior selected for investigation.

Allocative politics and political controversy

Our definition of politics determines whether we are willing to hypothesize that children acquire orientations of a political nature or whether we judge that what they absorb can reasonably be considered significant politically only for later life. In the personality literature, for example, the political phenomena to which modal (basic) personality traits are related frequently are part of what we would describe as the allocative processes in a system, the specifically partisan or controversial aspect of politics. Thus efforts have been made to understand the degree to which personality influences a vast body of party-political phenomena such as political apathy, involvement in and commitment to positions on issues, ideological postures, modes of participation, and styles of political leadership. Although there are notable exceptions, as, for example, in the considerable literature in which personality is brought to bear on an understanding of fundamental responses to political authority,[22] nonetheless allocative interests are prominent.

We find a similar restrictive if legitimate conception of politics in that literature dealing specifically with socialization of political orientations.[23] As has become clear from our previous discussion, the research that touches on direct political socialization is still very small in quantity. But the little that does exist has placed greatest emphasis on how and to what extent pre-adults acquire their right-left ideologies, political interest, party identification, and various other characteristics related to political participation. When children are described as having a low interest and concern for politics, what is normally implied is that they are not likely to get excited or have much information about current political events and issues. They are innocent of what to them is esoteric knowledge about who is running for office, how Congress conducts its affairs, what the parties stand for, how they operate in the system, what the different levels of government are, or the nature of the differences among the major world ideologies. It is these kinds of matters that both laymen and scholars frequently have in mind when they speak about politics.

There is little wonder then that students of socialization draw the conclusion that children are unlikely to be an appropriate subject for study. For the very reason of their immaturity we would expect children to receive relatively little preparatory training or experience that would be directly cogent for their participation in allocative processes. Ideological positions, policy preferences on issues, and most areas of political conflict probably do not make deep inroads into the child's consciousness, even though there is reason to believe that even in these areas, remote as they are for the child, some slight beginning is probably made in the United States.[24] But by and large allocative matters are difficult subjects for a child to grasp. In fact, in testing the younger child particularly, it is very difficult to find a way to open up such partisan topics without feeding the answers to the child, so far beyond his experience and knowledge are most allocative topics.

But if we were to join those who discount childhood socialization or see it as unlikely, and if we stopped at this point, we would be misled about what the child is acquiring in the field of politics. To conceive of politics solely as partisan activity dominated by conflict over the allocation of values is to restrict its content unduly. We would be omitting a whole range of political matters vital to the functioning of political systems, about which, as our data will amply attest, children have experience, opinions, and sentiments. What is even more to the point, it is an area of prime theoretical importance. We describe it as system politics.

System politics

In a way, in the United States and in most other politically self-conscious systems, we are prone to view various kinds of system-oriented behavior as somehow above politics. Patriotism, a commitment to the form of government and to the rules of the political game, the acceptance of certain fundamental aims for society, these all normally transcend the realm of partisan dispute in the United States and other similarly stable systems. We are reluctant to describe them as political matters in the usual meaning of the term.

We may demur at this, however, only if we insist on limiting the idea of politics to its party-political, controversial sense. If, however, we are prepared to consider that there may be many other kinds of activity that take place in a political system and that need not be a subject of controversy (although on occasion they are), we arrive at a different conclusion. It may be that we can appropriately designate as political even those activities that appear to be above politics. They may be just as much a part of political behavior as ordinary political controversy.

What we seldom discern, unless there is some public dispute about it, is that behavior particularly meaningful for system persistence is as integral a part of all political systems as any activity normally in the sphere of partisan strife. In addition to all those familiar processes through which particular authoritative allocations are made and put into effect, we can identify numerous other sorts of behavior that have a different kind of system relevance.

In *system politics* we would embrace *all those behaviors and orientations relevant for the persistence of some kind of system.* We refer therefore to the input of demands: At least some members of a system have to acquire those kinds of behaviors that lead to the making of demands and their conversion into issues, otherwise there would be no reason for a political system to continue in a society. We refer also to the input of support for some authorities, some kind of regime, and a political community. System politics includes such other areas as the orientation to the roles and rules of conduct relevant to the conversion of demands into outputs, and the implementation and acceptance of these as authoritative.

As we have mentioned, on occasion some of the behavior in and rules about these areas of a political system may be subject to political conflict, and they thereby become issues with which a maturing member may or may not be familiar. But what we are suggesting is that whether or not they are in dispute, they are areas of behavior found in all political systems, and it may be that here we are likely to find some early socialization. The probability of this is increased considerably when, as in hitherto stable systems such as the United States, these areas turn out to reflect political assumptions about which there has normally been the least controversy.

The special concern of our research will be with that area of system politics that we have called the input of support. As we have noted, this describes the behavior through which members express their approval of or discontent with the authorities, regime, and political community. Our conjecture will be that it is in childhood that a member, born into a system and, therefore, without previous political conceptions at all, first learns how to cognize, or "see," certain parts of the political world, how to feel about them, how to evaluate them, and how to identify and react to representative symbols of this world, such as "government," "party," "Washington," and "Uncle Sam."

Common sense alone would suggest that our area of special concern, supportive behavior, is clearly not so remote from childhood socialization as we might initially think. If we were to rephrase the matter and ask those who think about children and politics whether they believe that children develop any sense of loyalty to their government and country, or whether they acquire an ability to perceive some of the general properties of government, we would probably get a quick reply in the affirmative. We might even obtain acquiescence to the suggestion that it is reasonable to think of children as beginning to understand and develop feelings about such regime norms in the United States as those that exhort people to be interested in politics, to vote and be active in other ways, and to take partisan positions on public issues.

To insist on intuitive acknowledgment of this might, however, be asking too much.[25] But regardless of the range of subjects that this interpretation of the content of politics might include, we have to face the argument that even though we could expect children to acquire some appreciation of subjects such as these, this is not what we normally mean by the word politics. If nothing else, this word is normally laden with connotations of partisan strife.

For lay purposes we cannot doubt that this is so. But in the realm of general theory, especially in connection with a theory that searches for a fundamental understanding of the functioning of all political systems, topics such as those in the broad area of support are of central significance. They refer to behavior found in all political systems. They too are part of politics, if by this word we mean all behavior more or less directly related to the making and implementing of binding decisions.

This interpretation contradicts the normal assumptions in research about political socialization. We cannot agree that ". . . in examining the beginning of such political difference [primarily in the area of allocative politics] in childhood, we shall be treating of phenomena that are only *precursive* forms of politics, for politics as such is the prerogative of adults."[26] In our interpretation there is a level of politics that is as much the prerogative of children as of adults, and this we have called system politics.

If we can show empirically that children begin to acquire orientations relevant to one of the major kinds of system-related behaviors, such as to the input of support for a system, we shall thereby have demonstrated that political socialization does begin in childhood. What is true of this area of system behavior we would speculate is equally so for other major areas, such as the input of demands and the acceptance of outputs as authoritative (compliance behavior).

By redefining in this way what we mean by politics, both to expand it beyond its lay meaning and to enhance its theoretical importance, we simultaneously add the color of plausibility to the notion that childhood is vital for the acquisition of political orientations. We now understand politics to include more than just party-political matters, even though here, in anticipation of adult roles, some limited amount of early (anticipatory) socialization is not improbable. Through this reconceptualization we manage to open a new door of inquiry into the political aspects of childhood socialization. It is a door that offers us an empirical means of entry into problems that systems analysis has sought to elevate to a level of theoretical significance.

GENERAL SOCIALIZATION THEORY: ITS IMPLICATIONS FOR POLITICAL SOCIALIZATION

When we reassess and broaden the meaning normally given to the word politics, new areas seem appropriate for childhood socialization. It also happens that when we now consider a particular general theory of socialization (in contrast with a political theory of political socialization[27]), we find that it strengthens our conclusion that children are capable of acquiring orientations falling under the heading of system politics.

The kinds of subjects a child can absorb would seem to militate against the acquisition of those very orientations associated with partisan politics and would seem to throw the weight of probability to system politics. It has been argued, in one of the few attempts at a general theory of socialization, that childhood is a period peculiarly adapted to a concern with values and motives rather than with overt behavior, to the absorption of general rather than particular demands of society, and to idealism rather than realism.[28] Each of these areas describes characteristics that accurately reflect the general content of system politics, as will be borne out in detail in Part 3.

According to this theory, the socialization of children is likely to concentrate on fundamental motivations and the basic values in a society. Less attention is devoted to the overt behavior of specific roles and to the knowledge and skills that go with them. Childhood is thought to be a period when basic commitments (or, as we would qualify it, failure to make them) may occur. For example, the child will probably develop the general desire to assume a given role and an appreciation of some of the underlying values that the culture associates with it rather than learn the knowledge and skills actually required to perform the role. He will learn to want to work, for instance, rather than the skills to fulfill a specific occupation.

Complementing this is the probability that the values a child does learn will not be specific. Rather, he is likely to develop general values and motives which will characterize most roles in his culture. At a later stage in his maturation, as he begins to adopt specific roles, the style in which they are carried out will be colored by the general values that he has already acquired. As this theory of socialization puts it, general values learned in childhood, such as those related to achievement, nature, and the family, ". . . give shape and tone to the performance of many roles in society."[29]

Finally, in most areas of socialization, the child learns to see life in ideal terms. This is not idealism, in the sense of attachment to very high ethical goals, although an element of this may be present. It refers rather to the fact that children first learn the formal aspects of roles rather than the informal: how role occupants ought to behave rather than how they do in fact behave. Only as the child matures is he expected, in American society at least, to recognize the informal components. "In socialization the child is shielded from contact with the informal systems of society—or, at least, knowledge is not formally taught. This serves to maintain and legitimize the formal status differentiations and to protect them from change."[30]

If these qualities in fact describe the general nature of socialization in other basic social roles, it would be difficult to understand why we should choose to make an exception of fundamental political roles. It rests upon those who would argue otherwise to demonstrate that political interactions, of all areas of social existence, are somehow so profoundly different that here socialization does not occur in childhood, or if it does, then it is of negligible importance.

We shall propose on the contrary (in Chapter 18) that what is true for other basic social roles is equally so for introduction to the most general political role, that of "membership" in a political system. We may for this purpose disregard whether membership is in the form of subject, participant citizen, national, kinsman, or whatever. We shall see that a child begins to appreciate some of the general values implicit in the various basic political objects, that he acquires early motives and feelings about these objects, and that he seems to interpret them in general and idealized or formal terms.

Thus in the political sphere we may conjecture that he will be likely to acquire general orientations about support and begin to relate himself positively or negatively to the political community. In the United States he will probably be introduced to the notion of what it is to be an American as distinct from an Englishman or Frenchman, even though much more than political differences may be involved. But very early he undoubtedly learns that Americans have primary responsibility for deciding what happens in America. They share a division of political labor among themselves, and not with Englishmen or Frenchmen.

The child may also learn to commit himself (or otherwise) to the general range of goals associated with the regime of his system. He becomes familiar with the notion of democracy and may begin to absorb some general impressions about theoretically fundamental regime norms, already noted, such as the desirability of being politically interested, of feeling able to participate in the political process, and of adopting a partisan stance. [31] Only later may he acquire a minimal knowledge of and begin to learn the skills associated with the roles through which these general regime norms may be fulfilled.

On grounds of socialization theory itself, therefore, we ought not to expect children to begin to develop very many specific modes of behavior, even in anticipation, such as those involved in partisan politics. [32] The roles of voter, participant in campaigns, ideologue, party member, etc., are all so specific that we would be inclined to exclude them from a prominent place in early direct socialization. This is true at least if socialization of political roles is not substantially different from that of other social roles. For the moment we set aside the obvious fact that few children have the capacity to learn these roles in any detail. It may be that whatever a child learns of a specific sort is less influential for his later behavior than those experiences closer in time to adulthood, as the proximity theory has it. But before adolescence it seems safe to operate on the premise that, following what is known about orientations to other social roles, the child is probably ready to absorb knowledge and feelings of a general, formal sort about many adult political roles. He is probably learning fundamental ways of relating himself to the political sphere. It is during childhood that we may look for some of the basic commitments about a political system, whether they are positive or negative, to take shape.

NOTES

1. M. Argyle and P. Delin, "Non-universal Laws of Socialization," *Human Relations,* 18, pp. 77 - 86, 1965.

2. I. L. Child, "Socialization," in G. Lindzey (ed.), *Handbook of Social Psychology,* vol. II (Cambridge, Mass.: Addison-Wesley, 1954), pp. 655 - 692.

3. T. W. Adorno et al., *The Authoritarian Personality* (New York: Harper & Row, 1950); E. Fromm, *Escape From Freedom* (New York: Farrar & Rinehart, 1941); E. Hagen, *On the Theory of Social Change* (Homewood, Ill.: Dorsey, 1962); G. Gorer, *The American People* (New York: Norton, 1948); M. Mead, *Soviet Attitudes Toward Authority* (New York: McGraw-Hill, 1951); L. W. Pye, *Politics, Personality and Nation-Building* (New Haven, Conn.: Yale, 1962).

4. For a similar contrast, in educational psychology, between the place of childhood and adolescence — or theoretically between approaches that stress psychoanalytic premises and cognitive processes — see N. Sanford, "A Psychologist Speculates About New Perspectives," in F. Patterson (ed.), *The Adolescent Citizen* (New York: Free Press, 1960), pp. 271 - 287, especially pp. 274 - 275.

5. Pye, op. cit., p. 121.

6. Ibid., pp. 45 - 46.

7. Ibid.

8. See F. L. K. Hsu, *Psychological Anthropology: Approaches to Culture and Personality* (Homewood, Ill.: Dorsey, 1961), especially the essay by A. Inkeles, "National Character and Modern Political Systems," pp. 172 - 208.

9. For a serious challenge to the whole notion of a presumed basic personality as a significant determinant of behavior and an alternative explanation from the direction of structural or role theory, see O. G. Brim, Jr., and S. Wheeler, *Socialization After Childhood: Two Essays* (New York: Wiley, 1966); and O. G. Brim, Jr., "Per-

sonality Development as Role Learning," in I. Iscoe and H. Stevenson (eds.), *Personality Development in Children* (Austin, Tex.: University of Texas Press, 1960), pp. 127-159. For critical comments on this see E. Maccoby, "The Choice of Variables in the Study of Socialization," *Sociometry*, 24, pp. 357-370, 1961. For another alternative, see A. F. C. Wallace, *Culture and Personality* (New York: Random House, 1961).

10. See pp. 33ff.

11. See H. Hyman, *Political Socialization* (New York: Free Press, 1959), chap. 3. This is borne out by the survey by J. J. Patrick, "Political Socialization of American Youth: Implications for Secondary School Social Studies," National Council for the Social Studies, Research Bulletin no. 3, 1967; and R. E. Dawson, "Political Socialization," in J. A. Robinson (ed.), *Political Science Annual* (Indianapolis: Bobbs-Merrill, 1966).

12. Hyman, op. cit., p. 158.

13. S. M. Lipset et al., "The Psychology of Voting: An Analysis of Political Behavior" in G. Lindzey, op. cit.

14. G. A. Almond and S. Verba, *The Civic Culture* (Princeton, N.J.: Princeton, 1963), p. 324.

15. Ibid., p. 328.

16. Although these quotations perhaps reflect the dominant opinion, recently a few voices have been raised in behalf of the possible significance of earlier socialization, just as more than an occasional expression of this view may also be found in writings scattered through the ages. From Plato to modern times social philosophers have revealed an intuitive awareness of the potential impact of early political learning on later life. In both theory and practice authoritarian systems have sensed the necessity of bringing their ideologies to bear on members of their systems at the earliest possible age. Even democratic systems may devote more time in elementary and secondary schools to political matters than is true of some nondemocratic systems. See G. Z. F. Bereday and B. B. Stretch, "Political Education in the U.S.A. and the U.S.S.R.," *Comparative Education Review*, 7, pp. 9-16, 1963. More recently research has begun to catch up with insight and practice. Beginning with R. D. Hess and D. Easton, "The Child's Changing Image of the President," *Public Opinion Quarterly*, 24, pp. 632-644, 1960; and F. Greenstein, *Children and Politics* (New Haven, Conn.: Yale, 1965), an increasing number of publications have begun to hint at the possibility of primary political socialization with carry-over effect for adults. See R. Sigel (ed.), "Political Socialization: Its Role in the Political Process," *The Annals of the American Academy of Political and Social Science*, 361, 1965 (special issue on political socialization); J. Wahlke et al., *The Legislative System* (New York: Wiley, 1962), part 2, especially pp. 80-81; M. Wolfenstein and G. Kliman (eds.), *Children and the Death of a President* (Garden City, N.Y.: Doubleday, 1965); K. Prewitt et al., "Political Sociali-

zation and Political Roles," *Public Opinion Quarterly,* 30, pp. 569-581, 1966-1967; D. Jaros, H. Hirsch, and F. J. Fleron, Jr., "The Malevolent Leader: Political Socialization in an American Sub-Culture," *American Political Science Review,* 62, pp. 564-575, 1968; and R. E. Dawson, op. cit. See also M. Oakeshott, "Political Education," in P. Laslett (ed.), *Philosophy, Politics and Society* (New York: Macmillan, 1956), pp. 1-21, especially pp. 17-18.

17.   H. E. Wilson, *Education for Citizenship* (New York: McGraw-Hill, 1938).

18.   ". . . children tend to be shielded by society from the realities of life." O. G. Brim, Jr., and S. Wheeler, op. cit., p. 30. Some confirmation of this is offered by P. Peterson and K. Orren, "Presidential Assassination: A Case Study in the Dynamics of Political Socialization," *Journal of Politics,* 2, pp. 388-404, 1967. The authors show that adults reported a reluctance to tell their children about suspicions of a conspiracy behind the assassination of President Kennedy. In this way, we might suspect, an idealizing mythology is retained among children.

This is supported by other research. For example, neither children nor adolescents are likely to rebel against their parents politically, so low is the level of political interest among young people as well as among adults themselves. For children, see F. Estvan and E. Estvan, *The Child's World* (New York: Putnam, 1959), p. 19; for later age groups see E. Erikson, *Childhood and Society* (New York: Norton, 1950), pp. 323-324; R. E. Lane, "Fathers and Sons: Foundations of Political Belief," *American Political Science Review,* 24, pp. 502-511, 1959; R. Middleton and S. Putney, "Student Rebellion Against Parental Political Beliefs," *Social Forces,* 41, pp. 377-383, 1963 and "Political Expression of Adolescent Rebellion," *American Journal of Sociology,* 68, pp. 527-535, 1963; and D. Easton and R. D. Hess, "Youth and the Political System," in S. M. Lipset and L. Lowenthal (eds.), *Culture and Social Character* (New York: Free Press, 1961), pp. 226-251.

20.   Our unsystematic findings have apparently now been supported, if indirectly, by more intensive and controlled research. See K. P. Langton and M. K. Jennings, "Political Socialization and the High School Civics Curriculum in the United States," *American Political Science Review,* 62, pp. 852-867, 1968.

21.   Apparently there are equally "far-reaching" changes in attitudes about things other than politics in the elementary school years, so that it would indeed be strange if something of the same kind did not happen in the political sphere itself. *"It cannot be emphasized too strongly that attitudinal changes which take place during the elementary school years are far reaching.* The kinds of attitudes expressed by first and sixth grade children were significantly different in each phase of the interview except the last where greater uniformity would be expected in reasons given for selecting or rejecting pictures." Estvan and Estvan, op. cit., p. 262.

22. See the extensive literature on personality and political change. A useful review and analysis appears in G. J. Bender, "Political Socialization and Political Change," *The Western Political Quarterly,* 20, pp. 390-407, 1967.

23. See Hyman, op. cit., and Greenstein, op. cit. Although Greenstein deals with childhood socialization of basic system-oriented attitudes, his work too is devoted largely to those relevant to partisan politics.

24. The early awareness of party preferences, for example, has been documented for the United States, and our data show that this may influence the child's perceptions of basic political objects. But data such as these and others related to political participation need to be carefully interpreted. They may have a different meaning for children from that for adults. See D. Easton and J. Dennis, "The Child's Acquisition of Regime Norms: Political Efficacy," *American Political Science Review,* 61, pp. 25-38, 1967.

25. Although we do not report our data on these regime norms in this book, they are used as examples because we have found that children are familiar with them and have opinions about them. For our data on the norm of political efficacy—that a person should feel he is able to influence the course of government—see ibid.

26. Hyman, op. cit., p. 26. For the possible impact of political events even on children as young as four to five years of age see J. J. Zilbach, "The Impact of the Assassination of President Kennedy on Child Psychiatric Patients," in Wolfenstein and Kliman, op. cit., pp. 135-156, especially pp. 140-142.

27. We need to recall our discussion in Chapter 2 of the difference among the following types of theories: general socialization theory, a theory of political socialization, and a political theory of political socialization.

28. Brim and Wheeler, op. cit., pp. 24ff.

29. Ibid., p. 31. S. N. Eisenstadt, in *From Generation to Generation* (New York: Free Press, 1956), pp. 322-323, confirms this in more general terms.

30. Brim and Wheeler, op. cit., p. 29.

31. As we have repeatedly tried to indicate, socialization may be negative as well as positive. That is to say, it may lead children to feelings of disinterest, inefficacy, or political neutrality. The direction of socialization is always an empirical matter.

32. Since we began reporting our findings and interpretations, others have supported our premise here. M. K. Jennings, in "Pre-Adult Orientations to Multiple Systems of Government," *Midwest Journal of Political Science,* 11, pp. 291-317, 1967, points out that childhood is a period of basic commitments to various parts of a political system. Adolescence, he surmises, is a period of greater responsiveness to political inputs, of greater capacity to argue and reason about political positions, and of higher concern for political issues.

5

SOCIALIZATION OF
SUPPORT FOR
THE STRUCTURE
OF AUTHORITY

If in light of our preceding chapter we may now accept primary political socialization as plausible, we have still to decide on where we might begin empirical research. In that chapter we have observed that political socialization in childhood covers an extensive range of subjects, already identified under the heading of system politics. Any one of these might appear to be an appropriate topic with which to begin. In this book, however, we shall carefully narrow our focus to the structure of political authority.

Persuasive reasons account for this decision. First, political theory demonstrates that authority is a crucial and inescapable phenomenon in all political systems, regardless of type. Second, and of the highest importance, is our pretest finding that as the child begins to learn about the political system in the United States, the structure of authority offers him a number of easy points of contact with the system, however devoid he may be of orientations to other political objects. Theory and facts thereby join together in dictating the scope of our initial research.

THE THEORETICAL SIGNIFICANCE OF POLITICAL AUTHORITY

As we shall note empirically below, a child finds many paths of access to the political system. Our interviews, pretests, and final instrument give us hints about many areas in which socialization occurs. While being socialized, the child learns to extend support—whether negative or positive, high or low—to the political community, to the regime goals and norms, to the structure of authority, and even to the specific occupants of the authority roles. For theory, these are all vital aspects of any system. No system could persist for long without some minimal level of support for all these basic political objects.

But this is not all that the child is absorbing about the political sphere. If our group of children is not atypical, a child is also acquiring some understanding of the kinds of things it is appropriate to ask for through the political process. For example, our data indicate that initially children characteristically see the authorities as possible sources of nurturance, resources to which a person can turn in very much the same spirit that a child expects to be able to turn to his parents. As they grow older, many children come to learn that government plays a much more restrained role and, therefore, that many demands that one might make of one's family are "inappropriate" in the United States to direct toward government. We can see here the beginning of the growth of cultural restraints on the input of demands.[1]

Children also begin to acquire attitudes toward political outputs, especially in their form as laws in the United States, and toward their acceptability as authoritative. We can here detect the early sources of compliant (and noncompliant) behavior. These and many other kinds of political orientations are to be found during childhood.

Clearly there is much that is happening to the child politically in the broadened sense of the term. From among these varied and numerous areas of political socialization we have selected, as our first major subject of analysis, socialization about support for the structure of authority. We also have data on the child's orientation toward selected regime norms and some much less adequate data about his attachment to the political community, his conceptions of the political process, and his developing sense of compliance to outputs. But both because of the critical place of authority in the functioning of political systems and the richer and more extensive data we possess about this area, we confine our attention to it alone in this book.[2]

As heirs to centuries of recorded thinking about political authority we scarcely need to be reminded of its fundamental importance for politics. But systems analysis enables us to place the structure of authority in its broadest context.[3]

Put briefly, in most, if not all, systems we typically find formal or informal roles through which persons are expected to care for the daily business of running a group or country. The presence of some kind of structure or pattern of authority (or system of government, in ordinary but sometimes misleading language), however inchoate, is characteristic in most aggregates of persons that seek to take decisions and act on them. Without such a structure most groups would find it difficult to act in pursuit of any objectives.

The plausibility of this conclusion becomes evident if we recall our description of a political system. At the most general level we may interpret it as a type of system through which the human and physical resources of a society can be rallied and committed to specific objectives and general ends. In particular it represents a set of processes through which inputs called demands are converted into binding outputs called authoritative decisions and actions. But demands cannot be negotiated through to outputs without a variety of characteristic activities occurring in any political system. Among these we may identify three: the making of decisions, the obtaining of compliance, and the assurance of implementation.

The system must provide a way for considering alternatives as formulated in conflicting demands and for transforming them into decisions through some kind of settlement of the differences. It must also be able either to obtain the commitment of the relevant members of the system for the decided objectives or else to neutralize opposition. Finally, it needs to provide continuing energy to effect the decisions and to supervise their implementation. This variety of activities is as likely to be present in a small, nonliterate, tribal political system as in the largest and industrially most advanced type.

The means for accomplishing these tasks will vary. In some systems these means may take the form of diffuse, complex roles, such as lineage heads, through which many nonpolitical tasks are also performed. In other political systems at least some minimal specialization of political labor may occur, through which the power and responsibility for the day-to-day performance of the activities just mentioned is assigned. In most large-scale systems, special roles arise through which acknowledged members are able to take the initiative in considering demands, to help arrange for settlements among competing demands, and to implement decisions. The occupants of these roles give impulse and direction to action taken in the name of the system. The power and responsibility usually converge on some few, and this tends to be so even in the smallest political system, as among Bushman bands which may not exceed fifty persons.[4]

In some systems these roles may be set forth formally in a table of organization or written in the form of a constitution or other body of laws. In others, the roles may remain only informally recognized patterns of leadership and administration. But regardless of the extent to which they are affirmed, in writing or otherwise, few if any systems are able to do without some special roles to which are attached the ongoing responsibility and power for converting demands into accepted outputs, that is, for helping to bring about political settlements of differences in the system, and for implementing the outputs.

We could imagine a situation in which even though such structural means for meeting these special responsibilities existed, the occupants of the roles might need to justify each exercise of power in which they engaged. Each of their decisions and actions would have to receive specific endorsement from the politically relevant members in the system, those who count for most. But empirically it is difficult, if not impossible, to find a system of this kind. Usually some roles will have been traditionally endowed with continuing authority or will have acquired it through successful assertion. Normally the authority will not be associated exclusively with the individual person who occupies the role, aside from the case of the leader who arises at a moment of political crisis. Weber had argued that even then there is a tendency for the authority of the personal leader to become "routinized" and therefore for authority to become associated with the role.[5]

In most systems, authority usually becomes attached to the role itself rather than to the person. It is in part because of this that the paramount tribal chief, the lineage head, the monarch of a state, the administrators, legislators, and chief executives of a modern democracy, even the sole dictator, are all able to perform their routine tasks as they arrange for political settlements and convert competing demands into outputs. Without recognized authority, any and all of these political rulers would be in constant danger of exhausting their energies and resources in compelling or repeatedly persuading the members of the system to conform with the decisions. This capacity routinely to transform demands into outputs depends on the rulers' expectation, and the reciprocal expectations from the other members of the system, that within the limits of the roles of the rulers their actions will be accepted as authoritative or binding.

The occupants of these roles therefore have the special capacity, formally granted or implicitly acquired, to direct, order, or command, supported in many systems although not in all[6] by the power to compel through the use or threat of force. Hence the power associated with these roles consists of authority. It is the set of these roles in a system that we describe as the structure of political authority. The roles seldom stand discretely and independently; they tend to be related and complementary, part of some patterned division of political labor.

Whatever form of organization these authority roles take — democratic or authoritarian, representative or appointed, federal or unitary, etc. — they need to be distinguished from their occupants. The roles consist of rights and obligations with respect to the conversion process. They represent regularized patterns of behavior for the role occupants as well as expectations about their behavior and about the way in which others are expected to act toward them. Typically we designate the particular occupants of these roles at any moment of time as the political authorities, and the set of roles as the structure of authority. Political science has never developed a separate set of acceptable concepts to differentiate the role from the occupant, and in this lies much confusion.

There are usually many reasons for obedience to the occupants of these roles, that is, for the acceptance of the authority of the roles. Members of the system may accept decisions out of fear, expediency, habit, lethargy, or some combination of these. But typically, at least during periods when the political authorities are not being fundamentally challenged, their capacity to rule is closely connected to an ingrained belief that the occupants of the authority roles have a right to command and other members a duty to obey. The roles are considered to carry legitimate power.

In stable systems the major source of authoritative power for these roles is the prevalence of this conviction about their legitimacy; in changing systems this belief may be undergoing serious erosion. Stability and change will vary with the belief that it is right and proper to accept the decisions and actions of those who occupy the roles of authority. We may describe these varying convictions about the legitimacy of the authorities as one measure of the support for the structure of authority.

This does not exclude the possibility and indeed the probability that to backstop and supplement power derived from a belief in their legitimacy, the occupants of authority roles will have important other sources of power, such as force or rational persuasion. Nor should we ignore the fact that by virtue of their occupancy of these roles, the authorities cannot escape certain limitations on their powers. But these are aspects of a theory of political authority that do not concern our immediate research objectives and can be set aside.[7] Our sole point here is that no system can persist, regardless of its specific type or character, without some structure of authority, however limited or unrestrained the powers exercised through this structure may be. There must be some minimal input of support for the structure of authority, and a belief in its legitimacy empirically turns out to be the most dependable and continuing kind of support. Without this structure of authority the system could not sustain the minimal organization necessary to rally and commit, on any kind of recurring basis, the human and other resources of the system for the production and implementation of outputs. There could be no political system.

Hence we have selected socialization during childhood of orientations toward the structure of authority as a theoretically significant focus for our research. It opens the door to an understanding of how members of a system begin to acquire a sense of the legitimacy of the authorities. We assume that the attitudes toward political authority that are learned early will have some impact on the ability of any political system to operate and upon the future stability or change of the particular political system in which the socialization occurs.

THE CHILD'S POLITICAL IMAGES

Theoretically, the structure of authority, as part of the regime, stands as a postulated necessary condition for the persistence of any kind of political system. It turns out, happily, that what is theoretically of highest significance empirically plays a crucial part in linking the child to the political system in the United States. Theory and fact here converge. Among other things, primary socialization involves the acquisition of some knowledge about the structure of political authority and the development of attitudes toward its parts.

To discover how and where diffuse support has its origins it became imperative to inquire into the development of images about the structure of authority and its components. How do children see and interpret the points of contact that constitute the structure of authority? How do they feel about them?

An image itself is not a homogeneous object. We shall find that the images children form about authority have two basic dimensions, one essentially cognitive, the other affective (in the latter we shall include evaluative elements as well because of the difficulty of sorting out the two for children). Children have some knowledge about the figures and institutions of authority. Not that it is "accurate" by adult standards. This is less material than trying to understand the nature of the child's knowledge and its consequences for his developing support for political authority. Children also have feelings about political authority. They are able to rate it on what have been called "scales of better-ness and worseness,"[8] which necessarily include some evaluations. Thus we find that the child is able to express certain beliefs about the constituent parts of political authority and that these beliefs incorporate various kinds of feelings and judgments.

It is not a simple thing to differentiate these two aspects of an image empirically. At times it may be virtually impossible to separate the mixture. As will appear later, we do not suggest that our efforts have been entirely successful, so complex a psychic entity is an image in a child. But a major task of our pretests was to discover its basic dimensions.

What the child sees: cognitive image

If a child is to develop feelings about the political authorities, he must be aware of their existence in some shape or form. The child must be able to carry around in his mind a picture, how-ever fuzzy, obscure, and tentative, of something "out there," beyond the walls of home and school, about which he can develop ideas and feelings. The political system must take some kind of em-pirical or symbolic form for the child member, even if it is only of a great occasional force somewhere over the hills (as appears to be true for adults in some peasant societies[9]).

On a priori grounds we might have expected that the early ties of the child to the political system are few and simple. Chil-dren have a low interest in political matters of any kind when compared with other fields of activity. Their comprehension of this adult area would seem to be extremely circumscribed. Yet surprisingly, for the input of support the child finds no one clear and well-defined point of entry into the political system. From second through fourth grades, as the child becomes increasingly aware of things outside of his family, school, and immediate neighborhood, he is not led by the hand to one or two points of contact with the basic political objects. Extensive preliminary testing and interviewing revealed that as political matters unobtrusively begin to cross the child's horizons, several objects become sufficiently visible or meaningful for him to be able to hold opinions about them or to express some knowledge of them. He has spread before him aspects from each of the major levels of the political system—the political community, the regime, and the authorities—and develops some knowledge, however vague and inchoate, about them. In particular, for the input of support, the connective tissues between child and system are more varied and extensive, less delicate and tenuous, than we might have expected.

It became clear, from pretesting, that in our group the child very early began to think of himself as an American. We could see that he had begun to identify himself with what on theoretical grounds we have interpreted as the political community. At the same time, by fourth grade at least, he had also acquired the notion that somewhere beyond the family and neighborhood lay some force or persons called the government. In this concept we were able to identify the most comprehensive conception that the child possesses of the regime and the authorities. Not that the word government has a precise meaning for the child. Certainly in grades four and five, if not beyond, it would have defied the comprehension of the child to provide a description of the term more than modestly acceptable to knowledgeable adults. But, as we shall note in detail, even at these grades the child was not devoid of some understanding of what might be included within the idea of government.

"Government" will prove to be a central notion. It is the closest approximation to the theoretical concept "structure of authority." It is precisely through this symbolizing of the authority structure, we shall later estimate, that the child finds one way to begin to incorporate what adults often refer to as "our system of government." Because we could find no other idea that had as general an import for the child and that seemed, in one act of apprehension, to embrace the whole structure of authority, our search for the roots of support led us to probe more deeply into the significance of this notion for the child. Chapter 6 will analyze the child's image of government and its implications for his attachment to the system.

But simultaneously with his increasing awareness of something out there called the government, hovering over the country and caring for it, our pretesting revealed a peculiar phenomenon, one that we shall designate as the "head-and-tail effect" in political socialization. Traditional educational theory, currently subsumed in the curricula of many elementary school systems, has presupposed that the child broadens his range of awareness by moving through a series of neat and orderly concentric circles. At the core lies the nuclear family; it is about this social unit that he is first able to learn formally. From this, as he matures and his intellectual and emotional faculties together with his broadening experiences permit it, he gradually extends his range of knowledge and interests outward to the immediate neighborhood and school, and from there to the city, state, region, and nation as a whole. Finally, his perspective embraces even the international sphere. The content of the curriculum for the child is built on these assumptions. Instruction is geared to the state of readiness implied in each widening ring of experience and perception.

How accurately this pattern describes the growth of other areas of knowledge and interest we do not presume to know. But in the political sphere two things quickly became apparent in our pretests. First, there is no linear progression either from close to distant objects or, for that matter, from simple to complex ones. The introduction of the child to political life follows a much less orderly pattern. He proves capable of simultaneously making contact with both the inner and outer rings of traditional curricular theory, and at a number of different structural levels. We found the child to be absorbing ideas and expressing feelings about remote political things, such as the government and the President, even while he was becoming familiar with objects very close to home, such as the policeman, a staunch traditional symbol of authority.

Although in interviews children tended to disclose very little capacity to discuss politics or political structures in the city or state or, for that matter, until later grades, even to discuss national politics or structures, there was no doubt that they could readily talk about the head and the tail of the political system, the President and the policeman. These two were politically relevant objects about which most children had something to say. It was clear that in the area of the structure of authority, the child is likely to become aware initially of some distant objects and some closer to home. Those structures in between seem to remain, until later childhood at least, a truly blooming, buzzing confusion.[10]

Toward the older end of our age group, however, by grade eight, the child's political images contained many more details and certainly more figures and institutions. By that time most children had been exposed at the very least to some political history of the United States, including the Constitution, and often had had courses in civics. Few would have no knowledge of the existence of a mayor, if relevant in his locality, or of a governor, for example. But as we shall observe in a later chapter, the importance of these objects for children whom we tested and interviewed was sufficiently low to lead us, in settling on necessary priorities for research, to focus on what were obviously the most visible and salient political objects for the child. These turned out to be the President and the policeman for the younger children in our group. Chapters 7 to 11 deal with these figures as vital links between the child and the American political system for the input of diffuse support.

At the more distant, national level, the President does not cross the child's political horizon alone. When the child leaves the earliest grades, the President is accompanied, in the child's image, by such other political figures and institutions as senators, Congress, and the Supreme Court. They too become concrete political objects for the child and, like the President, seem to have sufficient meaning to come to the child's attention early and to lodge in his consciousness. In Chapters 12 and 13 we shall consider their place as links between growing children and the regime.

It is clear that, at least for politics, the child does not progress through those concentric rings of awareness that have been presupposed for other areas of social life. Indeed, if we had to choose among the structural levels at which the child is initially likely to become most thoroughly immersed in politics—always bearing in mind the relatively low interest children have in politics—we would point to the national sphere. Not only does the child feel able to talk about government in general, meaning thereby initially the national government, and the President in particular, but he acquires at least some knowledge of other equally distant national figures and institutions.

These political authorities have a degree of visibility or palpability that suggests how, if the child should know anything at all about political life, his knowledge might be of such well-defined objects. But we would be doing less than justice to the overall processes of political socialization if we were to leave the impression that in a system like the United States its maturing members become informed about the political sphere through these points alone. The resources that the American political system has at its disposal are far more varied and subtle. As we have already noted, our pretesting revealed that the child at the same time becomes quickly aware of the existence of certain expected behaviors (or norms) for persons in the political realm. He comes to realize that as an adult he will be expected to be interested in and to participate in politics, to feel as though he does or can have an effective voice in politics, and to sense that some degree of partisanship is viewed with approval. In other words, while he is learning to see and to develop feelings about one major component of the regime, its structure of authority, he is becoming apprised of the nature of another component, regime norms, and he is learning about them as well.

We can see that the child enters the political system through a number of different doors. What makes some doors more inviting than others, and what his feelings are while entering them, will undoubtedly depend in part upon the characteristics of the child himself, on his personality. But they will also be a function of the nature of what he sees. As we have already indicated, analytically we may treat the regime norms as distinct from the regime's structure of authority. Our political theory has accordingly proved to be a useful way of dividing our research efforts. In the present work we deal only with the kinds of images that children develop about the political authorities. We leave for separate and independent analysis the way in which children acquire knowledge and sentiments about regime norms.

What the child feels: affective image

Our purposes in baring the points of contact between a child and the political system are not solely to establish the resources available to a particular political order for socializing its young, although this knowledge in itself would carry us far beyond what is currently known about the sources of the input of support for a system. But once we establish the objects toward which maturing members of a system are capable of reacting, we need to inquire into how they feel about what they see. The image formed by children as they become socialized has affective and judgmental as well as cognitive components.

For the input of diffuse support, the feelings and associated evaluations incorporated in these images will be central. To the extent that children have positive feelings about and estimates of the political authorities, we can assume that they have begun to put in support for the regime. The folklore about the American system, especially about its relative lack of instability, presupposes a high level of input of positive support among adults. Even if we were to grant in advance that this has probably been correct, at least for much of the recent past, we can anticipate that there is some variability among adults. As we lack longitudinal studies of members of the system, carried forward from childhood through adulthood, we are unable to establish the precise linkage between child and mature member. Nevertheless we can anticipate that there ought to be some variability among children themselves. At the very least our research will raise the question of whether some significant association between childhood experience and adult outcome ought not to be suspected.

CONCLUSION

Our plan of analysis is therefore laid out for us. To probe into the sources of support for the regime structure, we seek to learn about the way in which children make their early contacts with the political system, especially with that part of it we call the structure of authority. On general theoretical grounds we see this as a central phenomenon in any ongoing political system.

To detect, document, and understand the significance of the precise way in which children reach out to the authorities, we need to discover those figures and institutions of political authority that the child first sees and the way he sees them and feels about them. In this way we shall be able to arrive at some judgment about how diffuse support for the political authorities in one system, the United States, emerges and perhaps begins to take the form it does. It will give us an empirical purchase on a difficult and amorphous concept in political inquiry, that of legitimacy. Those who are learning to support the structure of authority (negatively or positively) are also beginning to establish some attitudes toward its legitimacy. A sense of legitimacy, in turn, represents a major mechanism through which the political authorities in most systems are able to stimulate positive support for the regime.

It has become apparent by this time that throughout our analysis we shall be adopting an important assumption about the consequences of early socialization: Those children who begin to develop positive feelings toward the political authorities will tend to grow into adults who will be less easily disenchanted with the system than those children who early acquire negative, hostile sentiments.

We would not contend that this durability attaches to all political acquisitions in childhood. We have already suggested that in areas related to allocative politics, there may well be a different kind of outcome. Early political acquisitions there may only be selectively consequential for adult behavior. But for those subject matters that deal with the basic political objects, embraced in our notion of system politics, we shall presume that perceptions and feelings formed early in life are more difficult to dislodge than those of later life. They are likely to remain as underlying, latent sentiments that can be evoked in later years, under the proper circumstances, either on behalf of or in opposition to the basic political objects, depending upon their initial direction. Alienation may be as durable over the years as identification.

Not that early images will necessarily withstand the onslaught of all future events. Childhood events may be diluted and overridden by subsequent experiences. All we would contend is that basic childhood sentiments are less easily dislodged and modified than those acquired later in life.

We have already observed that this is a hypothesis supported mainly by a vast body of folklore but by extraordinarily little hard research. As has been noted,

> Most psychologists and social scientists agree that there is a special significance attached to first or early learning. There is good evidence for this assumption. What we do not know, and are unable to discover from the culture-personality [or other sources], is what precisely it is that is learned in early infancy and what its exact significance may be for later learning. As D. O. Hebb tersely remarks: "In such matters, our ignorance is virtually complete."[11]

Yet until reliable tests demonstrate otherwise in the political sphere, it seems to make sense to stand by this hypothesis as it applies to basic sentiments about the structure of political authority.

NOTES

1. See D. Easton, *A Systems Analysis of Political Life* (New York: Wiley, 1965), pp. 110ff.
2. As noted in the preceding chapter, we have already made a beginning at publishing some of our data about the socialization of regime norms. See Chapter 4, footnote 24.

3. Here we draw our materials from the discussion in D. Easton, op. cit., pp. 205-210, sometimes paraphrasing what is said there and sometimes quoting directly without benefit of quotation marks. See also an extended treatment of authority by D. Easton, "The Perception of Authority and Political Change," in C. J. Friedrich (ed.), *Authority* (Cambridge, Mass.: Harvard, 1958), pp. 170-196.

4. See references to nonliterate systems of various types in D. Easton, *The Political System* (New York: Knopf, 1953), pp. 139-141; D. Easton, "Political Anthropology," in B. J. Siegel (ed.), *Biennial Review of Anthropology* (Stanford, Calif.: Stanford, 1959), pp. 210-262; and I. Schapera, *Government and Politics in Tribal Societies* (London: Watts, 1956).

5. See T. Parsons (ed.), *Max Weber: The Theory of Social and Economic Organization* (Fair Lawn, N.J.: Oxford, 1947); and also a discussion of personal authority in D. Easton, *A Systems Analysis of Political Life,* p. 302ff.

6. For some exceptions, see Schapera, op. cit., especially p. 217.

7. For some remarks about these aspects, see D. Easton, *A Systems Analysis of Political Life,* pp. 207-208.

8. K. Boulding, *The Image* (Ann Arbor, Mich.: The University of Michigan Press, 1956), p. 11.

9. D. Lerner, *The Passing of Traditional Society* (New York: Free Press, 1958).

10. Special conditions may change the character of what is first seen by the younger members of a system. For example, the special image that Mayor Lee of New Haven had shaped for himself led children there to become more quickly aware of him than would appear to be true of mayors elsewhere. [F. Greenstein, *Children and Politics* (New Haven, Conn: Yale, 1965)]. Perhaps also in rural areas and small towns we might expect local officials to be better known to children than in more densely populated areas.

11. A. R. Lindesmith and A. L. Strauss, "A Critique of Culture-personality Writings," *American Sociological Review,* 15, p. 599, 1950.

PART **3**

IMAGES ABOUT
THE STRUCTURE
OF AUTHORITY

6

THE IMAGE OF GOVERNMENT

If on impressionistic grounds we had been called upon to advance an opinion about the candidates likely to act as concrete points of contact between the political system and children, we might have expected them to be figures that are prestigious and salient for adults, such as, at the very least, the President, senators, and perhaps even justices of the Supreme Court. In the United States without a monarch who might stand out as a single and major honorific symbol, it would not be farfetched that figures such as these step into the breach. We shall observe later that to some extent they in fact do, and this is especially true of the President. But it would not have been likely to occur to us that the mundane idea of government itself might somehow also take over part of the function that a highly prestigious, sometimes neutral figure such as a monarch may play in other systems.

Yet our data tell us that most children in our group do acquire an overview of the structure of authority, and at a very early stage. They achieve it through an ability to handle the idea of government and to give it some kind of concrete meaning. It is here that we find one of the first and major points of contact between children and the regime. It is certainly the only one that comes at all close to the theoretical notion of a structure or pattern of authority.

That the child may come very early to some ideas about government as symbol or substance has marked theoretical as well as empirical significance for his developing relationship with the system. If the child were only to apprehend the political authorities one by one, it would be difficult for him to arrive at the point where he could even visualize, much less articulate, some overall structure of which the authorities are part. To the extent that this area of political life remained structureless and fragmented for him, he might be linked to the political system only through individual isolated strands in the form of specific figures of authority. The child might have little initial sense of an enduring structure of authority that encompassed more than a summation of the individual authority figures familiar to him.

Furthermore, without some generalized conception of authority, it is difficult to imagine how a child would incorporate into his developing cognitive image any new political figure or institution about which he learned or that was created as he matured. We would expect that as he became aware of new political figures, he would have to be persuaded of their legitimacy on an ad hoc basis, instead of automatically attributing to them the same kind of legitimacy as he extended to the whole existing configuration of authorities. We are not prepared to say that the idea of government alone provides the child with a general intellective container, as it were, into which he can put each new object of authority. But we shall see that at the very least it serves to generalize his limited experiences with or perceptions of discrete political authorities.

The theoretical implications of a conception of government are therefore considerable. It would seem to provide the child with a conceptual device for grasping, however inchoately and awkwardly, the presence of some structure of authority.

THE CHILD'S EARLY RECOGNITION OF GOVERNMENT

Crystallization of the concept "government"

When do our respondents first begin to recognize the general category of things labeled government? One simple way of exploring this is to see whether the child himself thinks he knows what the word government means, even if no verbalization of his understanding is called for. On this simple test we find that even the seven- or eight-year-old child, in grade 2, is likely to feel that he has some rudimentary grasp of this general concept.

Table 6-1 Development of a Sense of Confidence in Under standing the Concept of Government (percent at each grade who mark that they are *not* sure what government means)*

Grade	Percent	Number of Cases
2	27	1655
3	19	1678
4	18	1749
5	11	1803
6	12	1749
7	8	1723
8	10	1695

*CA-9, page 12, item 55. [This reference indicates that this question is item 55, page 12 of our final questionnaire (Citizen's Attitudes No. 9). Instructions for obtaining a copy of the questionnaire appear in the Appendix, page 425.] "Some of you may not be sure what the word *government* means. If you are not sure what *government* means, put an X in the box below."

From the simple data presented in Table 6-1 we find that 27 percent of the second-grade children feel some uncertainty about the concept. This proportion declines rather regularly over the grades, however, so that for the eighth-grade children, only ten percent express this uncertainty. In general, these data suggest that a considerable portion of the youngest children felt it had already crystallized some concept of government prior to our testing. With each higher grade level the likelihood that the children did not feel they had formed some concept decreases. With these data—and similar data from other protocols—as a background, we can proceed to a more detailed consideration of the content of the child's understanding of government.

Symbolic associations of the government concept

As it appears that the child is rather likely to develop some working conception of government in these early years, we can move on to ask: What is the specific content of this concept? We might well expect that because of the inherent ambiguity and generality of the term, even for adults, considerable differences and disjunctiveness would characterize it for aggregates of children. Our findings do, in part, support this expectation. Yet there are clearly some dominant patterns in these collective conceptions, and these patterns vary to a large degree with the age and grade level of the children.

To get fairly directly at the dominant patterns in this period and at the way in which they change, we devised a pictorial representation of government. It took the form of the ten symbols shown in Figure 6-1. These symbols emerged distinctively in our pretest data when children were asked either to define government or to free associate with a list of words, one of which was government.

The pattern of response to these ten symbols is shown in Table 6-2. Several interesting facts are suggested. If we take

Figure 6-1 Symbols of Government.*

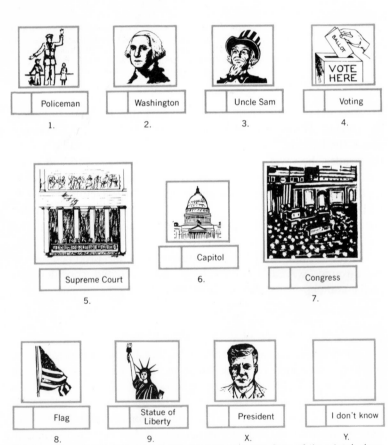

*CA-9 questionnaire, item 24, page 4. See Appendix, page 425. Some of the artwork above has been redrawn for reproductive clarity. The reader should examine the original questionnaire for the exact pictures administered to the children.

20 percent as a rough guide to what we might expect purely by chance as a maximum level of response to each of the ten symbol options (for two-answer format), we see that only four of these pictures were chosen with a frequency greater than chance. These four were George Washington, Voting, Congress, and President Kennedy. These are selected with considerably greater frequency than any of the others, although this dominance varies with grade level. For the youngest children, the two most popular options are the two Presidents, Washington and Kennedy. But these choices drop in the later grades. In Figure 6-2, the developmental curves for the four dominant options are plotted over the grade span in order to interpret more easily the major changes that are taking place.

It would appear that, in terms of these symbols, the youngest child's perception of government is quite likely to be framed by the few personal figures of high governmental authority that

Figure 6-2 Development of a Cognitive Image of Government: The Four Dominant Symbolic Associations.*

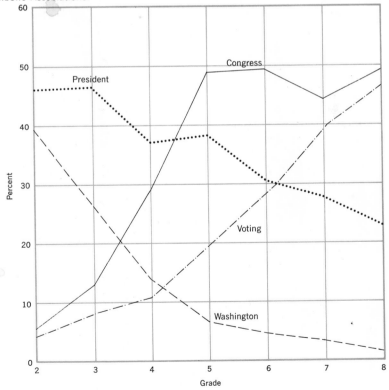

*The number of children responding at each grade level varies from 1,619 to 1,789.

Table 6-2 Development of a Cognitive Image of Government: Symbolic Associations* (percent of children and teachers responding)†

Grade	Police-man	George Wash-ington	Uncle Sam	Voting	Supreme Court	Capitol	Congress	Flag	Statue of Liberty	President Kennedy	I Don't Know	N§ Re-sponding	N Not Responding
Grade 2	8%	39	16	4	5	14	6	16	12	46	16%	1619	36
Grade 3	4	27	19	8	6	16	13	16	14	47	13	1662	16
Grade 4	6	14	18	11	10	17	29	13	13	37	13	1726	23
Grade 5	3	7	19	19	17	12	49	12	11	39	5	1789	14
Grade 6	2	5	17	28	17	10	50	11	17	31	5	1740	9
Grade 7	3	3	18	39	14	9	44	13	19	28	3	1714	9
Grade 8	2	2	16	47	16	7	49	12	20	23	2	1689	6
Teachers‡	1%	1	5	72	13	5	71	6	8	15	0%	390	1

*CA-9, page 4, item 24: "Here are some pictures that show what our government is. Pick the two pictures that show best what our government is."

† Percentages should add to 200 in the two-answer format, but do not, because of the failure of some children to make two choices; this is especially the case for those answering "I don't know."

‡ We have added the responses of the teachers of these children for the sake of comparison; the teachers were given a similar questionnaire at the time of administration of the children's questionnaire.

§N = the number of cases making some response. This number was used as the base for the percentages.

cross his cognitive horizon, probably both in the school (where the portraits of presidents are often prominently displayed) and outside. The young child focuses most directly upon personal or perhaps charismatic aspects of the political authorities for his interpretation of what government is. But as he moves into the middle years (grades 4 to 6), there is a greater likelihood that his attention will turn to rather different prominent aspects of the authorities. Thus he revises his notions to include the Congress and drops George Washington—who suffers a precipitous decline after his initial showing.

Undoubtedly, the growing response to Congress reflects an awareness of several things. (These conclusions are supported by various other data as well.) First, the older children become more aware of the group character of government and do not simply identify it with single persons. Second, the more frequent choice of Congress probably also reflects a greater awareness of governmental institutions—particularly the ongoing organizations engaged in lawmaking (as suggested undoubtedly in the beginning social studies, history, or civics texts). Children move from a very personalized conception of governmental authority to one that emphasizes the "legal-rational," institutionalized aspects, to continue the Weberian parallel. We may characterize this more generally as a shift from a personalized to an impersonal image of government. Third, children appear to reflect a greater awareness of the representative character of these institutions. Impersonalization of authority is coincident with some growth in the recognition of regime norms, in this case of the rules of behavior that contribute to representation. This conclusion is borne out to some degree by the marked age shift which occurs as represented by the older child's greater tendency to pick Voting as the best picture of our government. By grade 8 nearly half the children chose Voting. This suggests some beginning awareness of the regime rules associated with popular democracy and the expected role of ordinary people in it.

The child's conception of government is, therefore, brought in stages from far to near, from one small set of persons to many people, from a personalized to an impersonalized form of authority, and toward an awareness of the institutionalization in our system of such regime norms as are embodied in the idea of a representative, popular democracy. Not that all the children are going through these stages of cognitive development.[1] But the patterns which emerge seem very striking and are supported in various ways by our other data.

Generally, therefore, in these data about the cognitive development of this rather abstract category of the individual's political thought, we detect more than a mere glimmering of a concept. Furthermore, the emergent conception in this instance reflects some fairly wide and regularly changing comprehension for aggregates of children.

This suggests that society is probably expending considerable energy in an effort to transmit a concept deemed appropriate in the American political system. If we compare children with their teachers, for example (Table 6-2), we find that the latter most roundly endorse the two options dominant for the eighth-grade children. The proportions are even higher for the teachers—who may be important agents contributing to the child's political and general conceptual development—so that in terms of the statistical norms, they stand perhaps closer to the end state suggested by the direction of movement of the children. One could hypothesize, therefore, that a part of society's efforts to inform the child is reflected in the responses of the teachers.

The concept of government and the lawmaking function

A supporting piece of evidence which is connected to the general pattern of development just described, but which supplements it from the standpoint of governmental functions (rather than from the structural aspects of the concept alone), has to do with the child's changing awareness of the chief lawmakers in our system of government. One thing we found was that, of the various kinds of political or other functions that the child most readily associates with government, the making of laws is very prominent. When the child is asked "What does the government do?" he is quite likely to answer that he, it, or they make the laws. In one instance, Andrew, aged eight, son of a truck driver and loader and in third grade at a Chicago-area school, was asked in a personal interview "What is government?" He replied: "It's like governor. It keeps all the laws." In the same vein, but at a little older age, Patrick, ten, son of a commercial photographer and in fifth grade in the Chicago area, replied: "That's where they make the law, pass it on, and give it to the Supreme Court, then to the President, and then it is passed on to us and it—well, we are supposed to abide by it."

We could use this transparent awareness of the lawmaking activity to probe further into the child's image of government.

A questionnaire item that we presented in this connection read: "Who makes the laws? Put an X next to the one who does the most to make the laws." The options were: (1) Congress, (2) President, (3) Supreme Court, (4) I Don't Know. The same pictures as before were used. In Table 6-3 we see the patterns of change over the grade span for this aspect of the child's understanding.

Table 6-3 Development of an Awareness of the Chief Lawmaker* (percent of children and teachers responding)

Grade	Congress	President	Supreme Court	I Don't Know	Total	N Responding	N Not Responding
Grade 2	5%	76	11	8	100%	1627	28
Grade 3	11	66	17	6	100	1648	30
Grade 4	28	44	21	7	100	1723	26
Grade 5	57	19	20	3	99	1793	10
Grade 6	65	13	18	3	99	1743	6
Grade 7	72	9	16	3	100	1712	11
Grade 8	85	5	8	1	99	1690	5
Teachers	96%	1	3	0	100%	339	5

*CA-9, page 7, item 33. "Who makes the laws? Put an X next to the one who does the most to make the laws." A smaller set of the same pictures as in item 24 was used.

Here the President's early dominance is apparent, but Congress gradually supplants him by grade 5. Thus, by the middle grades the child is increasingly prone to identify Congress as both the chief source of lawmaking and a more representative symbol of our government than the President.

If this trend should continue into adulthood, we would expect considerable support for Congress as the primary institution of government vis-à-vis the President. We would expect that, of the opposing observations of Max Lerner and Robert Lane, for example, those of Lane would be given greater credence. Lerner observed (as cited by Lane) that "When the American thinks of his government, he thinks first of the President as its symbol."[2] If "first" means while he is a second or third grader, then Lerner is correct. But this does not appear to be the sense in which he is using the word.

In light of the developmental trends we see in our data, our respondents seem to resemble more closely the "common men" in Lane's Eastport study. Lane found that his respondents were more likely to perceive government in terms of its legislative functions than of its administrative or judicial ones.[3] Government is thought of in terms of its products, the laws it makes.[4] As far as the common men in Eastport were concerned, Congress was the most important focus of their concept of government. They considered government and Congress as benign, helpful, and responsive — an organization "working for the people, not merely restraining them."[5]

All these findings converge with our data as far as the developmental trends are concerned. The oldest children in our test group are those who most resemble the common men of Eastport. Our data are an indication that this image of government is not confined to the period of Lane's study but has more general application. Over the grades our respondents increasingly tend to see government with Congress as its center, law as its most visible product, and, as we shall later note, benign, helpful, protective, and responsive qualities in its manner of operation.

A further item bears out the child's emphasis on Congress in his conception of government. In our final instrument we asked our test group in the eight cities "Who does most to run the country?" This emphasis on executive activity is not as salient in the child's conception of government as is the lawmaking function. Nevertheless it is an important subsidiary one. As one ten-year-old child from fifth grade in a Chicago suburban school put it in reply to our question "What is government?": "A group of people that make the rules and sort of in charge of what's going on but not completely in control in the United States."

Table 6-4 indicates that among the options provided, the President is selected with highest frequency. Yet even in this question Congress moves from 4 percent at grade 2 to 35 percent by grade 8. We also need to note that the movement is in the direction of the collective opinion levels of the teachers, 61 percent of whom pick Congress.

Table 6-4   Development of an Awareness of "Who does most to run the country"*
(percent of children and teachers responding)

Grade	Congress	President	Supreme Court	I Don't Know	Total	N Responding	N Not Responding
Grade 2	4%	86	3	7	100%	1627	28
Grade 3	7	85	3	5	100	1662	16
Grade 4	13	77	3	6	99	1725	24
Grade 5	20	72	4	4	100	1796	7
Grade 6	25	66	5	4	100	1744	5
Grade 7	28	64	5	3	100	1711	12
Grade 8	35	58	4	3	100	1683	12
Teachers	61%	36	3	0	100%	338	6

*CA-9, page 9, item 41. "Who does the most to run the country? Put an X in the box next to the *one* who does the most to run the country: (1) Congress, (2) President, (3) Supreme Court, (4) I don't know." The same pictures were used as for page 7, item 33.

This question strongly hints at an executive rather than a legislative activity of government. Yet even with this emphasis, Congress develops considerable strength in these years in the cognitive map of government, in comparison with the President.

Differentiation of the public sector

Even though the children assert a growing awareness of government as an idea and object, are they able to distinguish it as separate from other areas of social life? If attitudes toward the authorities are relevant for later ties to the system, we need some evidence indicating that even in their earliest grades children are, in fact, able to recognize some minimal difference between that which is governmental and that which is not. Only under such conditions could we infer that attitudes toward government refer to distinctively political bonds.

To discover whether the child's own assertion that he knows what government means includes a capacity to discriminate governmental from nongovernmental objects, we chose to test his awareness of the difference between what we normally view as the public and private sectors of life. A variety of contexts could be used to explore this differentiation—activities of various kinds, organizations, symbols, or personnel. We chose the last for our test because we found that the formulation "people who do various jobs to help the community" is rather familiar to the child who has been exposed to the beginning social studies texts. The child learns that a variety of "community helpers" exist, ranging from doctors and nurses to firemen and street sweepers.

What we asked was very simple. Taking various occupations— milkman, policeman, soldier, judge, postman, and teacher—we said: "Here are some people. Which ones work for the government?" Then followed six questions with an appropriate picture for each, such as: "Does the MILKMAN work for the government?" The options were: (1) Yes, (2) No.

Only the milkman was considered by us to be clearly outside the governmental system as determined by his occupation.[6] Of the rest, two were more directly local-government workers— the policeman and the teacher; two were clearly national-government workers—the soldier and the postman; and one was indeterminate as among levels—the judge.

Several things are apparent from Table 6-5. Of these workers, the milkman is the one (as we would expect) who is least often identified as a member of the public sector. Around 70 percent

Table 6-5   Development of an Awareness of the Public and Private Sectors* (percent of children and teachers responding)

Grade	Milkman	Policeman	Soldier	Judge	Postman	Teacher	N Responding (varies by item)
Grade 2	29%	86	68	86	57	48%	1601-1626
Grade 3	31	89	79	88	63	55	1627-1656
Grade 4	28	91	83	89	71	58	1702-1730
Grade 5	21	89	90	90	80	63	1778-1792
Grade 6	16	88	93	92	86	64	1730-1747
Grade 7	13	82	96	94	89	64	1697-1718
Grade 8	8	81	98	94	93	59	1681-1692
Teachers	1%	77	100	91	99	45%	330-341

*CA-9, pages 11-12, items 49-54: "Here are some people. Which ones work for the government? Does the _____ work for the government?" Table entries are percent answering "yes."

of the youngest children were able to make an accurate assessment of his nongovernmental status. From grade 4 on, this proportion steadily increased so that by grade 8, less than 10 percent were in error.

For the rest, the youngest children most easily recognized that the policeman and the judge belong in the governmental sector. Then come the soldier, postman, and teacher in that order. Both the soldier and postman—the more nearly exclusively national government workers—increase in the proportions of children endorsing them at successively higher grade levels, until by grade 8 they are the ones who, with the judge, get the greatest governmental identification.

The teacher, on the other hand, does not really make any major gains over the grades; her governmental status remains somewhat ambiguous. This effect holds for the teacher respondents as well. Somehow the status of the teacher is a more complex one.

That something other than the capacity to discriminate between governmental and nongovernmental objects is probably at work in the children is seen when we compare their perceptions of the teacher and the policeman, both local-governmental in status, with the other figures. Over the grades both teacher and policeman suffer some net decline in the proportions of children endorsing their governmental status, whereas the other government workers show gains. Possibly the older child is more likely to direct his attention to the national level for his image of government, and, therefore, his differentiation is conflicted for local-government workers. This would fit other somewhat similar findings about the child's greater awareness of the national than of the lower levels of government.[7] It would also explain the markedly lower percentage of teachers who identify policemen and teachers themselves as working for the government.

In general, the child in his elementary years acquires the capacity to differentiate the governmental sector of behavior from the nongovernmental. This does not mean that he is able to do so in every conceivable way. Our data suggest only that he is increasingly able to distinguish government personnel from nongovernment personnel. His concept of government, therefore, does become differentiated at least in these terms. Again, this suggests a development beyond that of only a rudimentary grasp of this complex object in these early years of political awareness.

As the child matures, therefore, he becomes increasingly politicized, that is, his awareness of the political sector of life takes root and shows substantial growth. *Politicization* will prove to be a vital element in the socializing of children, as we move further along in our analysis. At this point, however, there is sufficient content in the child's perception of government for us to have some confidence that when we now come to talk about his attitudes toward government, we will be referring to attitudes toward genuinely political (that is, public) authorities. It will also prove significant for our interpretation that there is a tendency to think of government as at the national rather than the local level.

Views of the informal processes of government

It is apparent that as the children in our test group acquire some understanding of government, they see it largely in what as adults we would conceive to be formal terms. They see those roles that have official recognition in the American political system. These are well-defined offices for which requirements and behavior are formally prescribed.

That the child should become familiar with this aspect of the structure of political authority accords well with the more general theory of socialization already mentioned, which holds that adults tend to communicate the formal, recognized structure first.[8] According to this theory, only as children grow older do adults feel that they are equipped to understand and appreciate the other things that go in a structure, what in social science we recognize as the important informal processes and infrastructures through which the business of a group gets done.

However, it is not at all clear that the children acquire absolutely no knowledge about the informal areas of politics. We have some evidence that, at least for the overall structure of authority, the image gradually building up in the child's mind, about which he is beginning to develop feelings, also includes some discernible informal aspects. It is true, our pretest data suggested that this aspect of governmental awareness is relatively low in these early years. As a result, we found it difficult to devise instruments to tap the properties of the small degree of awareness likely to be present. Nevertheless we were able to detect some of the earliest beginnings of the informal parts of the image, if only from the fourth grade onwards.[9]

We had the children rate various people according to the extent that they helped to make laws for the country. We asked: "How much do these people help decide which laws are made for our country? Very Much, Some, Very Little, or Not at All? Put an X for each person or group of persons listed below." The choices included rich people, unions, the President, newspapers, churches, the average person, policemen, and big companies. We hoped to get some overall assessment of the child's relative awareness of participation by these various actors in the processes of government. The children's responses over the grades are shown in Table 6-6.

The children were clearly willing to assess differently the relative influence of these political actors, and there are marked age trends in some instances. The President was seen as far and away the actor of most importance in the lawmaking process. We might have suspected this from our knowledge of the children's previous emphasis on the formal aspects of government. This assessment remains high across the grades. At a considerable distance are various extragovernmental groups and strata, parts of the political infrastructure—rich people, unions, big companies, newspapers, and churches. Of these, unions (which were read out to the children as "labor unions") from the earliest grades evoke the greatest image of influence for our urban children.

Policemen, the other official government actors, do well at first, but quickly decline as participants in the lawmaking process. The child in this instance moves away from an overestimation of the role of policemen and thus toward the distribution exhibited by their teachers.

The interpretation of the average person's role is below that of the groups, strata, and official actors, yet it does show a gain just at the end of the period. Thus, there is some movement on

Table 6-6 "How much do these people help decide which laws are made for our country?"*
(percent of children and teachers responding)

	1. Very Much	2. Some	3. Very Little	4. Not at All	Total	N Responding	N Not Responding
"Rich People"							
Grade 4	18%	51	22	9	100%	1230	519
Grade 5	8	56	25	11	100	1563	240
Grade 6	5	58	26	11	100	1586	163
Grade 7	6	56	28	10	100	1609	114
Grade 8	8	59	25	8	100	1597	98
Teachers	19%	71	7	3	100%	323	21
"Unions"							
Grade 4	36%	53	9	2	100%	1141	608
Grade 5	34	56	8	2	100	1540	263
Grade 6	31	57	10	2	100	1582	167
Grade 7	26	61	11	3	101	1596	127
Grade 8	25	63	11	2	101	1612	83
Teachers	37%	59	3	1	100%	328	16
"The President"							
Grade 4	89%	10	1	0	100%	1499	250
Grade 5	87	12	1	0	100	1773	30
Grade 6	87	11	2	1	101	1728	21
Grade 7	85	13	2	1	101	1704	19
Grade 8	84	14	1	0	99	1674	21
Teachers	66%	33	1	0	100%	331	13
"Newspapers"							
Grade 4	14%	50	25	11	100%	1407	342
Grade 5	10	46	29	14	99	1695	108
Grade 6	10	44	31	14	99	1673	76
Grade 7	12	47	30	11	100	1676	47
Grade 8	15	52	24	9	100	1642	53
Teachers	38%	55	5	2	100%	328	16
"Churches"							
Grade 4	28%	38	22	12	100%	1365	384
Grade 5	18	45	25	12	100	1660	143
Grade 6	13	42	30	15	100	1611	138
Grade 7	11	45	32	12	100	1663	60
Grade 8	10	46	34	11	101	1615	80
Teachers	5%	60	29	6	100%	329	14

Table 6-6. (cont.) "How much do these people help decide which laws are made for our country?" (percent of children and teachers responding)

	1. Very Much	2. Some	3. Very Little	4. Not at all	Total	N Responding	N Not Responding
"The Average Person"							
Grade 4	11%	52	29	9	101%	1392	357
Grade 5	11	54	27	8	100	1703	100
Grade 6	10	51	30	9	100	1680	69
Grade 7	9	51	33	7	100	1681	42
Grade 8	14	53	28	5	100	1648	47
Teachers	14%	63	21	1	99%	331	13
"Policemen"							
Grade 4	35%	50	12	3	100%	1475	274
Grade 5	22	58	16	3	99	1731	72
Grade 6	15	59	21	5	100	1697	52
Grade 7	10	56	29	5	100	1684	39
Grade 8	7	58	29	6	100	1640	55
Teachers	2%	52	39	8	101%	327	17
"Big Companies"							
Grade 4	24%	47	20	9	100%	1314	435
Grade 5	17	51	23	8	99	1668	135
Grade 6	14	51	25	10	100	1646	103
Grade 7	10	56	26	8	100	1663	60
Grade 8	9	58	26	8	101	1627	68
Teachers	33%	63	3	1	100%	326	18

*CA-9, page 30, items 22-29.

The items appeared in the following format: "How much do these people *help decide which laws are made for our country:* Very much, Some, Very Little, or Not At All? Put an X for each person or group of people listed below."

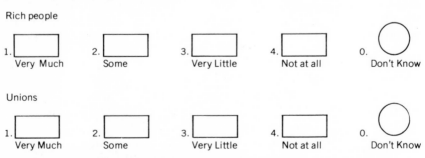

Each of the other persons and groups listed in the table was presented in the same way.

this item toward a greater assessment of the weight of the individual in the political process.

On most of these items, the teachers (who perhaps represent the adult view here) are at some distance from the child. Compared with the children's aggregate judgment, theirs slightly devalues the roles of the President, policeman, and churches. But the children are moving in their direction. For the other actors, the teachers are somewhat more inclined, as a group, to rate them higher in their level of participation. The teachers' awareness of the role of interest groups such as big companies, opinion leaders such as newspapers, and more heavily weighted social strata such as rich people is higher and perhaps closer to the one professional students of politics would endorse. The children would seemingly have some distance to go, therefore, in the development of an image of government which includes informal, group-related actors and the informal dimensions of American government. At least this is suggested by these somewhat indirect data.

In spite of this only partial realization of the existence of a political infrastructure, there is some sorting out of the informal actors in these years, even if the process looks as though it may be still subject to considerable later development. The President, as chief individual actor in the system, gets a very high rating and is clearly set off from the others. The child is thus acutely aware of the role of formal authorities. To this extent, the child has a developed orientation. The informal actors are not greatly differentiated, and all are allocated some influence. Thus the child's second major orientation seems to be a vision of political influence as diffuse, even if some actors are accorded slightly more influence than others. The children seem to lack, however, a third element which is likely to be present for the teachers. This is the heavier weighting of some of these actors, such as unions, big companies, and newspapers. But it is clear that in reacting to government as a political object the child has begun to pick up a few hints that its actions may not be entirely accounted for by the behavior of the President or other formal authorities alone.

Summary of the child's developing cognitive image

As a possible object toward which affect might be directed, the idea of government undergoes far-reaching changes in the cognitive development of the child in our test group. As he passes through grades 2 to 8, he begins with a rudimentary notion of government as personal in character, represented by a few high-ranking and visible leaders. But as he grows older, the child sees government in less personal terms. He becomes increasingly aware of its group character and its major institutions; he learns something about the norms (for example, voting) of a representative and popular democracy. In addition, the child becomes somewhat politicized and proves increasingly able to identify government as different from the private sector of life. All these perceptions suggest that, aside from any feelings that may be associated with government, the efforts by society to convey some cognitive representation of this abstract object are by no means in vain. Most children in our group have some conception of an overall structure of authority by the time they leave elementary school. Indeed they even begin to discern the far more subtle informal influences at work on the authorities, if only through a glass darkly.

THE CHILD'S AFFECTIVE RESPONSE TO GOVERNMENT

Although analytically we are able to separate the cognitive aspects of the image of government from accompanying feelings toward it, empirically they go hand in hand. For an understanding of the way in which the American political system stimulates diffuse support for the structure of authority, one must keep in mind that from the most rudimentary stage of his awareness, the child interprets government as something to further his welfare and that of the people around him. The benevolent, protective, helpful, and otherwise positive qualities of government constitute the first and continuing overall context of evaluation. Even at the end of our test period—when the child is thirteen or fourteen years of age, and government and the individual authorities, such as the President and the policeman, are beginning to be seen less ideally— the child still regards government and the individual authorities as great blessings, if slightly mixed ones.

The child thus continues to endorse government even though his understanding of it is changing. He seems reluctant to give up his initial, highly positive evaluation. In this we see, perhaps, the early formation of a bond that is hard to loosen. It is a bond that in the past may have predisposed adults in the United States to extend diffuse support for the governmental system, even in the face of deflective experiences.

The child's approval of government's role

In our pilot data we found such a uniformly favorable affective image of government, from the earliest grades onward, that we felt no special large-scale effort was necessary in our final instrument to demonstrate this sentiment. For example, in our early interviews and open-ended test questions, we found this feeling in statements ranging from "Government is a good man" or "Government is love" to "He [government] is a man that helps people when they are in need. He gets the taxes to help the people with. He sees that everything is all right in the United States."

But we do have some more systematic data which bear upon the question. First, however, we shall present a few examples of our considerable body of pilot data to show how highly consensual our younger children's approval of government is over the whole grade range.

In an instrument administered in the Chicago area, we proposed that the children either agree or disagree with statements such as these:

1 The government is getting too big for America.
2 The government meddles too much in our private lives.
3 The government has too much power.
4 The United States government usually knows what is best for the people.
5 The government ought to give money and food to people out of work.
6 The government should have more power over the people.

We attempted as far as possible to retain the original wordings of statements of children from our pretest interviews—but reversing the items in several cases. The patterns of response to these statements are shown in Table 6-7.

We see that children at all the grade levels tested roundly approve of government. They reject, at a fairly high level of agreement, the first three statements about the scope of government becoming too large. Statements 4 and 5, on the other hand, reflect approval of the role of government in guiding and caring for the people, and these statements elicit a high level of agreement. Only for the last statement do we see any impetus toward restricting the role of government; the children like it the way it is.

The overall response is one which is better characterized as a collectivist endorsement than individualistic disapproval of or restraint about government. In spite of the great myth of rugged individualism which is presumed to pervade the American consciousness, these children, at least, seem to be inclined toward

Table 6-7   Attitudes toward the Role of Government* (percent of children responding)

	1. "The government is getting too big for America."		2. "The government meddles too much in our private lives."		3. "The government has too much power."		4. "The government usually knows what is best for the people."		5. "The government ought to give money and food to people out of work."		6. "The government should have more power over the people."	
Grade	% Agree	N	% Agree	N	% Agree	N	% Agree	N	% Agree	N	% Agree	N
3	16	113	28	108	36	116	80	69	70	69	22	69
4	14	125	21	118	19	122	77	119	84	119	33	120
5	10	118	17	116	22	118	87	117	80	117	24	117
6	7	146	19	145	10	146	84	145	78	143	13	145
7	13	143	19	139	12	139	91	139	71	139	20	138
8	11	149	14	148	15	147	84	147	77	145	19	145

*These questions are from one of our pilot questionnaires, "In My Opinion #III," items 50, 125, 169, 170, and 151, respectively. For further information about our pilot tests, see Appendix.

the opposite kind of feeling about government. The government knows what is best and ought to care for the less fortunate (as do one's parents for members of the family, we may infer). The child as revealed in this limited test is inclined to see government as wise and succoring. He begins as something of a natural collectivist, and whatever individualistic tendencies he may exhibit are developed later on.

The sixth item suggests, moreover, that the child is likely to be a "conservative collectivist," in that he is not much in favor of extending the scope of government beyond what he sees as its present limits. He is rather happy with government as it stands and would not give it "more power over the people."

Thus, these and other pretest data reveal that the child's early contentment with government is fairly complete. He exhibits a high acceptance of government as a given, necessary part of the natural environment. If the child is to develop discontent and a desire for change, it is undoubtedly yet to be learned. But it will be overlaid upon an early base of high regard for the government.

The child's rating of government's qualities

The same early positive regard for the government is shown, as well, over a larger group of respondents in some ratings in our final eight-cities questionnaire. Using five role attributes and qualities of government as descriptions, we asked the children in grades 4 to 8 to "Think of the Government as it really is." The items read as follows:

Think of the *Government* as it really is . . . (Circle the number of your choice)*

1	2	3	4	5	6
Almost never makes mistakes	Rarely makes mistakes	Sometimes makes mistakes	Often makes mistakes	Usually makes mistakes	Almost always makes mistakes

1	2	3	4	5	6
Would always want to help me if I needed it	Would almost always want to help me if I needed it	Would usually want to help me if I needed it	Would sometimes want to help me if I needed it	Would seldom want to help me if I needed it	Would not usually want to help me if I needed it

1	2	3	4	5	6
Makes important decisions all the time	Makes important decisions a lot of the time	Makes important decisions sometimes	Makes important decisions seldom	Almost never makes important decisions	Never makes important decisions

1	2	3	4	5	6
Can punish anyone	Can punish almost anyone	Can punish many people	Can punish some people	Can punish a few people	Can punish no one

1	2	3	4	5	6
Knows more than anyone	Knows more than most people	Knows more than many people	Knows less than many people	Knows less than most people	Knows less than anyone

*CA-9, page 31, items 32-36.

A full explanation of why we used these ratings for unearthing the child's assessment of the government, as well as of specific authorities, will be presented at a later point.[10] Suffice it to say here that within the limits of testing time and the conceptual capacity of the maturing child as revealed through extensive analysis of pretest data, these ratings were selected. Each represented an attribute in terms of which children were capable of thinking about the role of government as well as other political objects. Thus, the item "Almost never makes mistakes" refers to the culturally approved virtue of infallibility; "Makes important decisions all the time" and "Knows more than anyone" to expected leadership qualities; "Can punish anyone" to perceived power (even though the term political power is not yet in the child's vocabulary); and "Would always want to help me if I needed it" to benevolence.[11]

Each rating represents characteristics of which our culture normally approves. To be close to infallible, to display qualities of leadership, to exert power, and to be benevolent in case of need are all qualities held in high regard by our culture, especially for those seen to be in a superior status. Hence to judge a person or object on rating scales pertaining to these qualities gives us a plausible if indirect measure of the degree of approval.[12] This is the way in which we interpret the child's evaluation of government on these characteristics.

On these premises, it is clear that children have considerable respect for the leadership role that they see government as playing. They rank it high on "Makes important decisions," with the mean moving from 1.87 to 1.51 over the grades. (See Table 6-8. The lower the measured value of the rating, the higher the approval by the average child in the test group.) Some ratings, both for government and, as we shall see later, for specific authority figures, drop off with age. But unlike these, the assessment of government on the leadership quality moves in the opposite direction. It suggests that the child comes to place increasing importance on the role of the government in the country. By grade 8, the proportion that sees government as making important decisions *all* the time rises from an initial low of 35 percent to 58 percent, the largest increment in any of the extremes on our government scales.

In addition, the older the children grow, the more likely are they to believe that government has greater knowledge than many people, coming close (for the mean) to knowing more than most. Fifty-nine percent at grade 4 say that government has more knowledge than anyone or most people, and this increases to 73 percent by grade 8. The mean rating rises from 2.37 to 2.15 across the grades.

Similarly, if we accept the child's perception of the capacity of government to punish as a rough indicator of his view of the government's general power, at the same time as he conceives of the government as playing an increasingly significant leader-

Table 6-8 Ratings of the Qualities of Government by Grade* (percent of children responding)

(a) "Makes important decisions"

Grade	1. All the Time	2. A Lot of the Time	3. Sometimes	4. Seldom	5. Almost Never	6. Never	Total	N Responding	N Not Responding	Mean Rating
4	35%	48	14	2	1	0	100%	1494	255	1.87
5	39	47	12	2	0	0	100	1783	20	1.79
6	48	40	10	1	0	0	99	1738	11	1.68
7	54	35	9	1	0	0	99	1714	9	1.59
8	58%	35	6	1	0	0	100%	1678	17	1.51

(b) "Knows"

Grade	1. More Than Anyone	2. More Than Most People	3. More Than Many People	4. Less Than Many People	5. Less Than Most People	6. Less Than Anyone	Total	N Responding	N Not Responding	Mean Rating
4	14%	45	36	3	1	1	100%	1491	258	2.37
5	11	52	34	1	1	1	100	1779	24	2.30
6	14	52	30	2	1	1	100	1733	16	2.27
7	16	54	27	2	1	0	100	1701	22	2.18
8	15%	58	24	2	1	0	100%	1662	33	2.15

(c) "Can punish"

Grade	1. Anyone	2. Almost Anyone	3. Many People	4. Some People	5. A Few People	6. No One	Total	N Responding	N Not Responding	Mean Rating
4	14%	29	24	19	9	5	100%	1489	260	2.94
5	14	34	25	17	7	4	101	1776	27	2.81
6	20	32	23	14	6	4	99	1735	14	2.69
7	22	32	24	13	5	3	99	1705	18	2.57
8	26%	31	21	13	6	3	100%	1668	27	2.50

(d) "Makes mistakes"

Grade	1. Almost Never	2. Rarely	3. Sometimes	4. Often	5. Usually	6. Almost Always	Total	N Responding	N Not Responding	Mean Rating
4	30%	43	25	1	1	1	101%	1499	250	2.02
5	24	46	28	2	0	0	100	1787	16	2.10
6	22	48	27	2	0	1	100	1740	9	2.12
7	17	49	32	2	0	0	100	1716	7	2.21
8	13%	46	38	2	0	0	99%	1681	14	2.31

(e) "Would want to help me if I needed it"

Grade	1. Always	2. Almost Always	3. Usually	4. Sometimes	5. Seldom	6. Not Usually	Total	N Responding	N Not Responding	Mean Rating
4	25%	32	24	12	5	2	100%	1488	261	2.47
5	17	31	28	16	5	3	100	1777	26	2.72
6	17	31	28	16	4	3	99	1735	14	2.70
7	16	29	31	16	6	3	101	1714	9	2.75
8	14%	29	32	16	6	3	100%	1676	19	2.81

*CA-9, page 31, items 32-36.

ship role, he considers that it has a growing power to do so. The mean rating of the government's capacity to punish increases from 2.94 to 2.50 (the lower the numerical value, the higher the approval), with 57 percent of our eighth graders alone considering that the government can punish anyone or almost anyone.[13]

Aside from any other meaning that these three ratings convey, the ability to make important decisions, knowledgeability, and the possession of power are themselves valued properties in our culture, as we have noted. At grade 4 most children already have a high estimate of the government on these qualities. The fact that the older the children the more likely are they to see government as improving in these terms would suggest a parallel growth in the respect with which government is held.

When we now add the last two scales, we can appreciate the very high positive affect with which children contemplate government. We interpreted the rating "Makes mistakes" as offering an estimate of dependability, or specifically of degrees of infallibility, if we may be permitted the grammatical misdemeanor of scaling an absolute. "Would want to help me if I needed it" we adopted as an index of the child's view of the responsive benevolence of government and therefore as an indication of his trust in it. Although, unlike the three characteristics just dealt with, assessment of both these qualities shows some decline with age, the two items nevertheless do elicit a high regard for government, in absolute terms, over the whole span of grades.

Most children in our group, in each grade, see the government as virtually infallible. The youngest wear the rosiest colored glasses and report that the government rarely makes mistakes, with a mean rating of 2.02. Although the eldest children, in grade 8, lose some of this rosy tint, they still are close to contending that the government rarely makes mistakes, dropping only to a mean rating of 2.31. Even at this grade, 59 percent still believe that the government almost never or rarely makes mistakes, a rare kind of response about anybody from the thirteen- or fourteen-year-old with his growing skepticism and worldly awareness. Confidence in the government's wisdom is amazingly high for this age group.

Of all our items about government, "Would want to help me if I needed it" is undoubtedly the least indirect measure of affect. It reflects the child's conception of the concern that government has for him, especially in time of need. As we might expect, with a growing sense of independence, the older child would be less likely to express any need for help from others. This is confirmed in the decline of the mean rating from 2.47 to 2.81. Nevertheless the absolute level, even for the eighth graders, remains fairly high. The percentage of those who see government as always or almost always willing to help, a strong expression of the expectation that government will respond in time of need, ranges from 57 percent at grade 4 to 43 percent at grade 8.

What significance, however, can we attach to the fact that as the ratings of the performance items—leadership, power, and knowledgeability—increase across the grades, the most affect-laden item, dealing with benevolence and responsiveness, declines (Figure 6-3)? Does this mean that the child is changing his relationship to government from one based largely on generalized favorable sentiments to one in which he simply judges

Figure 6-3. Mean Ratings by Grade on Five Attributes of Government.

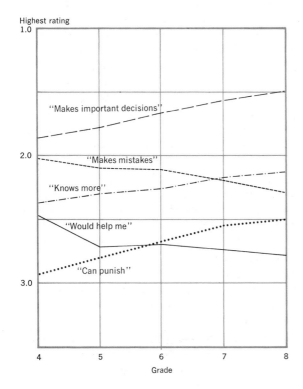

its capacities to perform well in various ways, a kind of efficiency rating?

As children mature they are increasingly able to differentiate qualities in the objects they see. We would therefore expect them to be able to make finer discriminations among the characteristics of the government. This is an essential part of growing up. But the fact that at the same time their least indirect expression of affect for the government, in our benevolence rating, falls off need not necessarily be interpreted as evidence that the child's attachment to or affection for government is also receding. Other things may be happening.

In the first place, the child may be responding faithfully to perceptions of reality. He may begin to see that government is not always at the beck and call of the members of society. The shift in the mean rating toward the somewhat less helpful end of the rating scale would reflect this.

In the second place, the child's way of expressing sentiments may also be undergoing a transformation. This interpretation is consistent with what we already know about the cognitive aspects of the child's image. As he grows older the child sees government in more impersonal terms, as institutions rather than as people. It seems plausible to infer that this too would inhibit the expression of the kind of sentiment normally reserved for people, such as that of seeing them as wanting to be helpful in case of need. But at the same time as the child depersonalizes his image of government, he does come to believe that government has more and more of the culturally approved capacities to do its job, such as leadership, power, and knowledge. These ratings are in themselves clear expressions of confidence and trust in government. It would seem, therefore, that even though the level of response to the one specifically affect-laden item, "Would want to help me if I needed it," drops off with age, this need not signal a parallel decline in the level of the child's attachment to government. What may be changing is only the child's mode of displaying his feelings. As the child grows older he becomes more reticent about expressions of emotions and more capable of detecting specific performance qualities. Positive sentiment is more likely to be revealed indirectly in his high estimate of the government's capacities to perform its roles than in measures that seek to test affect more directly.

The conclusion that we draw, therefore, is that the child's affect begins high and does not diminish but actually increases with age, as he learns more about the political world. Whatever later modifications and limits he may put upon his trust and approval, he begins in childhood with considerable sympathy for the government.

CONCLUSION

The findings which grow out of this analysis will, perhaps, surprise those readers who are accustomed to think of children as innocent of political thought. For not only does the child quite early begin to orient himself to the rather remote and mystical world of politics, but he even forms notions about its most abstract parts—such as government in general. Political marks are entered early on the *tabula rasa* and are continuously embellished thereafter.

We will, perhaps, disappoint those readers who are accustomed to think of the American as one who is brought up on the raw meat of rugged individualism. We find that the small child sees a vision of holiness when he chances to glance toward government—a sanctity and rightness of the demigoddess who dispenses the milk of human kindness. The government protects us, helps us, is good, and cares for us when we are in need, answer most children.

When the child emerges from his state of political innocence, therefore, he finds himself a part of a going political concern which he ordinarily adopts immediately as a source of nurture and protection. His early experience of government is analogous to his early experience of the family in that it involves an initial context of highly acceptable dependency.[14] Against this strongly positive affective background the child devises and later revises his cognitive image of government.

If a political system is to persist, it must somehow seek to provide a flow of information about and continuously create feelings about its basic forms. One of these is its general structure of authority. Although we typically do not think of the concept government in this way, it turns out to be a major device for introducing and orienting the child to structural aspects of the political system.[15] It is a stable term of reference for a system in which the occupants of leading authority roles may change frequently. Government thus appears as a primary focus in the generation of politically supportive orientations.

To maintain a social construct as varied, extensive, and demanding of social resources as government, a broad panoply of forces probably needs to be set in motion. The political socialization of new members is undoubtedly one of the most far-reaching and consequential of these forces.

Our data suggest that in the United States a positively supportive image of the general structure of authority is being widely and regularly reproduced for young new members. The average grade school child of our test group appears to experience some rather basic changes in his conception of government — changes which move him toward a cognitive image that harmonizes with adult formal conceptions of the American political system.

He begins, as a "political primitive," with a vision of government as the embodiment of a man or a small set of men who constitute a dimly recognized form of external authority. This authority applies to the immediate environment of the child in a rather abstract way as well as to the wider world beyond. Probably one of the first recognizable shadows that flickers across the wall of the cave of the child's unformed political mind is that of the President. He forms an initial visible image of the political world, and around him the child continues to build, gradually incorporating more and more objects until his political image becomes rounded and complex.

The child, moving toward a plural, complex conception of government (as our later chapters will continue to show), runs upon representative and popular institutions. He raises Congress and voting, as symbolic associations, to positions of dominance and thus unwittingly moves toward democracy in his interpretation of what his government is. At the same time, he is beginning to sharpen his knowledge about the boundaries of government by distinguishing what is outside the realm of government from what is within it. He is becoming politicized.

This finally adds up to a picture supportive of the American regime, a picture that becomes rapidly and forcefully exhibited in these years, as other data, not fully reported as yet,[16] confirm. The child is initiated into a supportive stance by what is probably high exposure to cues and messages about government, even while he is essentially unconcerned with such matters and too young to do much about them even if he wished. He learns to like the government before he really knows what it is. And as he learns what it is, he finds that it involves popular participation (voting) and that this is a valuable part of its countenance. It is further reason for liking it; and liking it is what the child continues to do. The child has somehow formed a deep sympathy for government even before he knows that he is in some way potentially part of it.

We know of course that such a process of changing understanding and feeling must go beyond these early years. Later experiences may also upset these earlier formed images. It could be, for example, that during the 1960s, the generational impact of the Vietnam war, racial conflict, urban deterioration, and poverty are slowly nibbling away at the expected level of support input from many sections of the adult population.[17] Yet from what little direct evidence there is about support for government per se, we can surmise that typically adult Americans have usually been highly supportive of their government (as distinguished from any given administration), whatever exaggerations may exist about their dislike of big government.[18] In these exploratory data that we have presented, we think we see growing the deep roots of this supportive sentiment in the past.

Furthermore, our data enable us to link up our discussions of the cognitive and affective aspects of the child's image of government, at least in a speculative way. Two things stand out in our data. First, the child begins with a view of government as composed of palpable, visible persons—such as the President or a past President, Washington. Second, as he makes his initial contact with government, it becomes a symbol of or orientation to political life that is charged with positive feelings. If we now make the plausible assumption that a child of seven or eight is less likely to develop such feelings about impersonal organizations or institutions, we can appreciate the significance of the fact that his first glimpse of government is in the form of the President. It permits the child to express toward a figure of political authority sentiments that he is already accustomed to displaying toward other human beings in his immediate environment.

From this we would draw the hypothesis that the *personalizing* of the initial orientation to political authority has important implications for the input of support to a political system—especially to its structure of authority—as the child continues through his early years into adolescence. As he fills in his picture of government, adding, to leading figures, such institutions as Congress and such regime rules as voting, we would suggest that the feelings originally stimulated by his personalized view of government subtly spill over to embrace other aspects of the regime itself.

But for this process it is difficult to see how impersonal, remote, and complex organizations, such as Congress, or practices, such as voting, could possibly catch the imagination of a child and win his approval. Yet our data show that positive sentiment toward government, even after the child has begun to see it in impersonal terms as he moves into the later grades of elementary school, continues high. When we add to this the fact that the children in our group tend to view government as national rather than local in its scope, we can appreciate the cementing strength that this image must have in a system such as the United States.

NOTES

1. Our note on research design in the Appendix provides our rationale for speaking in developmental terms, even though we did not undertake a real-time longitudinal study.
2. Max Lerner, *America as a Civilization* (New York: Simon and Schuster, 1957), p. 377.
3. R. Lane, *Political Ideology* (New York: Free Press, 1962), p. 146.
4. Ibid., pp. 147 - 148.
5. Ibid., pp. 145 - 149.
6. Pretesting had indicated that "the milkman" was as good an indicator as numerous other private roles such as farmer or uniformed service-station attendant.
7. See F. Greenstein, *Children and Politics* (New Haven, Conn.: Yale, 1965), pp. 60 - 61.
8. See Chapter 4.
9. Because children in earlier grades were less able to handle questions of this sort, we did not administer them below fourth grade.
10. See Chapter 8.
11. Since we are seeking evidence about the nature and degree of the child's attachment to the structure of authority, we would have preferred to obtain a simple, unambiguous measure of affect. We might have been able to do so if it had been possible to ask the child directly whether he liked the government or whether if was his favorite, two questions we found useful for individual authority figures, as will become evident in later chapters. But we found that this direct expression of feeling for government, even during the early grades when the image is personalized, did not occur in the natural idiom of the child. Hence we had to rely exclusively on a less direct means, through estimates of role qualities, to elicit the child's feelings.
12. Compare with the following procedure adopted for the study of images of federal officials, part of the structure of authority in the United States: "Our perceptions of the sort of people who are engaged in a given type of employment play a large role in shaping our image of that employment. What we think of the profession of teaching, for example, is based to an important degree on the stereotypes we have made for ourselves about teachers. One of the aims of this study was to get as precise a notion as possible of the images that come into people's minds at the mention of

'federal civil servants'. To the extent that these pictures embody qualities which are generally admired, respected, and sought after in an occupational setting, they can be said to exert a positive effect on the image of the federal service as a place of employment. To the extent that the perceived qualities are not admired, respected, and sought after, the effect can be said to be negative." F. P. Kilpatrick, M. C. Cummings, Jr., and M. K. Jennings, *The Image of the Federal Service* (Washington, D.C.: Brookings, 1964), p. 207.

13. For some evidence that adults continue to conceive of government as powerful and that this is an important ingredient of the general image, see Lane, op. cit., pp. 197 - 199.

14. For a suggestion about the broad, structural source of a child's "collectivist" orientations—from family and later from youth groups— see S. N. Eisenstadt, *From Generation to Generation* (New York: Free Press, 1956), p. 302. Lane finds a corresponding view among adults in his *Political Ideology*. He reports that his adult respondents charge the ". . . government . . . with unlimited responsibility for the general welfare," p. 191. See also his pp. 130 and 145 - 146.

15. For additional confirmation of the structural significance of government for the child, see F. Estvan and E. Estvan, *The Child's World* (New York: Putnam, 1959), p. 191. Their group of children, grades 1 to 6, interpret pictures of state and national capitol buildings in structural rather than functional terms. They talk about what the government is rather than what it does.

16. See, for example, D. Easton and J. Dennis, "The Child's Acquisition of Regime Norms: Political Efficacy," *American Political Science Review*, 61, pp. 25 - 38, 1967.

17. We have more to say about this in Chapter 14.

18. See V. O. Key, Jr., *Public Opinion and American Democracy* (New York: Knopf, 1961), pp. 28 - 32; M. Janowitz, D. Wright, and W. Delaney, *Public Administration and the Public: Perspectives Toward Government in a Metropolitan Community* (Ann Arbor: The University of Michigan Press, 1958), pp. 31 - 55; and Donald E. Stokes, "Popular Evaluations of Government: An Empirical Assessment," in H. Cleveland and H. D. Lasswell (eds.), *Ethics and Bigness* (New York: Harper, 1962), pp. 61 - 72.

7

VISIBILITY AND
SALIENCE OF
POLITICAL AUTHORITIES

In the preceding chapter we have seen that the closest the child comes to an overarching conception of a structure of authority is in his idea of government. But the tendency for children to see people and then institutions as constituting government gives us a further hint about other important points of contact between the child and the regime. It shows that children may relate themselves to more than just the symbol "government." They are capable of differentiating other concrete objects of authority. For them the faces of authority may be plural.

If we are to sort out the kinds of feelings children acquire about the political authorities in a system, we need to discover who or what stand as the major embodiments of authority. Political concepts or categories are tools by which the child organizes the political world. What he does not perceive or conceptualize he can have no feelings about. But what he does relate to emotionally we need to delineate in the child's terms, so that we may interpret the implications of the child's cognitive development for his attachment to the regime. We need to know what the child orients himself to if we are to discover any political significance to his emotional acceptance or rejection of the regime.

It is apparent that even with the limited intellective and emotional capacities of the child in the early grades, the political world is not the overwhelming confusion that we might have anticipated. We already know that the child sees an order in which government appears. In its concrete manifestations for the child it takes the forms of a President, historic figures such as George Washington, and, as the child grows older, institutions such as Congress and voting. But we must now push our inquiry somewhat further to determine the initial contact points between the child and the system. Is an image of government, however the child may define it, the only path he can take to apprehend the structure of authorities? Is this the only means at the disposal of the system to link the maturing member to it?

We shall find that in the earliest years of our age span, the child acquires more than just a sense of government with its emphasis on the primacy of the President. Our preliminary interviewing impressed on us the extent to which children gloss over other objects that we might have expected to appear on their cognitive horizons, such as mayors, judges, governors, senators, and organizations. Rather, they spy a figure of much lower status in the adult's hierarchy of authority, the policeman. It is as though at the outset the child saw the head and tail of the political animal with relative sharpness and salience. What lies between, such as a mayor, governor, senator, or judge, is not invisible or unimportant but just less distinct and less significant, except where special local circumstances may bring one or another of these figures to the foreground. Only as children move into the higher grades of elementary school do figures and organizations of authority between the head and the tail begin to fall into some kind of recognized place.

RELATIVE VISIBILITY AND SALIENCE

The data discussed in our previous chapter suggest that the child sees these two figures, the President and policeman, and considers them of some importance. We need say little at the moment about the significance of the President for the child. For the policeman, we need merely remind ourselves that no less than 80 percent of our group of children, in each grade, see him as an employee of government (Table 6-5), and therefore as a person somehow connected with political authority.

However, our knowledge of the presence of these figures in the mind of the child does not in itself help us to understand the relative visibility and salience of policeman and President. It could be that as prominent as these two figures are to the child, in comparison with other figures of authority not evoked by our questions about government they do not loom very large, even in the early grades. In this event, if we are seeking to understand the way in which children become attached to a political system, we would be misled if we concluded, without further evidence, that these are really the most effective avenues through which the child moves toward the political regime.

In this chapter we shall present data that will help us to draw some conclusions about which political authorities are most easily seen by the child and are accorded greatest status. These are also the political objects which will seem to us to leave the deepest impact on the consciousness of young children. We shall then be able to discuss the attributes of these authorities that seem most significant to the child. This will permit us to understand how a child comes to perceive some kinds of authorities and to attribute to them the sense of legitimacy that is vital for the input of long-term positive or negative support for the system.

THE VISIBILITY OF AUTHORITIES

From the time we began to collect our preliminary interviews, we were concerned with the comparative status of various figures of authority. We needed to discover who in the political sphere the child could be expected even to see, let alone cathect. It became quickly apparent that children in our group initially personalize authority and only later focus on institutions—something, as we have seen, that our final data confirmed. Hence we confined our attention to personal figures. Some of these were political and others nonpolitical in character. Our objective was to find out how the child assigned, relative to each other, such roles as those of father, teacher, policeman, and mayor; how important he considered each; and the ones he liked best and knew most about. We expected that questions like these would give us some idea of the visibility and salience of various figures of authority for the child. We could assume conversely that those figures, in the political sphere, visible and important for the child provide the system with an important means of access to the child's sentiments.

From our initial interviews we learned that the child by the earliest grades had already sorted out the relative weights of various figures in society. He also knew more about some of them and liked some better than others. One striking feature of these preliminary data was the degree to which the President emerged as a person of special distinction. One eight-year-old decisively expressed this sentiment in an interview.

Q. *"What does the President do?"*
A. *"He runs the country, he decides the decisions that we should try to get out of and he goes to meetings and he tries to make peace and things like that . . ."*
Q. *"When you say he runs the country, what do you mean?"*
A. *"Well, he's just about the boss of everything . . ."*

When presented with a set of cards bearing the pictures and names of eleven different figures—President, senator, governor, mayor, policeman, soldier, fireman, postman, judge, teacher, and father—interviewed children characteristically identified the President as the most important in general. But specifically they also selected him as being the most important in running the country, in making laws, and in helping the country, and as the one whom they would most like to be.

In our subsequent questionnaire data we found this effect repeated. For example, we had 338 children in the Chicago area rank ten figures of authority as first, second, or third on each of five questions. The questions were:

1 Who do you know the most about?
2 Who would you most like to be?
3 Who is most important in making the laws?
4 Who helps you and your family the most?
5 Who do you like the best?

These questions were intended to test for the importance of the authority figures as well as their visibility, although at the moment we are primarily interested in talking about the latter quality. The average ranking of each of the ten figures on the five questions appears in Table 7-1.

On the first question ("Who do you know most about?"), which can be thought to tap directly the familiarity of each of the figures to the child, the policeman and the President are second only to father and teacher for the youngest children. The policeman and President also score high for the third and fourth graders on "Who helps you and your family the most?"

The President, moreover, is a primary model, an ego ideal, for the youngest children. He ranks first for them on "Who would you most like to be?" They also consider him at the top of the list, across all grades, in response to "Who is most important in making the laws?" On the fifth question, "Who do you like the best?," the President is outranked only by father and teacher.

Table 7-1   Relative Visibility and Salience of Authority Figures* (average ranking within grade groupings)

"Who do you know the most about?"

Grade	Fire-man	Mayor	Pres-ident	Police-man	Soldier	Judge	Teacher	Sen-ator	Post-man	Father	N†
3-4	6.5	8	4	3	6.5	10	2	9	5	1	99
5-6	6	8	3	5	7	9.5	2	9.5	4	1	113
7-8	6	8.5	3	4	5	8.5	2	10	7	1	126

"Who would you most like to be?"

Grade	Fire-man	Mayor	Pres-ident	Police-man	Soldier	Judge	Teacher	Sen-ator	Post-man	Father	N
3-4	10	9	1	5	4	6	2	7.5	7.5	3	99
5-6	8.5	8.5	2	4	5	6	1	7	10	3	113
7-8	9	8	3	6	4	7	1	5	10	2	126

"Who is most important in making the laws?"

Grade	Fire-man	Mayor	Pres-ident	Police-man	Soldier	Judge	Teacher	Sen-ator	Post-man	Father	N
3-4	7	2	1	5	8	4	6	3	10	9	99
5-6	7.5	3	1	5	10	4	7.5	2	9	6	113
7-8	10	3	1	6	8.5	4	8.5	2	7	5	126

"Who helps you and your family the most?"

Grade	Fire-man	Mayor	Pres-ident	Police-man	Soldier	Judge	Teacher	Sen-ator	Post-man	Father	N
3-4	5	6.5	2	4	6.5	9	3	10	8	1	99
5-6	5	7.5	2	3	6	9	4	10	7.5	1	113
7-8	7	8	3	2	6	9	4	10	5	1	126

"Who do you like the best?"

Grade	Fire-man	Mayor	Pres-ident	Police-man	Soldier	Judge	Teacher	Sen-ator	Post-man	Father	N
3-4	5.5	8	3	5.5	4	9	2	10	7	1	99
5-6	6	8	3	4	7	9	2	10	5	1	113
7-8	7	8	4	3	6	10	2	9	5	1	126

*CA-5, pages 5-9, items 13-22, 24-33, 35-44, 47-56, 60-69.

†N = number of cases responding.

Overall the President stands out as one whom the child both knows about and sees as playing a major role in the system. The policeman is another highly visible symbol of authority of those listed, exceeded only by the child's parent, his teacher, and the President.

However little direct political meaning they may have for the young child, the policeman and the President are nevertheless fairly well known to him and accepted by him from the very beginning of these years. They elicit a sharper response, therefore, than do the mayor, the judge, and the senator. The policeman becomes a "significant other" in several respects more easily than do the soldier, fireman, and postman.

When we followed up some of these questions in later questionnaires, we found very nearly the same effects. Although our understanding of the child's awareness as revealed in the previous tests led us to narrow the range of authority figures in these later efforts, we did expand the size of our test groups. We were then able to extend the reliance we were willing to put on the data.

A question that we repeated, in slightly different form, provides a direct measure of visibility. We asked approximately thirteen hundred children in Chicago and Atlanta to "Put an X by the two people below that you know the most about." The options were: soldier, judge, senator, policeman, postman, and President. The results are shown in Table 7-2.

Table 7-2   Relative Visibility of Soldier, Judge, Senator, Policeman, Postman, and President in Chicago and Atlanta* (rankings within city and grade)

Grade	Soldier		Judge		Senator		Policeman		Postman		President	
	Chi.	Atl.	Chi.	Atl.	Chi.	Atl.	Chi.	Atl.	Chi.	Atl.	Chi.	Atl.
2	4	4	5	5	6	6	1	1	2	3	3	2
3	4	4	5	5	6	6	1	1	2.	2	3	3
4	4	4	5	5	6	6	1	1	2	3	3	2
5	4	4	5	6	6	5	1	1	3	2	2	3
6	3	3	5	5	6	6	2	2	4	4	1	1
7	4	3	5.5	6	5.5	5	2	2	3	4	1	1
8	2	†	6	†	4	†	3	†	5	†	1	†

*CA-8, page II-6, item 27. "Put an X by the two people below that you know the most about."
† No eighth-grade children in Atlanta were asked this question.

On this measure, the policeman and the President again dominate, even though the postman makes an early but declining showing. The early prominence of the postman—as one of the front runners in visibility—suggests that proximity may be one of the things that increases visibility for the child. The President, we may speculate, is visible because of his high status and the attendant publicity. Adults are likely to talk about him in the presence of children, and the mass media certainly pay more attention to the President than to Congress and probably than to other figures and institutions.[1] But the policeman and postman are much lower in the status hierarchy of society, and their prominence to the child, we would infer, derives in great part from everyday familiarity and propinquity. Familiarity of authority figures in the political sphere may depend in part, therefore, on formal status in the political structure; but it may also come from the simple fact of being close and ever present to the child.

Aside from the President and policeman, the other figures fall much where we might expect. The senator is quite invisible authority on this measure, the least well seen of all. The judge fares only a little better. These findings bore out our preliminary interviewing.

On the whole we could conclude from our pretesting that of all the figures of authority in the political system, there can be little doubt that children see the President and policeman first and continue to hold them in prominent view over the grades. In the pressure for space on our final questionnaire there seemed little point to belabor what by now had become obvious. We were prepared to take the high visibility of these two figures of political authority for granted without further special testing. We could build part of our test of the development in supportive sentiments toward the structure of authority around these two figures. In the complex world of politics they at least could be seen.

Nonetheless our final instrument gave us some supporting evidence about the perceptual primacy of the President and the policeman. As we have already witnessed in our analysis of the child's image of government, the President and the policeman both are strongly associated by the child with government, although in different ways. For the child at the beginning of the grade span, the President is the best overall representative of government. He is still relatively important in this respect even among our oldest respondents.

We have also seen in passing that although for the child the policeman is not very representative of government as a whole (Table 6-2), he is nevertheless regarded by the vast majority as a government worker (Table 6-5). This identification is fairly continuous across the grades. The policeman is also considered to be very important in making laws, and the young child, our interviews indicated, detects little difference in the source of the laws, whether they are local ordinances or national statutes. The item we examined in the preceding chapter, "How much do these people help decide which laws are made for our country?" (Table 6-6), begins to point up the high significance of the policeman for the child. From grades 4 to 7 the child ranks the policeman immediately below the President and unions as being influential. The mean ranking for policeman through grades 4 to 7 is higher than for any others except President and unions. Although the child senses the inappropriateness of associating policemen directly with the government, he does feel that this figure has something vital to do with laws—which in our conceptualization we designate as the outputs of political authorities.

Conversely, what is particularly clear from these data is that in the early grades the child is not likely to conceive of Congress or the Supreme Court as playing a very significant role among the authorities. When we asked the child to pick the two best pictures representing the government, only 5 percent and 6 percent in grades 2 and 3 chose the Supreme Court. What is more revealing, only 6 percent and 13 percent in these grades favored Congress, as against 49 percent by grade 8. In the lower grades, therefore, a number less than chance turned to Congress (Table 6-2). Similarly when we asked our respondents to indicate those who do most to make the laws (Table 6-3), in grades 2 and 3 Congress and the Supreme Court continued to draw fewer choices than we could account for by chance alone.

These data, reinforced as they are by interviews, leave little doubt about the low visibility of the various parts of the formal political structure for the younger child in our group. He gives little evidence of being aware of them, and if he is, they appear to have little meaning for him as part of the structure of authority in the system. It would appear that the younger child finds some difficulty in conceptualizing remote political structures and relating himself to them.

These findings give us confidence that the children in our group initially see personal figures, the President and the policeman, as especially prominent in the general structure of political authority. We are therefore able to consider these figures at least as appropriate starting points for further investigation of the child's developing relationship to the regime.[2]

What these tests did not answer, however, was whether the visibility of these figures for the children had enough meaning for them so that we might also consider the figures to be emotionally salient. Do they carry affective significance for the child even within the low limits of concern that children have for the political sphere? We can readily appreciate that children may see something in the political system and be able to talk about it. If, however, it has no relevance to their lives it could play but little part in relating them affectively to the system.

THE SALIENCE OF VARIOUS AUTHORITY FIGURES

We may surmise that if a person is considered nurtural and helpful, he probably has some importance for children that goes beyond mere familiarity. It was with this in mind that in our final, eight-city questionnaire we continued to ask a pretest question by which we intended to ascertain as directly as we could which figures of authority had most significance for the life situation of the child. We hoped then to know whether the visibility of the political figures of authority conveyed anything more than awareness alone. We were confident that among those figures tested, the child would have greater awareness of the policeman, President, postman, and soldier than of the senator and judge, and because of the poor drawing power of the last two figures we could conveniently drop them. We omitted the postman as well since the ramifications of his role for the relationship of the child to the political system appeared to be substantially less interesting than those of the other roles.

With a restricted list of characters in our final instrument, we repeated the question, "Who helps you and your family the most?" We added to this question the instruction "Put an X by the two who help you and your family the most." The options provided,

Table 7-3a The Relative Salience of Selected Authority Figures* (percent of children responding†)

Grade	Policeman	Soldier	Father	Teacher	President	Total	Total Number of Cases
2	51%	22	38	29	49	189%	1655
3	47	19	48	33	43	190	1678
4	38	16	59	35	35	183	1749
5	37	17	64	34	31	183	1803
6	34	15	68	36	30	183	1749
7	28	17	74	38	28	185	1723
8	30%	15	74	40	24	183%	1695

*CA-9, page 13, item 58: "Who helps you and your family the most? Put an X by the *two* who help you and your family the most."
†Not every child gave *two* answers to this question. Thus the percentages do not add to 200 percent. Every child did respond to this question at least once, however, so that there are none classified as "not responding."

Table 7-3b The Relative Salience of Selected Authority Figures*
(rankings within each grade)

Grade	Policeman	Soldier	Father	Teacher	President
2	1	5	3	4	2
3	2	5	1	4	3
4	2	5	1	3	4
5	2	5	1	3	4
6	3	5	1	2	4
7	3	5	1	2	4
8	3	5	1	2	4

*CA-9, page 13, item 58: "Who helps you and your family the most? Put an X
by the two who help you and your family the most."

with drawings of each figure, were the policeman, soldier, father, teacher, and President.

What we found suggests the high salience for the youngest children of the policeman and the President, among political and other authority figures. The changing pattern of relative perception of these representatives of authority is shown in Tables 7-3a and b.

Here once more it is the policeman, not the President, who receives the highest endorsement of all at grade 2, although the President follows closely. With succeeding grade levels increasing weight is given to the two more immediate authorities, father and teacher. The image of policeman and President as perhaps bigger than life is cut down, and the child works out what adults would no doubt think to be a more realistic conception of the relative roles of these authorities in his own life.

Nevertheless it is remarkable on this measure of salience for the child that the positions of policeman and President remain in exactly the same order of significance in almost all grades. A somewhat greater number of children nearly always sees the policeman as more helpful, regardless of the high prestige that the President would seem likely to command. The child seems to have fairly well-defined feelings about the policeman in his helping role.

We might be inclined to interpret this as a clue that the child thinks about helpfulness in a concrete, immediate sense. A policeman but not a President could be expected to be standing close by to help. Undoubtedly this accounts for the way in which the child orders policeman and President along this quality. But there appears to be more than a sense of presence or immediacy in the child's selection of these two symbols of political authority. For example, in grades 2 and 3 a larger percentage of children selects the policeman and President combined than selects father and teacher combined. If proximity and availability alone determined the younger child's choice, the higher percentage would have gone to father and teacher as most helpful.

An across-the-grades comparison of the percentages which see father and teacher combined as being most helpful with those which select the policeman and President together is shown in Table 7 - 4. In grades 2 and 3 the two political authorities outdraw the two personal authorities, as we have noted. But even though a reversal begins in grade 4, by eighth grade 54 percent (out of a possible 200 percent) still considers the clear political options to be more attractive.

Table 7 - 4 Relative Salience of Selected Authority Figures Combined* (percent of children responding)

Grade	Policeman and President	Father and Teacher	Total Number of Cases
2	100%	67%	1655
3	90	81	1678
4	73	94	1749
5	68	98	1803
6	64	104	1749
7	56	112	1723
8	54%	113%	1695

*See Table 7 - 3a.

The strength with which the political authorities in this question draw the youngest children testifies at the very least that they do more than just appear on the horizon of the child. The continuation for all ages tested of the appeal of the political figures at a relatively high level reveals the capacity of these symbols of the political system to impress themselves on the minds of children, at least for their quality of helpfulness.

In summary it would appear that, for the younger child in this age span, the President and the policeman are as somewhat special figures. Several sorts of questions over different samples of children reveal this. As representatives of political authority for the child—the policeman is seen as working for the government and the President *is* the government—both figures are highly visible and have some psychological importance for the child. Simultaneously the child in our group is able to relate himself to both extremities of the structure of authority. However spatially distant the President may in fact be, because the children sense that he may be helpful for them and their families he is brought psychically close to them. But the system does not rely exclusively on this mechanism for linking the child to it. The system spreads its risks, as it were, by also drawing the child into the ambit of the authority structure through the agency of a local representative with whom the child has frequent opportunities for face-to-face contact. Through the head-and-tail effect it is possible for children to be introduced to symbols and representatives of the political system—government as well as President—at the most inclusive level at the same time as they make even more direct contact with proximate manifestations, the policemen.

THE POLICEMAN IN THE STRUCTURE OF POLITICAL AUTHORITY

Have we been assuming too much in placing our emphasis on two figures, the President and the policeman? We are exploring the nature of the child's developing support for the structure of political authority. Have we any reasonable grounds for including both these figures as part of this structure?

The designation of the President as a political authority presents no difficulty, although in Chapter 9 we shall want to assure ourselves that the children orient themselves to the President in his structural role rather than in his personal capacity. But it is not equally clear that the policeman is part of the structure of political authority, especially in the American political system where this office is largely under local or state rather than national jurisdiction. Yet if we cannot reasonably consider the policeman to be an integral part of the structure of authority in the political system, his visibility or importance to the child would have little relevance for our study, important as it may be for other purposes.

From the perspective of a systems analysis of politics we must consider the policeman to be as central a part of the regime structure as are all the other, august figures and institutions usually included within it. Authorities are those who have the day-to-day task of formulating and implementing system outputs, what we have called policies and binding decisions. In a large-scale system such as the United States, the authorities are not concentrated at one level of the system alone. At the national level, in addition to executives, legislators, and the like, we find administrators, many of whom have little contact personally with the publics they serve. But in addition these national administrators include officials who are in close contact with members of the system at the local level, those who are most directly affected by administrative acts. A clerk in the local office of a Federal licensing agency or a county agent in the employ of the Department of Agriculture exemplify such figures of authority. They are part of the national organization of the political system, the output structure, through which policies or legal outputs are effected. The fact that typically they engage in specific personal and detailed interaction with members of the system may distinguish them from those who are typically more remote, such as higher officials whose range of activities forces on them a more impersonal role. But these administrators at the tail end of the hierarchy are no less part of the structure of authority than those at the top.

In the American type of federal system, the policeman, unlike terminal (locally based) officials in a national administrative structure, is not so easily located in the structure of authority. It is true, Federal police such as the FBI, Treasury officers, and revenue agents are part of the national organizational structure. Conceptually there would be little with which to cavil if we included these police as part of the structure of political authority. They are the operatives of national administrative agencies and as such are in direct contact with their publics.[3] Through the mass media, especially television, some national police agents, such as the FBI and G-men, have successfully impressed themselves on the minds of children as well as adults. But as we shall show in Chapter 10, the policeman, especially for our test children in the lower grades, is typically the cop on the beat, in the patrol car, on the motorcycle, at the school crossing, or at the intersection directing traffic.

From a theoretical point of view, however, this kind of policeman is part of the general structure of authority in a political system even if he functions at the local level. The American political system embraces a vast network of local subsystems—cities, towns, villages, and other municipal units—nesting within the broader system. Each of them produces a large variety of outputs in the form of traffic regulations, licensing, taxing, and the like. In part these are enforced through the efforts of the local police forces. Policemen therefore fulfill important roles in this part of the output structure of a political system. They apply the law, a form of output.

But they do even more. The notion of application or implementation obscures the processes that actually occur. In applying the law, policemen unavoidably also make decisions upon which they themselves and others, such as judges and jailers, may need to act. Policemen thereby produce outputs of an authoritative character. It is they who decide on the spot whether to write a ticket, to arrest an offender, or even to use the most fateful type of violence, the taking of human life. However narrow the scope of their decisions, these outputs are generically at one in their authoritativeness with the grand policy decisions of national legislatures.

In this sense we cannot exclude policemen, on theoretical grounds, from being important participants in the structure of political authority. Any kind of relationship that the child has with the policeman is a form of contact between the child and the regime. Even if children recognized policemen as local officials, this would not vitiate the role of the policeman as a link to one part of the total output structure of the regime.

But the fact is that the child is not a political scientist. He does not see political life through the eyes of the adult or the student of politics. In the early grades especially, the local political scene is hazy and obscure. As far as the younger child is concerned, the policeman is assimilated to the general structure of authority outside home and school. National, state, and local structures are not easily distinguished; all fuse into an ambiguous picture of authorities external to home and school. Chapter 10 will reveal that we found no preliminary evidence to suggest that children think of the policeman as any less compelling or authoritative than most other political authorities they perceive, regardless of structural level.

It is just at this point that theory and practice converge. For the child, especially the younger one, the policeman is out there, in the world beyond the family, with a power of a peculiar sort. Like the President and yet in a way the child knows to be different, as Chapter 10 will disclose, the policeman also represents something related to the political system and authority in it. Later the child may come to know much more about the status and role of the policeman as part of the overall structure of authority in a political system. But in the early part of the life cycle in which we see him, politics is still too ambiguous for us to expect clear structural distinctions to be present.

We are contending therefore that when he reports that the President is the government and when he considers that the policeman works for the government and exercises some special powers, the child is developing some image of the actual structure of authority in the system. Phenomenally both figures fuse into a composite if hazy picture of authority, something different and compelling out there beyond the boundaries of the family and school.

SOURCES OF VISIBILITY AND SALIENCE
OF PRESIDENT AND POLICEMAN

It is easy to speculate, even with few hard data, on why the younger child might find the President and policeman to be salient and visible figures of authority. Unlike Congress or the Supreme Court, which are complex impersonal institutions, President and policeman are individual persons much like many other human objects in the familiar environment of the child. We might expect to find that the child would respond more readily to them. Even for adults it has been argued that ". . . displacement of emotion on persons is easier for most people than displacement upon groups or issues or even symbols . . ."[4]

But much more than this is undoubtedly at work. There are many kinds of persons, political and otherwise, in the surroundings of the child. From among these we need to be able to account for the emergence not of just any kind of figure out of the total structure of authority but of the President and policeman in particular. Why from among all possible authority figures in the American system—administrators, governors, mayors, judges, and the like—should these two from the beginning catch and hold the attention of the child?

Here some probable reasons are not difficult to find. Sheer exposure alone would help to float these figures across the child's horizon. Policemen, for example, come into range from many different directions. In fantasy they appear in the guise of toy figures, bogeymen to induce obedience to parental demands, or characters in the game of cops and robbers. In life they are seen as crossing guards, as directors of traffic, or as guardians against theft and violence. The settings, real and imagined, in which the child encounters this symbol of authority are so numerous and varied that it would be the extraordinary child who entered school without the word policeman in his vocabulary.

Exposure operates to draw the President as well into the cognitive span of the child. Undoubtedly the child has fewer opportunities to see or hear about the President than about policemen, and yet by the time he enters grade 2, at about age seven, we have no evidence of any child who was unable to recognize the word President or its basic meaning.[5] It is not surprising that this should be so in the American system. Since the First World

War the Chief Executive has attained increasing prominence, and the child's awareness is probably related to the frequency with which adults themselves have occasion to discuss the Presidency. The role of political executives has been radically altered in modern political systems. The domestic problems of industrialized societies and the demands of foreign policy have everywhere dramatized the part of chief executives. But in part too the Presidency is thrown into sharp relief by the very nature of the American political structure, with its emphasis on the separation of powers and the grounds it thereby provides for recurring, open competition between Congress and the Presidency.

Empirically the prominence of the Presidency is reflected in the attention it obtains from the mass media.[6] Children may sense this current of interest among adults if only by overhearing the conversation of their own parents.

The drama of presidential-election campaigns undoubtedly also impresses the office on children. If we take five years of age as the earliest point at which a presidential campaign might leave some imprint on the child, all our children had undergone one campaign at least, by the time of our testing in late 1961 and early 1962, that between Kennedy and Nixon in 1960. In addition, all children in grades 5 to 8 had probably also experienced at a conscious level the Eisenhower-Stevenson campaign of 1956 and were therefore exposed twice. It seems plausible to assume that few children could pass through recurrent presidential contests without their curiosity being piqued, especially by the intense competitive element resonant of a similar feeling the child may experience in his own life, as in games and sports.

One indirect indicator of the child's exposure to the phenomenon of the election and its psychological importance to him is the response to the following question: "How much did you learn from the last election for President?" Answer options were: (1) I learned a lot, (2) I learned some, (3) I learned very little. When we cross-tabulated the responses to this item by grade (Table 7-5), we found a fairly stable pattern of relative salience over the grades. Only the lowest grade that we tested (grade 4) was different. But this one difference offers a little support for the hypothesis that the child who has been of school age during two general elections is likely to be more attuned to political affairs than the child aged five or over who has experienced only one election.

If this question is an indicator of the degree of sensitization of the child to politics through presidential elections, we can ask

Table 7-5   Salience of the 1960 Presidential Election* (percent of children responding)

Grade	I Learned a Lot	I Learned Some	I Learned Very Little	Total	N Not Respond-ing	N Re-spond-ing
4	36%	49	14	99%	1513	236
5	41	50	9	100	1783	20
6	44	47	9	100	1737	12
7	43	48	9	100	1710	13
8	41%	51	8	100%	1683	12

whether responses to the item are associated with the child's perceptions of the President in any way, and more particularly whether the child who says he has learned a substantial amount from the election is also likely to regard the President more highly.[7] Causality could of course run in either direction, but our guess would be that the child who becomes more aware of the election is more likely to generate positive feelings toward the winner.

Our test of such a possible effect is to cross-tabulate responses of the "how much learned" item with an index of the child's affective responses to the President. This is shown in Table 7-6.

We find an association at every grade level tested. The child who perceives himself to have been more affected by the election is also likely to see the President more favorably. There is at least a prima facie case for the hypothesis that the election has socializing effects (positive here), even though such effects may be confounded by other factors which predispose the child to pay attention to the election or to regard the President more favorably. Yet it is suggestive for future research into these questions that we do find evidence, however tenuous, that the drama of the presidential election sensitizes the child to awareness of political authority, and in particular to a more favorable reaction to the winner of the contest. Both cognitive and legitimating (supportive) consequences are suggested.

Furthermore, the classroom itself would seem to generate additional awareness and to provide historical continuity for the role of the President. It is the unusual school that does not have busts or pictures of past Presidents in the corridor and classrooms. Few curricula even in the early grades would fail to give some special attention to the office. As an indication of how much attention may be given to various figures and institutions of political authority we can turn briefly to some data obtained from a curriculum questionnaire sent to a sample of the teachers subsequent to the testing of the children. It is hard for us to estimate how representative this small sample of teachers might be. Yet

Table 7-6   Salience of the 1960 Presidential Election* versus Index of Child's Affect for President† (percent of children responding)

| | Affect for President | | | | N Responding | N Not Responding | Gamma Correlation |
	Low	Medium	High	Total			
Grade 4							
How much learned from election:							
A lot	23%	27	50	100%	546	6	
Some	32	36	33	101	731	14	.37
Very little	56	29	16	101	210	6	
Grade 5							
How much learned from election:							
A lot	30	33	37	100	716	7	
Some	40	35	26	101	888	4	.27
Very little	61	23	16	100	164	4	
Grade 6							
How much learned from election:							
A lot	29	34	37	100	750	7	
Some	40	32	28	100	810	6	.29
Very little	64	20	16	100	162	2	
Grade 7							
How much learned from election:							
A lot	33	35	32	100	732	11	
Some	44	33	23	100	806	13	.27
Very little	68	19	13	100	145	3	
Grade 8							
How much learned from election:							
A lot	40	28	32	100	679	13	
Some	53	30	18	101	849	15	.31
Very little	72%	21	7	100%	123	4	

*CA-9, page 31, item 30. "How much did you learn from the last election for President?"

†CA-9, pages 10 and 27, items 48 and 68 respectively. This index combines the responses on two ratings of the President, "He is my favorite" and "I like him." The index will be discussed more fully below (Chapter 16). High is equal to scores 9 to 11, medium is 7 to 8, and low is 1 to 6.

in Table 7-7 we see some trends in emphasis relative to the authorities we asked about, in the amount of time these teachers estimate that they spend on each authority in an average school year.

Dividing the sample by grade with which the teacher is mainly concerned (and bearing in mind the small numbers that therefore result for any one grade)[8] we find that there are more teachers who give more than minimal attention in the early grades to the President and policeman than there are those who give such attention to the other authorities. Thus the emphasis of the school no doubt reinforces whatever other stimuli might exist to make the two figures so salient to the young child.

Table 7-7 Curriculum Time Spent by a Sample of Teachers on Various Political Authorities* (percent of teachers responding)

Authority	Grade	Time Spent in Average School Year				Total	N Responding
		0 hr	0-1 hr	1-3 hrs	over 3 hrs		
President	2	13%	65	22	—	100%	23
	3	6	59	24	12	101	17
	4	6	24	65	6	101	17
	5	—	18	65	18	101	17
	6	4	8	52	36	100	25
	7	11	16	37	37	101	19
	8	24	24	—	53	101	17
Congress	2	71	21	8	—	100	24
	3	56	38	6	—	100	16
	4	18	47	35	—	100	17
	5	—	39	56	6	101	18
	6	8	36	24	32	100	25
	7	21	21	21	37	100	19
	8	33	11	11	44	99	18
Senator	2	78	22	—	—	100	23
	3	67	20	13	—	100	15
	4	24	59	18	—	101	17
	5	—	83	11	6	.100	18
	6	12	44	28	16	100	25
	7	32	21	26	21	100	19
	8	39	11	17	33	100	18
Policeman	2	—	29	33	38	100	24
	3	6	53	41	—	100	17
	4	29	47	24	—	100	17
	5	6	72	22	—	100	18
	6	32	44	24	—	100	25
	7	47	42	11	—	100	19
	8	44	39	11	6	100	18
Supreme Court	2	75	21	4	—	100	24
	3	62	31	6	—	99	16
	4	29	53	18	—	100	17
	5	6	44	44	6	100	18
	6	8	38	21	33	100	24
	7	26	16	26	32	100	19
	8	33	11	11	44	99	18
Mayor	2	57	39	—	4	100	23
	3	44	31	25	—	100	16
	4	18	76	6	—	100	17
	5	17	72	6	6	101	18
	6	12	50	29	8	99	24
	7	37	32	26	5	100	19
	8	33%	17	39	11	100%	18

*Curriculum Questionnaire, pages 1-3, items 2, 14, 19, 11, 15, and 20.

The simplicity and concreteness of the policeman and President as individual figures of authority and their immediacy for adults, in and out of the classroom, help us to understand why these figures should be prominent for young children. But these characteristics of the authority figures still do not explain an important phenomenon that we have ignored to this point. If we return to Tables 7-3 and 7-4, we see that even though the President is clearly a visible, salient figure for many children, he becomes decreasingly so over the years. The younger child is the one who is most impressed. In grade 2, one-half choose the policeman or President as being most helpful, whereas by grade 8 this proportion has declined to 53 percent (out of a possible 200 percent). Yet since the eighth-graders had witnessed two presidential elections as compared with only one for those in grades 2 through 4 and had had a longer time to hear from adults about the President and policeman, we might well have expected a reversal of these percentages. This clearly means that something more than sheer exposure to information about the Presidency and the emotional drama of campaigns is at work.

Here we can only speculate on the relevant forces. What draws the child to these figures of authority probably has something to do with the psychological context in which he interprets both policeman and President. As we shall see in the next chapters, younger children in particular conceive of these two authorities in highly glowing terms. They see them as providing, benign, and protective, almost in the image of an ideal father as he might be described in our culture. As the child grows older and learns more about these figures, some of this idealization may rub off. But there remains the question of why so many children in the early grades describe the President and policeman in hyperbole and correspondingly see them as very salient.[9]

The answer may involve in some measure the inner needs of the younger child. As he moves from infancy into early childhood and begins to be aware of the complexities of life beyond the family and of his own dependence on adults as a shield before this outer world, the accompanying sense of vulnerability may induce the child to attribute greater importance and more benign powers to figures of authority than in fact these authorities possess. Regardless of what the "real" significance of these authorities may be for the adult members of a system, if we accept the proposition that younger children feel a greater sense of vulnerability to the world outside the family, we can appreciate why, from among the political authorities, the child might choose those that seem best able to serve his immediate psychic needs. What he hears from adults about these figures dovetails with these needs. Hence we can understand why the political authorities should decline in importance as the child grows older.

By grade 8 he is more confident of his capacity to cope with life and is less inclined to attribute the same importance to political authorities, even though he still ranks them relatively high.

For the political system, however, the feelings of vulnerability that might have led him to elevate two authority figures to positions of considerable prominence have important consequences. They may help to lock the child into the political system and to provide the system with a mechanism for encouraging those kinds of sentiments without which, we have hypothesized, no system could hope to persist, whether in constant or changed form.

As we have already observed in Chapter 5, contrary to presuppositions built into elementary school curricula, children do not enlarge their knowledge of the world, at least in the political sphere, by working in concentric circles from far to near, if far and near are considered to be geographic terms. The least that we have found is that psychic distance differs from spatial distance.[10] Figures at the tail and head ends of the political creature — the policeman and the President — seem to be close to the child psychologically, however distant one of them may in fact be spatially. This capacity to incorporate even distant objects makes it possible, in the American political system, for the child to establish ties with the political system at the most inclusive level — the national unit — at the same time as he reaches out to a representative at the spatially closest point.

NOTES

1. See, for example, E. E. Cornwell, Jr., "Presidential News: The Expanding Public Image," *Journalism Quarterly,* 36, pp. 275-283, 1959, cited in F. Greenstein, *Children and Politics* (New Haven, Conn.: Yale, 1965), p. 76.

2. In earlier reports we have suggested other findings with which the present ones converge. See David Easton and R. D. Hess, "The Child's Changing Image of the President"; "Youth and the Political System," in S. M. Lipset and L. Lowenthal (eds.), *Culture and Social Character* (New York: Free Press, 1961); and "The Child's Political World," *Midwest Journal of Political Science,* 6, pp. 229-246, 1962.

3. In the police system of the United States three basic types prevail: the *local* police, which includes urban police forces, sheriffs, rural constables, county police, parkway police, and the like; the *state*

police; and the *Federal* police. Typically the latter fall into two classes: those concerned with the national revenue, such as the Intelligence Unit of the Bureau of Internal Revenue, the Enforcement Division of the Alcohol Tax Unit, and the Division of Investigations and Patrol of the Bureau of Customs; and those involved with protecting life and property and the enforcement of national criminal statutes, such as the FBI, the Secret Service Division, the Bureau of Narcotics, Post Office Inspectors, and the Immigration Border Patrol. See B. Smith, *Police Systems in the United States* (New York: Harper, 1949). Undoubtedly few adults, not to speak of children, have any clear picture of the multiplicity of police agencies in the country and their possible areas of overlapping jurisdiction.

4. R. E. Lane, *Political Life* (New York: Free Press, 1959), p. 138, and bibliography listed there in footnotes.

5. This is probably not equally true for all chief executives. In some scattered personal testing in Canada, the Prime Minister seemed to elude some younger children. They were more likely to know about the Queen, or in two instances the President of the United States!

6. For the visibility and salience of the President among adults see Greenstein, op. cit., p. 75; and "Popular Images of the President," *American Journal of Psychiatry,* 122, pp. 523-529, 1965; Lane, op. cit., pp. 318-319; R. E. Neustadt, *Presidential Power: The Politics of Leadership* (New York: Wiley, 1960). For some remarks on the latent socializing influences of the Presidential campaign, see J. Wahlke et al., *The Legislative System* (New York: Wiley, 1962), pp. 88-89.

7. Research on the effects of the Nixon-Kennedy TV debates upon adult perceptions of the candidates showed that simple exposure to the other party's candidate had the effect of reducing hostility and generating positive feelings toward him, especially for John F. Kennedy. We might expect a similar "campaign communication" effect for children. See S. Kraus ed.), *The Great Debates* (Bloomington, Ind.: Indiana University Press, 1962), especially pp. 218-219.

8. We sent out these questionnaires by mail to the teachers in six of the cities (excluding Jackson and Tacoma) and had a return rate of 59%. Some of our losses are due to the fact that our original sample contained a number of substitute teachers.

9. There is a suggestion that even black children respond to the President in similar glowing terms. See D. Jaros, "Children's Orientations towards the President: Some Additional Theoretical Considerations," *Journal of Politics,* 29, pp. 368-387, especially p. 381, 1967.

10. Another study involving political content reports the same kind of phenomenon. F. Estvan and E. Estvan, *The Child's World* (New

York: Putnam, 1959), pp. 260-261, indicate that ". . . both first grade and sixth grade pupils were more conscious of the nation as the setting for life situations than the state or region in which they lived. The former, it would appear, is 'psychologically' nearer than areas or divisions which are actually closer geographically speaking. In other words, children tend to skip such intermediate areas as the state or region in their expanding awareness of space rather than moving outward systematically in terms of size of unit." "Influence," the authors say on p. 39, "is not necessarily a matter of [spatial] distance."

8

THE PRESIDENT
AS A FOCAL POINT
OF POLITICAL SOCIALIZATION

To this point we have seen that children connect with the structure of the political system in two basic ways at least. Not later than grade 4 they acquire some idea that there is a general structure called government, and they are able to express a variety of feelings about it. We saw that initially attachment to the structure of authority occurred under a form of personalization of government. But at the same time our interviews and pretests put us on the path of two central figures of authority, the President and the policeman. Even children in grade 2 were fully aware of their presence. Since these are two of the first representatives of political authority from the world outside the family and school to become known to our children, we could easily anticipate that a child's perceptions of these two figures would play some important part in his overall relationship to the regime.

In what follows we shall try to explore the texture of the initial image that the child creates of the President and the policeman. We shall then be able to speculate on some of its implications for the bond between the child and the regime.

To anticipate the conclusion of this and succeeding chapters, there is little doubt that younger children particularly see these figures of political authority in highly idealistic terms. But we shall discover that more than a purely personal bond is being fashioned with the man who happens to be President or a police officer. From the earliest grades, we shall find that our test children typically see the incumbents of these positions as representative figures and that their attitudes pertain to the role, not to the persons who occupy it. From this we shall be able to conclude that our children are in the process of constructing an image of the structure of political authority. The sentiments incorporated in this image will permit us to make some informed guesses about the nature of the child's developing ties to the regime itself.

COMPONENTS OF THE CHILD'S IMAGE OF POLITICAL AUTHORITY

Our basic hypothesis has made the investigation of the child's image of these authority figures critical. The degree of input of support, we have presumed, is related to the complex psychological constructions of which a child's image is composed. As a first step in exploring this relationship, it is vital to design a way to fathom the child's conception of these salient figures of authority, President and policeman.

In our chapter on government we have concluded that the image children hold of political authorities contains a mixture of cognitive and affective elements. To a certain extent it proved possible to elicit either one or the other part of this mix. Yet because in most cases these elements exist as a package of orientations, it was hard to ascertain precisely what proportion of each was contained in the responses elicited by individual questions. Even those ratings which seemed to border on the most affective elements of the image were themselves subject to mixtures of content depending upon the precise context.

Bearing in mind the difficulty of sorting out affect and cognition clearly, we sought to select a variety of questionnaire items, in the form of ratings, that would accord with the child's own way of seeing and feeling about political authorities. But these items also had to bear upon the most theoretically interesting aspects of an image of authority, those that would help us to understand the way in which children begin to put in support, whether negative or positive, to a system.

Since the points of contact with the authorities proved to be numerous and varied, and included institutions (organizations such as government and the Supreme Court) as well as persons, at least some of the qualities to be tested by ratings had to be of a kind that would be appropriate for all types of objects of authority. Because we wished to know the object that the child does in fact react to, as well as how he feels about it, the ratings needed to elicit the cognitive as well as the affective components of the image. Furthermore, the literature on authority in general is replete with references to the relationship between attitudes to parental authority and those to authorities outside the home. It seemed appropriate to try to search out some of the connections between at least feelings about the authority of father as compared with those about some political authorities. The dimensions of authority that we selected for testing therefore had to be of a kind that would permit such comparison.

In short we sought to test for cognition and affect, to compare ratings of personal and impersonal political authorities, to relate these to nonpolitical authorities such as father, and to isolate qualities that were relevant for an understanding of our basic concerns with the input of support. These constraints governed our ultimate selections of ratings. Added to them were the limitations of available testing time and the capacity of children across the grades to handle the items.

Within these bounds we devised thirteen different item ratings for each of three authorities, the President, the policeman, and the child's father. We also used either five or six of the same ratings for government, as we have already noted, the Supreme Court and "the Average United States Senator," with a special set of ratings for "People who try to get elected." Given the restrictions on testing time as well as the relatively low tolerance of young children for a long series of rating scales, we were not able to use our series of thirteen ratings for each of the six authorities. Nor did we administer the questions about senator, Supreme Court, and government below the fourth grade. The second- and third-graders appeared, in our pretesting, to be relatively unfamiliar with these more remote and abstract embodiments of authority.

The thirteen ratings used, the grades to which they were administered, the objects to which they applied, together with the dimensions of the image of authority to which we presumed the ratings to be related, are presented in Table 8-1. These ratings depict the kinds of qualities that extensive pretesting and analysis of pretest data, including factor analyses, suggested as typical of the way in which children are apt to think about political authorities. The phrasing of the items, as shown on Table 8-1a, follows closely the actual words of children themselves.

Table 8-1 Outline of Ratings Used in Testing the Child's Images of Authority

Dimensions of Image of Authority	Ratings	Grades Tested 2 3 4 5 6 7 8	Father	President	Policeman	Senator	Supreme Court	Government
High Affective Content								
- Attachment or Affiliation	"He is my favorite of all" [likableness]	··········	x	x	x			
	"I like him more than anyone" [likableness]		x	x	x	x		
- Benevolence	"He would always want to help me if I needed it" [helpfulness]	··········	x	x	x	x	x	x
	"He protects me more than anyone" [protectiveness]		x	x	x			
- Dependability	"He always keeps his promises" [trustworthiness]	··········	x	x	x			
	"He almost never makes mistakes" [infallibility]		x	x	x	x	x	x
	"He never gives up when things are hard to do" [persistence]	·········	x	x	x			
- Power	"He can make anyone do what he wants" [control]	··········	x	x	x			
	"He can punish anyone" [sanctions]	·········	x	x	x	x	x	x
- Leadership	"He knows more than anyone" [knowledge-ability]	··········	x	x	x	x	x	x
	"He makes important decisions all the time"	·········	x	x	x	x	x	x
	"He works harder than almost anyone" [diligence]		x	x	x			
	"He is always a leader"		x	x	x			
High Cognitive Content								

Table 8-1a The Rating Questions

A. Objects of Political Authority

Think of the *President* [*Policeman, Average United States Senator, Government, Supreme Court, Your Father*] as he [it] really is . . . (circle the number of your choice)

1	2	3	4	5	6
Is my favorite of all	Is almost my favorite of all	Is more a favorite of mine than most	Is more a favorite of mine than many	Is more a favorite of mine than a few	Is not one of my favorites

1	2	3	4	5	6
I like him more than anyone	I like him more than most people	I like him more than many people	I like him more than some people	I like him more than a few people	I like him less than almost anyone

1	2	3	4	5	6
Would always want to help me if I needed it	Would almost always want to help me if I needed it	Would usually want to help me if I needed it	Would sometimes want to help me if I needed it	Would seldom want to help me if I needed it	Would not usually want to help me if I needed it

1	2	3	4	5	6
Protects me more than anyone	Protects me more than most do	Protects me more than many do	Protects me more than some do	Protects me less than some do	Protects me less than most do

1	2	3	4	5	6
Always keeps his promises	Almost always keeps his promises	Usually keeps his promises	Sometimes does not keep his promises	Usually does not keep his promises	Almost never keeps his promises

1	2	3	4	5	6
Almost never makes mistakes	Rarely makes mistakes	Sometimes makes mistakes	Often makes mistakes	Usually makes mistakes	Almost always makes mistakes

1	2	3	4	5	6
Almost always gives up when things are hard to do	Usually gives up when things are hard to do	Sometimes gives up when things are hard to do	Usually does not give up when things are hard to do	Almost never gives up when things are hard to do	Never gives up when things are hard to do

1	2	3	4	5	6
Can make anyone do what he wants	Can make almost anyone do what he wants	Can make many people do what he wants	Can make some people do what he wants	Can make a few people do what he wants	Can make almost no one do what he wants

Table 8-1a The Rating Questions (cont.)

1	2	3	4	5	6
Can punish anyone	Can punish almost anyone	Can punish many people	Can punish some people	Can punish a few people	Can punish no one

1	2	3	4	5	6
Knows more than anyone	Knows more than most people	Knows more than many people	Knows less than many people	Knows less than most people	Knows less than anyone

1	2	3	4	5	6
Makes important decisions all the time	Makes important decisions a lot of the time	Makes important decisions sometimes	Makes important decisions seldom	Almost never makes important decisions	Never makes important decisions

1	2	3	4	5	6
Works harder than almost anyone	Works harder than most people	Works harder than many people	Works less hard than many people	Works less hard than most people	Works less hard than almost anyone

1	2	3	4	5	6
Always a leader	Usually a leader	More often a leader than a follower	More often a follower than a leader	Usually a follower	Almost always a follower

B. Political Candidates

People who try to get elected are . . . . (circle the number of your choice)*

1	2	3	4	5	6
More honest than almost anyone	More honest than most people	More honest than some people	More dis-honest than some people	More dis-honest than most people	More dis-honest than almost any-one

People who try to get elected are . . . .

1	2	3	4	5	6
More sneaky than almost anyone	More sneaky than most people	More sneaky than some people	Less sneaky than some people	Less sneaky than most people	Less sneaky than almost anyone

People who try to get elected . . . .

1	2	3	4	5	6
Always keep their promises	Almost always keep their promises	Usually keep their promises	Sometimes keep their promises	Usually do not keep their promises	Almost never keep their promises

Table 8-1a The Rating Questions (cont.)

People who try to get elected are . . . .

1	2	3	4	5	6
More powerful than almost anyone	More powerful than most people	More powerful than some people	Less powerful than some people	Less powerful than most people	Less powerful than almost anyone

People who try to get elected are . . . .

1	2	3	4	5	6
Less selfish than almost anyone	Less selfish than most people	Less selfish than some people	More selfish than some people	More selfish than most people	More selfish than almost anyone

People who try to get elected are . . . .

1	2	3	4	5	6
Smarter than almost anyone	Smarter than most people	Smarter than some people	Less smart than some people	Less smart than most people	Less smart than almost anyone

*CA-9, page 36, items 55-60.

As we can readily see from Table 8-1, the ratings touch on a variety of aspects of authority and are designed to elicit a greater or lesser degree of cognition and affect. They run from two which most nearly approximate purely affective content ("I like him more than anyone" and "He is my favorite of all") to four dealing with leadership. The latter contain a high admixture of cognitive content. In between we have a number of items which evoke a fairly complex mix of emotion and knowledge.

HOW THE CHILD SEES THE PRESIDENT

Although the child's feelings about the President are scarcely distinguishable from cognitive aspects, it is nonetheless useful to examine in the child's image what it is that he sees the President as doing and the significance he may attach to this. From the earliest grade the child sees the President as on a commanding height, far above adults as well as children. The President flies in on angel's wings, smiling, beneficent, powerful, almost beyond the realm of mere mortals.

Our interviews disclosed that the child is aware of the President and is able to express an estimate of him before there is much understanding of or information about the actual role. A strong positive attitude prevails in advance of knowledge of the President's actual job, and this attitude colors the child's perceptions. Younger children especially see the President at the top of the whole system and in control of it. The mayor takes orders from him and Congress is his helper. Local, state, and national governmental structures fuse into a single pyramid of authority with the President at the top, supreme in power and authority. This appeared repeatedly in our interviews at various ages. As one eight-year-old child, the son of a lawyer, told us:

> Q. *". . . We were talking about laws earlier. What is the law?"*
> A. *"The law is something that you're supposed to obey. And if you don't usually something might happen, you know."*
> Q. *"Can you name a law?"*
> A. *"Don't go through a red light."*
> Q. *"Who makes the laws?"*
> A. *"Usually the President. Or if the President doesn't he'll tell somebody, a least bit lower—like a vice-president or so—and they'll discuss the law."*

A ten-year-old from a different school responded in a similar fashion.

> Q. *"And what does the President do?"*
> A. *"He decides what people should do and things like that."*
> Q. *"Tell me more about that. I don't quite understand."*
> A. *"Well, he decides usually what laws people should go by, and things like that. . . . He makes the street laws so that you could stop at the red light and people won't crash or anything, and he makes the state laws."*

The other side of the picture, however, is that the President is seen as using his power and unbounded knowledge to help people, protect them from whatever dangers may lurk in the great unknown beyond the habitat of the child. Yet this powerful and virtually omniscient figure is within easy reach. Children feel they can write to him, call him on the phone, even visit him in Washington. As one nine-year-old put it:

> Q. *"Can you ever tell the President of the United States what kind of things you think he should do?"*
> A. *"Yeah, you can talk with him . . ."*

Q. *How—just call him up on the telephone and tell him, or what?"*
A. *"Yeah, you go to the White House, most people do . . ."*
Q. *"Some people do go and tell him what they want?"*
A. *"Yeah . . ."*

Although as the children grow older they draw him closer to the position of an ordinary mortal, they never quite bring him down to earth.

From an operational standpoint, there is a great variety of properties of the Presidency which could serve as points for testing the child's changing conception. In a number of different preliminary excursions in this area, we tapped a few of these. Fragile as some of these data have been, they give us some flavor of the shifting knowledge embodied in the child's early image.

The importance of the President's role

A few questions from one of our pilot questionnaires show us parts of the cognitive base underlying the child's earliest image. We asked some children to respond to a variety of statements about the President in a simple agree-disagree fashion. Three items are relevant to the cognitive image. They concern the relative importance of the President's role in the system. These items were formulated from statements taken almost verbatim from an early series of individual interviews. They are shown in Table 8-2.

Table 8-2   The Child's Assessment of the Importance of the President's Role*

Grade	1. "If the President made a big mistake in his job, it would hurt America a lot."		2. "If the President does not approve of a law, it should not be passed."		3. "The mayor should get his orders from the President."	
	Percent Agree	Number of Cases	Percent Agree	Number of Cases	Percent Agree	Number of Cases
3	85	116	83	113	67	69
4	81	123	68	122	54	119
5	89	118	42	118	31	117
6	86	146	47	146	33	145
7	81	140	30	142	17	140
8	86	145	19	147	12	145

*Pilot test, "In My Opinion #III," questions 113, 112, and 157, respectively.

From the overall pattern of response to the question in column 1, we can discern that children regard the President right from the beginning (grade 3 in this case) as highly important. There is little doubt in the minds of most that the President has grave responsibilities. This does not change as the child grows older and acquires increasing knowledge about the Presidency, even though with age many other evaluations shift significantly, as we shall see later. By grade 3, the children have put the President in a central position in the country. The importance they thus attribute to him seems to color all other attitudes and perceptions. There is at the same time a growing realization of the limitations of his role as an authority, as shown in columns 2 and 3.

In our final instrument, we included a question which confirms this conception of the President's high significance in the political system and adds some further dimensions to it. We asked the following question:

> Here are some things that boys and girls have said about what the President's job is. What do you think the job of the President is? Put an X beside the *two* things below that say what you think the job of the President is:
>
> 1 His job is to keep us out of war.
> 2 His job is to make friends with other countries.
> 3 His job is to help people in our country.
> 4 His job is to stand for our country.
> 5 His job is to make people obey the laws.
> 6 His job is to make sure our country is run well.

These data indicate that in all grades a solid majority of our children see it as the task of the President to make sure that the country is run well. They interpret this as his general responsibility. But in grades 3 to 5, the next two most popular choices

Table 8-3 The Child's Perception of the President's Job* (percent of children and teachers responding)

Grade	1. Keep Us Out of War	2. Make Friends with Other Countries	3. Help People in Our Country	4. Stand for Our Country	5. Make People Obey the Laws	6. Make Sure Our Country Is Run Well	Total	N† Responding	N Not Responding
3	41%	35	26	22	11	54	189%	1645	33
4	37	38	27	21	8	59	190	1726	23
5	32	45	27	23	5	58	190	1791	12
6	27	41	33	25	3	60	189	1742	7
7	22	36	32	30	2	64	186	1704	19
8	17	30	33	33	5	69	187	1678	17
Teachers	2%	16	28	36	4	86	172%	370	21

*CA-9, page 22, item 44. "Here are some things that boys and girls have said about what the President's job is. What do you think the job of the President is? Put an X beside the two things that say what you think the job of the President is."

†N = number of cases making some response. This number was used as the base for the percentages.

represent relatively specific tasks such as keeping the country out of war and making friends in the area of foreign relations. The younger group of children is less certain that the President has an overall obligation to care for the country. They see his job as divided between this and some narrower tasks in foreign affairs.

As we move into the upper grades, however, the children are more likely to interpret the President's job in overarching terms. By grade 8, the three most preferred items all stress the general executive responsibility of the President for running the country. Helping people in our country, standing for our country, and making sure our country is run well (columns 3, 4, and 6) are diffuse functions identifying different aspects of the most general nature of Presidential responsibilities. Combined, these options draw 102 percent out of a possible 200 percent in grade 3 and rise to 135 percent by grade 8, with each of the items increasing continuously over the grades. Correspondingly the children tend to give somewhat less importance to the more specifically defined parts of the President's role. But without necessarily denying the other kinds of jobs that the President may have, almost three-quarters of our group, by the end of the elementary school years, in a forced-choice situation as represented by this question attribute the greatest weight to his general responsibilities. The President is not only one of the first to be seen among all public institutions, as we noted in the preceding chapter, but being seen, his major work is also considered to bear the most general, and therefore the most onerous, responsibilities. As the last row in Table 8 - 3 shows, in this the children look much like their teachers, who completed a questionnaire very similar to that of the students.

The President's authority status

Although consistency is not necessarily any more a mark of the child than of the adult, it would seem only reasonable that if children in general tend to aggrandize the role of the President, at least the younger children who have little knowledge of the President might interpret his status as including the power to meet his apparent position and attendant responsibilities. In our final survey we have some data on the extent to which children see the President as a powerful person, and this will appear shortly. But our pretest findings are suggestive about the location of the President in the authority structure, an aspect we did not test in our final instrument.

The child, at least in the early grades, sees the President as at the top of the authority structure in the country. The President is the one who should decide on what is to be done. As the questions reported in columns 2 and 3 of Table 8-2 show, a large majority of the children in grade 3 sees the President as the person who should be the great lawmaker, almost the same percentage as attributes outstanding importance to his job as President. This conception changes quite rapidly, however, and only a small percentage of the children in grade 8 continues to believe that the President should have a final veto in lawmaking. Apparently knowledge tempers the image of the kind of power the President should have. We know that as children grow older they realize that representative bodies exist and that these bodies help to make the laws. We can now see that children also begin to understand the correspondingly more limited legal powers of the President.

Another rapid revision occurs in the child's conception of the position of the President in the hierarchy of political authority. A majority in grades 3 and 4 agrees that "The mayor should [and for younger children especially this is usually equivalent to saying that he does] get his orders from the President." We found this also to be the case in our interviews.[2] By grade 5— ages nine and ten—there is a marked decline in the number who see the mayor as subordinate. Only a minority thinks that he ought to get his orders from the President, and presumably they attach some degree of autonomy to the mayoral position.

These limited data from our pilot studies and our final questionnaire suggest that in the early grades children may view the President as the person upon whose shoulders lie the primary responsibilities for running the country. If anything, this perception spreads to increasing numbers of children as we move into the upper grades. At the outset, the child may innocently expect that since the President has the overall obligation to care for the country he ought also to be top boss. But as the child grows older, he learns that the President's authority does not extend fully to making all laws or to giving order to lesser executives at lower levels of government. Our pilot data at any rate suggest that, from an adult viewpoint, on most items the child's cognitive map becomes less distorted with age. The older child shows signs of finding his way among the rather abstract and complicated contours of authority that exist for the Presidency in the diffuse federal system of the United States.

Cognition and support

At the same time that these changes in cognitive orientation are taking place, the child seems to be accumulating a store of affect. This becomes apparent at times even in the more cognitively relevant kinds of questions. In ascribing towering status and authority and in placing the care of the country in his hands, there is little doubt that the child must be expressing latent approval of the President. Logically we could also argue that it would be possible for him to see the President in a position of power and responsibility and yet refuse to think well of him. But psychodynamically this is as little likely to be the case for children as it is for adults. If they see a person in an elevated status, they very probably also will believe that he is a wonderful person, especially if the status is approved by adults and remains so distant that little capacity exists for a child to test his evaluations through direct experiences.

It would appear therefore that some of the kinds of knowledge children acquire about the President help to provide a hard-rock base for the input of support. The limited areas of the child's cognitive map of the President that we have explored are at least not inconsistent with the inference that children think he is worthy of considerable esteem.

But the picture delineated here only sketches out roughly how the child sees and feels about the President and therefore only begins to tell us about the nature of the support to which the child is being socialized. We need to look at numerous other ways in which we sought to elicit as directly as possible the kinds of feelings the child learns to extend toward the President. Incidentally we will learn much more as well about the knowledge he has of the President insofar as information and affect are here distinguishable.

HOW THE CHILD FEELS ABOUT THE PRESIDENT

In all our testing and interviewing, we were unable to find a child who did not express the highest esteem for the President. The descriptions of him were universally so approving that we must describe them as a form of idealization. What this idealization means will be discussed at a later point, but here we need to ascertain the various terms in which the child expresses his sentiments.

Most children have little difficulty in describing the President in glowing phrases. He is seemingly a storehouse of inexhaustible virtues—wisdom, benevolence, power, trustworthiness, and exemplary leadership. Figure 8-1 shows the mean ratings, by grade, given by the children on each of the thirteen qualities listed in Table 8-1. Tables 8-4a to 8-4m provide the distribution of opinion for each point on each of the rating scales about the President.

Figure 8-1 Mean Ratings of the President on Thirteen Attributes by Grade

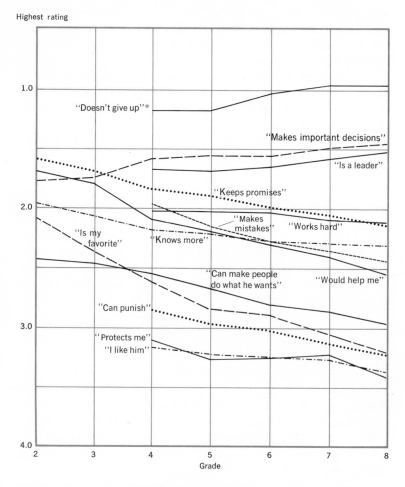

*Means of this rating were subtracted from 6.0 to make them more comparable with the rest.

Table 8-4   Ratings of the Qualities of the President* (percent of children responding)

(a) "I like him"

Grade	1. More Than Any-one	2. More Than Most	3. More Than Many	4. More Than Some	5. More Than a Few	6. Less Than Almost Anyone	Total	N Re-spond-ing	N Not Respond-ing	Mean Rating
4	10%	27	23	23	9	8	100%	1727	22	3.17
5	7	26	29	22	10	7	101	1785	18	3.22
6	5	29	29	21	10	7	101	1739	10	3.24
7	4	27	30	23	11	5	100	1706	17	3.26
8	3%	22	31	26	12	5	99%	1676	19	3.37

(b) "He is my favorite"

Grade	1. Of All	2. Al-most of All	3. More Than Most	4. More Than Many	5. More Than a Few	6. Not	Total	N Re-spond-ing	N Not Respond-ing	Mean Rating
2	51%	21	11	6	6	4	99%	1642	13	2.08
3	39	27	14	8	7	6	101	1667	11	2.36
4	28	30	17	11	7	7	100	1732	17	2.60
5	21	29	21	13	9	8	101	1787	16	2.83
6	22	26	20	14	9	9	100	1741	8	2.88
7	17	25	23	16	9	10	100	1706	17	3.03
8	14%	23	22	21	11	9	100%	1673	22	3.18

(c) "He would want to help me if I needed it"

Grade	1. Al-ways	2. Al-most Al-ways	3. Usually	4. Some-times	5. Seldom	6. Not Usually	Total	N Re-spond-ing	N Not Respond-ing	Mean Rating
2	67%	14	10	5	2	3	101%	1642	13	1.70
3	58	18	14	6	2	2	100	1673	5	1.81
4	46	21	20	9	3	2	101	1732	17	2.09
5	39	24	21	11	3	2	100	1794	9	2.20
6	34	25	23	12	3	3	100	1742	7	2.32
7	33	24	23	15	3	3	101	1708	15	2.41
8	27%	25	26	14	4	3	99%	1677	18	2.54

(d) "He protects me"

Grade	1. More Than Any-one	2. More Than Most Do	3. More Than Many Do	4. More Than Some Do	5. Less Than Some Do	6. Less Than Most Do	Total	N Re-spond-ing	N Not Respond-ing	Mean Rating
4	13%	26	23	22	7	9	100%	1720	29	3.10
5	9	23	26	25	9	8	100	1780	23	3.27
6	9	22	27	25	8	8	99	1724	25	3.25
7	9	24	28	23	9	7	100	1701	22	3.22
8	8%	20	26	28	10	8	100%	1670	25	3.29

(e) "He keeps his promises"

Grade	1. Always	2. Almost Always	3. Usually	4. Sometimes Not	5. Usually Not	6. Almost Never	Total	N Responding	N Not Responding	Mean Rating
2	68%	16	10	5	1	1	101%	1642	13	1.60
3	57	25	13	4	1	1	101	1670	8	1.69
4	43	34	18	4	0	0	99	1733	16	1.85
5	37	41	18	4	0	0	100	1793	10	1.90
6	32	43	19	5	0	1	100	1747	2	2.01
7	24	52	20	4	0	0	100	1714	9	2.06
8	21%	49	25	4	0	0	99%	1679	16	2.14

(f) "He makes mistakes"

Grade	1. Almost Never	2. Rarely	3. Sometimes	4. Often	5. Usually	6. Almost Always	Total	N Responding	N Not Responding	Mean Rating
4	38%	34	25	2	1	1	101%	1732	17	1.97
5	25	38	33	2	1	1	100	1793	10	2.16
6	19	41	36	3	0	1	100	1743	6	2.28
7	14	42	41	3	0	1	101	1713	10	2.35
8	10%	41	45	3	0	0	99%	1687	8	2.44

(g) "He gives up when things are hard to do"

Grade	1. Almost Always	2. Usually	3. Sometimes	4. Usually Not	5. Almost Never	6. Never	Total	N Responding	N Not Responding	Mean Rating
4	6%	4	6	13	29	42	100%	1726	23	4.81
5	4	4	7	13	32	39	99	1788	15	4.82
6	4	2	5	14	34	41	100	1733	16	4.95
7	3	2	5	12	35	43	100	1697	26	5.05
8	3%	2	4	12	37	42	100%	1669	26	5.05

(h) "He can make people do what he wants"

Grade	1. Anyone	2. Almost Anyone	3. Many People	4. Some People	5. A Few People	6. Almost No One	Total	N Responding	N Not Responding	Mean Rating
2	36%	23	19	11	6	5	100%	1633	22	2.43
3	29	28	22	10	6	4	99	1668	10	2.47
4	24	32	24	12	4	5	101	1728	21	2.55
5	17	35	28	11	3	7	101	1791	12	2.67
6	13	37	26	13	5	7	101	1738	11	2.80
7	11	35	30	13	4	7	100	1708	15	2.86
8	8%	32	35	15	4	7	101%	1673	22	2.96

(i) "He can punish"

Grade	1. Any-one	2. Al-most Any-one	3. Many People	4. Some People	5. A Few People	6. No One	Total	N Re-spond-ing	N Not Respond-ing	Mean Rating
4	20%	30	21	11	9	9	100%	1723	26	2.85
5	15	33	20	13	8	11	100	1784	19	2.97
6	14	31	21	16	8	10	100	1733	16	3.02
7	10	32	24	13	10	11	100	1704	19	3.12
8	9%	28	27	15	10	11	100%	1679	16	3.21

(j) "He makes important decisions"

Grade	1. All the Time	2. A Lot of the Time	3. Some-times	4. Seldom	5. Almost Never	6. Never	Total	N Re-spond-ing	N Not Respond-ing	Mean Rating
2	46%	37	13	2	1	1	100%	1646	9	1.78
3	47	39	11	1	0	1	99	1671	7	1.71
4	51	41	7	1	0	0	100	1736	13	1.60
5	52	41	7	1	0	0	101	1800	3	1.57
6	53	40	6	1	0	1	101	1748	1	1.57
7	56	38	5	0	0	0	99	1715	8	1.51
8	58%	37	4	0	0	0	99%	1685	10	1.47

(k) "He is a leader or a follower"

Grade	1. Always Leader	2. Usually Leader	3. More Often Leader	4. More Often Fol-lower	5. Usually Fol-lower	6. Almost Always Fol-lower	Total	N Re-spond-ing	N Not Respond-ing	Mean Rating
4	52%	34	10	1	0	2	99%	1730	19	1.69
5	48	39	11	1	1	1	101	1794	9	1.71
6	50	38	10	0	1	1	100	1741	8	1.67
7	52	38	9	1	0	0	100	1710	13	1.60
8	56%	36	7	1	0	0	100%	1682	13	1.53

(l) "He knows"

Grade	1. More Than Any-one	2. More Than Most People	3. More Than Many People	4. Less Than Many People	5. Less Than Most People	6. Less Than Any-one	Total	N Re-spond-ing	N Not Respond-in	Mean Rating
2	43%	33	17	2	2	3	100%	1640	15	1.97
3	30	44	21	3	1	2	101	1672	6	2.07
4	18	50	29	1	1	0	99	1733	16	2.18
5	11	57	30	2	0	0	100	1798	5	2.22
6	8	57	33	1	0	1	100	1744	5	2.30
7	7	58	34	1	0	0	100	1712	11	2.30
8	5%	60	34	1	0	0	100%	1685	10	2.31

(m) "He works harder"

	1. Than Almost Anyone	2. Than Most	3. Than Many	4. Less Than Many	5. Less Than Most	6. Less Than Almost Anyone	Total	N Responding	N Not Responding	Mean Rating
4	37%	35	20	4	2	2	100%	1726	23	2.03
5	35	39	19	3	1	2	99	1788	15	2.04
6	35	38	21	3	1	2	100	1743	6	2.04
7	30	41	23	4	1	1	100	1716	7	2.10
8	27%	43	24	4	1	1	100%	1684	11	2.12

*See Table 8-1a for exact wording of these ratings.

If we scan the tables, the first thing to observe about the ratings is that although we offered the child a 6-point scale on each item, in virtually no instance are more than a very few children able to bring themselves to make the kind of negative or low-keyed judgment that would lead them to select the last two positions.[3] The responses are overwhelmingly skewed to the positive side of the ratings in each instance.

For only two items ("He protects me" and "I like him") do the means fall between 3 and 4, and in only two other instances ("He is my favorite" and "He can make people do what he wants") do the means for any grade fall below the midpoint of the scales. Thus in all but four of the thirteen ratings, on the average the child ranks the President exclusively on the upper half of each scale. This is true even though none of the attributes remain constant over the age span. This one datum alone impresses on us the high esteem with which our children have come to regard the President in their first thirteen or fourteen years of life.

Figure 8-1 permits a second general observation. Most of the mean ratings decline as the child moves toward grade 8. Only three show any increase, and this will prove to be an important fact. With these general comments in mind, let us now examine each of the ratings to see what they suggest about the child's assessment of the President.

Attachment or affiliation

The rating "I like him" is a forthright test of the child's sense of attachment to the President. It draws the lowest mean ranking, between 3 and 4 (Table 8-4a). That is, on the average the children in grades 4 to 8 feel that they like him more than some people, but they would not go so far as to say that they like him more than most or even more than many people.

In comparison with the extreme statements selected on other scales, this expression of affection appears to be restrained, and perhaps two reasons help to account for this. We administered this item only at grade 4 and up, and it is the children in the lower grades who typically select the most positive values on most scales. But even more important, liking is probably a term that the child confines to persons with whom he is in primary contact, well within the range of his daily experiences and comprehension.

This interpretation of the less extreme level on this quality is partly supported if we look at "He is my favorite." At grade 2 the mean for this rating is about 2 and does not fall below 3 until grade 7. If we look at the distribution of choices (Table 8-4b), 72 percent of the children in grade 2 consider the President their favorite of all or almost all, and this drops below 50 percent only in grade 6 when the child is ten or eleven years old. Even in grade 8, with children thirteen and fourteen years old, 59 percent still count the President as at least more a favorite than many people. But in comparison with other scales the child's feelings here drop most precipitously, as Figure 8-1 reveals. This suggests that where a public political figure such as the President is involved, older children are more reluctant to wax so enthusiastic as to exclaim that he is their favorite or best-liked person. Nonetheless it is apparent that a large majority of our younger children was able to extend a rather high level of affection toward the President even in the kinds of vocabulary more likely to be reserved for movie stars, baseball players, or similar public entertainers dear to their hearts.

Benevolence

Not only do most of our group of children feel warmly toward the President, they also feel that he is benevolently disposed toward them and would respond to their needs. This would seem to be the obverse of the coin of affection. Those who the child feels would help him are likely to be the same ones of whom he would be fond; and those he likes he is apt to think would be ready to help him.

Children seem relatively convinced that the President would always or almost always want to help them. Beginning with 81 percent in second grade, 52 percent continue to express this sentiment in grade 8 (Table 8-4c).

On our final instrument, we included an additional item designed to evoke some of the same sentiments, yet from a little different perspective. We wanted to get a further idea of the extent to which the child perceives that the President would be benignly responsive to his own needs and requests. If the child were unable to envision that the President would care about him as an individual, then the kind of global affect which typifies his image of the President would probably not have any very direct or intense meaning for him. The attachment to the President would have been somewhat superficial.

A way of judging the depth of the personal significance of the President was suggested by interview responses from several children about the possibility of writing letters to the President.[4] Many children felt that they could write letters to the President and that he would be interested and concerned on receiving them. If the child could perceive that his writing to the President would be noted and that the President would actually heed his requests, the affect generated would therefore be quite tangibly based. The child would have a valid personal rationale for liking the President in much the same way that he might come to regard his parents or Santa Claus or a guardian angel as both good and useful.

What we proposed therefore was comparatively simple. We asked,

Which do you think is the most true? (Choose one.)
1 If you write to the President, he cares *a lot* what you think.
2 If you write to the President, he cares *some* what you think.
3 If you write to the President, he cares *a little* what you think.

In Table 8-5 we see the pattern of response to this question over the grades. We find that the younger children overwhelmingly pick the option reflecting an image of the President's high concern for them. This sense of responsiveness is depleted over the grades, but even at grade 8, for close to half our group, the image is remarkably positive.

The child is somewhat less certain about the protective help that he can expect. As Figure 8-1 shows, 39 percent in grade 4 and 28 percent in grade 8 consider the President more protective than most other persons (Table 8-4d). We can assume here too that if we had used this scale in the second and third grades, a substantially larger percentage would have chosen the higher rankings.

In these items we get a firmer feeling for the overall tone of the sentiments our children display for the President. He is not

Table 8-5   The Child's Perception of the President's Responsiveness to Individual Requests* (percent of children responding)

If you write to the President . . .

Grade	he cares a lot what you think	he cares some what you think	he cares a little what you think	Total	N Re-spond-ing	N Not Respond-ing
2	75%	20	5	100%	1639	16
3	69	26	5	100	1664	14
4	56	36	7	99	1738	11
5	51	40	9	100	1795	8
6	46	42	11	99	1744	5
7	45	44	11	100	1710	13
8	43%	43	14	100%	1686	9

*CA-9, page 7, item 34. "Which do you think is the most true? (Choose one) (1) If you write to the President he cares a *lot* what you think. (2) If you write to the President he cares *some* what you think. (3) If you write to the President he cares a *little* what you think."

just out there to be observed and admired. The children feel an intimate connection with him. The President is concerned enough to help and protect children. Clearly they consider that the bond between themselves and the President is reciprocal. Their affection for him and his benevolent guardianship of them go hand in hand.

Dependability

The President is also dependable. We can expect him to keep his promises and not make mistakes, and we can rely on him to persist in what he is doing. Among adults we would have expected that statements such as these could be made on the basis of observation and therefore would reflect some knowledge about the President, either first- or secondhand (historical) in origin. But certainly our youngest children, those who have little actual information about the President, can only be projecting their expectations about him. Their estimates of general dependability are likely to represent more feelings than actual knowledge. As the children grow older, new information may temper their earlier unrestrained enthusiasm.

Thus although few of the youngest children would know whether the President does in fact keep his promises, their expectations about him are such that this item reports the highest mean for second grade (1.60), and even by grade 8 it has dropped only to 2.14. In aggregate terms, 84 percent in grade 2 feel that the President always or almost always keeps his promises, and even with what the child must learn from history, civics courses, and incidental sources, this falls off only to 70 percent by grade 8 (Table 8-4e). Trustworthiness appears to be an outstanding characteristic of the President.

But he is also dependable in another sense, in his expected infallibility. The younger children, in grade 4, again were the most positive, with 72 percent saying that he almost never or rarely makes mistakes (Table 8-4f). If we had been able to test in grades 2 and 3, we would undoubtedly have found that a considerably larger number of children felt the same way. To most of the younger children the President is very unlikely to fall into error. Even by eighth grade, 51 percent continue to share an extraordinary confidence in his judgment. Only an insignificant proportion can harbor the thought that the President might often take the wrong course of action.

Finally, the President is also trustworthy and reliable by virtue of the fact that he is less likely to give up when things are hard to do. Here we have one of three of our scales that moves in a direction opposite from most. The mean rating rises with the grade, if only slightly. Well over 70 percent of the children across the grades, beginning with grade 4, hold the opinion that the President never or almost never gives up, with 71 percent in grade 4 rising to 79 percent in grade 8 (Table 8-4g). Persistence in the face of adversity is a Presidential virtue for an increasingly larger number of the children.

Power

Likableness, benevolence, trustworthiness, and reliability are all personal qualities with which the child colors in his picture of the President. But our group of children perceives another property that may seem to have more direct political implications. The President is considered to be a person with not inconsiderable power over others. Adults take this for granted in an era when the chief executives in most industrial political systems have achieved positions of preeminence. But it comes as not a little surprising that at an age when adults would imagine children are innocent of a social phenomenon such as power, our children are in fact sensitive to this kind of potential in a President, even though it is expressed only in very concrete terms, within the limits of a child's conceptual abilities.

In our interviews the youngest children, in grade 2, were already talking about the President as one who directs and orders people, makes laws, keeps the peace, works for the good of the people, and does important things such as taking trips around the country and abroad. There was little doubt about the President's prominence in the country. With it goes the impression that he has the capacity to execute his wishes.

For operational purposes we did not find that the term power was very useful. The child is not familiar with it, at least with the way in which we wished to use it. But to present the underlying meaning of the word, we used both a connotative and a denotative description. The child is able to comprehend the basic idea of power—being able to have other people to do what one wants them to do—even if the word is normally outside his vocabulary in the early grades. To get at this suggestion of the President's general control over others, we asked the child whether "He can make people do what he wants." The child is also able to understand what it means to be able to enforce one's will through the employment of sanctions. We therefore asked him whom the President "can punish." In our interpretation this is clearly an important instance for the child in the exercise of power. These two aspects, general control and sanctions, seemed to cover the kinds of subjects children typically mentioned in the area of power during our pretesting.

We probed the first dimension of power by asking the child to rate the President (and other authorities) according to his capacity to make people do what he wants them to do. As Figure 8-1 reveals, the youngest children, in grade 2, on the average hold that the President falls somewhere between being able to make almost anyone and being able to make many people do what he wants. Even by grade 8 this estimate of the controlling capability of the President has not dropped very much. In aggregate terms the child's image of this capacity stands out with greater prominence. In second grade, 59 percent feel the President can make anyone or almost anyone do what he wants. This declines to 40 percent by grade 8, with most of the difference shifting toward the opinion that he has control only over many persons (Table 8-4h).

When we look at the coercive component in this perception, we find that children are less certain of the President's power. On the average, children from grades 4 to 8 hover in the neighborhood of the relatively restrained opinion that the President can punish only many people, not everyone or most. But again, if we look at the actual proportions, we have slightly more information. In grade 4, our earliest grade, 50 percent think that the President can levy sanctions on anyone or almost anyone, and even by eighth grade 37 percent continue to stand by this conviction (Table 8 - 4i).

However benign the President might be seen in other respects, there is little doubt that many younger children consider him to be a relatively powerful figure. It is equally clear that a sizable minority even think of him as virtually omnipotent, with 36 percent in second grade, 29 percent in third grade, and 24 percent in fourth grade indicating that the President can make anyone do what he wants, and even 20 percent in grade 4 holding the opinion that he can punish anyone (Table 8 - 4i). Most older children, however, express a more moderate opinion on this capacity to manipulate and punish people.

Leadership

We have already learned that however poorly informed younger children may be about politics, they do have some knowledge about possible activities in which the President engages. From grade 3 on, children were able to select meaningfully among the possible activities of the President that deal with domestic and foreign affairs (Table 8 - 3). Our discussion of the image of government has also demonstrated the extent to which children associate the President with making laws and running the country.

Implicit in these data is the suggestion that the child interprets the President as a person who offers some kind of leadership to the country. If for many young children he best represents what our government is, makes laws, and does the most to run the country, these activities may be accepted as virtual definitions of leadership. But we were also able to obtain a direct evaluation of the President as a possible leader.

In our leadership ratings it appears as though we are asking the child exclusively for information about the President. In fact, as we have already indicated, although there is undoubtedly some informational content in these items, there is also a high evaluative component. For children, leadership is not an emotionally neutral idea. It connotes approval, especially in the American cultural setting. In the abstract many children might want to be a leader. It is reasonable, then, to interpret our ratings about leadership traits as reflective of the child's feelings for the President.

When we asked about the extent of the President's knowledge, his capacity for hard work, the importance of his decisions, and forthrightly about his leadership abilities, the image was amazingly stable over the grades. On the average (Figure 8 - 1), most children think that he knows more than, and works harder than, most people. As we move into grade 8, the mean ratings on these items decline only slightly. When asked about the frequency with which the President makes important decisions, our children thought that he did so a lot of the time. As they grow older they tend to move toward the opinion that the President does so all the time. The proportions believing that he makes important decisions all or a lot of the time rise from 83 percent to 95 percent from grades 2 to 8 (Table 8-4j). Similarly in grades 4 to 8, the mean ratings of the children range between assessing the President to be a leader "all the time" and "usually," moving somewhat toward the former as they grow older. Thus 86 percent in grade 4 see him as always or usually a leader rather than a follower, and this increases to 92 percent by grade 8 (Table 8-4k).

It is clear that, from the moment we are able to test them, children are impressed by the special role of the President. Not only is he knowledgeable and persevering, but by grade 8 they are virtually unanimous that the President is never a follower, that he possesses the qualities of leadership, and that his duties are always or usually of supreme importance.

IDEALIZATION AND SUPPORT

In summary, the evidence is overwhelming that young children view the President through rose-colored glasses. No taint of criticism, mistrust, or indifference creeps into the picture. Even those who rank lowest on our scales are nonetheless positive in their evaluations. Most of these children think the President is inherently likable and benevolent, since he would help and protect them more often than not. He measures up to the cultural ideals of being very trustworthy, not too fallible, and very persistent in his effort. He has the power to perform whatever it is that he does, and in doing so, he displays qualities associated with leadership. For most of these judgments the child as he ages revises the original benign image. But he does so from the direction of high initial approval. He has already committed himself to the judgment that the President is a benign helper, protector, and leader.

It is important to recognize the full meaning of the positive assessment of the President with respect to these various qualities.[5] These are all properties that our culture tends to value. We consider people to be good and virtuous if they are protective, helpful, trustworthy, correct, persistent, knowledgeable, hard-working, and possessed of leadership qualities. Our culture is more ambiguous about power. Might does not always make right. But power is also a mark of success where it is not clearly associated with evil. For our test children, it would seem to be a positive attribute in the President.

If we cluster all these properties together in this way and bear in mind the high rating that the child extends to the President on almost all of them, it is evident that behind them there is something more than just an acquired affection for the President. With little knowledge about him, especially in the earliest grades, the child may be reporting less about what the President is than what he is expected to be. And to fill in the gap in his actual knowledge he may be falling back on the ideas in which his culture has already begun to instruct him. The President should have the cultural ideals associated with good adults.

What the President should be is therefore probably expressed in the child's cultural ideals for the good adult. Idealized, the President should be protective, helpful, trustworthy, strong, and so forth, and this is therefore what he is for the child. Certainly these perceptions are encouraged to some extent by adult judgments. The child may learn directly from adults in his environment to feel this way about the President. We can easily imagine that the child would arrive at a different assessment if adults typically considered Presidents timid, fearful, vacillating, unable to place their imprint on the affairs of state, and thwarted in every major effort to exercise power. But adults are not likely to hold this image in general, although they may feel this way about a particular President.[6] Hence children would not be likely to learn from them to deny the cultural ideals to the President.

It seems plausible therefore to assume that for the children in our group, the President has become an authority object on which they feel able to project certain ideals absorbed from the culture. When we deal with other authority figures, we shall return to this notion. But at the moment, whether this is or is not an acceptable interpretation of how the child comes to hold the President in high regard, it is indisputable that he does have a strongly idealized image of the President.

The children are responding to the system in terms of the person who for them best represents it, even if for them this relationship is not apparent and even though they have little consciousness of the political relevance of their ideas and feelings. For the youngest of our test children at least, their acceptance of this symbol of political authority appears to come well before their awareness of and therefore before their acceptance of the myriad of institutions that underpin and surround the Presidency. Attachment to the President would seem to give these broader and more diffuse institutions through which political authority is expressed, called the government, a visible and personal incarnation. If the President is indeed the living symbol of the political system—"our government"—for the young child, the main conduit through which a child moves into the fuller stream of political life in the United States, we may suspect that support for the regime arises easily and naturally.

In our further analysis of the child's image of political authority figures and agencies, we shall be presuming these findings. Our further data will involve a variety of ratings of authorities other than the President. In these ratings we shall repeatedly see the exceptional comparative position the President enjoys in the eyes of the child. But before this analysis is undertaken, we need to examine more carefully what it is that the child is being connected to when he admires the President.

NOTES

1. See Chapter 6.
2. As one nine-year-old put it in an interview:

   Q. *"Do you think the mayor should get his orders from the President?*
   A. *"Yes."*
   Q. *"Why?"*
   A. *"The President is smart, and one ought to do the things the President wants us to do."*

3. Table 8-4m appears to be an exception. But this was only because the scale was reversed in order to assure ourselves that the children were not checking the higher points solely because of acquiescence response set.
4. For an interesting and amusing collection of letters which actually were written, see W. Adler, *Kids' Letters to President Kennedy* (New York: Morrow, 1962).
5. For reinforcing data related to reaction of children to the assassination of President Kennedy, see essays in M. Wolfenstein and G. Kliman (eds.), *Children and the Death of a President* (Garden City, N.Y.: Doubleday, 1965), especially R. Sigel, "An Exploration into

Some Aspects of Political Socialization: School Children's Reactions to the Death of a President," pp. 30-61.

6. We say this somewhat tentatively, given the state of research on public attitudes toward the President and Presidency. Popular reaction to the assassination of John F. Kennedy certainly suggests that the public is apt to idealize the Chief Executive and to hold some fairly far-reaching, if ordinarily unconscious, feelings about him. See, for example, B. S. Greenberg and E. B. Parker (eds.), *The Kennedy Assassination and the American Public* (Stanford, Calif.: Stanford, 1965). For data about the reaction of children and youth see Wolfenstein and Kliman, op. cit. Neither of these books gives a precise answer to our question, however; nor does any other research that we have been able to locate. Information has become available more recently which is suggestive, however, if not an exact answer to our question. Sigel reports, using a 1960 sample from Detroit, that respondents more often than not favor a strong President and prefer Presidential to Congressional leadership (52 percent versus 40 percent respectively). For these and other relevant findings see R. Sigel, "Image of the American Presidency," *Midwest Journal of Political Science,* 10, pp. 123-137, 1966.

9

THE PRESIDENT, THE PRESIDENCY

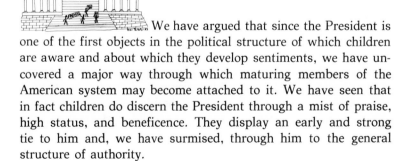 We have argued that since the President is one of the first objects in the political structure of which children are aware and about which they develop sentiments, we have uncovered a major way through which maturing members of the American system may become attached to it. We have seen that in fact children do discern the President through a mist of praise, high status, and beneficence. They display an early and strong tie to him and, we have surmised, through him to the general structure of authority.

THE PERSON versus THE ROLE

But are we taking too much for granted? It is not enough to demonstrate that the school child has put the President on so lofty a pedestal. Could it be that we have only been picking up clues about the way in which the child was reacting to the particular person who happened to be President during our test period? If the children were reporting only that the incumbent, President Kennedy, was as a person likable, powerful, dependable, etc., this gives us little direct information about their orientation to the role of the Presidency as one of the critical components in the American structure of authority. To the extent that the child is responding only to the qualities of the occupant of the Presidency and not to the characteristics that he associates with all Presidents, we learn little about how he evaluates the presidential role.

Even if our findings were limited in this way, they would still have considerable value. If we had been driven to the alternative conclusion that the children in our group were evaluating only the personal characteristics of Kennedy as President, we would be required merely to add another link in our interpretive chain of reasoning. Conceivably the way the child feels about a person who holds an office would in due course spill over to the office itself. Children who were fond both of Eisenhower and of Kennedy uniquely as persons might in time come to think well of the office of the President itself, or they might at least develop similar expectations about all Presidents. Undoubtedly even among adults admiration for the man helps in some part to sustain a belief in the validity of the office. But if we were forced back to this interpretation, it would prohibit us from drawing direct inferences from our findings about the way in which the child feels about the structure of authority. Yet it is exactly statements about the child's relationship to the structure of authority that we would like to be able to make, and have in fact made.

We are left with a problem then as to what we have been testing. If we can show that the child is capable of directing expressive attitudes toward the presidential role rather than merely to the President as the particular occupant of this authority role, we will be able to say that we have established something about the evolving relationship between the child and the structure of authority. This in turn will make it easier for us to adduce some probable connection between the child and the regime.

THE ROLE RELEVANCE OF OUR FINDINGS

We have no decisive proof one way or the other, but we do have several kinds of evidence suggesting that the child is reacting to the presidential role. To begin with, at the time of our earliest preoccupation with the child's image of the President, the incumbent of the role was a Republican, Eisenhower. Since this was in the initial stages of our thinking about socialization, we do not have test items strictly comparable with those administered in our survey when a Democrat, Kennedy, held office. But some similar ones have already been reported in detail.[1]

We asked the child to express his views comparing the President with most men, about how hard he works (diligence), how honest he is (honesty), how much knowledge he has (knowledgeability), and how much he likes people (friendliness). We also asked the child to rate the President as the best in the world, a good person, or not a good person. Although the number of children tested is small, the ratings move in a direction similar to those for our study made after Kennedy became President. The child's evaluations during the Eisenhower test period are uniformly high over the grades, with the more affective items declining somewhat as the child grows older and the more cognitive ones, such as "works hard" and "knows more," increasing. These findings give us some confidence that at least one important personal quality of an incumbent of the Presidency, his party identification, need not be the decisive determinant of the child's perception.

But this conclusion does not permit us to go to the opposite extreme and to argue that the role of the Presidency must therefore account for all the variance, that it is the only factor shaping the child's image. Data from our present study indicate that some part of the child's attitudes toward the President can be accounted for by his party preference. Where he is of the same party as the President, the child is more enthusiastic about him. If this is so, at least one personal characteristic of the President, his party identification, contributes something to the intensity with which the child approves of him.

Thus when we combined the items "I like him" and "He is my favorite" to form an Index of Affect for or Attachment to the President[2] and correlated this index with the party preference expressed by the child,[3] we found a significant, even if fairly weak, relationship between them. At grade 4, the earliest grade for which we were able to develop this index, the correlation between affection for the President and the party preference of the child is scarcely significant. But as we move through the grades, the correlation increases in a negative direction for those children identifying themselves as Republicans, as we would expect (see Table 9-1). For those children who in effect declared themselves to be Independents,[4] there was no significant correlation with affection for the President, either positive or negative. It is apparent therefore that the party of the President does influence in some degree the extent to which the child approves of him.[5]

Table 9-1 Correlation between Party Preference* and Index of Affect for the President† (Pearson r)

Party Preference	Grade				
	4	5	6	7	8
Democrat v. other	.11	.14	.18	.16	.17
Republican v. other	−.11	−.13	−.18	−.17	−.22
Independent v. other	.00	−.01	.00	.00	.03

*Each category was scored on a dichotomous variable, namely, Democrat or other, Republican or other, Independent or other. Party preference is determined by answers to CA-9, page 9, item 42 (see footnote 3 of this chapter).
†The Affect Index is fully discussed in Chapter 17.

The effect of party is brought out even more vividly in Table 9-2, which shows the distribution by grade of Republican and Democratic children on our Index of Affect for the President. In each grade a larger percentage of Republican children consistently falls into the low category. In this category (low), the percentage difference between Republicans and Democrats in each grade remains relatively constant through grade 7 (at an average 15 percent), but in grade 8 it leaps about an extra 10 points (to 25 percent). This would seem to reflect the growing capacity of the child to appreciate the significance of party alignment and therefore to take it more into account in his estimate of the President.

Table 9-2 Relation of Republican or Democratic Party Preference to Affect for President,* by Grade (percent responding)

Grade	Party	Low Affect	Medium Affect	High Affect	Total	N† Responding	N Not Responding
4	Republicans	39%	26	35	100%	520	3
	Democrats	24	33	43	100	329	2
5	Republicans	43	30	28	101	534	4
	Democrats	31	31	38	100	450	2
6	Republicans	44	32	24	100	489	3
	Democrats	27	32	40	99	497	5
7	Republicans	49	31	20	100	415	5
	Democrats	34	31	36	101	537	10
8	Republicans	64	22	14	100	336	9
	Democrats	39%	31	30	100%	542	6

*High is equal to scores 9 to 11, medium is 7 to 8, and low is 1 to 6.
†N = number of cases responding. This number was used as the base for the percentages.

But even this conclusion about the impact of party identification on expressions of approval needs to be interpreted with caution. We may well doubt whether it applies to our younger children. It would seem reasonable to project downward our correlations for grade 4. In this event since a significant correlation[6] between party preference and attachment (Table 9-1) just begins to emerge at grade 4, we could assume that the lower grades would show none higher. Yet we will recall that in all but a small number of instances it is in the lower grades that our ratings reach their peak and children report their highest evaluations of the President. We can safely assume then that the party identification of a President would have little meaning for our youngest children.

Two possible inferences may be drawn on these assumptions. We could argue that children originally base their judgments purely on the kind of person they take a particular President to be. If so, as they learn to assert a party preference and as they also learn that the President stands with one or the other party, their initial estimates may be influenced somewhat. This would account for the less positive assessments, during the Kennedy period of our test, by the children who identify themselves as Republicans.

An alternative explanation seems more plausible. The children, especially those in the earlier grades, have very little knowledge about the Presidency. It is unlikely that they have enough information about the personal qualities of a given individual to be able to make judgments about him. They must therefore be making assumptions about the characteristics of all Presidents as persons who hold this office. In effect they are describing what they see as aspects of the typical personality in that role, the role personality. As the children grow older, we can expect them to acquire a better sense of their own party identification and also to be able to understand something about what the President's own party coloration may mean. They should gradually be able to modify their evaluation of the general presidential-role personality with information about the particular President. In this interpretation the acquisition of party preferences by the child represents a very early opportunity to introduce personal criteria into his previously learned expectations about the role.

The kind of evidence we have presented leads us toward the conclusion that the child is probably less concerned with the President as a particular person than as a symbol of political authority. If the child is indeed reacting to the symbol in large measure, it is highly probable that he is expressing sentiments about the Presidency, a part of the structure of authority.

The fact that the child absorbs expectations about the personal qualities of the occupant of the presidential role is not at all unusual. It is well known in other spheres of life. As we mature in the American society, for example, we anticipate that physicians as such will have certain personal properties regardless of individual idiosyncracies. However ill-tempered, intolerant, self-centered, or even mercenary he may be in other spheres of life, we expect the physician to listen patiently and sympathetically to our complaints, to provide honest diagnoses and treatment, and even to sacrifice some of his own comforts, such as sleep and regular hours, to help us in distress. We also expect him to be motivated by more than a mere desire for financial gain.

But as we become acquainted with a particular physician we usually have to alter our expectations in light of the actual personal characteristics that we encounter. We may also modify our generalized expectations about the role personality of physicians by what we now know about this particular physician. Nonetheless, the relationship between physician and patient and in fact the position of the physician in the social structure are very dependent upon the initial and subsequent generalized perceptions that we develop about him.

Similarly for the President, what we find is that at the outset the maturing member of society, as represented in our group of children, acquires sets of dispositions toward this political role, which also happens to be a central unit in the structure of political authority. In the immaturity of childhood it is the personal qualities that are most easily perceived and understood. There is little reason to be surprised that children should seize not upon the complex duties and behavior of a President but on his clearly personal qualities as elements of the role that help them to orient themselves to him and, we would infer, through him to the political structure.

THE MEANING OF PERSONALIZATION OF THE PRESIDENCY

Probable as this inference may be, it does leave us with an apparent contradiction. In Chapter 6, on "The Image of Government," we argued that it was very meaningful to find that the child initially personalizes government by seeing it best represented in such figures as the President. Only later does he turn to such impersonal institutions as Congress or voting. Yet here we are proposing that initially the child's image is shaped largely by the Presidency as an institution with only some small influence being exercised by the qualities of the incumbent President as a particular person.

The contradiction is apparent only. To say that the child personalizes authority is not the same as asserting that he sees only the person or incumbent in the authority role. In Chapter 6 we were trying to show only that in the whole range of objects of political authority, the child is drawn to that object which could be most easily symbolized by some person. Given the marginal status of political things in the daily concerns of the child as well as his acute inability to cope with a concept as abstract as political authority, he is able to deal only with very tangible manifestations. Among other things, initially the child sees not some complex, imposing, and overarching structure of authority but an Eisenhower or a Kennedy. To some limited extent he may be impressed by them as partisans, and the older he grows the more does partisan identification constrain his judgment. But to a much larger extent it does not matter what the idiosyncratic qualities of the incumbents are. To the children a named President is more than the man. An Eisenhower or a Kennedy is *our* President and this growing awareness evokes a set of generalized expectations about his benevolence, dependability, and the like, that is, about his role personality.

Transparently most younger children at any rate are not able to distinguish consciously between the Presidency and the role occupant. For this reason in designing our questionnaire we felt free to use a hand-drawn sketch of President Kennedy to represent the general role of President without fearing that the child would really be relaying to us his image only of Kennedy the man. As our data indicate, children are able to talk about the particular incumbent as though he were "the Presidency" in adult parlance, that is, the institutionalized role.

Peculiarly it appears that the child begins political life not by concentrating on the unique person, although this is not entirely neglected, but rather on the occupant as representative of the country and government. The general symbolism of the role overpowers the particular characteristics of the occupant. We are able to conclude for this reason that the child begins to be aware of an important part of the structure of authority. The fact that previously we concluded that he does this through personalization of the structure is not inconsistent with our conclusion in this chapter that the child is able to see and cathect the role.

THE SYSTEM EFFECTS OF PERSONALIZATION

What are some of the consequences of this high degree of personalization of the Presidential role? To recapitulate the essence of our findings in this area, we have discovered that a large proportion of younger children waxes so enthusiastic about the President that he seems to become something just less than a paragon of virtue as measured by our various criteria. It might be suggested that this is not surprising, since children are known to be prone to exaggerate and to see things in black and white. But for the Presidency at least, this is not the case. Usually something less than 50 percent hold the most highly positive notions; the remainder of our group distributes its opinions over a gradient, even if the children's judgments seldom fall below midpoint on our rating scales. Furthermore, as we shall see later, children are also able to discriminate between the President and other authority figures such as father, policeman, and senator. Their judgment of the President is not part of a wholesale, uniform, and extreme idealization of all authorities.

Our data also suggest that children are not thinking in these exceptional terms only about a particular President. At the young age that we tested them they were already able to see numerous expected generic qualities of the presidential office rather than the man.

The implications of these findings for the political system are varied. We shall now examine a few of them.

Personalization as the child's mode of contact

Personalization identifies a process whereby the child is able to establish contact with the structure of authority in a way that is plausible for and congenial to his mental and emotional capacities. Without some connection such as this, it is difficult to imagine how a child would begin to develop an identification with the system in which he finds himself.

When he is born and begins to mature in a society, as we suggested earlier, the child is in many ways similar to an immigrant who has just entered the system. Unlike the immigrant, however, he does not undergo a resocializing process. The child does not have to learn to transfer his allegiance; he has no political preconceptions and predispositions to cast off or revamp. But like an immigrant, the child for the first time does have to learn to recognize parts of an unknown map about political authority. Depending upon what he sees and his experiences with it he will then extend some measure of support, positive or negative. The fact that in the American system the child's eye first catches not some impersonal institution such as Congress or even the Supreme Court but rather a figure of authority, and the fact that he sees this figure as a bundle of personal qualities associated with the role, make it relatively easier for him to reach out to the structure.

One of the reasons for this is that the President is the kind of element in the political structure that can bring the child's image of the regime to a sharp focus. The idea of government, of which some children are simultaneously aware by grade 2, is certainly much more diffuse, more difficult to grasp, for both adults and children. Indeed, insofar as children do comprehend it, we have seen that it is often initially in terms of the President as its best expression. The President's singularity, eminence, visibility, and power give the child a handle to grasp as he seeks to interpret the phenomenon of an authority external to the family, a kind of authority that he is quickly aware of as his eye and mind wander beyond the home.

The personalization of the President reflects the fact that what the child sees are warm, palpable characteristics, much like those of human beings with whom he already has developed primordial ties. Personalization facilitates the development of those very elemental kinds of feelings of which children are capable: love and hate. It incorporates a host of other attributes that children are accustomed to associate with ordinary people, such as leadership, power, and benevolence.

Structural versus personal legitimacy

But in spite of the extraction of personal characteristics in the presidential role, in our interpretation the child relates himself not to the occupant as a man but to the role itself. This is of vital significance for the input of diffuse support for a political system. It may be a singular mainstay of the Presidential structure in the American system.

If the child fixed his attention only on the man and revered the particular qualities of the incumbent, one of his first lessons in politics would be that the legitimacy of the authorities depends on their individual qualities. He would be acquiring a sense of the personal legitimacy of the President, his charisma. Presumably if he retained his orientation, on the change of the President the child would need to start afresh and would renew this support only if he considered the new President also had admirable qualities. Each President would be faced with the task of revitalizing a belief in his legitimacy. To command acceptance, each President would have to stimulate a belief in his personal adequacy. Leadership succession would be a constant source of political strain. In Weberian language, the routinization of charisma would have difficulty in developing.

Undoubtedly there are systems, even in a mass, industrialized society, in which the qualities of the man rather than the position he occupies may temporarily be basic to his acceptance. Some would argue that this is indeed the case with de Gaulle. But our data suggest that in the United States personalization is not the same as the acceptance of the legitimacy of a figure of authority on purely personal grounds. Children are able to accept the President because they have certain idealized expectations about the occupant of the presidential role, regardless of who he may be. Tensions and crises of succession resulting from the need for each occupant to re-create a loyalty uniquely due to him — the Weberian charismatic type of base for legitimacy — are thereby avoided for the child. Any President merits his esteem because he is President, even if he is of an opposite political complexion.

We cannot overemphasize the surprising nature of this finding.[7] Here we have stumbled upon a possible means through which a political system manages to transmit respect for at least one of the principal offices in its structure. We are tapping a major source of continuity in a regime. In most large-scale political systems, persistence requires some popular belief in structural legitimacy, the acceptance as right and proper of the basic organization of political relationships, formal and otherwise.[8] Our findings hint at the dynamic forces that enable maturing members to learn for the first time that persons may come and go but that the structure — or more cautiously, one basic structural component, the Presidency — can go on, if not forever, at least beyond the incumbency of the current occupant.

Thus we may interpret the image of the President as an indication of the kind and level of support that our group of children is prepared to put into the structure of authority. Certainly this is a plausible conclusion for the younger children in our group. For them the President is the one who does most to run the country, and he is one of the best symbols of the government — itself a vague, omnibus term for the authorities as a whole. We have been arguing in a Freudian vein that emotions experienced this

early are apt to color behavior in later life. In this may lie the ultimate significance of childhood attachment to and belief in the
legitimacy of the structure of political authority (in the past, at
least) as represented in the President and, as we shall see, in other
figures and institutions as well.

Political controversy and structural legitimacy

We may also have some clue here about the origins of that
capacity among adults that permits them to criticize and con-
demn the President and yet retain respect for the office. In the
short run at least, the passions surrounding the role do not seem
to undermine support for it or for the rest of the structure of political authority. If it were not that as adults we have become so
accustomed to considering the controversy surrounding the office
as normally immaterial to the acceptability of the Presidential
system itself, we might long ago have been struck with wonder
at the ease with which we can differentiate man from role. We
might otherwise have felt an urgent need to inquire into its source.

In party politics, the specific qualities of the man as a nego-
tiator, arbiter, leader, strategist, and policy maker may be paramount for judging an incumbent.[9] But for most adults, regardless of the degree of competence of the President, the office as
a symbol of the whole regime continues unimpaired. Furthermore, however much members may differ about the qualities
of the man, once he steps into office they anticipate that he will
conform to certain personal standards in meeting its requirements.

We have seen that this is not a capacity that is left to adulthood for its development. Our group of children has already
acquired this posture toward the Presidency before it has left
elementary school. We might expect that in this respect the adult
is but the child writ large. Our research has guided us toward
an understanding of how in childhood the future adult members
of the American political system learn to distinguish between
the role and the man. Not that we would contend that adults have
the capacity to keep the two so separate that what they think
of the man does not ultimately influence their judgment about
the role. Spillover from one to the other undoubtedly occurs. It
contributes perhaps to a certain ambiguity in adult perceptions
of the Presidency, something we know little about as yet. There
always remains the latent fear in the United States that excessively harsh condemnation of a President may undermine the
authority of the Presidency as an institution. But without the

capacity to make the distinction between men and role, it is unlikely that a sense of structural legitimacy could be maintained. In this event other sources of support for the political structure would have to be sought.

Without doubt it is useful for a regime that combines in one office the figurehead of the system and the active executive to train its members to distinguish the role from the man. But our findings imply more than this. They also contain a hint about the source of diffuse support for the structure of authority, not among children alone but among adults as well.

It is conceivable that idealization during the early years of life will leave a residue of positive sentiment within the later adult. Manifest affect in childhood may continue as latent affect in adulthood. If this is indeed true, it may be an added reason why, among adults, criticisms of the occupant do not readily shake their confidence in the Presidency. However much members of the system may despair of the man as President, early idealization of the office may leave enough respect as a latent force to sustain a belief in its legitimacy. If so, we have come upon a major taproot of diffuse support in a system.

Personalization and personal political identification

Consequences for the system may also flow from what personalization does for the child himself. The Presidency may be a point in the complex social world which guides the child toward a sense of political identity. The President is *his* President, even though partisanship does introduce some distracting noise into the system. We may suspect that personalization of the office helps the child to become aware of who and what he is politically; he sees himself reflected in the President. We might even hazard the guess that in the past the assured and cocky air of some Americans at home and abroad, their national brashness, has been not only a product of national wealth and power but of a deep feeling of political assurance, a strong air of self-confidence that they knew who they were politically. We are led to wonder whether the psychic roots of this phenomenon do not lie partly in the opportunity to attain a secure sense of the political self through the early personalization of authority in the Presidency. If so, in this respect as well, early socialization through the Presidency may have far-reaching consequences for the input of diffuse support to the American regime.

THE UNIVERSALITY OF PERSONALIZATION

Our interpretation of the possible system effects of personalization carries us far beyond its immediate significance for socialization in the American political system. In effect, we may have encountered here a central mechanism available to many political systems for building up diffuse support in each wave of children as they enter a political system through birth into it. The fact that the new member is a child rather than an adult with a preexisting set of attitudes toward political life creates a need for special devices to build support for the regime and authorities. Each system will, of course, have its own specific mode of personalization. It may take the form of a monarch, a paramount chief, a renowned elder or ancestor, a charismatic leader, or a forceful dictator.[10] But the pattern of making government or the structure of authority a warm and immediate object through its initial symbolization as a person, the high affect that this permits for a child, and the possible subsequent overflow of this feeling to cold and impersonal institutions and norms may be vital. They provide a complex yet not unfamiliar mechanism for attaching to the system those members who are new to it by virtue of their birth in it.

From the peculiar position that the President comes to hold in the American system, however, we cannot directly infer that every system must provide some kind of personal point of contact, central in the political structure, if the maturing generation is to learn to put in support for the regime. Certainly we would be going beyond even the broadest implications of the data to argue from our knowledge about the visibility, salience, and idealization of the American President that every system requires some estimable personal chief executive.

There is a confluence of several forces that projects the American President into the foreground. The first is the considerable importance of chief executives in all modern industrialized systems; the second is the prominence of the Presidency because of the peculiar nature of the American political regime; the third is the child's own sense of vulnerability and need for a powerful protector. It is difficult if not impossible in a one-system study such as ours to disentangle what may be common to all systems from what is unique to a single system. We cannot tell whether in the American system the President arises as a point of contact for the child because of the growing visibility of all chief executives in modern times, because of the special properties of the

American political structure, because of the child's need to feel protected, or because of some peculiar combination of these factors.

If, however, we subscribe to the idea that the personalization of authority for the child represents a phenomenon that transcends this time and place, the prominence and importance of personal figures such as the President raise some interesting questions about the input of support to political systems in general. Suppose a system developed a structure of authority that contained no central personal figure to which the maturing members could direct their attention and affection. How then would a child make contact with the regime, especially if, as we assume, in his earlier years his ability to conceptualize and relate himself emotionally to impersonal objects, such as organizations or institutions, is very low?

It is clear that under these conditions, with our assumptions, the system would probably have considerable difficulty in socializing its members so that they developed positive sentiments early in life. But if the system did *not* show signs of weakened support, it would alert us to the need to look for other kinds of mechanisms that might have come into operation and through which the members could begin to accent the legitimacy of the political authorities.

For example, if there is a low level of support in the early years, it might be compensated for by mechanisms in later years that serve to increase the input. In some systems the maturing members might put in no direct support at all to the structure of the regime. Intermediate figures and organizations might exist through which the child is bonded to the system. The child might learn to esteem the head of a lineage who might mediate between the system and the child. A church, ethnic group, linguistic unit, or the like might similarly play a mediating function. Regardless, however, of the specific devices through which a system might seek to encourage the input of diffuse support for the structure of authority, the means it developed would have to take into account the apparently low capacity of younger children, if our test group is typical of most children, to relate themselves to impersonal institutions.

Whatever the way in which other systems might handle the socialization of support, in the United States the President as a personalized figure is a towering, glittering mountain peak for the younger child, easy to single out from the whole range of authority. As the child grows older, his eyesight becomes stronger and hidden peaks appear that may even soar higher, such as Congress. But we have suggested that what he initially sees and the feeling he develops for it may remain as an undercurrent of his attitudes toward the authority structure. Even though the older child may see authority in more critical and less enthusiastic terms, early idealization may create latent feelings that are hard to undo or shake off. This is the major significance of the first bond to the system through the Presidency. The positive feelings for political authority generated there can be expected to have lasting consequences.

This does not deny the patent possibility and reality of change. Children as well as adults may be loosened from their ties to the system. But our data on the regime in the United States do not permit inferences about the nature of the processes of change insofar as they are influenced by childhood socialization. Our sample of white urban children shows little evidence of their being disconnected even marginally from the structure. Neither for that matter would we imply that this is the whole story and explains how socialization has contributed to the stability of the American system. The political structure is only a limited, although significant, aspect of the political system. Regime values and norms, the political community, and the specific authorities as such are other parts which may also endure or change; and these, it must be recalled, we do not explore in this work.

NOTES

1. R. D. Hess and D. Easton, "The Child's Changing Image of the President," *Public Opinion Quarterly,* 24, pp. 632-644, 1960.
2. We did so after undertaking a series of factor analyses which isolated these two items as measuring a separate attitudinal dimemsion. See Part 4.
3. Our party-preference item read as follows: "If you could vote, what would you be? (Choose one) (1) A Republican. (2) A Democrat. (3) Sometimes a Democrat and sometimes a Republican. (4) I don't know which I would be. (5) I don't know what *Democrat* and *Republican* mean." CA-9, page 9, item 42.
4. They selected the option "Sometimes a Democrat and sometimes a Republican."
5. The impact of partisanship is demonstrated in other studies. "We further predicted [after the assassination of President Kennedy]

that children who identified with the President's party (those children who said they would vote Democratic if they were old enough to vote) would show more signs of grief and fear over the future of the country than those not so identified . . . this was indeed the case, although it showed up mainly in the area of emotional responses. Democratically inclined children reported more trouble sleeping, more loss of appetite, crying, etc. More of them identified with the President — 'worried how the U.S. would get along without its leader' (Democrats 66 percent, Republicans 58 percent). And, not unexpectedly, more of them showed feelings of aggression toward Oswald (Democrats 50 percent, Republicans 38 percent). The President may have a firm niche in American children's affections and admiration, but partisanship is apparently an intervening variable, which either strengthens or loosens the bond. Even in death and tragedy children are aware of their partisanship — although not to a very marked degree." R. E. Sigel, "An Exploration into Some Aspects of Political Socialization: School Children's Reactions to the Death of a President," in M. Wolfenstein and G. Kliman (eds.), *Children and the Death of a President* (Garden City, N.Y.: Doubleday, 1965), pp. 52-53.

6. A correlation of .08 would, for our size *N*, normally be considered significant at the .01 level.

7. This was first suspected and reported in our preliminary research in 1960. See Hess and Easton, op. cit.

8. For difference between personal and structural legitimacy, see D. Easton, *A Systems Analysis of Political Life* (New York: Wiley, 1965), chap. 19.

9. R. E. Neustadt, *Presidential Power: The Politics of Leadership* (New York: Wiley, 1960).

10. Compare with the relationship of the British monarchy to affect about the system as developed in E. Shils and M. Young, "The Meaning of the Coronation," *Sociological Review,* 1 (new series), pp. 63-81, 1953; and the Earl of Balfour in his introduction to W. Bagehot, *The English Constitution* (Fair Lawn, N.J.: Oxford University Press, 1928).

10

HOW THE CHILD SEES THE POLICEMAN

The policeman, we have already discovered, joins the President as one of the figures in the political world first apparent to the child. For the child the policeman may be only a person with some special power. But for the student of political socialization the policeman carries far deeper meaning. He helps to link the maturing child to the political structure. This will form the subject of the present and succeeding chapters.

With respect to the policeman we shall find that several politically significant things happen to the maturing children in our group. Through this figure, they discover that there are persons outside the family who have authority. They recognize that these persons are persuasive and powerful enough to impose their will on other adults, as well as on children. Finally, they learn to respect policemen and by implication the legitimacy of their power. Although our data do not permit us to trace out the full set of relationships through which our group of children receive vital messages like these about the presence and legitimacy of political authority in general, we can clearly discern one of the important sources of such messages in the image of the police. The policeman starts the child well along the road toward becoming politicized—developing an awareness of the political sphere and its significance.

POLICE IN THE POLITICAL SYSTEM

Vital as the police are as an institution in a legal society, it is strange that they have never been considered of central significance in the functioning of political systems. As a result they have always fallen into a position so peripheral to the core of political science that it is virtually impossible to find a sustained theoretical discussion of the varied functions they fulfill in political systems.

Historically, the limited attention they have received from students of politics falls into two major theoretical areas, more through the accident of practical interest than from the conscious design of theoretical analysis. On the one hand, the police have been implicitly conceptualized as agencies for the enforcement of law and order, especially for those systems committed to the rule of law. But a theoretical proposition such as this is normally just assumed rather than explored. There is little conscious effort to expand on the implications, for the political system as a whole, of police activity directed to the maintenance of law and order, or to compare police forces with parallel and alternative institutional devices.

The main thrust of research in this area is typically normative in character rather than analytical. The underlying goals hinge on current policy concerns. Standards of performance are posited, and the task is to discover the conditions that will permit the police to measure up to them. The central question would seem to be: How can a democratic, humanitarian society encourage the development of a police force that is expert, incorruptible, highly motivated, and intent on the reduction of crime, yet cognizant of the limits of its authority in such a society and restrained in the use of force?

From this perspective a few sociologists have recently explored the major dimensions of the police as a professional occupation and the impact of society upon their operations.[1] The administrative sciences have inquired into the kind of organization and regulations necessary for recruiting the appropriate personnel and enabling them to perform their duties in an efficient and morally acceptable way. Students of public law have analyzed the legal norms and rules that crystallize what is conceived to be a desired relationship between the powers of the police and the goals and values of members in a democratic system. Research in urban politics has mapped out the connections among crime, the police, and politics and has looked for a pattern of relationships that would promote effective civilian control but prevent unwarranted interference with specifically police activities.

On the other hand, the police have sometimes been approached from a different theoretical perspective, one that is particularly apparent in the literature on political development and change and on authoritarian systems. Here there is less concern about the effectiveness of the police as a law-enforcing institution. Implicitly they are interpreted as an instrument of political power, one that groups in a political system may manipulate to their own advantage. For Marx and others exploring the conditions of social change, the police are weapons of control in the hands of the ruling class or an elite. For students of developing societies and authoritarian systems, the police may represent social agencies which join with the army in the application of violence. From this standpoint, interest in the police as an agency for the suppression of crime and for the enforcement of the law recedes visibly.

But even in these two respects—as institutions for the preservation of law and order and as paramilitary organizations for the maintenance of power—there has been little sustained theoretical inquiry into or conceptualization about the overall relationship of the police to the political system. Equally important, efforts to probe for other ways in which the police might be significant in the functioning of political systems have been seriously lacking. As a result of such investigation, we might hope to round out a theory of the police as a *political* institution and draw the study of the police more intimately into the general framework of political research.

It testifies to the dividends of theory in general and of systems-persistence theory in particular that from it we can deduce some additional critical consequences of police institutions. These institutions do more than enforce the law, provide services of various kinds, or, in some systems, openly partake in the political struggles of the day. In posing questions about the sources of support in any political system, persistence theory leads us to inquire into the function of policemen as central connecting points between maturing members of a system and the structure of political authority. Indeed, from our limited data we shall be led to hypothesize that probably few regimes in mass societies would be able to obtain the minimal level of cognition and approval they require without the contribution of such local representatives as the police in awakening the appropriate sentiments of its members. Not that the police as such need be considered an inescapable part of all political structures. But, our findings impress on us, if a political system in a mass society does not provide for a police establishment, some other visible local representative of authority may well be necessary as a substitute.

Thus theory alerts us to the need to broaden our perspectives about the part that the police may play, at least as a specific kind of institution in large-scale political systems. Over and above the obvious and vital consequences they may have for helping to sustain or change a prevailing system of law and order, they may also be serving as a bridge between maturing members of the system and the broader political structure. This is demonstrably true for the American political system.

THE CHILD'S COGNITIVE IMAGES OF THE POLICEMAN

A peculiar and interesting aspect of the introduction of our test children to the American political system, as we have already hinted, is the immediacy of their contact with the system. Not only do they see a President somewhere off in the geographical distance but psychically close, they also come into direct contact with the policeman who, it turns out, is both spatially and affectively close. For the child, we shall see, the policeman also becomes a physical symbol connected with a felt obligation to obey something outside the family circle.

Objectively the policeman is a part of the structure of authority in a political system. He belongs to the output structure helping to implement the decisions of other governmental agencies. But he also produces outputs of his own. He makes decisions on what rules to invoke in a given situation and on whether or not to apply a rule in a given instance. "The role of the police as decision-makers," it has been observed, "must be expressly recognized."[2] In this sense the policeman represents an important unit in the general structure of authority in the United States. Insofar as a person relates to a policeman in any way at all, objectively he would be establishing ties of some sort with the structure of authority, at its tail end, as we have observed in Chapter 7.

This link to the political structure may occur unwittingly. It is not necessary that members of the system be aware that their contacts with the policeman and the way they feel about him help to shape their ties to the structure of the political regime. This is true for adult members in general and would apply with even greater force to children. The objective position of the police in the political structure in no way guarantees that the child will see them in that position or have any understanding of what their role involves politically. The policeman can serve as a vital relay point between the child and the structure of authority, and yet neither policeman nor child need have any inkling of this function.

But to the extent that the child has some understanding of the place that the policeman occupies in the structure of authority, our argument that the policeman is a significant link between the child and the system will have greater force. Perception can be expected to reinforce objective reality.

As the data in this chapter will suggest, empirically it turns out that the child has some important cues about where the policeman stands in the political state of things. The growing child increasingly develops an image that puts the policeman close to the government. If children understand the policeman to be related somehow to the government, we can expect that sentiments about him will have some direct bearing on how we can interpret their feelings for the structure of authority.

Who is the policeman?

Before we can proceed to explore how the child relates the policeman to the political structure, if he does at all, we need to ask: Whom does the child have in mind when he entertains our questions about the policeman? Is he thinking of all police, from the neighborhood cop to the FBI agent or sheriff?

In our final instrument we did not test specifically to identify the object of the child's responses. Evidence from our preliminary interviews convinced us that most children probably think largely of the local policeman, typically on view in uniform in school books during the early grades and as he moves about the neighborhood.

Very early in our investigations we interviewed a small number of children in a middle-class suburb of Chicago. Our discussions with them were not without some ambiguity; typically, showing little knowledge of the political sphere or even of the broader neighborhood, the responses tended to be vague, sometimes apparently contradictory. Thus when we asked our small pretest group of children whether the policeman is part of the government, almost all those from grade 2 and above replied affirmatively (Table 10-1). But when we asked the same children whether their town has a government, the great majority grade 1 to 4 replied either no or that they did not know. Not until grade 5 did a majority give an affirmative answer.

Table 10-1   Two Items from Informal Interviews of Children in Town of Riverside, Illinois (frequencies)

| | "Does Riverside have a government?" | | | | "Are the police part of the government?" | | | | |
Grade	Yes	No	Don't Know	NA*	Yes	No	Don't Know	NA*	N† for Each Item
1			3	1					4
2	2	1	7	2	8		2	2	12
3	1	1	2		4				4
4	3	2	4		7	2			9
5	3	1	1	1	5	1			6
6	5				5				5
7	4				3				4
8	3				3				3

*NA = not ascertained.
†N = number of cases.

It would appear therefore that for the younger children, at least, the government was not local in character. As we know from our chapter on "The Image of Government," younger children do tend to see the President or some other national, personal figure as most representative of the government. We might infer that for younger children all government seems to be national in character; the distinction between national and local is not one that has much meaning for them. All government tends to fuse into one mass, undifferentiated as to level.

If we could expect children to be consistent in the adult sense of the term, we might infer that if the younger ones see government as national and if they acknowledge that the policeman is part of government (noted earlier in Table 6-5), they would be inclined to think of the policeman as somehow unconnected with the local scene. But the child is not so certain or informed about differences in the levels of government or so interested in the policeman as to be concerned with consistency in the logical sense of adults. Hence when we inquired into what he thought the policeman does, it was clear that regardless of the child's failure to see government as locally based, police activities were certainly viewed from a local perspective. In this suburban town the few children tested from grade 1 considered that the police take care of people, get mad at them, put them in jail, tell them where places are, and give them tickets. The "people" to whom the children referred seemed to be somewhere in the immediate environs. In grade 2, the child was likely to think of the police as catching criminals and helping people. Grade 3 added keeping traffic rules to the list, and grade 4 conceptualized more broadly by indicating that the police enforce the laws or run this suburban town.

It would seem, therefore, that however little information children may have about government and the relationship of the policeman to it, they intuitively think of the policeman as a local person; he performs activities associated with the neighborhood or local community. The word policeman did not seem to arouse in the child's mind an image of the multifarious police agents and agencies at other structural levels in the United States, such as the sheriff, state trooper, FBI, G-man, or lawman of western movies. In spite of the fact that in metropolitan regions in the United States policemen tend to travel in cars or on motorcycles rather than on foot, the child's early picture of him is close to what we would have expected in a prior period when foot patrols were more prevalent. In part we might suspect that his localized image comes from the crossing-guard police and uniformed surrogates.

This is not to imply that the younger child has any awareness of the position of the police in the political structure. In fact, he appears to be more alert to what he thinks the police do than to their structural position. He is functionally rather than structurally oriented. Yet in the specification of the activities in which the police engage, the limited group of children whom we initially interviewed did seem to detect a peculiarly immediate and local aura about the policeman. If the younger child has any idea at all of the structural location of the police, he places them at the local level, even though with apparent illogic he sees the police as working for the government and cannot as yet disentangle government itself from the national sphere. The evidence in various subsequent interviews confirmed this inference so decisively that there was no incentive to consume valuable space in our final instrument for further testing of the object of reference in the child's idea of the policeman.

The child's location of the policeman among the authorities

The object of our inquiry is therefore the ordinary neighborhood policeman. He is the political object the child is most likely to see, in the earliest grades, together with the President and a vaguely defined government. But even though the children in our group place the policeman in their local community, it would appear from our data that for them the policeman blends into the diffuse structure of political authority, or "the government," in their own vocabulary.

Here again, however, we have to work through the child's way of seeing and interpreting the position of the policeman and infer from this the consequences for the child's ties to the political system. Even though in the end we shall maintain that the children connect the policeman explicitly with the political authorities, this unadorned conclusion would not tell us enough. In what way do the children make this connection? Do they go so far as to consider the policeman part of the authorities who stand at the center of the decision-making process, those whom the child looks to as the government? Or is the policeman only peripherally related? Does the nature of the observed relationship affect the way in which the policeman may operate as a linkage point? Although we cannot answer these questions definitively, we may from our evidence draw some plausible inferences.

There is little doubt that for the children the policeman is neither a good representative of the government nor a person who plays a significant part in running the country, as a lawmaker. Thus in contrast with the symbolism he attaches to the President, the child rejects the policeman as a good overall representative of government. On our question about the best representative of government, among the youngest children a percentage less than chance selects the policeman[3] even in grade 2, at an age when, if at all, we might have expected the child to value the policeman as a close and visible symbol of government.

Furthermore, even though, as we would expect, the child links the policeman in an important way with laws, he does not go so far as to consider that the policeman has an important part to play in the making of laws. Indeed, our pilot studies indicated that children associate the policeman with this task so seldom that we did not find it worth including the policeman as an option in one of our basic questions on who makes the laws. (The options we finally settled on were Congress, the President, and the Supreme Court, the most frequent choices.[4]).

This low ranking of the policeman on a lawmaking function emerged strikingly in one of our pretests. Here we asked the child directly whether or not the policeman is involved in making laws;

Table 10-2 presents two such items. We see that the younger children more easily rejected the broader statement that "Policemen make laws" than perhaps the more credible statement that "Traffic laws are made by policemen and highway patrolmen." By grade 8, nearly all these children turned down both statements.

Table 10-2 The Child's Understanding of the Role of the Policeman as One Who Does *Not* Make Laws*

	"Policemen make laws."		"Traffic laws are made by policemen and highway patrolmen."	
Grade	Percent Agree	N Responding	Percent Agree	N Responding
3	16	69	51	69
4	15	118	25	118
5	8	116	15	117
6	7	145	13	142
7	9	141	10	139
8	5	145	4	145

*Pilot test, "In My Opinion #III," items 144 and 165.

But the child does not fully disassociate the police from the making of laws. We ought perhaps to expect that in a legalistic society such as the United States, law and police would be inextricably intertwined and children would very early sense the presence of some kind of relationship without necessarily being able to articulate it very well. In fact our group of children do feel that even though the police are not to be held directly responsible for making laws, they help in some undefined way.

When we asked the children to indicate how much each of a number of persons and organizations "helps to decide what laws are made for our country," the police are seen to fall somewhere between having some and having very little part. Figure 10-1 shows that, among the options offered, for grade 4 the policemen are exceeded in their influence only by the President and unions. This emphasizes the strong connection that the younger child is apt to see between lawmaking and police, and the curves in Figure 10-1 suggest that if we had tested the children in grades 2 and 3 on this set of items, policemen might have ranked next to the President. Although the child starts out rather impressed by the involvement of the police in the making of laws, by grade 8 the police recede to a more modest position. Nevertheless even at the latter grade, they seem to carry about as much weight,

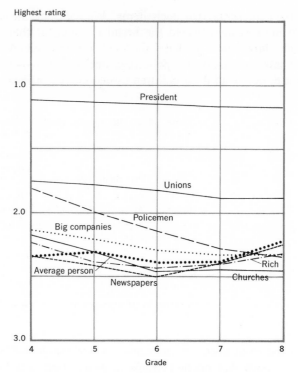

Highest rating

Figure 10-1. Mean Ratings by Grade on Who Helps Decide Which Laws Are Made for Our Country.

in the child's mind, as rich people and big companies, somewhat more than churches, and somewhat less than newspapers and the average person. However, for grade 8 all these persons and organizations, aside from the President and unions, are thought to possess a relatively low measure of influence in shaping the laws, on the average less than "some" on our scale.

It is clear therefore that for most of the children the policeman does not directly participate in the legislative processes in the manner of Congress, the President, or the Supreme Court, even though because of the close association of the police with law it would have seemed easy for the child to have thought otherwise. The child rejects the notion that the policeman occupies the foreground of the formal political stage.

But it is one thing to exclude the police as good representatives of government and as potential lawmakers of importance and another matter to disassociate them from the governmental (political) structure entirely. Even though the child may not conceive of the policeman as possessed of legislative powers, he has little doubt that the policeman is part of the overall, vague structure of political authority apparent to him. However uncertain the child's image of government may be and however much the younger child may confound local with national structures, as we have already seen, our children do recognize that the policeman is a person who works for the government. Nor is this conception peculiar to any grade level. As we have already noted, over 80 percent in each grade describe the policeman in this way (Table 6-5).

It would have been enough for our purposes to demonstrate only that the child has some conception of the existence of the policeman or relates to him in some manner. As long as in objective, theoretical terms we can assign the policeman some place in the political structure—as we did in Chapter 7—this is enough to justify our further inquiry into the child's interpretation of and feelings about the policeman, as we pursue our study of the sources of support for the political authorities.

But we now see that we can go further. It is clear that the child has acquired a subtle, discriminating awareness, at even the earliest grades, of the location of the policeman in the political structure. Even though the local policeman is a figure well known to all our children, they do not give him excessive prominence in the direct lawmaking processes. We might have anticipated the contrary for the early grades at least. The children seem to have a relatively modest conception of the part that the policeman plays in the system. They have learned to discriminate between having something to do with government, as an employee, and running the country, as in the case of the President—between what we would call a narrow administrative and a broad legislative-executive location in the structure of authority. The older the children are, the more clearly they are able to capture this difference. But even though the policeman recedes in importance in this sense, all children, whatever their grade, do continue to connect him with the government and thereby, in our terms, with the structure of political authority. This subjective awareness reinforces our theoretical grounds for identifying the policeman as a meaningful point of contact between the child and the authorities.

THE AUTHORITY OF THE POLICE

Support for the structure of authority includes more than just an awareness of the presence of a figure or institution as part of that structure. It involves at the very least a readiness to accept the object and its actions as valid or authoritative and perhaps even some understanding of what that figure or institution does.

It is a basic assumption of our research that no system could persist without some means for making allocations that are accepted as binding, or *authoritative,* by most of the politically relevant members of the system most of the time. We can assume, without fear of contradiction, that children in our age group generally accept the authority of their parents, even if specific decisions may be questioned. But how does it happen that maturing members of a political system are able to identify and accept the right of persons outside the family, even those whom they may not know personally, to exercise authority over them and over adults as well?

The problem

Authority we interpret as just one kind of power. Power in general we see as the capacity to bend another to one's will. Person A can be said to have the kind of power we call authority over B if A sends a communication to B and B accepts it as a basis for action regardless of his independent judgment about the advisability of doing so. The communication carries with it a quality of oughtness; B feels he *should* obey even though he may strongly disagree with the wisdom of the specific message. Why he feels this way can be ignored at the moment, although typically, in political systems, the sense of obligation derives from the attitude that it is right and proper to do so, that the authority is legitimate.[5]

Children are typically subject to the power of the authority of most adults in their environment. The child learns that he is expected to obey certain types of adults, that they have the power to tell him what to do, and that it is right and proper to accept their judgments within some undefined limits.

But in the United States, as in most other systems, we take it for granted that as the members of a system grow up, somehow they learn that there is a power external to the father and mother and even to most other adults they know. All persons, not only children, are subject to it. What is usually assumed we here consider problematic. How is it that the members of a society are indeed prepared to accept the authority of persons external to the family, such as those who are part of the political structure?

We might reply that in most modern political systems a person would soon realize his error if he failed to obey. Typically force would be applied in no unmistakable sense to seek to bring about conformity. But we also know that in the normal course of events adults do not live in fear and trembling of political authority, even as it may be represented in law-enforcement agencies. Most people usually abide by the injunctions of the authorities because they think it is right to do so, within vague but definable zones of obedience. They come to consider the authorities as legitimately endowed with power. It is this sense of legitimacy that constitutes a fundamental source of support for most regimes.

Yet members of a political system are not born with this propensity to accept authority. Such acceptance is a product of a complex set of attitudes and perceptions that they acquire in varying degrees by virtue of membership in a system. How does this form of support come about?

We have found one major source to be associated with the upper reaches of the structure of authority in the United States. Something looms over the children with power and virtue, and they perceive this as the government; a person is closely associated or identified with it whom they call the President. As they grow older, other institutions such as Congress enter the increasingly complex image of these external authorities. But simultaneously the system impresses its authority on the child from another direction, from the tail end. It is as though the remoter objects, visible in part, intangible but symbolically present, could not be depended upon to assert the dominance of the political sphere on all appropriate occasions. Thus we find the policeman, closely tied as he is to law, playing an important function in molding the child's understanding of and feelings about political authority. The policeman is a tangible, personal agent of authority, and to the child therefore a plausible one. Through the policeman, we shall conclude, the child is impressed with the presence of a power over and beyond that of father or mother and one that even parents, as potent as they may appear to the child, cannot escape. Here lies a seed out of which a sense of the legitimacy of the authority structure springs.

Police authority as an external power

That the policeman is a compelling force, one whom there is a special obligation to obey, is apparent to the child from the earliest moment at which we have been able to test him. When given a number of options about what is important for the policeman to do (Table 10-3), 77 percent of our test children in grade 4 considered that his job was to "Make people obey the law" and

"Catch people who break the law" as against "Help people who are in trouble." Even in grade 8 a clear majority, 61 percent, continues to hold these views. The power of enforcement is paramount in the minds of the children, even though it is estimated that in reality about 90 percent of the time the local police perform services only marginally related, if at all, to enforcement.[6]

Table 10-3   The Child's View of the Most Important Job of the Policeman* (percent of children responding)

Grade	Make People Obey the Law	Help People Who Are in Trouble	Catch People Who Break the Law	Total	N Re-sponding	N Not Respond-ing
4	38%	23	39	100%	1526	223
5	42	30	28	100	1787	16
6	43	33	25	101	1731	18
7	45	34	21	100	1709	14
8	42%	40	19	101%	1680	15

*CA-9, page 31, item 31. "Which is the most important for the policeman to do? (Choose one): (1) Make people obey the law, (2) Help people who are in trouble, (3) Catch people who break the law."

This emphasis on the power of the policeman, especially for the enforcement of the law, appeared time and again in our pretests. One of our preliminary investigations proved to be particularly revealing along these lines. At the outset we had assumed that many if not most adults held rather disparaging opinions about the police and that one way or another these might be subtly transmitted to children. Yet we did not seem to be picking up anything but positive sentiments from them. We speculated that perhaps the trouble lay in our techniques of inquiry. Could it be that by virtue of our mere presence in a question and answer setting, we inadvertently constrained the child from expressing honest opinions? An argument could be made that in the presence of one adult authority, the interviewer, a child would be somewhat reluctant to give verbal answers expressing hostility toward or some depreciation of other adult authorities, such as policemen.

We sought to overcome this possible limitation of the interview and questionnaire format by asking over six hundred children to draw pictures of various authority figures, including the policeman. Although interesting additional feelings and judgments of the child could be inferred from their drawing, the small increment in knowledge did not seem to justify extensive further use of this method.[7] On the whole the new information gained in this way merely reinforced what we had already learned through interviews. In their drawings the children depicted the policeman as physically dominant, suggesting the magnitude of his power. With relatively few exceptions the children, in the two lowest grades especially, drew the policeman as several times larger than other objects such as cars or ordinary people. This suggests that he is in command of the scene, and indeed the action of the drawings clearly made this point.

The police were rarely drawn as inert figures; they were commonly shown in both verbal and motor activity interacting with other persons. We divided the pictures into three functional areas of activity: protective, as when a policeman helps a child across the street; prohibitive, as when a policeman appears with arms extended directing traffic and saying "Stop"; and punitive, as when a policeman is apprehending or jailing a criminal.[8] Although the children portrayed the police in a multitude of situations and evoked many facets of their activities, over 50 percent of the drawings have distinctive elements of an interpretation that emphasizes prohibitive and punitive qualities. The propensity of the police to direct and punish rather than help looms large. It would appear to be the power of the police that captures the free-flowing imagination of the child.

Essentially the same kind of message comes through, although less dramatically, in the child's response to our ratings (Figure 10-2). They also convey his early sensitivity to the special power of the police. The children are perhaps a little doubtful about the punitive component in the power of the policeman, although the views are relatively stable over the grades. On the average, as the mean ratings over the grades show, they consider that the policeman can punish close to the point on the rating labeled "Many people." But a comparatively large proportion of the children do attribute considerable punitive capacity to the policeman. From 37 percent in grade 4 to 30 percent in grade 8 declare that the policeman can punish anyone or almost anyone (Table 10-4).

The children are, however, more convinced of the power of the policeman to order people about. On the average our grade-2 children feel that he can make many people do what he wants, and this conception drops only slightly over the grades (Figure 10-2). Table 10-5 fleshes out this mean rating. About 48 percent in grade 2, falling gradually to 36 percent in grade 8, consider that the policeman can make anyone or almost anyone do what he wants, a considerable measure of control over others by any standard. This is particularly significant for the older child. Many at

Table 10-4   Power Rating of Policeman: "He can punish"* (percent of children responding)

Grade	1. Any- one	2. Almost Anyone	3. Many People	4. Some People	5. A Few People	6. No One	Total	N Re- sponding	N Not Respond- ing	Mean Rating
4	10%	27	29	21	10	4	101%	1724	25	3.05
5	8	27	33	21	8	4	101	1793	10	3.03
6	9	29	34	17	6	4	99	1744	5	2.94
7	8	29	36	17	6	4	100	1714	9	2.98
8	6%	24	39	19	5	7	100%	1679	16	3.14

*CA-9, page 29, item 76.

Table 10-5   Power Rating of Policeman: "He can make people do what he wants"* (percent of children responding)

Grade	1. Any- one	2. Almost Anyone	3. Many People	4. Some People	5. A Few People	6. Almost No One	Total	N Re- sponding	N Not Respond- ing	Mean Rating
2	26%	22	20	16	7	8	99%	1632	23	2.80
3	18	25	25	18	8	7	101	1666	12	2.93
4	13	30	26	18	7	6	100	1730	19	2.94
5	11	28	32	18	6	5	100	1783	20	2.95
6	11	31	31	17	5	5	100	1737	12	2.87
7	12	32	31	16	5	5	101	1702	21	2.83
8	9%	27	36	17	5	6	100%	1669	26	2.98

*CA-9, page 6, item 30.

age thirteen or fourteen are still convinced of the extraordinary compulsory capacity of the policeman. From their earliest years, therefore, the children recognize the ability of the police to impose sanctions and to exercise some considerable measure of control over people.

This is no subterranean, amorphous feeling. Children are able to express it clearly in more than one way. When we compare the child's image of the power of the policeman with that of his own father, for example, we find that for both ratings we have been considering the father ranks much lower on the average. However powerful the father may be for children, he does not measure up to the policeman.[9] This inferiority of parental authority emerges even more forcefully and directly in the child's response to another item. We sought to elicit a direct comparison of the degree of rightness or wrongness in disobeying various figures of authority: mother, teacher, father, and policeman. Table 10-6 reports the exact wording of the item and the pattern of response.

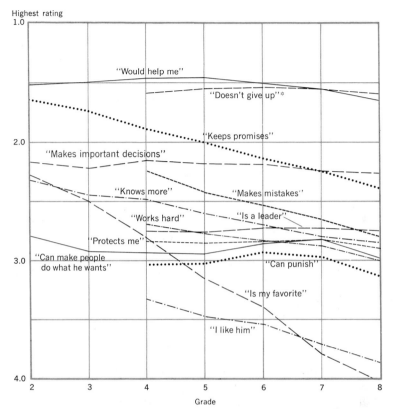

Highest rating

Figure 10-2. Mean Ratings on Thirteen Attributes of the Policeman by Grade.
*Means of this rating were subtracted from 6.0 to make them more comparable with the rest.

Three-fourths of the youngest children choose the policeman as the one most wrong to disobey. External political authority in the guise of the policeman apparently has special weight for the young child. He rather clearly recognizes that the policeman's authority is high and that his demands for obedience are to be respected. As the children get older, they reevaluate somewhat this great weight of the policeman and become more responsive to family authority. An increasing number feels it is less wrong to disobey the policeman. But in all grades a minimum of about 50 percent considers it most wrong to disobey the policeman.

The pattern changes in an opposite manner to what we might have expected. We might have thought that the acceptance of law-enforcement authority would be higher as the child learns

Table 10-6 The Child's Perception of Relative Need for Obedience to Various Authority Figures* (percent of children responding)

| | Which of these is the most wrong to disobey? | | | | | | |
Grade	Mother	Teacher	Father	Policeman	Total	N Responding	N Not Responding
3	10%	8	8	75	101%	1605	73
4	10	6	12	72	100	1653	96
5	14	5	16	65	100	1715	88
6	14	4	21	61	100	1673	76
7	16	3	25	56	100	1645	78
8	19%	4	28	49	100%	1595	100

*CA-9, page 24, item 54: "*Disobey* means to do something someone tells you not to do. *Which of these is the most wrong?* Put an X beside the *one* that is the most wrong: (1) To disobey your *mother*, (2) To disobey your *teacher*, (3) To disobey your *father*, (4) To disobey the *policeman.*"

more and more about the political system. This is clearly not the case. It is the younger child who sees this authority as most compulsory, and it is the older child who resists this idea. The family comes increasingly to offset the authority of the political system as it is represented by the policeman.

In part this shift away from police authority may be due to generic tendencies in the maturation of the child. Piaget notes the inclination of younger children to accept rules as sacrosanct but to question them and begin to exercise rational judgment in assessing them as they reach eight and nine years of age.[10] But in connection with the policeman, this decreasing concern for his authority may also be a special effect related to the ambivalence with which he is probably regarded by adults. Regardless of the kinds of positive feelings adults may express about the policeman—and we shall touch on these in the following chapter—we can assume that often they view the policeman as a person who is at least occasionally wrong or corrupt. At times he may be regarded as the enemy who has to be outwitted, as in the area of traffic violations. These kinds of sentiments in parents may help the older child to modify his own acknowledgment of the superior authority of the police. Yet although we see perhaps a modest tendency toward the abrogation of police authority, it occurs nonetheless in the context of initial acceptance that comes relatively early in the child's cognitive development.

The item we have just discussed substantially confirms the continuing awareness over the grades of the presence of an authority external to the most familiar world of the child, a power that for most younger children dominates over the injunctions of such close figures as mother, father, and teacher, individually considered. We can have little doubt that the tail end of the structure of political authority—the policeman—has left a distinctive imprint on the mind of the child. Through the policeman the child learns an important lesson about the power of external authority and about the need to accept as obligatory or binding the actions or decisions of others from the broad world beyond the family.

Here, we suspect, lies an important source of that support for the structure of authority that we may call recognition of the legitimacy of its authorities. Of course the child has no consciousness of the policeman as a representative of political authority on the output side. Neither have most adults. But this is of little significance compared with the child's clear awareness of the authority of the policeman. He does not question its appropriateness. The large majority of our test children indeed initially see it as superior to that of close adults. Therein may lie a vital mechanism for generating support for the authorities at large. Through the policeman the child is encouraged in the belief that external authority should and must be accepted. It reinforces a similar posture that he is early encouraged to adopt toward government and the President. Thereby the policeman contributes significantly to the politicization of the child.

NOTES

1. M. Banton, *The Policeman in the Community* (London: Tavistock, 1964); J. J. Preiss and H. J. Ehrlich, *An Examination of Role Theory: The Case of the State Police* (Lincoln, Nebr.: University of Nebraska Press, 1966).
2. W. R. LaFave, "The Police and Nonenforcement of the Law," *Wisconsin Law Review*, 9, p. 239, 1962 (quoted in Banton, op. cit., p. 145).
3. See Table 6-2.
4. See Table 6-3.
5. For a full discussion of this point see D. Easton, "The Perception of Authority and Political Change," in C. J. Friedrich (ed.), *Authority* (Cambridge, Mass.: Harvard, 1958); *A Systems Analysis of Political Life*, part 4.
6. "It has been estimated that at least 90% of all police business is not of a strictly criminal nature." G. D. Gourley, "Police Public Relations," *The Annals of the American Academy of Political and Social Science*, 291, p. 136, 1954. See also The President's Com-

mission on Law Enforcement and Administration of Justice, *The Challenge of Crime in a Free Society* (Washington, D.C.: GPO, 1967), pp. 91ff., especially pp. 97-98; E. Cumming, I. M. Cumming, and L. Edell, "Policeman As Philosopher, Guide and Friend," *Social Problems,* 12, pp. 276-286; 1965; W. H. Parker, "The Police Challenge in Our Great Cities," *The Annals of the American Academy of Political and Social Science,* 291, pp. 5-13, 1954.

7. Aside from the difficulty of administering a test of this sort to large populations, there is the additional difficulty of stable interpretations and coding of pictures. It seemed useful to adopt the technique only for limited exploratory purposes. Our assistant, Albert Robles, was responsible for the initial coding and analysis of the drawings.

8. In a free drawing exercise such as this it is interesting that crime detection and prevention, a favorite way of depicting police activity on television, seldom appear.

9. See Figures 12-11 and 12-12.

10. J. Piaget, *The Moral Judgment of the Child* (New York: Free Press, 1948), Chap. 1.

11

HOW THE CHILD FEELS ABOUT THE POLICEMAN

In the last chapter we saw that the children in our test group, especially the younger ones, have little knowledge of the policeman's position in the formal structure of political authority, even though to some extent they realize that the police operate outside the centers of decision making. In addition, the child perceives rather clearly that the police are a power to be reckoned with in the world beyond the family.

It will appear in this chapter that the American political system does not rely only on perception of police power to bring about the acceptance of authority by maturing members. Cognition is reinforced by affect. In the socialization process we shall find that, as for the President, the child acquires feelings for the policeman that are very significant for the growth of an attachment to the structure of political authority.

We need to turn from perception to feeling, for good reason. It is entirely conceivable that under certain circumstances the child might well recognize the authority of the police, as in an autocratic system in which the police impose a virtual reign of terror; yet if fear and disaffection were widespread among adults, the child might be as resistant to this authority as his parents. The police might be a symbol of fear and hatred. It would be doubtful that children growing up in this kind of climate would express much esteem for the police, however fully they might be compelled to recognize police power. The texture of the acceptance of political authority and its validity will be vastly different where it is underpinned by positive feelings from where there is only an acknowledgment of its inescapable power. By moving beyond the cognitive level to the affective we may hope to capture the full flavor of the reception of police authority by maturing members of the system.

THE POSITION OF THE POLICE IN MODERN SOCIETY

The police hold a special place in modern democratic societies, one that arouses an unusual combination of feelings among adults. If we were to deduce the child's feelings about the police from those that people often assume adults hold, we might imagine that what is a well-recognized authoritative role for the child is not necessarily well thought of.

What is there about the role of the police that gives them a unique position in society? Above all else, the peculiarity of their role in democratic systems flows from their capacity to use violence in the pursuit of occupational ends.[1] No other public servants aside from the military are permitted to apply force to the individual members of the system. In the last resort, as we have already noted in Chapter 7, the police have the extraordinary power of life and death.

> "I'm only a cop," says Patrolman Frank Foucault, 41, of Precinct 10, Livernois and Elmhurst, in Detroit. "But you look at me real close and you will see something that has more power than even the President of the United States. I don't mean me, Frank Foucault; I mean me, the cop. I have the power of life and death. In ten seconds, I can kill someone or let him live, and I don't have a jury or judge or anybody there to say Yes or No."[2]

Although legal rules and conventions impose severe restraints on the exercise of this power, ultimately it is of the very nature of crime detection and prevention and law enforcement that a wide range of discretion must belong to the police. The individual policeman, often entirely on his own, must produce certain kinds of outputs in the system. It is he who makes the final decision, whether to write out a ticket for an offence, order an action to cease, or undertake whatever force may be necessary to effect an arrest.

In a society that values individual freedom and responsibility and in which the frontier disregard for law still plays an important part in its traditions, neither police nor the ordinary individual ever feels completely at ease about the possible relationships that may flow from these powers.[3] The police are one of the few representatives of authority who are ubiquitous and in continuous potential contact with the individual members of the system. At the same time the visibility guaranteed by their uniform leaves them particularly vulnerable "as easily identifiable targets for the expression of hostility toward authority."[4]

Probably because of the peculiarity of this position of the police, adults do not display totally unmixed feelings about them. Indeed, so ambiguous does the role become in some systems that it carries over to the policeman's family, which may suffer varying degrees of social isolation.[5] In the United States, if we were to rely on popular and even professional conceptions about how people feel, we would be forced to conclude that adults generally hold the police in very low esteem. It would appear that the police are seen as venal, prone to roughness if not brutality, tainted by the very criminals with whom their occupation forces them into contact.[6] We are apt to believe that suspicion and fear rather than trust and respect would characterize the overall popular image of the police.

The evidence that we shall present will dispute this folkloric interpretation of the popular view of the police. But at this point we can at least accept as plausible the notion that adult attitudes toward police authority are not without ambiguity. We would expect therefore that the cross-generational transmission of this ambivalence would become apparent in children's responses to questions about their affective orientations toward the policeman.

What in fact we find among the children in our group is a surprisingly favorable reception of the policeman. This affect declines as the child grows older. But overall feelings about the policeman are fairly positive on most measures.

This approval will raise a puzzling problem for us. If the popular adult conception of the police were indeed deprecatory, it would be most unlikely that parents could conceal their view entirely from their children, even if they wished to. We would expect that younger children particularly, least exposed as they are to competing views from outside the family, would mirror these sentiments of their parents. Yet it is the youngest children in our test group who turn out to be most favorably disposed toward the policeman. The data will therefore pose a conundrum for us that we shall have to resolve at a later point.

OVERALL RESPECT FOR THE POLICEMAN

In face of the unusual position occupied by the policeman in modern society, how do we find the children of our test group feel about him? Can we say that their general regard or respect for him is predominantly positive?

Overview of the rating scales

We administered the same thirteen rating scales about the policeman that we had used for the President. As we saw from Figure 10-2, the most positive response on the ratings occurs among the youngest children. This image continues over the grades, except that some of the high idealism is lost. The decline in the level of favorable sentiment takes place, however, upon a base of fairly high affect.

From Figure 10-2 we saw that a few of the average ratings on the policeman are relatively high and stable over the whole span: his benevolence (willingness to help, protectiveness), his power (capacity to control others and to punish), his leadership (as represented by our leadership rating and the perceived frequency of making important decisions), and even to a limited degree, his dependability ("He doesn't give up when things are hard to do"). On these qualities the child's impressions of the policeman seem to become fixed early in life and to remain at about the same level.

The remainder of the ratings begin fairly high on the scales, but the changes that take place in these perceptions as the child grows older are striking. The ratings that directly express the child's attachment to the policeman ("I like him," "He is my favorite") decline markedly, as do some of the items that are involved in the child's perception of the policeman's dependability ("He keeps his promises," "He makes mistakes") and some aspects of his leadership ("He knows a lot," "He works hard").

If a higher rating is a measure of the average child's greater readiness to accept the policeman as an authority figure, it is instructive to note that regardless of the constancy or decline of the perceptions over the grades, on the average all qualities are rated above the midpoint on our scales, with the lone exception of the attachment items. Few children have developed a negative image of the policeman, even by grade 8.

As we have already argued for the image of the President, all the ratings probably represent ideal qualities or virtues in the American culture. Few people would contend that it is *not* desirable for policemen to be benevolent and dependable and to exercise qualities of leadership. The children display differences in the degree to which they incorporate elements of these general cultural characteristics in their image of the policeman. As with the President, we have a comparatively idealized picture of the policeman at the outset, although at an overall lower level. It would appear therefore that the children see the policeman possessed of all the cultural virtues and that any diminution by grade 8 does not seriously interfere with the fairly high esteem in which they continue to hold this figure of authority.

Direct attachment to the policeman

It might be argued, however, that the most general measures of affect for the policeman, our attachment items, run contrary to the general trend of all other items and that this apparent contradiction cannot be ignored. If we look at the proportions of the children who rank the policeman at various points on the two ratings "I like him" and "He is my favorite," we can indeed see the low affiliative sentiment that the policeman evokes. Apparently by grade 4 the child has begun to develop some relatively well-defined feelings about the police, and these prevent him from expressing a strong personal attachment to them. Although in second grade 65 percent of our group could say that the policeman is their favorite either of all or almost of all, by grade 8 this falls to a mere 16 percent (Table 11-1). Similarly only 27 percent in grade 4 are able to declare that they like the policeman more than anyone or than most, and this recedes to 10 percent by grade 8 (Table 11-2). Clearly the policeman has little personal charisma for the child, especially as he grows older.

How can we account for this low level of attachment as compared with the patently higher regard that the child displays on the other ratings? An explanation that readily comes to mind is that the child has an ambiguous image of the policeman. Whatever the source of his conflict, it manifests itself in these contradictory ratings.

Table 11-1 Children's Ratings of Policeman: "He is my favorite"* (percent of children responding)

Grade	1. Of All	2. Almost of All	3. More Than Most	4. More Than Many	5. More Than a Few	6. Not	Total	N Responding	N Not Responding	Mean Rating
2	42%	23	15	10	7	4	101%	1636	19	2.29
3	31	29	16	11	9	4	100	1666	12	2.51
4	21	28	20	15	11	5	100	1722	27	2.82
5	12	25	24	19	12	7	99	1781	22	3.16
6	9	24	23	20	13	11	100	1732	17	3.40
7	6	15	22	24	18	15	100	1693	30	3.79
8	4%	12	20	25	21	19	101%	1662	33	4.03

*CA-9, page 6, item 31. (We would remind the reader to refer to the note in Table 6-1 for the meaning of this kind of reference.)

Table 11-2 Children's Ratings of Policeman: "I like him"* (percent of children responding)

Grade	1. More Than Anyone	2. More Than Most	3. More Than Many	4. More Than Some	5. More Than a Few	6. Less Than Almost Anyone	Total	N Responding	N Not Responding	Mean Rating
4	6%	21	28	27	12	5	99%	1725	24	3.33
5	4	17	30	31	13	6	101	1784	19	3.48
6	3	18	31	29	12	7	100	1738	11	3.53
7	2	13	31	30	16	9	101	1711	12	3.72
8	1%	9	28	35	18	9	100%	1679	16	3.87

*CA-9, page 29, item 19.

What lends an air of plausibility to this line of reasoning is the general impression that one gains, from the folklore, of the feelings of adults toward policemen. If, as it is thought, adults do have little respect for them, we could anticipate that children would find themselves somewhat in conflict about the kinds of signals they were receiving from adults. Adults might want them to think well of the police — on the principle that children need to be sheltered from the harsh realities and sordid details of life — and yet the adults might not be able to conceal their true feelings entirely.

As we have already hinted, however, available information on adults would seem to refute the notion that they hold the police in low regard. On the contrary, most adults normally have considerable respect for the police, as we shall see in Chapter 14. There is little need for them to transmit conflicting messages to the children. Rather, children are probably being socialized by adults to think well of the police because this is the way most adults genuinely feel. If this is so, the level of our attachment items needs to be explained in other terms.

In part there may be a simple explanation for the low attachment ratings. At the same time as the children are learning about the policeman, they observe that he is responsible for punishment and enforcement of the law. They may develop mixed feelings about this. He is helpful but also a person to be feared in some measure. This may interfere with a direct expression of affection for the policeman. However, this conclusion needs to be tempered by what we shall have to say later about the policeman as a figure of power. We cannot take it for granted that for children the possession of power necessarily breeds distrust.

There may be other reasons that better account for the low level of the attachment ratings by grade 8. We have already witnessed and discussed the same tendency for the likableness rating about the President. There, "I like him" and "He is my favorite" also drop sharply to what we would regard as a relatively low point. However, for the President these two attachment ratings do not fall relatively so far as they do for the policeman. This difference in levels between the ranking of the President and the policeman is not difficult to explain. In doing so, it will help us to understand why both attachment items may fall so low for the policeman.

For the obvious reason of differences in occupational importance, we would expect the President to fare much better than the policeman. Both figures are salient for the child, as we have seen, but for different reasons. The President runs the country, and the child cannot help but pick up cues from his environment about the critical importance of this role. The policeman is not so distant spatially, it is true, and in this sense may be better known to the child. But those in the child's environment are unlikely to attach the same significance to the policeman's role. This alone would help to account for the lesser decline of the President on our attachment ratings.

Although this difference between President and policeman does not tell us why the child should express so little direct attachment to the policeman, it does point us in the proper direction. Unlike the President and unlike entertainment figures in the movies, television, or the sports world, there is little that is vividly unique about the policeman or that would be especially appealing to the child, particularly as he grows beyond the cops-and-robbers stage. Although television and the movies do dramatize the role of lawman in various ways, it is not usually the cop on the beat or in the patrol car but the sheriff, FBI agent, G-man, private detective, or special-forces officer. The average child is less likely to come into personal contact with these kinds of police. Perhaps is we had asked the child to relate to a particular policeman by name or other specific identification—such as a known crossing guard— he might have been more prone to assert a personal attachment. But in the normal course of events, the policeman in the general role being tested is too undramatized a figure, without real individuality, at least in the form in which we posed our ratings, to evoke a high assessment on our attachment items.

To say that a person "is my favorite" or that "I like him" is an extremely personal thing, especially as the child grows older. It would appear that however much the child may respect a figure, there may be only certain types of public figures—those that are dramatized in one way or another—that are able to forge this kind of restricted relationship with the child. The fact that the policeman ranks relatively low on the attachment items need not of itself discourage us from concluding that he may nonetheless be in a position to provide an effective point of contact for linking the child to the structure of authority.

The benevolence of the policeman

When we look at the other ratings, it is clear that the low level of affiliative sentiment does not interfere with the child's more positive image of the policeman in other respects. What stands out from among the other ratings is the high degree of benevolence that the child attributes to him. Likable or not, he is seen as very willing to help the child personally. In second grade, 85 percent of the children indicate that they think he would always or almost always want to help in case of need, and this remains almost at the same level in grade 8 (Table 11-3). The realistic quality of this assessment was noted in the previous chapter.[7] Furthermore, between 60 and 70 percent of the children in all grades tested also consider that the policeman protects them more than most or many people do (Table 11-4). That he is seen as a benign, responsive figure needs no further comment.

However, this outcome of our analysis was more than a little surprising. We might excusably have expected otherwise. Adults in the American culture tend to be suspicious of persons with power—or so it is thought. We might have inferred that children follow their parents in this. If so, because for them the policeman is a powerful figure (Tables 10-4 and 10-5), he would also be a person to fear and suspect, not one to whom a child could be expected to turn for help. But this is not what happens, and we shall return to this theme in Part 4 when we seek to explain

Table 11-3   Children's Ratings of Policeman: "He would want to help me if I needed it"* (percent of children responding)

Grade	1. Al- ways	2. Almost Always	3. Usually	4. Some- times	5. Seldom	6. Not Usually	Total	N Re- spond- ing	N Not Respond- ing	Mean Rating
2	71%	14	9	3	1	1	99%	1634	21	1.53
3	72	15	8	4	1	1	101	1667	11	1.51
4	74	12	10	3	1	1	101	1729	20	1.47
5	72	15	10	2	1	0	100	1796	7	1.46
6	71	15	11	2	1	1	101	1738	11	1.51
7	65	19	11	3	1	0	99	1709	14	1.57
8	58%	23	15	3	0	1	100%	1670	25	1.66

*CA-9, page 6, item 26.

Table 11-4   Children's Ratings of Policeman: "He protects me"* (percent of children responding)

Grade	1. More Than Any- one	2. More Than Most Do	3. More Than Many Do	4. More Than Some Do	5. Less Than Some Do	6. Less Than Most Do	Total	N Re- spond- ing	N Not Respond- ing	Mean Rating
4	10%	32	30	21	5	2	100%	1727	22	2.85
5	8	32	31	22	4	2	99	1782	21	2.87
6	8	35	31	20	3	3	100	1736	13	2.85
7	7	36	34	18	3	3	101	1709	14	2.83
8	6%	33	33	21	3	3	99%	1676	19	2.91

*CA-9, page 29, item 20.

more generally why children should have so high a regard for political authorities. Here, however, we need to note that at the same time that the child is learning about the power of the policeman, he appears to seize on that power for his own purposes, as it were, and to be convinced that it will be used benignly, to help and protect him.

Dependability

The policeman is also interpreted as a fairly dependable person. Very few children feel that he is anything less than very persistent in his efforts, and this sentiment remains stable at a high level across the grades ("He doesn't give up when things are hard to do," Figure 10-2). He is trustworthy. The younger children on the average locate him somewhere between always and almost always likely to keep his promises. Although this mean rating drops considerably by grade 8, the children still feel that they can

Table 11 - 5 Children's Ratings of Policeman: "He makes mistakes"* (percent of children responding)

Grade	1. Almost Never	2. Rarely	3. Sometimes	4. Often	5. Usually	6. Almost Always	Total	N Responding	N Not Responding	Mean Rating
4	22%	38	35	3	1	1	100%	1735	14	2.25
5	13	38	45	3	1	1	101	1795	8	2.44
6	9	36	50	3	0	1	99	1744	5	2.53
7	6	31	57	5	1	1	101	1714	9	2.66
8	3%	24	66	6	1	1	101%	1686	9	2.81

*CA-9, page 29, item 74.

rely on him to keep his promises more than just "usually." Finally, they are not convinced that he is infallible. In grade 4, however, 60 percent of the children feel that he almost never or rarely makes mistakes, an unusually high level of trustworthiness (Table 11 - 5). If we project this proportion downward to grade 2, we might expect an extremely high percentage to select these two options. Although by grade 8 a preponderance of children expresses a more modest trust in the policeman, a substantial 27 percent of the thirteen- and fourteen-year-olds continue to retain the high level of trust of earlier years. On the whole therefore the image of the policeman does not tarnish readily in the area of his dependability.

Leadership

As we would anticipate, the children do not imagine that the policeman shines as a leader. They are somewhat restrained in their assessment of the qualities that we have assumed are associated with leadership (Table 8-1 and Figure 10-2). Nevertheless even though the child is not convinced that the policeman is outstanding for the leadership he displays, he is not thrown unceremoniously into the category of nonleader. Apparently the child sees the policeman as possessing a sufficiently different and prestigious role to merit something better than average in an assessment of leadership qualities. Hence in no instance does the average rating fall below the midpoint.

Furthermore, it is interesting that this conception the children have of the policeman is not modified radically by age. Although grade-8 children are clearly more likely to see the policeman as fallible than are those in grade 4, little change takes place in the evaluation of the other qualities over the grades. Little "disillusionment" would seem to occur. Even though the children think the policeman is only a moderately important decision maker and even somewhat less significant as a leader, they retain this estimate of him through grade 8. There is a rather unshakable conviction among the children of all grades that the policeman possesses something a little better than average prominence as a leader.

Summary

In comparison with the President there is little doubt that the child's feelings about the policeman are considerably muted. But if we look at the policeman ratings independently, it is clear that the child ranks him fairly high on all the cultural virtues to which the ratings refer. Certain qualities stand out in the child's image. The policeman is dependable by virtue of his capacity for persisting in what he does, he is quite trustworthy, and he plays some role as a decision maker. Above all else he is a benign figure, one who will help the child.

It is difficult to conclude that in comparison with the President the child idealizes the policeman. By *adult* standards the children are more "realistic" here. But if we had been able to construct some index of respect by collapsing all our ratings into a single measure,[8] we would have found that the child has a fairly high level of respect for the policeman, one that declines somewhat over the years but not substantially.[9] The child feels positively about the policeman but not overwhelmingly so except perhaps for some aspects of his benevolence and dependability.

RESPECT AND LEGITIMACY

It would be reasonable to infer from the general respect children show for the policeman that they would probably accept his authority on the grounds that it is right and proper to obey him. It would scarcely be likely that a child, or for that matter an adult, would express even such moderately favorable sentiments about a policeman without at the same time accepting the appropriateness or legitimacy of his powers. Piaget argues for the same point:

> It is not the obligatory character of the rule laid down by an individual that makes us respect this individual, it is the respect we feel for the individual that makes us regard as obligatory the rule that he lays down. The appearance of the sense of duty in a child thus admits of the simplest explanation, namely that he receives commands from older children (in play) and from adults (in life), and that he respects older children and parents. [10]

But if this is true, we have succeeded in exposing one of the taproots of support for any regime. It is axiomatic that few systems could persist if, for each decision, the authorities had to persuade or compel the members of the system to conform. In most systems the members do in fact come to accept the validity of the power of the authorities, within varying limits. The police represent an output terminus of the authority structure that is personally nearest to the daily lives of the members of the system.[11] If as children matured they came to despise, distrust, scorn, or reject the police, the probabilities would be considerable (assuming no compensatory mechanisms came into operation in later years) that acceptance of the whole structure of authority at all levels would suffer.[12]

Not that esteem in childhood for the police necessarily guarantees a continuing high level of input of support in adulthood. There are many years of experience ahead of the child which may deflect his sentiments away from the regime, about which we shall have more to say in Chapter 14. But if in the United States the nearest representatives of authority were rejected at the outset, because of the very few connecting points between the child and the structure of authority a major impediment would stand in the way of the growth of feelings about that structure. The Presidency might remain virtually alone for the earliest years of childhood, forced to carry the full burden for generating (or failing to generate) diffuse support among younger children. However unaware socialization research has been of this probable systemic consequence of the police, it is apparent from our data that they play a vital role in laying part of the foundation for the input of support.

Our analysis also incidentally points up the extent to which a major set of institutions—the law-enforcement agencies—have been neglected in political research and the need to bring the police into the study of politics in a more meaningful way. As we mentioned at the outset of our discussion, scholars have paid considerable attention to other aspects of the police but have generally failed to appreciate the central part that the police may play as a component of the authoritative output structure of a political system. As producers of outputs they are in a peculiarly appropriate and visible position to mediate between the members of a system and the rest of the structure of authority. It is a mediation that reveals itself particularly through the way in which the police may or may not contribute to the growth of a sense of legitimacy. By focusing on this aspect of the police we are able to bring knowledge of this institution to bear on an understanding of the process of legitimating political authorities, a central phenomenon in all political systems.

As important as the police, along with the President, may be for the generation of support, the importance of other possible major points of contact between the political system and the growing child, especially as he moves out of the early grades, is not diminished. We find a number of alternative objects crossing his political horizon as his attitudes toward political authorities continue to evolve. It is to these objects that we shall now turn.

NOTES

1. W. A. Westley, "The Police: A Sociological Study of Law, Custom, and Morality," in E. Burgess and D. W. Bogue (eds.), *Contributions to Urban Sociology* (Chicago: The University of Chicago Press, 1964), p. 307.
2. B. Gavzer, "The Policeman's Lot," *Wisconsin State Journal,* sec. 4, p. 5, September 5, 1965.
3. See R. Williams, "The Relations Between the Police and the Public," appendix 4 in Royal Commission on the Police, the *Minutes of Evidence* (London: H. M. Stationery Office, 1962); M. Banton, *The Policeman in the Community* (London: Tavistock, 1964); G. D. Gourley, "Public Relations and the Police," *The Annals of the American Academy of Political and Social Science,* 291, pp. 135-142, 1954.
4. Royal Commission on the Police, op. cit., p. 41.
5. Ibid.; Banton, op. cit.
6. Gourley, op. cit., p. 136; Banton, op. cit., pp. 95, 170-171.
7. In practice by far the largest percentage of the policeman's time is in fact spent not in crime detecting and prevention and law enforcement but in helping others: giving directions, providing emergency medical and ambulance services, regulating traffic, rescuing lost children, assisting stranded motorists, intervening in family quarrels, reporting neighborhood needs to the proper authorities, and the like.
8. We did not construct such an index in fact. Our various correlational and factor analyses indicated that these ratings do not combine into a single stable attitude across the grades. Hence we speak here only of an a priori index.
9. Six of the ratings decline with age, and the remaining seven are fairly stable (Figure 10-2).
10. J. Piaget, *The Moral Judgment of the Child* (New York: Free Press, 1948), p. 101.
11. This has at times been intuitively observed. "Mechanized police forces have by their very nature taken away some of the closeness that prevailed when beat men were the rule rather than the excep-

tion, and this naturally has taken away to some extent the personal contacts that policemen formerly had with neighborhoods and their peoples. In fact, the whole tenor of life has tended to get people away from the 'neighborliness' that was prevalent years ago. This in my opinion is responsible for some of the delinquency today among both juveniles and adults. Years ago, the beat man knew most of the people on his beat. Today, the police car is the symbol of authority, and the car and its occupants must now relate to the children in some positive way. This can and is being done." A. A. Ballard, "Policeman—the Children's Friend," *Childhood Education*, 35, p. 109, 1958.

12. We must bear in mind that our study includes almost exclusively white children. There may be some question about the way in which black children would respond to our items. With the mounting numbers and intensity of riots in the black ghettos during the 1960s and the hostility that all law-enforcement agencies have drawn down upon themselves, black children might be undergoing some important new generational experiences. But some very preliminary drawings by black children in one major slum suggest that they too may hold the policeman up as a model worth emulating, although, as we would expect, some important ambivalences begin to creep in. But even if young black children have absorbed white attitudes toward the police in the past, we would expect that if the polarization of the races continues significant changes in the orientations of black children will also occur. The potential impact on the early generation of support among blacks for the structure of authority is self-evident. For some hints about the attitudes of black children toward political authority see R. Coles, *Children of Crisis* (Boston: Little, Brown, 1967); and D. Jaros, "Children's Orientations Toward the President: Some Additional Theoretical Considerations and Data," *Journal of Politics,* 29, pp. 368-387, 1967, especially p. 381.

12

AUTHORITY OBJECTS IN LATER CHILDHOOD

The initial major points of contact between the children in our group and the structure of authority, we have seen, are to be found in the symbol "government" (personalized at first), in the President, and in the policeman. In the early years no other objects of authority loom so large for the child as to merit special treatment.

We could conceive that in some systems feelings and perceptions about the various figures of authority might come into serious conflict with each other. This would be especially likely where the individual authorities were themselves in open opposition — as where a monarch might be struggling against a parliament, a tribal chief against a new secular representative, or local officials against a strong centralizing government. In the face of contradictory messages sent out by authorities in the throes of conflict, primary socialization would undoubtedly leave a residue of tensions and uncertainty in children's developing political outlook.

As the children matured, their early experiences might help to push them in any one of a number of directions. Some might find themselves in an ambiguous state of mind about whom to regard as the legitimate authorities. Others might drift aimlessly about in the contradictory political currents. Still others might even be repelled by the regime entirely and retreat into an apolitical existence.

But it is apparent that in the American system for most children their orientations to political authority, whether at the national or local level as represented by our figures, or whether on a personal or institutional plane, are not antagonistic to one another. Indeed, if anything, all move in common to bolster up diffuse support. Any cursory inspection of the discrete analysis of the three objects of authority already completed testifies quickly to this essential congruence in outlook. Even with the decline that occurs by grade 8 for most items concerning the three objects, the level of overall respect remains fairly high, as we have observed.

Nonetheless we have unobtrusively been taking several matters for granted, and it is time that we brought these to the foreground for more careful scrutiny. We refer to three interrelated matters, each of which will help us to understand more fully the way in which our subjects continue to maintain their respect for the structure of authority as they move through childhood, even in the face of their declining enchantment with the personal facets of authority.

How acceptable is our assumption that the child is indeed aware of political authority as contrasted with authority in general? What happens to the child who may be unmoved by one or another of the objects of authority? How does the system manage to keep the respect of the child for the structure of authority after the earliest years, when the personal component no longer exercises its pristine powers; that is, does the process of political socialization then cease or fall into desuetude, or do other mechanisms arise to carry on the task?

Answers to these questions will help us to follow the political socialization of our subjects through the later years of their childhood. We shall briefly examine the nature of the problem posed by each question and then search for answers in this and the succeeding chapter.

ANALYSIS OF THE PROBLEMS

Political versus parental authorities: politicization

We have assumed that through the three objects of authority, the child is being connected in some way with the political system. But what evidence have we that those whom on theoretical grounds we designate as political authorities the children do in fact treat differently from other kinds of authorities? We have already touched on this in our consideration of the policeman. There we found some indication that in the policeman the child sees a power outside the family to which even adults are subordinate. Certainly in our interviews there was no question of the youngest children mistaking the policeman for a member of the family, nor was there any sign that the child thought either he or adults could escape the long arm of the law.

However, we require more evidence than this to demonstrate that the child has the capacity to differentiate at least between family and external authority. If the child is just evaluating the political authorities as father surrogates, this would lead us to suspect that all authority is homogeneous for him and that we are really not tapping any specifically political orientation in process of development. Yet without making some beginning not only in identifying political authorities but in differentiating them from parental authority, a political system would have to leave initiation into the political realm—early politicization—to some postchildhood phase of the life cycle.

The risk of support failure

Furthermore, although our assertion that because most of the children pile up on the positive side of the scales there is thus a pyramiding of respect for the three authority objects is certainly true for the children in the aggregate, it neglects a simple yet vital consideration. What happens to those children who find themselves in a minority for one or another of the figures of authority and who therefore may be less than enthusiastic about these authorities? Is their support lost to the system? Can the system hope to win them to a supportive stance toward political authority only at a later stage of life?

We are raising here the matter of how a system manages to cope with the risk that some children will be negative or indifferent to some of the authorities or about some of their qualities. To this point we have ignored these children. Now however we can take our phrase "most children display a favorable image toward the political authorities" and reverse it by asking: What provisions, if any, are found in the system for those who rate one or another authority low on one or another item? Do we find in the system any general way of compensating for the low regard that some children may have for some specific authorities?

Personal versus organizational objects of authority:
institutionalization

Finally, although we have emphasized repeatedly the personal nature of the initial bond between the child and the structure of authority, we have also seen that for the older children this mechanism seems to operate less effectively. For most qualities their estimates of the objects of authority tend to decline. It is possible that the process of positive socialization might stop at this point. The members might be so approving of the authorities as to require no further reinforcement. But even if they were, we would be left with the problem of understanding how a maturing member acquires the capacity and will to relate himself not to the personalized authorities but to those very impersonal institutions (organizations) by which at least all large-scale systems are governed. We can scarcely assume that just because the child may favor personal figures, such as the President and the policeman, or those organizations of authority to which he attributes initially some personal content, such as government, he must automatically spread his positive evaluations to cover impersonal institutions, such as the Supreme Court. About these he usually knows little even by grade 8. Yet without the member's attachment in some way to these organizational aspects of political authority and acceptance of them as legitimate, the system could scarcely operate except through constant coercion.

It is of course possible that all socialization about these impersonal units might be relegated to a later phase in the life cycle, one beyond our period of concern. We need however to test whether this is indeed so or whether even during the pre-adolescent period some beginning is made toward linking the child to these impersonal points in the system. Does personalization yield to what we might call the institutionalization of authority?

We plan, therefore, to explore the extent to which children as they grow older are able to differentiate parental and political authority, the process through which the system copes with unsuccessful efforts to generate diffuse support for some authorities some of the time, and the way in which orientations shift from personal to institutional objects of authority. To do so, we shall find it profitable to undertake first a systematic comparison of the child's images of various authorities. From it we shall understand better how in the American political system some of the possible gaps in the earliest phase of the socialization of diffuse support are closed.

THE SUBJECTS UNDER COMPARISON

In entering upon a comparison of the ratings of the various authorities, we shall seek to increase the potency of the analysis by adding to the kinds of authorities considered, over and above those we have already examined. Although the primary points of contact between the child and the political system are the policeman and the President, along with the idea of government itself as an overarching symbol of the structure of authority, this does not mean that these are the only objects through which the child relates himself to the structure of the regime. Other figures and institutions embodying political authority come within view of the child, especially as he progresses into the higher grades of elementary school. Indeed we already know that he is aware of the existence of Congress,[1] and we can reasonably suspect that several other major figures and institutions of authority leave some imprint on him.

Nevertheless for purposes of our inquiry several matters militate against any extensive analysis of the child's orientation to other objects. The President and the policeman represent without question the most salient and visible objects for the child from grade 2 upward. On occasion, as we have already noted, because of special circumstances a mayor, an alderman, a governor, or some other public official may gain sufficient prominence to be important in the political socialization of the child. But we suspect that these are idiosyncratic events and that concentration on them would have led us into too great a degree of specificity in our study before the broad trends had been sketched out. Most other major objects of political authority, such as the government, Congress, the Senate, or the Supreme Court, normally become known to the child during a period somewhat later than grade 2. In a developmental study such as ours, such objects therefore did not lend themselves as readily to cross-grade comparison through the elementary school span. Among those that emerge in midchildhood years, we selected government for more intensive analysis because it was the only concept through which the children seemed to be reaching out directly, even if vaguely and hesitantly, to the whole structure of authority.

Yet it did not seem wise to omit all other objects entirely, however late they moved into the child's range of vision, if only because we could obtain some preliminary ideas about the extent to which they joined the early objects as major socializing devices. Examination of other objects to which the child is exposed would help us to detect any special socializing experiences associated with them.

For the purpose, therefore, of adding to the variability of our authorities, we selected two additional objects of authority known to most children from at least grade 4, "the average United States senator" and the Supreme Court. As we shall presently learn, even the slight attention we gave to these two objects paid off handsomely. We discovered, to our surprise, that the average senator has far less salience in the political socialization of the child than any of the other figures and institutions examined. The inclusion of the Supreme Court, by contrast, enabled us to gain some new insight about an entirely different means through which, in the American political system, the child may be impressed with the virtues of the authority structure. Although originally we expected to use the Court primarily for the analysis of orientations toward legal rules—the regime norms and outputs of a political system—we found that the Court occupies a unique place in the process by which children relate themselves to the structure of authority.[2]

In one instance we have also gone beyond the political authorities for purposes of the additional light that comparison might shed on the development of the child's orientation to the political structure. On the assumption that there might be a relationship between the child's attitude toward political authority and parental authority, as Freudian-oriented psychology has been insisting for decades, we added "father" to the figures of authority. Although we leave to a later chapter discussion of the influence of the child's attitudes toward father on his orientations toward political authorities, we shall find it helpful here to introduce the data on father as something of a base line against which we can compare orientations toward political authority. In particular these data will help us to reexamine the notion, advanced in the analysis of the policeman, that the child is able in the earliest years to differentiate political from familial authority, a critical capability if support is to be generated for the political sphere directly.

In all, therefore, we shall be able to compare six objects of authority toward which the children in our group orient themselves: government, the President, the policeman, the average United States senator, the Supreme Court, and father. For some of these, it will be recalled, we have thirteen different qualities on which we have solicited the child's ratings. For others, because of certain requirements related to the child's mental capacity and to the availability of testing time, we do not have data at all grades, either for each characteristic or for each object.[3]

These data provide the basis for a comparison of the way in which our test children view the authorities. At the outset, it is important to bear in mind that the congruence of orientations already encountered for the government, President, and policeman continues for the other political objects we now include. Yet even though all ratings for all authorities lie at the positive end of the scales, there is considerable variability. Rating by rating and figure by figure variations unavoidably complicate the presentation of the findings. Nevertheless some patterns in orientations can be discerned, and these will help us to answer the questions we are posing about the developing ties between the children and the structure of authority as represented by our objects.

DIFFERENTIATION BETWEEN POLITICAL AND PARENTAL AUTHORITIES

If we look at the previous graphs for each figure of political authority and at Figure 12-1 for father as well, one difference stands out prominently.[4] For father, the average ratings on each of the thirteen items at the different grade levels are fairly constant. The average child at grade 2 is likely to rate his father somewhat the same as does the average child at grade 8. A few ratings do show some trends, and this is especially so for "He makes important decisions." But by and large the variation in any rating is slight. The relative stability of these feelings and perceptions implies that most children in our group are not likely to modify very much their expectations of their fathers' behavior or general personal attributes. This holds true even as these children grow older and learn more about their fathers.

The situation is notably different for political figures and institutions. If we now include the data we have on the average ratings for senator and Supreme Court (Figures 12-2 and 12-3), and if we briefly scrutinize again the ratings we have already presented for government, President, and policeman, it is apparent at once that the orientations of the older children toward these political authorities are quite different from those toward father. Most of the average ratings on the political items do not remain constant; they either rise or fall, as shown in Table 12-1. It would seem that as the average child in our group matures, what he learns about the political authorities encourages him to modify the points of view he held in an earlier grade.[5]

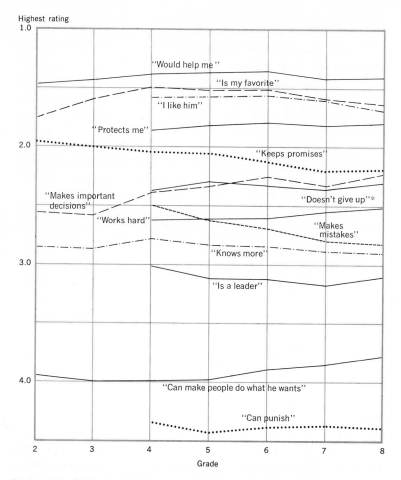

Figure 12-1. Children's Ratings of Their Fathers on Thirteen Attributes by Grade.
*Means of this rating were subtracted from 6.0 to make them more comparable with the rest.

This single datum reinforces a conclusion that we have already had occasion to draw from our findings on the child's orientations toward the policeman. The children in our group do not confuse familial authority, as manifested by father, with the political authorities in the outside world. Their feelings toward and perceptions of these external authorities change for the dimensions we examine; those about father either remain constant or shift to a far more limited extent.

Furthermore, if we look ahead for a moment to the figures compared in the rest of this chapter and note the rank in which

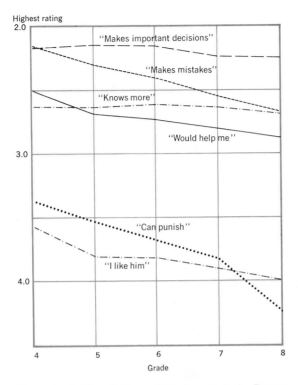

Figure 12-2. Mean Ratings of the Average U.S. Senator on Six Attributes by Grade.

the children place father on each item, we discover a strikingly uniform pattern. On those items that best express affectional content, such as the ratings about attachment and benevolence (Figures 12-4 to 12-7), father consistently ranks higher than any of the figures or institutions of political authority. The children display a higher level of affection for father and view him as more benevolent than any of the political authorities. As warmly as they may feel toward the President in particular, but toward other political authorities as well, there is little doubt that father merits their highest affection.

But as we move toward the more heavily cognitive items, where the child is asked to judge the extent to which both father and the figures and institutions of political authority possess certain role-performance properties, the child discriminates decisively in favor of the political authorities. On almost every item father recedes toward last place. Whether we look at the ratings denoting dependability, power, or leadership (Figures 12-8 to 12-16),

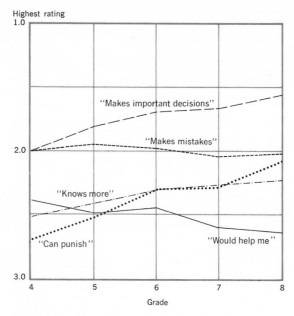

Figure 12-3. Mean Ratings of the Supreme Court on Five Attributes by Grade.

father consistently ranks lowest at each grade, with one or two exceptions. For persistence ("He never gives up when things are hard to do") and diligence ("He works harder"), father occupies a position between the President and the policeman. In the only two other cases (out of nine) in which father does not fall into last place in the rank order—trustworthiness ("He keeps his promises") and importance as a decision maker—the difference between father and the lowest object of political authority is slight.

Certainly by grade 4, the young child whose knowledge of the political sphere is not yet very extensive has nonetheless grasped the basic notion that the political authorities are different from father in important respects. They may be less lovable, but they are more capable. The children in our group are obviously not reacting to the authority figures—parental or political—without some pronounced differences in expectations about their behavior and outright likableness. They have taken an important step toward becoming politicized, toward recognizing a difference between the familial and political spheres.

We are of course not surprised that children should like father more; we would have expected this to be so. But common sense might have led us to assume that proximity of father and gen-

Table 12 - 1   Differences in Mean Ratings of Authorities for Earliest and Latest Grades Available*

Set Name	Item	Govern- ment	Pres- ident	Police- man	Senator	Supreme Court	Father
Attach- ment	Is my favorite†		− 1.10	− 1.74			.12
	I like him‡		− .20	− .54	− .44		−.10
Benevo- lence	Would want to help (helpfulness)	− .34‡	− .84†	− .13†	− .39‡	− .22‡	.06†
	Protects me‡ (protectiveness)		− .29	− .06			.06
Depend- ability	Keeps promises† (trustworthiness)		− .54	− .74			− .24
	Makes mistakes‡ (infallibility)	− .29	− .47	− .56	− .54	− .02	− .32
	Gives up‡ (persistence)		.24	− .01			.10
Power	Can make others do† (control)		− .53	− .18			.19
	Can punish‡ (sanctions)	.44	− .36	− .09	− .88	.64	− .03
Leader- ship	Knows more (knowledgeability)	.22‡	− .34†	− .53†	− .06‡	.31‡	− .05†
	Makes important decisions (decision maker)	.36‡	.31†	− .09†	.09‡	.44‡	.32†
	Works harder‡ (diligence)		− .09	− .30			.12
	Is a leader‡		.16	.01			− .09

*A minus sign (−) indicates that the eighth-grade rating is less positive or favorable than that of the earlier grade. Except on the persistence item, the eighth-grade mean would actually be a higher number on the rating scales used.

†Grades 2 through 8.   ‡Grades 4 through 8.

eral admiration for him that we attribute to the average pre-adolescent would have induced the children to have ranked him equal with or above all the political figures on most other characteristics as well. At the very least we might have imagined that the President alone, because of the peculiar position the Chief Executive plays in the American system, might have surpassed father. But such is not the case, and this perhaps helps to explain the very early stage in life at which diffuse support seems to take root in American society. If children confused political and familial authority, there would be little opportunity to begin the acquisition of supportive sentiments about specifically political objects. Not that the child spontaneously has the vocabulary to articulate the difference that he senses between the familial and political worlds. It is enough that he is able to identify specifically different feelings and perceptions about these orders of existence. In the next chapter we shall return to the significance of this differentiating capacity as it affects the input of support for the structure of authority.

DIFFERENTIATION AMONG AND INSTITUTIONALIZATION OF POLITICAL AUTHORITIES

Not only does the child sort out political authorities in the aggregate from father, he also gradually becomes aware of the existence of differences among political authorities themselves. He does not like all political authorities equally well. Nor does he consider them all to be endowed with similar degrees of role competence. He develops a finer level of discrimination, one that is of considerable consequence for the extension of support to these authorities.

Aside from any consideration of the child's subjective capacity to discriminate in the political sphere, there are objective, theoretical grounds why we could not be satisfied with the idea that maturing members simply orient themselves to political authorities in the aggregate, undifferentiated as to type or characteristics. If this were so, we would have to conclude that a political system depended entirely on one omnibus set of objects for socializing its members with respect to authority. Although it is possible that in a given system all eggs might be put in one basket in this way, it is more likely that the risks in a system would be spread more widely. It might not be essential for the maturing member to hold all authorities in uniformly high regard; his support might still be won if he held a favorable image of only some of the authorities.

Whether or not the risks are spread in all systems in this way, we find that in the American political system the maturing members of our test group are offered alternative paths for relating themselves to the political authorities. If the child fails to develop supportive sentiments about the general structure of political authority from his understanding of one object of authority, he might develop them with another. We shall conclude among other things that the availability of these alternatives may be one determinant of system stability in the United States, although both system comparisons and intrasystem longitudinal research would be necessary to confirm this speculation.

High affect ratings of the authorities

We can appreciate the differential impact that varying objects of political authority might have, and therefore the way in which the American system in fact manages to spread the risk of failing to generate diffuse support, by comparing the ways in which children see and feel about authorities. We shall begin with the area of the developing sentiments the children express for various individual figures of authority. This will again point up one device for linking the child to the system: the emphasis in the earlier grades on personal figures of authority rather than impersonal organizations. But we shall now find that not all personal figures act with equal potency on the child across the grades and that in this variability lie alternative routes, for the child, to the structure of authority.

As we have observed, father emerges at the top of the list on all attachment and benevolence ratings (Figures 12-4 to 12-7), commanding far more affection than any of the political authorities. He provides us with a maximal level of affection against which others may be compared. But among the political authorities not all objects are able to elicit a uniform measure of affective response. For our most openly affective items (Figures 12-4 and 12-5), as we would expect from our previous detailed analysis, the President stands closest to father in the degree of affection displayed by the child. The President evokes far more affiliative sentiment than does the policeman or senator. What is also noteworthy is the position of the senator. He falls well below the policeman on our scale of likableness. By grade 8 he lies for the aggregate somewhere near the weak statement that the children like him only "more than some people."

Thus to the extent that affect spills over from our political objects to the regime structure as a whole, the President as a linkage point for the child would seem to be of considerably greater potency than either the policeman or the senator. To be sure, the feelings for all figures move in the same positive direction, even if there are clear differences in level, depending upon the object and attribute being considered. But from these differences we can infer that the President has greater potentiality for tying the child to the structure of political authority than either of the other figures of authority tested on these items.

The real diversity and multiplicity of mechanisms available in the system for stimulating diffuse support are evident from

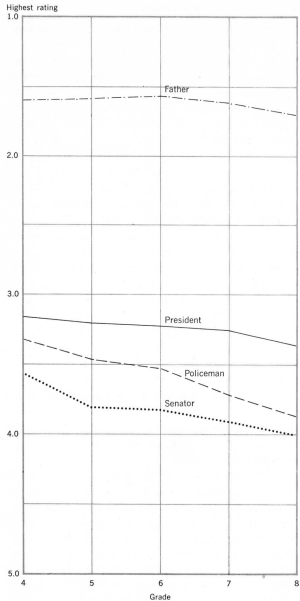

Figure 12-4. Mean Rating by Grade on "I like him" for Senator, Policeman, President, and Father.

the changing rank order of the political objects. We see this with special clarity in the area of perceived benevolence. The system does not need to rely on how each child feels about or sees the

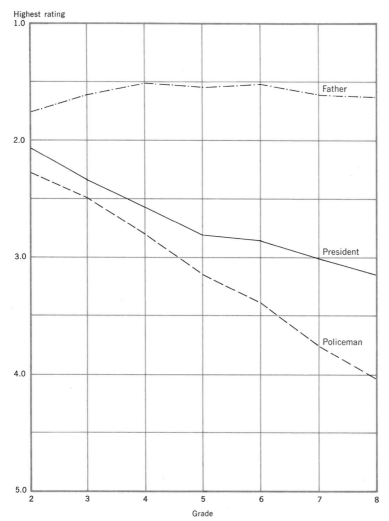

Figure 12-5. Mean Rating by Grade on "He is my favorite" for Policeman, President, and Father.

President. Other objects of authority move in and become prominent in the positive socialization of new members about the structure of authority.

In Figure 12-6 we see a comparison of father, policeman, and President on our protectiveness rating from grades 4 to 8. We find here that the child on the average thinks the policeman is more protective of him than is the President, and the father is most protective of all three. All these authorities are fairly stationary in the level of endorsement on this rating across the grades. The President drops a little, but for the most part the order of perceived protectiveness of each is established early and continues at the same level to grade 8.

For helpfulness, on the other hand, Figure 12-7 shows that a somewhat greater sense of psychic distance appears for the President. After the earliest grades the policeman and father remain at the same general higher level. The child regards these two closer authorities as more likely to help him than are the spatially more remote figures of President and senator, or than are the impersonal authorities, the Supreme Court and government.

Figure 12-6. Mean Rating by Grade on "He protects me" for Policeman, and Father.

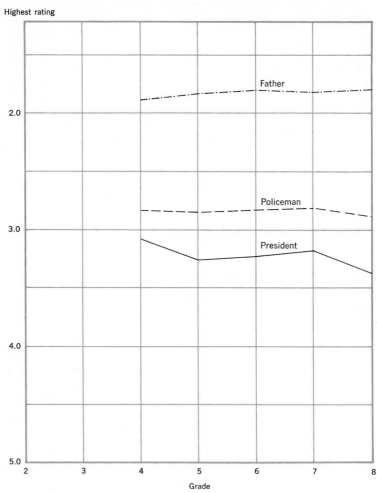

Again the senator is the most remote of all, even more so than the impersonal Supreme Court. We see how radically different is the perception of these authorities in this part of the child's affective image.

Physical proximity seems to be highly important for perception in this area. The expectation that the child has of aid and comfort varies with the spatial distance of the authority in question. Among the remote authorities, however, the President is still the most salient and the senator the least. For benevolence— help and protection—therefore there is a fairly sharp degree of sorting out of authorities.

Generally speaking, then, the child readily distinguishes among authorities on the various ratings for affection and benevolence. For all authorities the high level of regard rules out any possibility of the encouragement of negative support, but feelings run higher in the earlier grades for all the political authorities. Although the average child shows a fairly clear pattern of image differentiation for affection and benevolence, the precise rating of each figure depends a good deal on the specific item. Each is somewhat different. The child likes the President better than the policeman but regards the latter as a more likely source of assistance. The senator ranks considerably lower on all items, and the institutions do not fare much better.

Figure 12 - 7. Mean Rating by Grade on "Would help me if I needed it" for Senator, Government, Supreme Court, President, Policeman and Father.

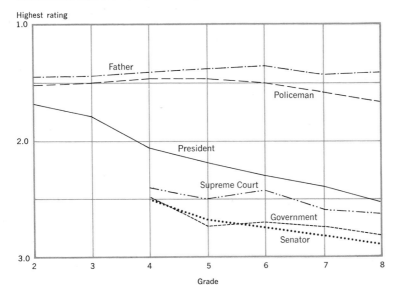

To catch the younger child's sentiments, therefore, the system places heaviest reliance on two different representatives: the President when direct affect is at stake, and the policeman in the matter of direct benevolence. On the limited measurements that we have, the Supreme Court and government as institutions and the senator make far less of a contribution. But they do draw favorable responses, even if at a lower level. It is clear therefore that, objectively speaking, there is some spreading of the risk here, ensuring that a favorable affective contact is made at one or another point in the structure of authority.

High cognitive ratings

When we move on to those items that reveal a more complex mixture of affect and perceptions, several things are clear. First, the child evidences a continuing ability, even when dealing with attributes other than those representing high affect, to distinguish his perceptions of father from those of political authorities. Second, the child displays a subtle capacity for differentiating among the individual political authorities themselves. He does not blanket them with a single, monotonic evaluation or locate them all in a uniform role of authority; he reports authority-specific kinds of perceptions, revealing thereby a capacity to differentiate among political authority roles. Third, especially as we move to the older child, we find that he gradually reorders his orientations toward personal figures of authority compared with institutional representations. The last two conclusions will be supported particularly by the items having highest cognitive content, those touching on performance in political roles (power and leadership).

To present these findings we shall now examine the ratings set by set. We shall then be in a position to draw in the next chapter some of the possible general implications for the socialization of diffuse support.

On the dependability items as a whole (Figures 12-8 to 12-10), covering trustworthiness, fallibility, and persistence, the tendencies just noted begin to emerge. However, as we have seen before,[6] because these items entail a considerable commingling of affect and cognition, we would not expect the effects to be as pronounced as with other items of higher cognitive content.

In Figure 12-8, the child's rating of policeman, father, and President are shown for their trustworthiness ("He keeps his promises"). This figure also reports evaluations about an additional category of political actors, "people who try to get elected," that is, politicians who are candidates for public office. Candidates are of course not political authorities. But we included them on our questionnaire for a different theoretical reason, and on this rating we have data comparable with those for the three authorities.

Of these the President is thought most apt to keep his promises, even though all the authorities are close over the whole range. Father drops to third place until sixth grade, when he moves up into second place. Political candidates, on the other hand, remain at some distance, receiving a considerably lower average rating than any of the other three. We see here the first suggestion of a theme that other data, unreported in this book, bear out more fully. There is a distinctive gap between the child's evaluation of the formal political authorities and of those political actors who participate in the system more informally.

Thus the child rates candidates lower than his own father in trustworthiness. Even the ten- or eleven-year-old child has inter-

Figure 12-8. Mean Rating by Grade on "He keeps his promises" for Candidates, Father, Policeman, and President.

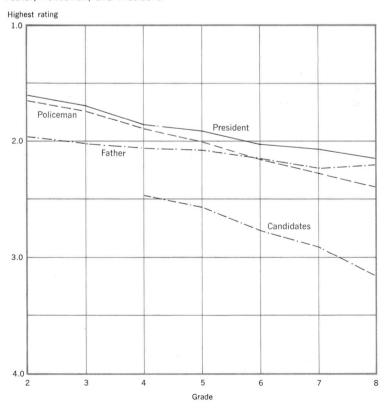

nalized a view of a person running for public office. The child is by no means as unequivocally positive about political candidates as he is about those who are already in public office. By the middle grades a little distrust and skepticism have already crept into the consciousness of the average child in our sample. The candidates come off second best right from the beginning, even before the child has very much of an idea of what electioneering is about. As he grows older and presumably learns more about what a candidate is, his regard for them drops. For present purposes the item on the candidates helps to confirm our conclusion about the early capacity of children to differentiate rather finely various types of objects in the political sphere and to react to them differently.

A full understanding of the implications of this assessment of candidates for the political system must await some future analysis of the child's perceptions of the political process. But in this work it can be said that there is no necessary inconsistency in the child's holding a positive image of the political authorities and a more jaundiced view of the occupants or potential occupants of these roles as they act in a somewhat different capacity. He may be skeptical about the trustworthiness of candidates or perhaps even of authorities acting as politicians or contenders for office. But he may at the same time hold these very persons in high esteem while they act within the expected limits of an authority role. This is a rather fine discrimination, one that a child might not be able to understand intellectually. But in practice it would seem that the child is indeed groping for it intuitively.

On our persistence item (Figure 12-9), all three authorities are rated fairly high. Here too the President outranks father. But father in turn is perceived as less likely to give up than is the policeman. Only for the President is there much change over the years, and it is in a positive direction.

Fallibility (Figure 12-10), the last item of those connected with the general trait of dependability, is a quality that children show they associate specifically with political objects, in this case, political institutions. The Supreme Court emerges as the authority least likely to make mistakes, with the government running a close second, followed by President, senator, policeman, and father in that order. At grade 4 the young child is least able to distinguish the performance of two institutions (the Supreme Court and the government) from that of the President, placing all three at about the same average position on the scale. But

Highest rating

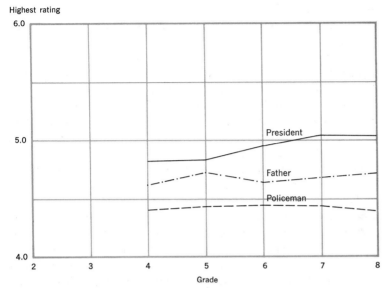

Figure 12 - 9. Mean Rating by Grade on "He doesn't give up when things are hard to do" for Policeman, Father, and President.

in grade 5 the child is able to discriminate among these authority objects clearly, and this continues to the end of our age span.

The special position of one institution, the Supreme Court, is emphasized. All the authorities except the Court show an increase in their fallibility as the age of the children increases; the evaluation of the Court is virtually constant. Somehow the aura of wisdom

Figure 12 - 10. Mean Rating by Grade on "Makes few mistakes" for Father, Senator, Policeman, Government, Supreme Court, and President.

Highest rating

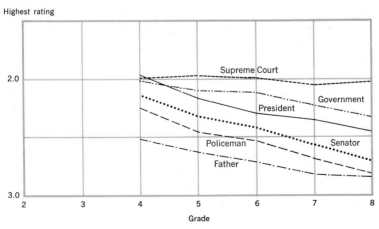

which most adults probably associate with the Court[7] becomes apparent very early and continues undiminished throughout childhood.

This special status for the Court seems to be part of an orientation that leads the children, the older they become, to attribute lower degrees of fallibility to institutions than to persons in the political sphere. Aside from the Supreme Court all authorities decline at about the same rate. Of these, the institution of government holds up best and maintains second place at grade 8.

In these ratings we get the first inkling of the possibility that age brings with it a reorientation in the salience of objects of authority. The younger children, below grade 4, find it hard to grasp the meaning of institutions as well as they do that of personal figures. Institutional names are not known to most of them, or when they are, as with government, a personal meaning is imputed to them. But among the older children there is little difficulty in coping with such political concepts as the Supreme Court or government. More importantly, they clearly treat these institutions differently from the personal figures. We can only wonder whether if we had been able to include institutions in the previous two items of this set, the same pattern in favor of institutions would have arisen.

What is first noticeable in our analysis of the previous dependability ratings becomes fully apparent in the more highly cognitive items, those reflecting judgment of performance through power and leadership. For the three ratings on which we were able to seek evaluations about the institutions (Figures 12-11, 12-13, and 12-14), there is a tendency for these objects of authority to obtain an ascendant position over the personal figures. In two out of three ratings, by grade 8, government and the Supreme Court stand highest (Figures 12-11 and 12-13). In the third, although the President emerges supreme, government and the Supreme Court follow very closely on his heels (Figure 12-14). Furthermore, the differentiation of parental from political authority continues unabated.

On our power ratings the institutions quickly assert their primacy in the eyes of the children. On our item dealing with the ability to punish (Figure 12-11), by grade 5 the average child concludes that the Supreme Court and the government have the greatest capacity. The policeman and the President run closely behind with the senator and father falling far behind. This ordering suggests that if we had included the institutions on our next rating, the power to make others do something (Figure 12-12), we would probably have discovered somewhat the same ranking for institutions and personal figures.

But these power items tell us something more. In Figure 12-12 we observe the average ratings for the three primary authorities on "He can make anyone do what he wants." Here father is considerably below the President and the policeman over the whole range. There is some narrowing of the differential in the later grades, but it is still large. The child thus sorts out once again very early the relative capacities of the political authorities with respect to father. But unlike the items tapping affect, here father ranks well behind the political authorities. This reversal itself gives unmistakable evidence again that the child makes

Figure 12-11. Mean Rating by Grade on "Can punish people" for Father, Senator, President, Policeman, Government, and Supreme Court.

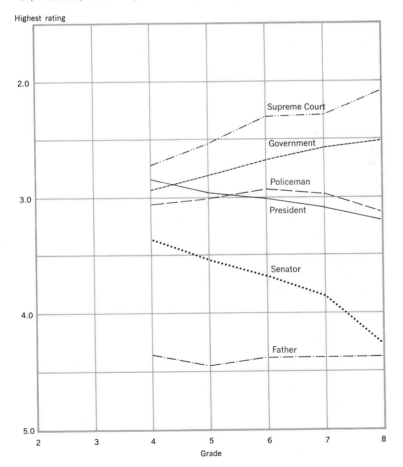

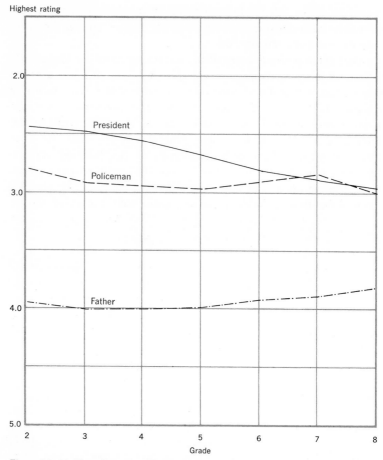

Figure 12-12. Mean Rating by Grade on "He can make anyone do what he wants" for Father, Policeman, and President.

fairly well-defined assessments of parental authority. He has some well-articulated ideas about what it can and cannot do in comparison with other authorities such as the political.

It is interesting, moreover, that the child underrates the power of the President relative to the policeman. The child is not so much in awe of the President as to gloss over his limitations, and this propensity increases in the later grades. The policeman as seen by the child is a moderately powerful agent of law enforcement. His coercive capacities seem to the child to be fairly high.

There are plausible reasons for the child to assess policemen close to the President in his punitive and coercive potentials. As we have observed in our chapter on the policeman, the child has the opportunity, in his own experience or from mass media, to perceive the policeman in the process of exercising his powers. The most usual category of observed acts has to do with controlling the actions of others. But the President's power, although much greater in scope, is considerably less visible. He is not usually observed in the performance of punitive or coercive acts, nor are such acts as intimately and directly associated with his role as they are with that of the policeman. Rather, the President is generally seen by the child as smiling, waving, talking, shaking hands, or in other agreeable postures.

The effect of these different images of the President and the policeman is clearly reflected in Figure 12-11; here the policeman's rating on the capacity to punish is somewhat higher than that of the President from grade 6 on. He is exceeded only by the government and the Supreme Court. Of the authorities included, it is the latter which is perceived by the growing child to have greatest punitive powers, and this becomes ever more apparent as he matures. The President, on the other hand, loses ground, but not as precipitously as does the senator. The government takes on a kind of average value between policeman and Supreme Court and increases in a linear fashion on perceived capacity to punish. Father, by contrast, is low and stable in the child's perception across the grades.

Thus, even by grade 4 the child has sorted out quite clearly, on the power dimension, the general role of political authorities from that of parental authority. He already knows that the representatives of political authority (even if he cannot identify them explicitly) far exceed his own father in power, in the limited sense of our items. Among the personal figures the policeman, for special reasons associated with the attributes tested, vies even with the President in this perception. But the President holds his own very well relative to the senator, who declines very rapidly. Finally, from grade 4 on there is again a well-defined differentiation among the political authorities. The institutions begin to loom large in power and the personal authorities to decline.[8]

In our other major set of performance characteristics, those included in our general category of leadership, we find similar tendencies for the child to view institutions of authority with the highest regard. On knowledgeability, father is clearly in the lowest rank across the grades (Figure 12-13). President and policeman stand at the top. But when we test for all authorities in grade 4, we find that the ranks of these two personal figures have already declined, and by grade 8 the government and the Supreme Court edge out even the President in the extent to which

Highest rating

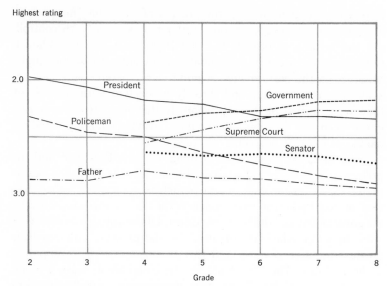

Figure 12-13. Mean Rating by Grade on "Knows more than others" for Father, Senator, Supreme Court, Policeman, Government, and President.

children consider them to possess expertise. Similarly, in the matter of making important decisions (Figure 12-14), although the President always stands out as the paramount decision maker, for obvious reasons, the increasing authoritativeness of institutions becomes manifest. The government and the Supreme Court run a very close second and third by grade 8.

Some important shifting to institutional authorities therefore begins to take place by grade 8, which represents a highly significant change in the points of contact with the child for the American system. We shall pursue this further in the succeeding chapter. But now if we add our two other items on leadership— "He works harder" (Figure 12-15) and "He is a leader" (Figure 12-16)— to the two just discussed we can appreciate that the child never drifts too far from what was one of his very earliest objects of political awareness, the President.

On his working capacity and leadership ability the President draws some of the highest mean scores among all the ratings. Unfortunately we do not have comparable data about institutions on these items, but it would be surprising if either government or the Supreme Court would surpass the President. The strength of the President's appeal here and on "He makes important decisions" would lead us to believe that however much the child may revise his estimate of those authorities he initially considered worthy of the highest esteem, the President continues

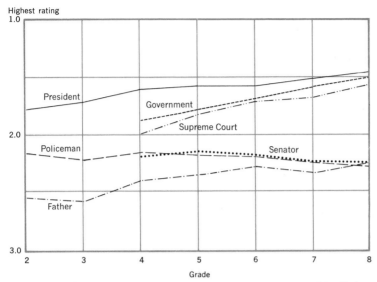

Figure 12-14. Mean Rating by Grade on "Makes important decisions" for Father, Senator, Policeman, Supreme Court, Government, and President.

to have a great deal to do, even in grade 8, with linking the child to the structure of authority. Whether this is so because he is the President or because he is a personal figure of authority and the child can consequently relate to him with relative ease is a question to which we shall return in the next chapter.

Figure 12-15. Mean Rating by Grade on "He works hard" for Policeman, Father, and President.

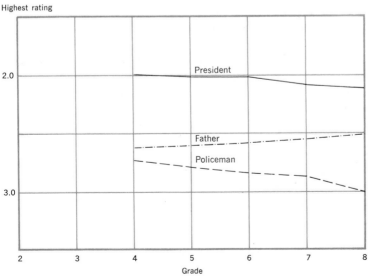

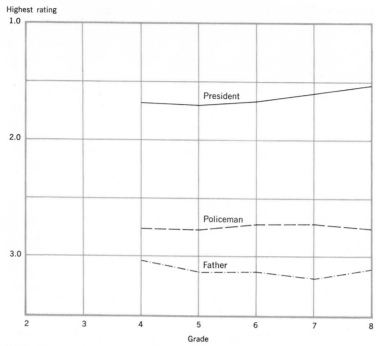

Highest rating

Grade

Figure 12-16. Mean Rating by Grade on "He is a leader" for Father, Policeman, and President.

CONCLUSION

To sum up what we learn from a comparison of the ratings, our test children do not see or feel about all objects of authority in identical terms. Especially as they move into the higher grades, they are able to discriminate among these objects, and in three different ways. First, they clearly consider that there is a sharp difference, on affective and performance characteristics, between father as an authority and that kind of authority outside the family that we have designated as political. Political authority is not just parent writ large; some politicization, or capacity to differentiate political from familial authority, has begun. We have here reaffirmed a previous finding of the same sort.[9]

Second, the children differentiate among the political authorities themselves. There is not just one universal role of political authorities. The child sees a variety of political roles and has little difficulty describing their differences. He has varying expectations dependent on the object and the quality. We have perhaps discovered a way in which some systems, if the American is not unique, may vary the contacts between children and the structure of authority. The availability of a number of attractive authorities in a political system may enable it to hedge against the risk of support failure, which might easily follow from excessive reliance on any single means to win the respect of the maturing member.

It is significant that by grade 8 the child has acquired a considerable ability to identify and describe varying kinds of political roles and to distinguish them from the parental role. It reveals a relatively high level of socialization during childhood about structural phenomena in politics. However much or little the child may have absorbed from his environment about partisan (allocative) politics, he has achieved some degree of sophistication in breaking down his external world into some of its components, one of which is the political structure. In the next chapter we shall find how vital this capacity is as a means for ensuring diffuse support during childhood.

Finally, even though the children are initially attracted to personal objects in the political sphere, and this tendency persists in some degree across the grades, they do not remain fixed in this mold. Somewhat earlier we had some forewarning of what we could expect to occur. In our chapter on "The Image of Government" we witnessed a decided shift from persons as the best representative of government to institutions such as Congress or practices such as voting. We have now discovered that this is symptomatic of a more general capacity, with age, to establish ties with and to take note of impersonal units of authority. *Institutionalization* begins to displace personalization of political authority.

But of what significance are these findings for our understanding of the early sources of support? As intrinsically interesting as these findings may be, we know that our main purpose does not lie in determining how children come to distinguish the political from the nonpolitical world or how they acquire knowledge and feelings about the political world. In themselves these matters could scarcely offer a justifiable primary focus for political research. Our concern rather is with a theoretical problem in understanding the functioning of political systems: How do systems, such as the American, create support, whether positive or negative, with respect to the regime structure? Unless our comparative analysis of the ratings points toward some significant consequences in the area of diffuse support, it will have little meaning for our objectives. It is to the system implications of the data, therefore, that we turn in the following chapter.

NOTES

1. See Chapter 6.
2. We now suspect we might profitably have included Congress as another institution for intensive analysis, especially in light of its prominence during later years in the child's image of government.
3. See Table 8 - 1.
4. For government, see p. 135; for President, see p. 178; for policeman, see p. 225.
5. We would draw attention again to the major assumption of our synthetic longitudinal design: that in their political orientations, our younger children look like our older children would have looked if we had tested them at the appropriate chronological age. See Appendix.
6. See Table 8 - 1 and discussion about it.
7. See K. M. Dolbeare, "The Public Views the Supreme Court," in H. Jacob (ed.), *Law, Politics and the Federal Courts* (Boston: Little, Brown, 1967), pp. 194 - 212; K. M. Dolbeare and P. E. Hammond, "The Political Party Basis of Attitudes Toward the U.S. Supreme Court," *Public Opinion Quarterly,* 32, pp. 16 - 30, 1968; W. F. Murphy and J. Tanenhaus, "Public Opinion and the United States Supreme Court: A Preliminary Mapping of Some Prerequisites for Court Legitimation of Regime Changes," a paper delivered at the Shambaugh Conference on Judicial Research, University of Iowa, October, 1967; and "Public Opinion and Supreme Court: The Goldwater Campaign," *Public Opinion Quarterly,* 32, pp. 31 - 50, 1968; and J. Kessel, "Public Perceptions of the Supreme Court," *Midwest Journal of Political Science,* 10, pp. 167 - 191, 1966.
8. We could perhaps speculate that it is law-enforcement and application which hold special sway in the child's early judgments about which authorities are the punishing kind. This function is not so much associated with the President or the senator probably because their main functions are focused elsewhere — upon initiation of policy or making of the laws, according to which transgressors can be punished. Somehow lurking beneath the surface of the child's response to political authority is a triad of law, crime, and punishment. Research is needed to probe more fully into this aspect of political socialization. For the time being we can only guess at the meaning of Figure 12 - 11 and at how it reflects the significant roles of law, lawmaking, law-abidingness, and law-enforcement in the young child's introduction to the power of political authority in the American system.
9. See Chapters 10 and 11.

13

SHIFTING IMAGES
AND SUPPORT
FOR THE SYSTEM

 The comparative analysis of the ratings for
the various objects, in the preceding chapter, reveals the way in
which during later childhood images of the political authorities
undergo some substantial changes. These changes open the door to
some suggestive speculations about the implications of our findings for the input of diffuse support to the structure of authority.

What we have to say applies of course only to our 12,000 children. However, until further research demonstrates the contrary,
we may temporarily assume that the distribution of orientations
in our subjects is not atypical of white, metropolitan, public school
children in the society as a whole. At a minimum this assumption
will provide us with a set of hypotheses for subsequent testing;
at most, it will help to illuminate some probable early sources
of diffuse support in the American system as a whole.

EARLY POLITICIZATION AND THE INPUT OF SUPPORT

Let us turn first to the support implications of our findings about the child's capacity to differentiate political authorities from persons such as father and from political candidates. This capacity has been confirmed in two ways: by the consistency with which the children favor father on the affective attributes and the political authorities on those dealing with performance, and by the clear difference that children discern between the formal political authorities and would-be authorities, the political candidates. This has helped to reinforce the earlier evidence we found for the policeman in Chapters 10 and 11. There we had noted that through the police the child conceives of a power outside the family and superior to it. It is clear that the child has little difficulty in discriminating rather narrowly between qualities that he would associate with parental authority and those he would use to describe the external authority we have been labeling political. He orients himself differently to each type, and this presents us with some important evidence about the growth of a consciousness of a uniquely extrafamilial sphere of authority. In this sense the child learns to be sensitive to the political dimension of his world; he is becoming politicized. Indeed his awareness has been so sharply refined that he is able to distinguish rather precisely his image of political candidates from that of formal political authorities. The latter stand out as unmistakably different and more laudable.

More than this however is implied in our data. We clearly have here the beginning of a discrimination of roles. The child has different levels of expectation for father and the external authorities. We cannot say that he has qualitatively different expectations about the characteristics of their behavior, for we have tested both father and the external authorities on the same attributes. But our investigation does demonstrate that the child expects father to be more lovable and benign, with the political authorities displaying greater dependability, power, and leadership. These are marked and systematic differences in expectations. Their frequency distribution among our subjects suggests that these expectations have the regularity about them that we find in other kinds of role identifications.[1] At the very least the child is distinguishing between internal roles of authority, those found within the family, and external roles, those found outside.

This is a phenomenon of fundamental importance for a political system, especially for the input of support. Undoubtedly in some systems—such as those in which there is little structural differentiation between parental and political authority, as where the basic social unit is the extended lineage group—the political system can claim no support that is readily distinguishable, formally, from the family head.[2] But in structurally differentiated societies such as the United States we can now identify the way in which an autonomous support base may begin to evolve.

As the child at an astonishingly early period begins to discern a difference between familial and external authority roles, a solid base is laid down in the system for the development of two different capabilities critical for its persistence. First, the growing child has increasing, regularized differences in expectations about authorities. Thereby he is in fact being socialized about structural elements in the political system. He is coming to recognize specific components in the political structure as contrasted with the family.

For so highly differentiated a social system as we find in the United States, this is a central outcome of the socializing processes. As in all other modern industrialized societies, if the child confused political with familial authority roles, the political system would find itself hard put to draw the child out of the family environment. This would impair the ability of the system to activate him, at a later period in his life, for nonfamilial, society-wide purposes, unless of course in the interval some other kinds of socializing experiences were to bear the whole burden for moving the maturing member in the same direction.

Indeed in many developing political systems in which lineage groups are carried over from the original tribal societies, it is this very reluctance of members to acknowledge authority outside the extended family group that interferes with the capacity of the newly formed political system to win enough support to provide viability for its political authorities. Where lineage groups are able to lay prior claim to the loyalty of their members, one may well wonder whether primary socialization does not help to produce this result by reversing the process we find in the American system. That is to say, we would expect to find that children in lineage-dominated systems probably learn to view external authority as inferior to lineage authority.

To return to the American system, however, it is true that we have not determined whether external authority is itself broken down by the child into different spheres. If he did not so break it down, he would not be able to distinguish *political* authority from the authority that others, such as a church, scout organization, gang leader, or musical director may exercise over him from time to time. Our study leaves this a moot point. But the weight of evidence would indicate that by grade 4 or 5 the child is not likely to confuse the authority of other institutions with that of the President, policeman, or Supreme Court. We would conclude, therefore, that there is a strong probability in the American system that through the central elements in its structure of authority the child develops very early a sense of the political sphere.

As the child becomes aware of the structure of political authority and can relate to it in role-specific terms, conditions in the system make it possible to begin to evoke diffuse support from him. At the same time as the child begins to perceive authorities beyond the small circle of the family—as he becomes politicized— he develops positive sentiments about them. This occurs during childhood, well before the maturing member has the capacity for rational evaluation of alternatives. The system thereby begins to build up diffuse support on which, if later experiences do not deflect the child, authorities and others in the system may subsequently call. If what is early impressed on a person endures, the early origins of support fortify the probability that this support will be available later in the life cycle. This may be an important source of the relative durability of the American structure of authority in the past.

THE INSTITUTIONALIZATION OF AUTHORITY

In the previous chapter we adduced some considerable evidence of the child's capacity to shift his attention and regard from personal to institutional objects of political authority. We shall now return to this point to establish it more firmly and to pursue its implications for explaining a further source of diffuse support.

Our earlier comparison of the individual items revealed that the older the child, the higher is his evaluation of the institutions of authority (government, Supreme Court) on our measures of role performance likely to be. We can now see this even more clearly in Table 13 - 1, which presents the way in which the child ranks each object of authority, at all grades, on each of the attributes. If we confine our attention to those attributes tested for all five objects of political authority, we can observe that the older children tend to give a higher ranking to our two institutions on the performance items.

Thus for infallibility, at grade 4 the rank order was President, Supreme Court, and government. By grade 8 President drops to

Table 13-1   Rank of All Objects of Authority on Each Attribute (by grade)

Set Name	Item	Grade	Govern- ment	Pres- ident	Police- man	Sen- ator	Supreme Court	Father
Attach- ment	Is my favorite	2		2	3			1
		4		2	3			1
		8		2	3			1
	I like him	2						
		4		2	3	4		1
		8		2	3	4		1
Benevo- lence	Would want to help (helpfulness)	2		3	2			1
		4	5	3	2	6	4	1
		8	5	3	2	6	4	1
	Protects me (protectiveness)	2						
		4		3	2			1
		8		3	2			1
Depend- ability	Keeps promises (trustworthiness)	2		1	2			3
		4		1	2			3
		8		1	3			2
	Makes mistakes (infallibility)	2						
		4	2.5	1	5	4	2.5	6
		8	2	3	5	4	1	6
	Gives up (persistence)	2						
		4		1	3			2
		8		1	3			2
Power	Can make others do (control)	2		1	2			3
		4		1	2			3
		8		1	2			3
	Can punish (sanctions)	2						
		4	3	2	4	5	1	6
		8	2	4	3	5	1	6
Leader- ship	Knows more (knowledgeability)	2		1	2			3
		4	2	1	3	5	4	6
		8	1	3	5	4	2	6
	Makes important decisions (decision maker)	2		1	2			3
		4	2	1	4	5	3	6
		8	2	1	6	5	3	4
	Works harder (diligence)	2						
		4		1	3			2
		8		1	3			2
	Is a leader	2						
		4		1	2			3
		8		1	2			3

third place. In the matter of sanctions ("He can punish"), ranking in grade 4 is Supreme Court, President, and government; by grade 8 government moves up to second position, and President is fourth. Perhaps the greatest reorientation in favor of institutions is for knowledgeability. At grade 4, President is first, government second, and Supreme Court fourth. But by grade 8, government has moved to first place, Supreme Court to second, and President to third. Only in the making of important decisions do government and Supreme Court not improve their position, but they do retain second and third place.

On these performance ratings, therefore, the institutions or organized roles of authority most frequently succeed in winning the highest esteem of the children by the end of our age span. This is displayed in Table 13-2. For this table we have excluded father and reassigned rank order on each attribute accordingly. We have then calculated the average rank on each attribute for the objects of political authority. At grade 4, the average rank of the President exceeds that of the Supreme Court and government. But by grade 8, the Supreme Court has moved up to first place followed by the government and the President in that order.

Table 13-2   Rankings and Average Ranks for Political Authorities on Selected Ratings

Set Name	Item	Grade	Govern- ment	Pres- ident	Police- man	Sen- ator	Supreme Court
Benevo- lence	Would want to help (helpfulness)	4 8	4 4	2 2	1 1	5 5	3 3
Depend- ability	Makes mistakes (infallibility)	4 8	2.5 2	1 3	5 5	4 4	2.5 1
Power	Can punish (sanctions)	4 8	3 2	2 4	4 3	5 5	1 1
Leader- ship	Knows more (knowledgeability)	4 8	2 1	1 3	3 5	5 4	4 2
	Makes important decisions (decision maker)	4 8	2 2	1 1	4 5	5 4	3 3
Average ranking over all above items		4 8	2.7 2.2	1.4 2.6	3.4 3.8	4.8 4.4	2.7 2.0
Rank order of average rankings		4 8	2.5 2	1 3	4 4	5 5	2.5 1

The elevation of the impersonal institutions to a paramount position of respect is particularly evident for the Supreme Court. Our data do not penetrate very deeply into the child's attitudes toward this body. But even with the cursory material we have, the esteem the Court commands from the children is of a very special sort, as we can see from Figure 12-3. Unlike many of the sentiments for and perceptions of other objects of authority, in this case all but one of the ratings are relatively stationary or increase with age. The Court is seen as rarely making mistakes, and this holds up across the grades. In grade 4 the children consider that it makes important decisions a lot of the time, and this judgment increases to all the time by grade 8. Similarly its power ("He can punish") and knowledge ("He knows a lot") increase markedly with the age of the child.

Whether in each new generation of adults this is an important source of the public image of a special sagacity, wisdom, and prudence not enjoyed by other authorities, and of the peculiar sanctity that has surrounded the Supreme Court even in the face of unpopular decisions, we cannot say. Nor can we even begin to speculate whether this sentiment has anything to do with the willingness of many members of the system to tolerate decisions by the Court that run ahead of popular conviction, as the school-desegregation decision *Brown v. Board of Education.* But at the very least we can infer that a high level of regard for this impersonal unit in the structure of authority has been built up in children by the time they are ready to leave elementary school.

What is the significance of this increasing tendency to lift the impersonal institutions to a position of high esteem? For the American system, with its emphasis on the power of the office, not of the occupant, and with its commitment to collective participation in the making of political decisions, the capacity of the maturing member to reorient his thinking from personalized figures of authorities to institutions is critical.

A system that sought to attach its members to its structure of authority solely by relying on the culturally approved virtues of its personal representatives of authority would undoubtedly run the danger of overpersonalizing its whole regime. We might then expect each leadership succession to precipitate a "crisis of authority" for other political institutions. It raises the question as to whether this kind of emphasis on personalization does not find a significant place in the socializing of each new generation in systems such as Spain and France, and in many Latin American systems. Certainly the excessive stress on personalized figures would encourage the maturing members to attach themselves ultimately to persons rather than to organizations as the appropriate wielders of authority.

Of course for a system that depends largely upon personal legitimacy[3] — charisma, in Weber's terminology — and seeks to perpetuate itself, emphasis on personalization would not only be satisfactory; under certain circumstances it might be mandatory. But where the regime depends upon the legitimacy of organized institutions, as does the American, some way must be found for attaching the members to the roles involved, not to their occupants. Institutional support, not personal support, is clearly a defining condition for the continuity of such a system.

The capacity to identify and admire faceless organizations is no easy or ordinary achievement for children, particularly in an area that has little intrinsic interest for them, such as politics. The difficulties standing in the way have already been implied. We have looked at a considerable body of data demonstrating that for our group of children the personal figures of authority became almost inescapable initial points of contact with the regime. We have, it is true, concluded earlier that the younger child shows signs of relating not to persons as such but to the institutionalized role, to the Presidency rather than the specific President, for example. Nevertheless we were also impelled to propose that the child can more easily make a meaningful contact with those roles that are personalized in the form of some palpable human being, such as a visible President or a nearby policeman.

But not all objects of authority lend themselves to such a personalization. Political organizations such as the Supreme Court consist of an aggregate of persons, and it may be difficult to personalize its organized collection of roles. Few adults, much less children, know the name of its Chief Justice, to say nothing of its associate justices. Hence in some systems, such as the American, the maturing members may somehow need to acquire the capacity to esteem impersonal institutions.

To a limited extent this may be equally true of all systems, even of those in which personal legitimacy dominates as a bonding device. It would seem plausible to expect that at some point in his development, a member of most systems will lose his early childhood dependence upon personal elements among the various objects of authority and accept those objects as well that display less personal, more institutional qualities. Somewhere in the socializing processes therefore we can expect a shift in orientation to take place, wherein the member finds he no longer needs to have his senses excited by the personal component of the authority but is able to accept (or reject as the case may be[4]) the more impersonal authority of organizations.

What has surprised us is that the process begins so early, in the American system at least. To all appearances, as the child develops the general intellectual and emotional capacity to relate to nonpersonal, distant things such as institutions, he does so in the area of political authority as well. We do not have to wait until adolescence or adulthood for the maturing member to acquire a sensitivity to the exercise of authority by organizations in the regime.

As a specific consequence, systems, such as the American, which attribute authority to offices and organized institutions rather than to men are able to orient the maturing member increasingly toward these impersonal objects. But the child is not only able to react to the institutions of authority as he grows older. The favorable sentiments first extended to the personal figures he now tends to shift toward those very organizations that he previously had failed to notice.

The import for the system needs little elaboration. These positive evaluations undoubtedly reflect and simultaneously help to reinforce the large measure of stability the American regime has achieved. Positive support is socialized firmly for the structure through which authority is exercised, even without the mediation of the personal element. The danger is correspondingly diminished that the persons who happen to occupy positions of authority for only a limited time will draw off the child's support.

THE PERSONALIZATION OF AUTHORITY

Our data have repeatedly brought us back to the refrain that the personal figure involved in an object of authority—as in government, during the early years, and in the Presidency and the policeman—eases the generation of positive support among younger children. Our comparative analysis in the preceding chapter now bears this out decisively—and yet forces a certain qualification on the hypothesis.

Table 13-2 shows us the reasons for the reinforcement of our previous conclusions. It indicates the undisputed primacy of the President in grade 4 for those five attributes on which we have a comparison with institutional forms of authority. There is little reason to believe that if we had been able to test the child's evaluation of all objects on all attributes the President would have fared any less well. We know that the child has reordered his perceptions in favor of the impersonal institutions by grade 8.

But our comparative analysis now compels us to modify our conclusions about personalization in the early grades to a modest yet important degree. But not all personal figures of authority serve with equal impact as points of contact between the average child in our test group and the regime. This is particularly clear for the policeman. As the child grows older, he has changing expectations about the policeman. Even by grade 4 the policeman ranks only fourth, and he continues steady in this position through the later grades (Table 13-2). But the senator is even more revealing of the limitations of personalized authorities. He is an undisputed personal figure of authority, and yet of all our five objects he evokes the lowest degree of positive sentiments from the children.

If we return to Table 13-1, we can see that of the six qualities on which we have ratings for the senator, the children consistently put him toward the last. His rank ranges between third and fifth place, if father is excluded. Not even at grade 4, the more personalizing phase among children, is he ranked among the first. In spite of his elevated position in the political system for the professional observer, the children do not esteem the senator, on our measures, so highly as they do the lower-status (for adults) policeman. At grade 4 the children rank the policeman higher on five out of the six attributes on which we have ratings. Even in grade 8, when the thirteen- or fourteen-year-old child has considerably more knowledge about government, for three out of the same six attributes the policeman still draws a higher rank than the senator. The lower rating for the senator may perhaps be partly a function of the kinds of qualities we rated. But when we consider that even the impersonal institutions of government and the Supreme Court also call forth a more favorable response on most qualities, we can see that the inferior evocative power of the senator must also be a function of the nature of the role as perceived by the children.

This is not to say that the children are hostile to or suspicious of senators. Figure 12-2 shows that the average senator does rate high on our scales, somewhere above the midpoint for four out of the six qualities tested. But in comparison with the rankings given to other objects of political authority, the senator tends to bring up the rear. The personalization of authority that the senator represents is apparently not enough in itself to draw the higher regard of the children in face of other figures that have some greater cultural meaning at work for them. As a mechanism of attachment to the structure of authority the senator operates as a considerably less influential point of contact with the child.

Clearly not all personal figures of authority play an equally prominent part in the socializing process. Although the child is able to attach to personal figures earlier than to other objects of authority, only some figures of authority possess the qualities necessary to catch his eye and elicit highly positive assessments. Personalization is a necessary but not sufficient condition. For the personal element to be activated as a link between the child and object of authority, apparently the system must already have provided the figure of authority with some psychic or physical prominence for the child. Perhaps the figure needs to be dramatized in some way, as by the periodicity of elections for the President or by the crime-busting folklore surrounding police activities. The culture thereby harmonizes with the capacity of the child to relate to personal, nonfamilial objects. In practice the culture sets before the child only select figures of political authority, and the senator is clearly not an important one of these.

THE HEDGE AGAINST FAILURE

In brief, therefore, the system does not concentrate its efforts in one direction alone in stimulating diffuse support for significant elements in the structure of authority. It is protected against failure, as it were, by the presence of a number of open doors through which the child may enter supportively into political life.

Image congruence

We must bear in mind what we have already noted well, that in spite of the relative position of the authorities among themselves, all the authorities are rated fairly high on most attributes. We continue to assume that high ratings reflect a positive evaluation, because most of the rated attributes represent American cultural values. In this sense each object at the very least adds a modest increment to the growth of positive support. Negatively put, no object presents an adverse image to the majority of children that might discourage them from viewing the authorities favorably. However poorly a figure shows up comparatively, there is no question of the child developing a sense of distrust of political authority. Even for the senator, who fares worst in this respect, the ratings remain relatively high.

It is also evident that however differently the child may see the various political authorities and however his perception may shift with age, his images as reflected in our ratings do not reveal any fundamental inner tensions. They all move in a congruent direction, toward some overall and consistently favorable interpretation of the political authorities.

The significance of this homogeneous outlook in each child cannot be overstated. Assuming our tested children are not atypical, the high level of unconflicted evaluation of all authorities severally, and in the aggregate, would seem to reflect and at the same time help to account for the hitherto relatively stable character of the American regime.

Variations of appeal

Furthermore, the socializing processes seem to work in such a way as to spread the risk for the system over a number of figures. This is a consequence of the fact that the degree of esteem the child builds up for the authorities depends on the kind of characteristics he associates with them. He likes the President, considers him very trustworthy and persistent, sees him as a very powerful person, as an important decision maker, increasingly as a hard worker and leader. But even though he does not rate the policeman so high on these attributes, the child does consider him to be particularly benign (helpful and protective). He finds the Supreme Court admirable at least for its infallibility and power to punish. The government as a whole stands out, particularly in the oldest child's mind, for its wisdom—it knows more than any of the other figures or organizations of authority. With the exception of the average senator, it appears that at some point across the grades there is always some quality in which one or another of the authorities excels relative to the others. If a child is not of the majority's opinion on one object of authority, he is not lost to the system. The system has a hedge against failure to win the diffuse support of this particular child; he may join the majority in regarding highly one or more of the other objects of authority.

The socializing processes also take advantage of the capacity of the child to orient himself to things political. The political system need not rely exclusively either on personal figures of authority or on institutions to begin the process of attaching members to the political authorities. Because of the clear incapacity of the very young child to handle impersonal units in the structure, there is no recourse but for the generation of diffuse support to begin through the emphasis of personalized components. The child develops a high estimate of the President and policeman; he also begins to reach out to institutions, such as government. But at this early stage in the political socializing processes, the child's limits of conceptualization lead him to interpret the institution in personalized terms.

Nevertheless even though the primary socializing processes in the American system take advantage of the personal components in the structure of authority at those stages in the child's maturation when palpability of the occupant counts for most, the general thrust of these processes is in a different direction. They move decisively toward stimulating diffuse support for institutions, either initially for institutionalized roles (the Presidency as against a particular President) or later for impersonal organizations of authority. As the child grows older, this shift in orientations protects the system from any failure to capture some kind of favorable response. Without abandoning personal figures entirely as a linkage point, the child no longer needs to lean so heavily on them alone. As the child acquires the capacity to orient himself to the impersonal institutions, he begins to reorganize his perceptions somewhat. The organizational component in the political authorities—such as the Supreme Court and government—comes closer to the foreground of his feelings about the political world.

From this analysis we are led to conclude that in some part the persistence of the authority structure in the American regime in relatively stable form over the generations is not alone a product of any "success" in meeting routine political problems and intermittent crises or of any peculiarity about its institutional arrangements, such as the separation of powers and its federal structure. Early politicization seems to free the child from his family or other group ties at least sufficiently to enable him to begin building up some ideas and feelings about the political authorities. His subtle introduction through the personalized elements of these authorities yields with age to esteem for institutions. If our findings also apply to the recent past, they suggest that for each rising generation alternative ways have been provided in the system for hedging against the chance of failure in keeping the reservoirs of diffuse support full. But aside from the validity of so broad a generalization, we can say that no effort to explain the consequences of political socialization in the American political system can afford to neglect the impact that early political experiences may have in these specific ways for the input of diffuse support for the structure of authority.

NOTES

1. See N. Gross, W. S. Mason, and A. W. McEachern, *Explorations in Role Analysis* (New York: Wiley, 1958); and B. J. Biddle and E. J. Thomas, *Role Theory: Concepts and Research* (New York: Wiley, 1966).

2. See D. Easton, "Political Anthropology" in B. J. Siegel, *Biennial Review of Anthropology 1959* (Stanford, Calif.: Stanford University Press, 1959), pp. 210-262, and the literature cited there.

3. For this term, see D. Easton, *A Systems Analysis of Political Life* (New York: Wiley, 1965), pp. 302-307.

4. Although the monotony of repetition forbids it, in each case where we speak of the input of support or acceptance of authority, unless the context indicates otherwise we assume that the maturing member may be acquiring either negative or positive support. That is, he may be acquiring disaffective as well as conforming sentiments. Without this caveat about the use of the notion of support, it would appear that we are examining only the conditions of stability, whereas we are in fact seeking to understand change as well. Unfortunately—from a *theoretical* point of view—the American system has been relatively stable and research on it does not offer much help in understanding the nature and conditions of political change. Because of this bias of the system toward stability, it becomes more important than ever to bear constantly in mind that in speaking of support for the system or of the bonding of members to the system, the negative character of the support (alienation or disaffection) may in other systems be the major consideration.

14

POLITICAL STABILITY
AND CHANGE
AFTER CHILDHOOD

 If our sample of children is at all typical, in the American system the child becomes tightly linked to the structure of authority. The overwhelming thrust of primary socialization in this system must therefore be toward political stability. Early orientations provide a solid supportive base for the regime as the members grow older. Even if later events should disillusion members about the structure of authority, the rate of decline in support might at least be restrained somewhat by the pull of latent childhood sentiments.

However complex the process through which this support is built, it can be succinctly summarized in the concepts of personalization, institutionalization, politicization, and idealization. The child reaches out to the political system through the structure of authority and at the beginning finds palpable human objects such as the President, the policeman, and government (interpreted in a personal way). His contact points have been *personalized*. Simultaneously most children quickly become sufficiently *politicized* to distinguish between the internal authority of the family and the superior, external authority of society as represented in these personalized political figures. The older the child in our test group grows, the more likely he is to extend his perceptions to embrace other figures and institutions such as the Supreme Court. At this stage personalization tends to give way to or join what we have called the *institutionalization* of political authority. The child now possesses the emotional and perceptual equipment not only to take cognizance of the existence of impersonal institutions (such as the Supreme Court or government, which is now interpreted as Congress or voting) but also to acquire and express decided sentiments about them. The *idealized* image he initially developed for the personal figures he is now able to extend, in more moderate but nonetheless still relatively high measure, to these impersonal political objects. Although regard for all authority declines as the child ages, it never falls to a very low average point. In this esteem, we have concluded, lies the potential source of positive support for that part of the regime we have designated as the structure of political authority.

We are of course not surprised that in the United States the overall tendency of primary socialization should be toward the political stability implied in these processes. For better or worse, this system has been relatively stable over the years, and we would expect children to mirror the behavior and hopes of their parents. If in a stable system we would look for the beginnings of political change, we would not be likely to find it during the stage of childhood socialization.

The fact that we interpret primary socialization in the American system in this way, however, raises certain dangers. It might be thought that we are implying that socialization always tends to act as a stabilizing factor in political systems. Nothing could be further from our intentions. Indeed in Chapter 2 we were clearly loath to accept any assumption like this, in principle; we even suggested that in some systems childhood socialization might conceivably be an important means for inducing change. Now, however, with a solid body of data behind us, we propose to go further and to inquire whether our study of children gives us any hint at all about where we might expect socialization to be hospitable to political change and innovation. Here we will need to digress somewhat from our main theme, the childhood sources of diffuse support for the structure of authority. But this is necessary if we are to appreciate the conflicting systemic consequences political socialization may have for support, at different ages, in the same system. Even in the United States, we shall find, stable as it has been, a person is not coupled to the system with the same strength in every phase of the life cycle.

Here events of the 1960s in the United States can help us out. The child begins his contacts with the political system in a strongly positive spirit. But the increased rate of political activity of young people in the 1960s may indicate that something happens by late adolescence and early adulthood to change substantially the political sentiments of maturing persons. The mood among many young people in the 1960s has been one of too great defiance of political authority for us to believe that early sentiments always or necessarily continue unimpaired.

Can socialization with regard to authority possibly help us to account for this change between the affiliative mood in which we leave the child in grade 8 and the numerous less than enthusiastic adolescents and young adults of the 1960s? If so, we may appreciate more fully the limits on the consequences of childhood socialization for a political system. We may also better understand those special age groups through which political innovation and change, the frequent consequence of instability, are most likely to have their beginning.

It is clear that we cannot explain the rebellious sentiments and activities of many young people in the 1960s and the political climate among them critical of political authority solely by what we know about political socialization in childhood. These early political orientations should lay a restraining hand on adolescents and young adults, if we assume that sentiments acquired in childhood are not easily dislodged. Yet the new political spirit among young adults in the 1960s seems to run contrary to the warm attachment to the structure of authority characteristically acquired by our test children.

The failure of the tendencies so dominant in childhood to persist at least among many young people suggests that we look at postchildhood stages of the life cycle for some assistance in understanding how tight bonds to political authority may begin to loosen. Because of the lack of any significant data about public regard for most authorities, we shall find it extremely helpful to pick up the threads of our discussion about the police from Chapters 10 and 11. The availability of some data about adult attitudes toward the police will give us some rich new leads — although no firm inferences — into why it might be that during the 1960s it is young adults who break out of the stabilizing restraints so clearly applied during childhood.

INSTABILITY AND POLITICAL SOCIALIZATION

In contrast to the 1960s, in most earlier periods the United States has been a relatively stable political system. Not that many changes have not come about. But with two or three exceptions these changes have resulted from slow accretions rather than from sudden transformations or violent intrusions. The American system has moved from a decentralized federal type to one in which considerable power over states and localities resides in the national government, from a system in which government was involved only marginally in the economy and other social spheres to one in which government is the largest employer, and there is large-scale governmental regulation, direction, and innovation in many major areas of life. We have also in recent years witnessed the transformation of the rules governing the rights of some minorities, especially the blacks, under revised interpretations of the Constitution without formal modifications of this document. Even with the far-reaching transformations in political life that these changes represent, in comparison with other political systems the United States has hitherto appeared to be quite stable. From our data we would assume that childhood socialization has contributed its share to this outcome.

An unfolding decade of instability

But events in the 1960s, at least, permit us to pose the question of whether the United States may not be about to enter a vastly different decade, one in which political change may move far more quickly and in which the path of change will be strewn more frequently with open and violent conflict. Could the United States be on the threshold of an entirely new epoch of political unrest in which even the style of political participation will shift radically from debate, the hustings, and the ballot box to the street, the bullet, and the torch? In the 1960s there has already been visible a clear progression in the frequency and intensity of violence. At first street demonstrations and sit-ins began to supplement open debate. In the face of hostile opposition, these noisy but peaceful assemblies gradually shifted to freedom marches and to the use of force in self-defense. From here it was but a step for political frustration and anger to express themselves positively through open resistance to authority. Street demonstrations blended into urban riots, nonviolent dissent against policies in Vietnam into outright resistance, and conformity with legal rules into civil disobedience in the name of higher moral law. Dissent in turn has at times been met with the all-too-ready use of the billy club, massive police force, and provocative rumors of arming by parts of the citizenry.

Does this new and apparently growing propensity to turn to civil disobedience and to the dramatic use of force for the expression of political demands and for signalizing the withdrawal of political support—a new politics of confrontation—mean that the United States is entering a period in which basic attitudes toward political authority are undergoing profound changes? Even though only a minority of young people and concerned adults, both white and black, have been directly engaged in these events, it can be argued that this is not a phenomenon confined only to these small percentages across the country. We would expect organized signs of unrest to be concentrated initially within the narrow confines of campuses and ghettos. When modern industrialization brought labor together in the factory, for the first time it offered conditions conducive to collective action for the labor force. Similarly in the 1960s, campus activity has been less a reflection of the limited scope of discontent than of a significant residential concentration of concerned young people.[1] For them collective action and organization become physically feasible in a way not possible for others who may feel just as strongly but who are more widely dispersed throughout the population. We would expect to find that, as the youth put it, the campus or the ghetto is "where the action is."

Furthermore, when even a minority of a people takes to the streets regularly, when a leadership arises to justify this in passionate moral terms, when the governmental response is circumspect, and when even the churches, normally the bulwarks of authority, join in the fray, there is ample evidence that suspicion and distrust of political authorities are more widespread than the numbers engaged in actual demonstrations might suggest. Urban violence, student activism, and opposition to the war in Vietnam during the 1960s have been possible only in the context of an underlying deep and more widespread urban discontent and popular frustration with the war, with poverty, and with the loss of individuality in modern civilization.

Does this then portend a new phase of American life, one in which instability may for some time become an intrinsic part of the political fabric? Clearly it is too early to say whether the unrest of the 1960s marks the beginning of a long period of civil turmoil in which the threat of violence backstops the vote, even though as social scientists we cannot escape raising the question for objective analysis. There have been other periods of violence, during the 1860s and the 1930s particularly, when it also might have appeared that the basic texture of political life was being unalterably transformed. Yet a noncoercive, constitutional political style was able to reassert itself within a decade in each case. It is entirely possible that the unrest in the 1960s will be equally short-lived.

We cannot help but acknowledge, however, that the political climate of the 1960s has been unusually disturbing. There have been deep political crises in the past. Yet not all these have sparked a passion that carried opposition into the streets, as has been the case in this period, and that have aroused so great a show of suppressive force. We are prompted to ask whether there may be something unique about the conditions of the 1960s that can help us account for the changing attitudes toward the legitimacy of the policies of the political authorities, if not indeed toward the legitimacy of the very authorities themselves.

It goes almost without saying that there are many reasons for the increasing political malaise of the 1960s. A world that seems doomed to hang precariously on the edge of atomic self-destruction is not likely to be one in which reactions to international crisis will follow past "normal" patterns. A political system, as in the United States, that has placed a high priority on political involvement by its people and participation in decision making is not likely to be one in which fateful policies will be accepted without fundamental challenge. Furthermore, the events of this decade have perhaps themselves been sufficiently unsettling if not traumatic to help undo the bonds so tightly welded in childhood. But in spite of these obvious causes, if our study of childhood socialization has sketched a political profile of a child who is deeply attached to the structure of authority as he sees it, and if in the succeeding phase of youth and young adulthood we see signs that many have become wary of if not openly hostile to political authority, we may credibly ask whether socialization in these later phases of life may not also help to explain this phenomenon.

The police as a generic symbol of authority

Unfortunately the scope of our inquiry into the child's perception of the Presidency and other political authorities did not permit us to pursue the process of political socialization into the later stages of the life cycle. In addition, very few data are available from other sources that could be construed to tap the adult's attitudes toward the office of the Presidency as against specific Presidents and toward the other institutions and figures of authority with which we have dealt.

But we are in a somewhat better position for the policeman, understood as a symbol of political authority. Here the very nature of our investigation concerned not the specific policeman but the general role as perceived by children. Recently there has been a growing number of efforts probing for the views of adults about police in matters that overlap with ours for the child. We are therefore able to take advantage of studies on the images adults hold of the policeman to see whether the available data can shed any new light on the later systemic consequences of the socialization of children. In the process we shall find some clues about the way in which socialization itself helps to leave youth and young adults in the 1960s susceptible to some loosening of their bonds to political authority.

We shall find that political crises in the 1960s, domestic and international, have been occurring at a time in the life cycle of the younger generations when the latter may be most likely to question their earlier attachment to the political authorities and when their numbers may enable them effectively to act out their doubts. This happenstance could contribute significantly to the forces making for instability in the American political system.

Lacking comparable data about other figures and institutions of authority, we are forced to rely exclusively on the maturing person's attitudes toward the authority of the police as a rough indicator of possible incipient feelings about the legitimacy of political authority in general. However adequate this assumption may be for children, we recognize its greater questionableness for older persons. Yet this decision need not be as hazardous as might appear on the surface. The police symbolize the law, and in a constitutional, legal society like the United States, the authorities assert their power formally through the law. It is not farfetched therefore to interpret orientations toward the authority of the police at least as symptomatic of those that may be developing toward political authority in general. Furthermore, most of the curves on our ratings for all authorities other than the policeman move in the same direction, during childhood, as do those for the policeman himself. We might expect that they would continue to be parallel even beyond childhood.

But having gone this far with our assumptions, we are nonetheless very much alive to their speculative nature. Not all curves of respect for all the authorities need follow the same path, especially as we move into adulthood. Hence, however useful our assumptions may be for breeding what we feel are significant and provocative hypotheses, we do not pretend that even with the hard data we are able to present, we have gone beyond insight and informed speculation. It is in this spirit that the analysis in this chapter is presented.

THE IMAGE OF THE POLICE AMONG ADULTS

It will be recalled that at the point where our inquiry left the child, at age thirteen or fourteen, however favorably he may think of the policeman on the whole, the glow is beginning to dim. What kind of consequences might this early respect have for the stability of a system if it is slowly being displaced by a far more depreciative image? Have we any data that would throw some light on whether later experiences accelerate the downward trend of the curve of respect, arrest it, or even reverse it?

Before examining these data, however, we need to bear one reservation in mind. In a strict sense, we have made our major point, regardless of how we may discover adults to feel about the police. Even if it should turn out that adults are distrustful of the police and resist their authority, these findings would have little bearing on the initial meaning of the police as a bridge between the child and the structure of authority. The child gets his first view of the political system by looking at the policeman and other personalized objects of authority, and builds up early sentiments based upon how he interprets these objects, but the childhood experience may later be overpowered. However, it need not be automatically erased. It will have to be taken into account in assessing the consequences of later experiences. Whatever the nature of these experiences, we would surmise that a person who is favorably disposed to political authority in childhood is not likely to be as easily disillusioned with authority in later life as one who begins his membership in the political system in a state of cynicism. The general effect of these early positive orientations should be to increase the level of tolerance of subsequent unfavorable experiences with authority and to act as a brake on instability and change.

Nonetheless if we try to find out what does happen during various phases of adulthood, we may better understand the contribution of socialization to change. The striking thing, we shall discover, is that the image of the police held by older adults looks more like that of our children than like that of teen-agers and young adults. Between childhood and late adulthood—after age fourteen and before about thirty-five—the modest evidence available reveals a pronounced dip in respect for the police. We will be in a better position to interpret the potential systemic consequences of postchildhood socialization if we ascertain the nature of this dip and examine some of its more likely causes.

We have already intimated that the literature on adult perceptions of the police repeatedly speaks of the very low opinion that most people hold. There are, it is commonly said, ". . . widely held beliefs that policemen are uneducated and of low mentality; that they are selected for physical strength and courage alone; that they are of doubtful honesty and integrity; that they are engaged in a continuous offensive against society; that they are often rude and domineering . . ."[2] It may be that these beliefs accurately reflect prevailing attitudes in some localities in the United States. But strangely enough the few national, urban, and statewide studies that have been undertaken do not confirm this. From the fragmentary and varied measures that we have, it would appear— with some ambiguity due to divergent findings, varying time periods, and differences in the specific qualities being appraised— that there is a considerable gap between what writers think is the popular image of the police in recent times and the findings of local and national surveys about actual beliefs. In fact, as we look at adults, undifferentiated by age, we are impressed by the close similarity of their views to those we have already found in children.

One component of the general image that adults hold of the police consists of their status, or general standing in the community as compared with other occupations. Numerous studies have included the police in the prestige structure of occupations. One review of these studies concludes that these ". . . prestige rankings of occupations have yielded surprising consensus in the ranking of 'police' as an occupational category. In general, the police are placed in the middle ranks. What is surprising is that these ratings of the police appear relatively stable through time, are relatively constant across national boundaries, and seem relatively unaffected by differences in scaling techniques."[3] In one of these national surveys in the United States, in 1947, 41 percent of the sample gave the policeman an excellent or good status rating; in a replication in 1963, the figure had risen to 54 percent.[4]

Occupational prestige is not necessarily synonymous with respect, even though in many instances prestige and respect may go hand in hand. It is possible, for example, to place the military high on a status scale and yet to have little fondness or respect for the military as an occupation. Typically, occupations considered necessary evils may acquire some glamour and prestige from their social importance or influence, yet personal esteem need not accompany the judgment. But it is not too farfetched to see in occupational ratings of the police some modest admixture of respect.

There are many components in an image of the police, and other studies have tapped a number of these. They all definitely add up to an unexpectedly favorable adult assessment of the police. During the fifties in a survey of the city of Los Angeles, 29 percent of the population considered the police to be persons of unquestionable honesty, and 53 percent felt that they are usually men who are fairly honest. All in all, on such ratings as courtesy, dedication to their job, competence, and impartiality, with some important reservations, this police force at the time seemed to elicit a favorable reaction from its public.[5]

In another sample, this time about attitudes toward the police of a particular state, the image that emerges appears to be about as positive as among the children in our sample. The state police are viewed as

> . . . an honest, impartial, objective police organization whose job in general is about the same as most with respect to the time and effort involved, but one which involves frequent exposure to risk and danger. What they do is important and they do it well. Their rewards are an above-average income and high prestige in their community. . . 87% of the responses describing the nature of public-police contacts depict that interaction as "friendly, helpful, and courteous."[6]

Finally, a national survey in 1965 posed a question that forthrightly sought the opinion of the adult on his respect for the police he is most likely to know best. In response to the question "How much respect do you have for the police in your area?" 70 percent of a national sample indicated that they had a great deal of respect, with only 22 percent and 4 percent replying "some" or "hardly any," respectively.[7] In a repetition of the question in 1967, those answering "a great deal" rose to 77 percent.

It is of course risky to generalize from these few studies. There are said to be 40,000 separate and distinct police agencies in the United States, with 420,000 policemen.[8] It may be that attitudes are to some extent agency-specific and variable by community and region. We know little about the specific referents that the word policeman calls up in the minds of adults. Nevertheless the little evidence we do have unmistakably affirms that most people have higher regard for the policeman as a generalized role than we might have anticipated from the folklore in the literature.

We can now see that from our evidence on children alone we would have grounds for making an intelligent guess about the attitudes of adults. If children tend to acquire the attitudes of their parents, we might have anticipated that, regardless of the contrary indications of the literature, adults would be favorably disposed toward the police. The puzzling disparity between the presumed low estimate of the police by adults and the more positive views of our test children is revealed only as a product of misinformation. The children and adults in the aggregate do not seem to be too far apart in their estimate of the police.

THE TROUGH IN THE EARLY YEARS AMONG ADULTS

If adults do indeed take a positive view of the policeman, we are immediately confronted with what might appear to be a new puzzle. By the time the children in our group reach age thirteen or fourteen their favorable image of the policeman is either stabilized or declining, depending upon the component that we select. If we assume that our ratings for children tap the same general qualities, summarized in the notion of respect, as the kinds of items already noted in the studies for adults, it appears that even though the child's regard for the police is on the whole declining, that of adults is relatively high. How can we explain an apparent rise in the curve of respect at some point beyond childhood?

Since we lack strictly comparable data for adults and children, we can only speculate about the answers. But the speculations are useful in drawing out several alternatives, and even the limited data we have on adults will enable us to make some informed guesses about what may be taking place and its possible implications for the political system, especially for its stability or change.

There are several possible explanations for the discrepancy between the declining level of respect we find in our thirteen- or fourteen-year-olds and the high level reported for adults. First, as depicted by Model A in Figure 14-1, the respect of the children may begin at so high a level that even if it does continue to decline slowly with age, it never falls below a relatively high point. We would therefore expect to find that adults assess the police very favorably even if somewhat less so than children.

But second, as represented by the upper curve in Model B, Figure 14-1, it could be that in the past, when the present generation of adults were children, they learned a high level of respect for the police and have maintained it. However, the present generation of children, which we are testing, may be different. With them respect may begin to decline at an early age and it may continue to fall as they move on through the adult phases of life (lower curve in Model B). The differences between the children in our group on the one hand and present adults on the other could therefore be attributed to generational shifts in attitudes toward the police.

Finally, we might hypothesize that both past and present generations are not too dissimilar. Esteem for the police declines with age among children and even beyond, but at some point it stabilizes itself and then reverses direction and climbs to the level of regard which the surveys among adults report. It is possible that there is a middle-years dip in respect, with this low point extending from the late teens to somewhere in the thirties, as illustrated in Model C, Figure 14-1.

Although the indeterminacy of the evidence in the face of complex socializing processes does not rule out any of these explanations or variations on them, the available data lend some greater credence to the third interpretation. The reason for believing that during the early adult years there may be a trough in respect resides in the relationship between age and contact with the police. In the United States the child is apt to see the policeman as something of a model of the "good guy." In cops and robbers, for most children the cops stand on the side of virtue and the robbers are the outlaws. But as the child moves into the teens and young adulthood, his experiences with the law begin to change. In the modern age he becomes part of the car culture; and this together with the greater mobility, assertiveness, and exuberance of youth raises the probability of increased conflict with the police over safety and order. Most recent studies report the highest rate of contact between members of society and the police occurs in the teens. Generally, beginning with the late teens, contact with police varies inversely with age. In one study, 75 percent of those over sixty-five reported no police contacts in the past five years, but only 4 percent under twenty-one fell into this category.[9]

But as the young adult grows older and, we would assume, takes on the responsibilities of job and family and acquires addi-

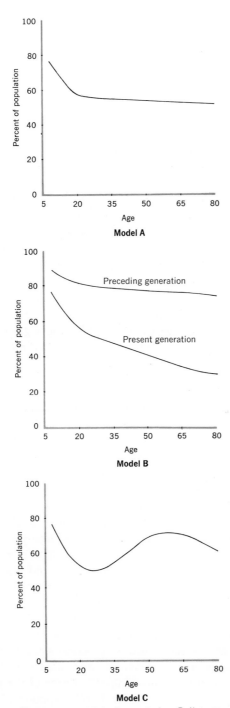

Figure 14-1. High Respect for Police as Representative of Political Authority: Theoretical Distributions.

tional stakes in life, he probably also revises his relationship to the immediate enforcement agencies. He comes down somewhat more heavily on the side of law and order, and his previous conceptions may be reawakened. Not that they need to or are likely to stand out as prominently as in the past. Adults may not be so favorably disposed toward the police as are children. But the curve of respect ascends again.

The data we have are at least consistent with this kind of explanation, although we hasten to add that there are some disturbing additional analytic problems. Because of the complex interlacing of the major socializing influences over time, it is impossible to disentangle, through survey data of the kind available, the relative influence of biological aging, social aging in the sense of the particular pattern of influences through which a person moves as he matures, and generation of birth. A generation we interpret as an age set that has been exposed to similar major temporal events which leave a deep imprint on the outlook of that group. But the serious if inescapable limits of this sorting problem for interpretive purposes do not reduce the significance of the various studies to which we refer. They reveal a middle-years dip in respect for the police.

This tendency for the policeman to rank low with teen-agers and younger adults and to improve with age in recent years, is confirmed in a number of studies. In the previous 1953 survey of public attitudes toward police in Los Angeles, the older people, fifty-five years and above, were found to be the most favorably inclined, and the severest critics on a variety of traits were those between fifteen and forty-four (Figure 14-2). Of these, the respondents in the twenty-five to forty-four age group were inclined to feel least favorably disposed toward the Los Angeles police. If we assume a much more favorable evaluation among children, as estimated for the seven- to fourteen-year-olds in Figure 14-2, decline in approval sets in at age fifteen, reaches a low point between ages twenty and forty-five, and then begins to ascend again. The younger and older groups are more accepting of the police, the middle groups more rejecting.[10]

In the 1959-1960 study of state police cited earlier, on a ranking on close to twenty characteristics the rank order of favorableness by age showed a direct, practically linear relationship. "Younger persons are less favorable and older persons are more favorable with respect to this composite image of the police."[11]

In the American Institute for Public Opinion (A.I.P.O.) national survey referred to, a similar kind of association between age and respect for the police emerges. As Figure 14-3 shows,

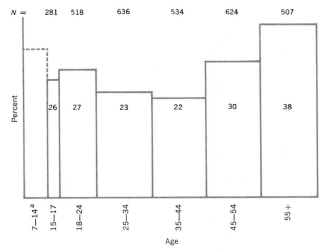

Figure 14-2. Overall Evaluation of Los Angeles Police by Age. Percent Who Answer, "One of the very best police departments in the country." (Adapted from G. D. Gourley, *Public Relations and the Police* [Spring-field, Ill.: Thomas, 1953], p. 65.) [b]

[a] Estimate of where children would be.
[b] This histogram is drawn with unequal intervals on age and heights proportional to percent giving favorable evaluation.

the proportion that has a great deal of respect for the police rises from 53 percent for those between twenty-one and twenty-five to 84 percent by ages fifty-six to sixty where some decline occurs.[12]

Figure 14-3. Percent Responding that They Have "a great deal" of Respect for the Police.*

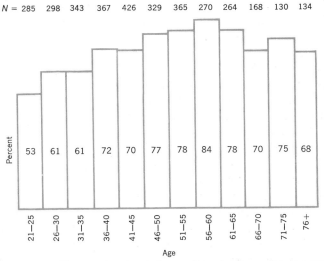

*Question: "How much respect do you have for the police in your area—a great deal, some, or hardly any?"
Source: A.I.P.O. Survey no. 0709 (March, 1965), Question 011.

A national sample in Great Britain also reveals a close relationship between respect and age. The proportions having great respect for the police move from 63 percent for those eighteen to twenty-one years of age to 88 percent for the forty-five to sixty-five age category, as shown in Figure 14-4. (It may be that the closer connection between age and respect in Britain is a product of the greater respect that tradition seems to give to the British policeman.) Even when length of potential contact with police is controlled, age still dominates as a determinant. Thus among motorists, the group most likely to have contact with the police and to come into conflict over the enforcement of traffic regulations, analysis shows that the tendency for respect to increase with age persists.[13]

If we now join together the bits and pieces of evidence about how aging correlates with the image of the police, we seem to

Figure 14-4. Percent Who Have "great respect" for the Police in Great Britain.*

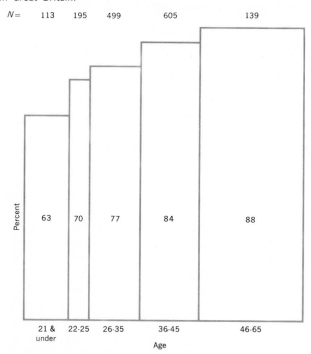

*Question: "Considering everything about the way the police do their job, would you say that you had great respect for the police, little respect, or mixed feelings about them?"
Source: Royal Commission on the Police, Appendix 3 to the Minutes of Evidence (London: H. M. Stationery Office, 1962), p. 6.
Note that this histogram is drawn with unequal intervals on age and heights proportional to percent giving favorable evaluation.

have a pattern of the following kind. Children, such as those in our group, on making contact with external authority, as represented by the police, acquire a relatively high level of regard. We have only a slight hint about the movement of this sentiment between ages fourteen and twenty-one. But if we may interpolate, we would think that given the nature of teen-age culture in the United States, regard for the police might continue to drop. This declining feeling seems to bottom out somewhere in the late twenties or early thirties, when it reverses direction and slowly rises again to some high point among the sixty-year-olds. Even after it declines beyond the latter age on the one measure we have reported for this group (Figure 14-3), it does not drop to the low point of the twenties. If we were to construct a curve to represent our speculations about fluctuations in respect for the police over the whole life cycle, it would look something like Model C in Figure 14-1, given the kind of data we have examined.

THE SIGNIFICANCE OF THE EARLY-YEARS TROUGH

Of what significance for attachment to the structure of authority is this trough of respect during the early adult years? It discloses several noteworthy things about the relationship of the individual member of the American system to the regime and thereby about possible sources of instability and change.

The police as a continuing linkage point

In the first place, the existence of this trough helps us to understand the implications of the decline in respect for the police that we detect in grade school. The diminution in the child's positive image as he moves through the grades may not be just a temporary phenomenon. It probably parallels the general decline in the growing child's proclivity for idealizing persons. It undoubtedly also in part reflects the growth of a youthful sense of independence and social autonomy, expressed through opposition to adult authority in many areas of life. But in addition, the child's initial feelings are probably deflected by specific kinds of experiences and values associated with special periods in the immediately succeeding phases of his life. We have already observed this in the nature of the kinds of contact many teen-agers are likely to have with the police.

As the individual moves out of these early stages of his life into later adulthood, however, some of his positive sentiments toward the part of the structure of authority represented by the police revive, either because they had continued in latent form, waiting to surface again, or because they are reinvigorated through new experiences. Perhaps both influences are at work. Whatever the source, however, of primary significance to us is the probable continuity in the United States of the police as a positive linkage point between the members of the political system and the structure of authority.

Whether for the present generation of young adults the police will continue to serve a stabilizing function, as they probably have prior to the 1960s, will of course depend in part on the extent to which respect survives the strain being put upon it during the 1960s. The periodic violent confrontations between police and young adults on campuses and in the inner cities may so disturb the growing generation as to create a new breed of disillusioned older adults in the years ahead.[14] The ascent of the respect curve, therefore, cannot always be taken for granted. It may depend in part on the particular experiences of young adults during their typical early-years dip.

But we must bear in mind a caveat mentioned previously. Even if the data had pointed toward a possible continuation of the decline we found in grade school, with no subsequent reversal of direction, we could not allow this in itself to lead us to underestimate the kinds of sentiments generated to that point. Respect for the police as a symbol of authority is still relatively high in grade 8. If feelings acquired early in life are not easily shed, they will serve at least to cushion the impact of later negative impressions.

In the second place, these fluctuations in sentiment about political authorities may have the deepest significance for the fate of the political system. The accessibility of a member of a system for mobilization for or against political authorities could be partly a function of the phase of the life cycle in which one catches him. If, for example, the decline in grade school continued for the President and other major political institutions, as it does for the policeman, and only during the late forties began to surge back, this could have profound implications for stability and change in a political system. If the low point in attachment were indeed the same point in the life cycle for all objects of authority — a big assumption indeed but not implausible — it would mean that one part of the population, the fifteen to thirty-five age group, would be more susceptible than others to appeals leading toward opposition to political authority and toward a modification in the regime. The ties of young adults to the structure of authority (and perhaps to regime norms — but about this we do not know) would be at their lowest ebb. Empirically these members in the political system would be in a greater state of readiness to disengage themselves from the existing regime than they were when younger and than they will be when older.

Age distribution and stability

An interpretation such as this throws a new light on the possible significance of the age distribution in a population for the stability and change of a political system. The larger the percentage and absolute numbers of the population in, say, the fifteen to thirty-five age bracket—assuming the validity and generality of our tentative inference—the greater the proportion of the members of a political system that can be more easily detached from it. Systems with a younger population of this kind should turn out to be more volatile. Indeed it may be that from these younger ranks are recruited the counterelites. This may help to explain the phenomenon of youth and relatively young adults at the forefront of many changes, revolutionary and otherwise. They are at an age when we can expect them to be least committed to the support of authority and most prepared therefore to challenge tradition.[15] This gives new meaning to the notion that older persons tend to be ideologically more conservative than they were during their youth. It reveals that the basis may lie in part in a general maturational pattern of fluctuations in sentiments toward the political authorities.

Some plausibility for these inferences is offered by events in the 1960s. It does appear that as the proportion and absolute numbers of young people in the population of most societies in the West and elsewhere have increased during the 1960s there has been a corresponding heightening of the political activity of youth in opposition to authority. Confrontations with political authorities through peaceful dissent, street demonstrations, and other forms of active protest have been appropriated as the hallmark of youth. Passionate concern for substantive justice has often taken the place of unquestioning confidence in traditional social forms, legal rules, and symbols of authority.

At one time we might have thought that the new political activism of young people in the United States was a product of a few universal issues: the war in Vietnam, poverty in the ghettos, feelings of despair about the future, and a sense of powerlessness over their own destiny. But when we look beyond the horizons of the United States, we see very similar activity among young people on foreign streets and campuses; yet in few instances have the issues been the same. In Moscow young people have protested for increased literary freedom; in Warsaw, on behalf of freedom for drama and for the protection of the university as a sanctuary against the authorities; in Prague, for a more liberal spirit in the Party and for a cleansing of the old guard; in Paris and in Rome, for improvement of the academic curriculum and for a greater share of the national resources on behalf of education as a whole; in Tokyo, for a foreign policy independent of the United States. In Louvain, Belgium, students have periodically taken to the barricades for the preservation or extension of linguistic rights. In Holland they have mobilized for increased student power. Not even China has been spared a marked increase in youthful participation, manifesting itself there in a massive student movement, the Red Guard, the spearhead of the Cultural Revolution.[16] Even in the United States the National Advisory Commission on Civil Disorders described the typical rioters during the summer of 1967 as ". . . late teenagers or young adults."[17]

It is clear that teen-agers and young adults appear to be the bearers of political discontent, the harbingers of possible instability in many countries. We can hardly explain this phenomenon *solely* in terms of issues at stake; there is such variability among these issues that we might suspect that they are as likely to be the occasion as a contributing cause.

From our discovery of the middle-years dip in respect for authority we may derive a more plausible explanation. It may be that in many large-scale societies it is in the nature of social maturation that young people become infused with a floating distrust of political authority, a distrust that seeks some issue on which to alight. In previous epochs when the proportion and absolute numbers of young persons in the population were smaller and perhaps when the issues seemed less critical, there was little opportunity for these young persons to do anything about these issues. But in the 1960s the situation is different.

In the United States, for example, as shown in Table 14-1, the pool of young people aged fifteen to twenty-four (in whom esteem for police authority should be nearing its lowest ebb) has increased from about 13 percent of the population (24,000,000) in 1960 to 16 percent (over 31,000,000) in 1966 and a continued rise is projected through 1975.[18] An increasing number of these young adults is concentrated geographically—on campuses and in the black ghettos. As we suggested before, labor itself did not begin to flex its muscles and strive for political power until indus-

Table 14 - 1 U.S. Population, 1930 - 1975*

	1930	1940	1950	1960	1966	Projection	
						1970	1975
Median Age	26.4	29.0	30.2	29.5	27.8	—	—
Total Population‡	123,203	132,165	151,326	179,323	195,857	207,000 †	221,000 †
15 - 24‡	22,507	24,032	22,220	24,020	31,362	36,361	40,106
15 - 24 as % of Total	18.3%	18.2%	14.7%	13.4%	16.0%	17.6%	18.1%

1930 - 1960 data: *Statistical Abstracts of the United States,* 1967, p. 26.
1966 data: *Statistical Abstracts of the United States,* 1967, p. 10.
1970 - 1975 data: *Statistical Abstracts of the United States,* 1967, p. 8.
†Estimated
‡In thousands.
Source: W. J. Cohen and B. Gross, *The Learning Force* (New York: Basic Books, forthcoming).

trialization brought people together in the factories, where organization and collective action first became feasible. The educational factories of today and the narrow streets of the black ghettos have served the same purposes for contemporary young people. Swelling numbers, combined as they are with opportunities for collective action on the one hand and with critical, youth-related issues as the sparks for action on the other, offer the occasion for open dissent and protest. The "natural" suspicion for authority during these years that we have found seems to add to the incentive.

SOURCES OF YOUTHFUL DISCONTENT

Of course our inference from the patterns for the police to all other parts of the structure of political authority and to other elements of the regime as well represents a sizable speculative leap in the dark. But even if we accept its plausibility for the moment, this does not imply that just because the younger age brackets in the population may have weaker feelings of attachment the system need under all circumstances experience change. Negative sentiments may not be sufficiently intense to leave members readily available for action against the authorities. Furthermore, even if their attachment has sunk to a very low level, there may be no issues or conditions to make them sufficiently dissatisfied with political life to lend their support for any significant change. Beyond that, even if discontent were rife, there need not always be the institutional and organizational resources and the absolute numbers needed to achieve a "critical mass" for effective protest. Nor need there always be waiting a competent leadership to initiate any plausible effort for change.

Thus even if we had evidence that belief in the legitimacy of the authorities had declined temporarily, it would only describe a significant condition for political transformations. We have no basis for predicting what would in fact occur historically. This would depend upon these other factors—the numbers, resources, leadership, and provocative circumstances. But it is the fact that these other factors *are* present in the United States (and other countries) during the 1960s which makes this combination of circumstances politically so inflammable.

We are not of course suggesting that the emergence of critical issues at home and abroad at a moment in time when young adults constitute an increasingly larger element in the population of the United States represents a single valid explanation for the rising political discontent among young people during the 1960s. To do so would be to rest our whole case on a demographic hypothesis, and this we do not intend. We subscribe neither to monocausality nor to demographic determinism. Present discontents among the young are clearly not a product of age and numbers alone. Increased numbers of young people provide only a necessary condition for visible and effective political action. But they are not sufficient. There need to be vital issues to arouse young people and to give them a cause around which to cohere. Of these issues there has been no shortage in the 1960s. Even if young adults had remained an unchanging proportion of the population, the issues themselves have certainly been urgent and provocative enough to penetrate into deeper layers of the population than ever before and to stimulate novel political activity.

Furthermore, even if we were to add the prevalence of deep concern among young people to the demographic hypothesis, we would still not begin to exhaust the supply of possible supplementary explanations for present discontents among the young around the world. Youthful activism is a complex, multicausal phenomenon. For example, it may be, as some have argued, that among American whites at least, the middle-class activists who form the core of the New Left on campuses are playing out the liberal sentiments of their parents, who had been close to the old left of the Great Depression during the 1930s. Perhaps, too, the loosening of family ties has led young people to seek a new sense of identity based on age consciousness and age solidarity. It might also be argued that in the 1960s more young people have more years of education than ever before, and there are reasons to believe that the more educated a person, the less likely is he to submit uncritically to authority.[19] The National Advisory Commission on Civil Disorders reported that in the riots in the ghettos in the United States during 1967 ". . . those with some high-school education were more likely to riot than those who had only finished grade school."[20] Finally, outbreaks of civil disorders throughout the world under the leadership of young people may well be due partly to the effects of cultural diffusion through imitation, rather than exclusively to parallel independent but similar kinds of stimuli. Nor is it in the least immaterial that youthful dissent has frequently been met with lack of understanding and repressive measures, including violence.

But in addition to all these plausible sources of present discontents and pressures toward political instability, we would be overlooking a vital confluence of contributing causes if we failed to take into account: first, that young people constitute larger numbers in the population of the United States than ever before; second, that they are residentially more concentrated than in the past; third, that they represent an age group in which respect for and attachment to political authority may typically have declined to its lowest ebb; and fourth, when this is coupled with urgent, frustrating issues such as have been present during the 1960s and a proneness among adults themselves to turn to force, we have a combination of circumstances ripe for swelling the number of those ready to defy political authority in behalf of what they consider just.

Through the erosion of support for the structure of authority in this way, stability could be undermined. But what is instability for one man may simply be the harbinger of change for another. If our chain of inferences withstands the assault of further research, we have here possibly put our finger on one of the age groups whose socializing experiences may prepare it to serve under certain circumstances as a major vehicle of political change. But regardless of the specific implications of our analysis for attachment to the political authorities in the 1960s, our research does press more generally for a massive increase in attention to several different aspects of the regime. There is an urgent need for a far better understanding, first, of the early origins of a sense of legitimacy for the structure of political authority; second, of the pattern of change in these sentiments as members age; and third, of the implications of age variations in these sentiments for the stability and change of regimes under differing conditions.

What relevance has this discussion for our broader theoretical interest? After all, we did note in the early chapters that our major preoccupation is not with an analysis of socialization as a means for producing stability in a system or, for that matter, for bringing about change. What we have been searching for is some understanding of the processes underlying the attachment of members to a structure of authority, on the assumption that unless this linkage occurs no political system, stable or unstable, can persist. As we will note in our final chapters the stability or instability of the structure is of concern to us only as it can help us understand better the process of attachment to the structure of authority.

But it happens that the American system has been relatively stable, at least for the period in which we tested our group of children. This has created certain problems of interpretation for us. The findings in our previous chapters were unavoidably and heavily weighted toward pointing up the stabilizing consequences of primary socialization. We have feared that this emphasis of our interpretations could easily leave the entirely false impression that socialization must always and inevitably perpetuate the status quo.

The present chapter has helped indicate that this need not be true. Aside from what the consequences might be if primary socialization occurred under conditions of political instability — and we have little data on this — even in as stable a system as the United States has appeared to be, socialization may work in one or another direction, depending upon the phase of the life cycle under examination. If we had remained with our data for the childhood stage, we might easily have concluded that socialization inevitably encourages stability. What is now also suggested is that secondary socialization, during the period beyond childhood, may under certain circumstances work in an opposite direction. As a result, we can anticipate that the early adult years may reflect some tension between childhood affect and later disenchantment, with the net outcome dependent on the particular situational events.

To suggest that there may be unstabilizing consequences associated with certain phases of socialization is not to imply of course that the system must therefore show signs of instability. The general stability of a system depends on more than what happens in this area alone. Manifestly we should not expect to be able to conclude from our analysis only of socialization in the postchildhood phase that the members would necessarily become so detached from the structure of authority that they could not support any authorities. Even if disenchantment set in with respect to one type of authority structure, this might simply be the signal for a change of structures. In that event there would be a shift of allegiance to a new way of organizing political authority. Hence the outcome of the discontent in the 1960s need have little relevance for the capacity of the members of the American system to cathect some kind of structure of political authority. Only under very special conditions, where succeeding structures repeatedly fail to capture the support of the members, might a situation arise in which some kind of system would be unable to continue.

In this chapter, however, we have hoped to nip in the bud any thought that we might be implying that socialization must always reinforce support for the structure of political authority. Although in Chapter 2 we had already denied this, with the analysis of our data still ahead of us we could not make the point too persuasively. We still cannot argue from our data alone that primary socialization may contribute to change or instability; this must await research in a different kind of political system, one in which instability is pronounced. But we now have some tentative grounds for estimating—if only through scattered and patently preliminary data—that socialization beyond childhood, even in a system that has been as stable as the American, may operate to dampen rather than to heighten the ardor for the structure of political authority. In the American system, as elsewhere, this may be a critical period, so far as socializing processes are involved, for the introduction of change and innovations.

NOTES

1. In the United States higher education (graduate and undergraduate) quadrupled between 1940 and 1965 alone and promises to increase over sixfold by 1975, from 1.6 million to 10.7 million. See W. Cohen and B. Gross, *The Learning Force* (New York: Basic Books, forthcoming).

2. G. D. Gourley, "Public Relations and the Police," *The Annals of the American Academy of Political and Social Science*, 291, p. 136, 1954. Compare also: "The fact of public distrust of the police is, we feel, not to be disputed. A survey of the attitudes of social workers, union stewards, Negro leaders, and lawyers made by students drawn from a criminology class in the local college indicated that the vast majority thought the police too ignorant, corrupt, and brutal . . . Public distrust is, therefore, the major occupational problem of the po-

lice," W. A. Westley, "The Police: A Sociological Study of Law, Custom, and Morality," in E. Burgess and D. W. Bogue (eds.), *Contributions to Urban Sociology* (Chicago: The University of Chicago Press, 1964), pp. 306-307.

3. J. J. Preiss and H. J. Ehrlich, *An Examination of Role Theory: The Case of the State Police* (Lincoln, Nebr.: University of Nebraska Press, 1966), p. 125. The text contains an extensive listing of references to these studies of occupational rankings.

4. R. W. Hodge, "The Public, the Police and the Administration of Justice," National Opinion Research Center, University of Chicago, December, 1965, p. 4.

5. Gourley, op. cit., chap. 4.

6. Preiss and Ehrlich, op. cit., pp. 128-129.

7. American Institute for Public Opinion, Gallup, Survey no. 0709, March, 1965, Question 011; and *Gallup Opinion Index*, Report no. 27, September, 1967, p. 19. The findings of G. Almond and S. Verba in *The Civic Culture* (Princeton, N.J.: Princeton, 1963), pp. 108-109, suggest that Americans regard their police as highly as do all other peoples in this cross-cultural survey. The British alone view their police more favorably.

8. Preiss and Ehrlich, op. cit., p. 125; and The President's Commission on Law Enforcement and Administration of Justice, *The Challenge of a Free Society* (Washington, D.C.: GPO, 1967), p. 91.

9. Preiss and Ehrlich, op. cit., p. 130.

10. On two qualities, however, liking and fearing the police, the youngest group tends to drop below the level of the average for all respondents. See Gourley, op. cit., pp. 65 and 71.

11. Preiss and Ehrlich, op. cit., p. 130. The sample included persons under twenty-one years of age.

12. The reduction of respect among the very old, those beyond 70, may be partly a function of the general disengagement process characteristic of the aged, although we would need to know more about aging to explain this decline adequately.

13. *Royal Commission on the Police* (London: H. M. Stationery Office, 1960-1962), p. 6 and appendix 5. Comparable results were obtained in a study in Australia, using a question identical with the one in the British survey. The research workers report that "The differences between age groups is quite impressive; of those interviewed in the 17-20 age group only 25% said they had great respect for the police as compared with 58% of the 21-30-year-olds; in the 31-45 group 75% had great respect while in the over 46 group 82%. The older you get the more respect for the police you profess." P. R. Wilson and D. Chappell, "Police Public Relations," *Politics*, 2, pp. 258-259, 1967.

14. Apprehension along these lines is already implicit in testimony before the President's National Advisory Commission on Civil Disorders (1967). The *New York Times* (November 24, 1967) reports

that the Commission heard testimony recommending ". . . that the National Guard members be substituted for policemen as soon as possible after major civil disturbances begin . . . This would lessen animosity toward policemen taking part in 'actual combat' and thus permit them, when order is restored, to 'go on the next day picking up the pieces, putting it back together . . . The police then perhaps are in a better position to move in and assume their rightful role as the over-all law enforcement agency and crime prevention agency in the area, without quite as serious a stigma hanging over them.' "

15. To obtain some initial insight into the impact of age variations, it would be useful to correlate age distributions in a population with some indicators of the propensity of a regime to change. Similarly studies could be undertaken of the extent to which parties seeking changes are more likely to be composed of younger generations. Research might also be usefully devoted to analyzing the age composition of elites on the assumption that they might be consistently recruited from the least attached generations, in our terms.

16. See *New York Times*, March 13, 1968, p. 3.

17. See *Report of the National Advisory Commission on Civil Disorders* (New York: Dutton, 1968), p. 129, and chap. 2, footnote 115.

18. It is true that before 1960 the proportion of fifteen to twenty-four-year-olds was greater, but because of a smaller population base, the numbers in this age group are notably fewer.

19. We are indebted to Philip Auerbach, a graduate student in the department of political science at the University of Chicago, for drawing this point to our attention. Also see footnote 1 above.

20. See *Report of the National Advisory Commission on Civil Disorders*, p. 132, and chap. 2, footnote 126.

DETERMINANTS OF DIFFUSE SUPPORT IN CHILDHOOD

15

EXPLANATION OF THE CHILD'S DEVELOPING IMAGES

Our analysis thus far has been directed toward illuminating several of the most important processes through which diffuse support arises among young new members of the American political system. To that end we have focused primarily upon maturational trends in the child's capacity to relate himself to political authority, represented by such key objects as the policeman, the President, and the overarching structure of government. As we have progressed in this analysis, a series of hypotheses has evolved, and these have led to a variety of suggestions about the possible systemic impact of early orientations toward political authority.

What now remains is to push the analysis back, insofar as possible, to the factors that influence and shape these processes that we have detected. To accomplish this, it is first appropriate to restate briefly our major developmental hypotheses about these processes. Second, we shall attempt to suggest some broad categories of explanation for these propositions. After these preliminary steps, we can move on to a further and more detailed analysis of our data for explanatory purposes, employing independent variables that seem appropriate and are available within the limits of our study. Hence a restatement of our problem in relation to various possible types of explanations will occupy this chapter; the consideration of specific explanations available from our data will constitute the next two chapters.

In our attempt to give an account of the early developmental trends in the emergence of diffuse support, we have used several basic descriptive hypotheses. These have involved both cognitive and affective aspects of images of various authority objects. Our findings have permitted us to draw important inferences about the relative levels of diffuse support among children in different grades and about the processes through which children acquire their perceptions of and sentiments about the authorities.

Our analysis, however, calls for more than an elaboration of these inductions. We need to be able to advance some explanations that will help us to account for the origins, processes, and precipitating factors that lie behind the phenomena we have described. Our central hypotheses and findings offer the most appropriate entry points for this next stage of our analysis.

Our data, it will be recalled, have led us to hypothesize that the government, the President, and the policeman constitute especially salient points of contact for the young child in his growing acquaintance with the structure of political authority. Through these, and later through other objects of authority, the child begins to be politicized. This was substantiated by our discovery of the child's ability to recognize the difference between the public and private realms of life, the superior authority of persons and institutions external to the family, and the difference between political authority on the one hand and parental authority on the other. Given his level of maturity, we have hypothesized, the young child at first personalizes political authority, but by the middle grades he begins to shift to a more institutionalized interpretation of this authority. We have proposed that the idealization associated with early personalized perceptions carries over in modified form into the later years of childhood, as well as extending to political institutions. In sum, socialization during childhood is characterized by processes that we have labeled politicization, personalization, institutionalization, and idealization. All these processes seem to interlock in such a way as to contribute to a relatively high level of diffuse support for political authority.

These hypotheses about primary political socialization in the United States form our major dependent variables. But we may now ask whether all the children in our test sample, in any given age category, are necessarily socialized in exactly the same way, or whether there may not be important group differences. We may go even further and ask why the socializing processes themselves take the form they do. In these two different but related ways we may be able to obtain some additional understanding of how primary political socialization occurs and of the factors that influence it.

Hence for purposes of explaining the socializing processes we are now faced with two major tasks. One will be to elaborate some of the discernible group differences among those being socialized. Through this we will become aware of variations in the way members of different sex, social status, and other social categories respond to authority during childhood. Another main task will be to turn to these as well as to other independent variables —such as attitudes toward father, region, party preference, religion, and IQ—to help explain those processes, already identified, through which children become politically socialized.

However, in anticipation of our later discussion of these group variations and basic determinants, we shall find it useful if not imperative to turn to a general consideration of strategies that might be appropriate for explaining the key hypotheses that we have already evolved. As we indicated, this will occupy us for the remainder of the present chapter.

STRATEGIES OF EXPLANATION

As originally conceived our study did not place a high priority upon locating and measuring the effects of explanatory variables. Because we began at a very early stage in the investigation of political socialization, there was a prior task to be undertaken. Phenomena can be appropriately explained only after they have been accurately identified and described, and consequently the greatest share of the research resources was devoted to giving a better description of what the young child learns about the political realm and of when and how he learns it. Once the basic aspects of the socializing processes were established, we felt, it would be appropriate to explore their circumstances and causes.

Without such a strategy, the investigator could easily be caught in the endless confusion of attempting to identify, measure, and connect causes (early family influences, for example), the effects of which might turn out to be remote from actual political behavior.[1]

Consequently, it seemed to us profitable to attempt first to pinpoint the periods of basic change in political orientations and only then to mount a major effort to locate the proximate causes. Indeed, we have assumed that the changes we sought were likely to occur over a somewhat extended period of the life cycle. If this assumption is valid, then a likely corollary is that there exists a fairly complicated set of causal circumstances. A further implication would be that the tactic of deciding a priori when the most crucial time of socialization might be, then observing causal conditions existing at that time, would, given the strong probability of choosing the wrong point in the life cycle, be uneconomical and possibly a complete waste of time.

When in the next chapter we consider our own set of explanatory variables, therefore, we do so in the realization that this part of the analysis does not represent our main effort but that it necessarily constitutes only a secondary objective for the time being. *We regard our data only as precursory and suggestive for some later, specifically designed investigation of causes.*

From our data, however, we are able to obtain some guidance for the future. They enable us to estimate and outline what some of the explanatory variables of high merit might be. In the course of our research we did become keenly aware of a number of major causal circumstances underlying the development of authority images during childhood. Hence it has seemed appropriate to sketch out briefly an overall strategy of explanation suggested to us by our experiences in this area; to this strategy we will relate our own explanatory data as we present them in the succeeding chapters.

As we emphasized in the early chapters, political socialization is a long-term process of change in political attitudes and behaviors. It is probable that a complex set of forces acts to induce these changes. General cultural conditions, structural properties of the system, the available means of political communication, system-level changes in politics, certain patterns of individual and social attributes that exist at a given time, and many other influences may help to account for changes in what a given set of new members of the system think and feel about politics and in the initial input of diffuse support. But these various determinants need to be specified more discretely and operationally.[2]

Let us discuss them in what we would guess to be their approximate order of importance.

Developmental change

Grade (or its close correlate, age), as we have used it, represents an essential causal nexus and summary independent variable. Grade serves as the surrogate for several maturational forces. From one point of view the variable is the rough analog of level of educational attainment used so widely in studies of adult political behavior. It provides a convenient, if implicit, summary of the many influences of formal education upon the child—teachers, curricula, textbooks, school activities, the social, cultural, and economic milieu of the school, and the like. But in our study, grade in school is conceived more broadly to mean more than the formal and informal contributions of the educational system. That is, grade contains variance from a specified number of years of nonschool experiences. The fifth-grade child is normally in his sixth year of exposure to the educational system but in his eleventh year of direct family influence and probably in his ninth year of heavy exposure to television. Thus, in temporal priority and frequency of exposure, the school is merely a third force reflected in year-to-year changes of political orientation. In addition, by the middle years of elementary school, a child's peers are probably beginning to mark his thinking about the social world.[3]

The child also becomes cognizant of where he and others stand in various social hierarchies, defined by race, social class, religion, sex, national origin, etc. He must learn, therefore, to respond to a number of different roles: son or daughter, sibling, pupil, male or female, playmate, and so forth. Through any of these roles, the child may increasingly begin to relate himself to the wider political system. As he gains such consciousness through these several means, changes which take place will reflect his location on the educational and age-level hierarchies.

Moreover, grade in school indicates a significant level of intellectual development. This should perhaps be emphasized. In a rough way, society represents the standardized intellectual-development scores of young individuals by their placement at various school-grade levels. Thus, when we refer to grade-level changes in perceptions, we are in part referring (implicitly) to the child's arrival at various levels of intellectual maturity. His increasing capacity to understand subtleties such as the political system is no doubt reflected in his answers to our questions — and his sophistication is a result either of the overt actions of the educational system or of the indirect effects of other agencies that enhance his intellect.

Of possible special consequences as well is the grade-related introduction of specifically political or "civic" education in the schools. One way of interpreting grade-level changes is to connect them to the child's early introduction in the schools to the concepts of American citizenship — in beginning social studies, history, or civics instruction. There is at least a prima facie case for asserting a connection between such school inputs and the political awareness that we observe. In fact, if there is to be such a connection, it almost has to be in the pre-high-school years of the kinds of children included in our test group, given the recent intimation of a general lack of correlation of basic attitudes with civic education in high school.[4]

Grade as an independent variable therefore includes a number of specific, underlying conditions affecting political socialization. These are not only the general program of the school for promoting social learning and the more directly political aspects of school education, but also factors such as increasing intellectual maturity and the contributions of family, mass media, and peers. Grade represents, therefore, some "linear transformation" of a number of influences that accumulate from year to year as the individual and society attempt to adjust the individual's responses to the political and other social realms of behavior. Grade takes us a certain distance in the direction we want to go; but its main explanatory use is to suggest a number of influences that lie behind it. It is to the latter that we need to turn.

Before doing so, however, one final point should be made about age and grade. Looking for the moment at political socialization from the standpoint of its uses in explaining system-level phenomena (rather than as something in need of explanation) we can point to some further hypotheses. The major utilization of grade or age is in connection with the familiar hypothesis that what is learned earliest is fundamental to further behavior and will have most lasting effects. In moments of crisis in later life the likelihood that a person will regress to his basic beliefs is high.[5] Part of this effect is no doubt connected to the special psychological circumstances of early learning. The child learns from those who protect him from the hazards of the world and whose authority he is most apt to accept without question. Thus, in an atmosphere of warmth and protection, the young child is susceptible to appeals for his allegiance that enter his consciousness through the auspices of those people closest to him.[6]

The main thrust of our analysis has been to present a description and an explanation of the nature of changes in the child's images of political authority more precise than have hitherto existed, and to relate these to system-level processes. But we have attempted also to draw certain inferences about patterns of exposure reflected in grade-related changes that we observe, particularly for the profound system consequences of early exposure to political structures. There is much more to be said about what age trends represent in the way of causal circumstances than we have adumbrated. To some extent we shall be able to pursue these further possibilities as we consider some explanatory variables, such as IQ and subgroup memberships of the child. We will attempt, that is, to drive the analysis back to these underlying and intervening variables. To say that political attitudes are deep-seated when formed early and that they are in fact formed early, although essential to the tasks we have set ourselves, is nevertheless only a first step in causal exposition. Let us turn to some other possibilities.

Political structure

In addition to employing age-related developmental factors as explanations at a number of points, we have also used explanations related to the nature of the political structure. We proposed that certain key features of political authority are important to the way the young child becomes acquainted with the system and simultaneously begins to acquire supportive orientations. We have spoken at some length of the "head-and-tail" effects in the early personalization of political authority and of the way the robust image of benevolence begins to fade as the child matures. The psychological cementing functions of the personal images correspondingly decline in importance. Part of what one can say about long-term change of political orientations in the United States concerns certain distinctive features of the political system which provide the opportunity for early political learning—for example, representatives of authority who uniquely combine simplicity, personal palpability, visibility, and salience. The availability of such tangible, appealing incarnations of political authority as the policeman and President in the United States allows the child to be introduced to the system at a very early age, and thus with greatest potential long-term impact.

In systems where authority objects are less capable of losing their abstract character—where they are less amenable to being personalized, to being made highly visible and salient, or where the collectivity of authorities cannot readily be typified by a few strategic individuals or types of roles—we would expect the child to establish contact with the system less readily, more clumsily and abstractly, and probably at a later, less impressionable age. It would be interesting, for example, to test our generalizations through cross-cultural research in such collegial regimes as Uruguay or in other systems which lack one or another of the properties that we have hypothesized as important to the manner in which the young child becomes or fails to become attached to the system in the United States.

The trappings and symbolism of those objects in the structure of authority that serve as contact points, moreover, may be very important later on in establishing the terms of legitimacy. For example, if the chief figure of authority—say, the king or premier—is always seen by the child in military uniform, then incursions by the military into civilian politics may subsequently be resisted less readily than they would be in a system where political authorities usually appear in civilian dress. Military force may be more readily accepted at an early age as a legitimate instrument of political authority. Rule of law, which limits military intervention in politics, and civilian elections, political parties, and other devices may become less firmly based if the main myths and symbols of the system unite warrior and ruler.

In the American system, where civilian rule at the "head" and the means of violence at the "tail" are separate and yet both apparent to the child, the possibility of the preeminence of violence is limited—especially since the contact point for legitimate violence has generally been the police rather than the military. The police are interpreted as enforcers of the law while themselves subject to it. The new experiences during the urban riots of the 1960s in which the military as well as the police were involved may, of course, have new and different socializing consequences.

These are all structural interpretations along the lines that our analysis has suggested. Much needs to be done in these terms to distinguish different types of early contact points and to detect their possible results. It may make a considerable political difference which points of contact are most visible and salient— both for the symbolization of authority and for the way the child becomes assimilated to the system at an early age, which in turn has consequences for the deep-rootedness of support for a given structure of authorities. Our analysis just begins to scratch the surface of the possibilities that exist for this level of analysis as a strategy of explanation. But, however little we have done with it, we would think it a most compelling explanatory approach for future research.

Learning processes

Whatever the child's contact points with the political world, there must be certain processes in which he participates in order to find them. He does not come to them and extend diffuse support simply because they exist. Rather, the child engages in specific activities and interacts with others in such a way that he learns who the authorities are and what they are like. Thus part of the variance we need to bring into our explanatory equation is described by these activities and interactions.

From one point of view, age itself, or aging, is a process. In this sense our grade-level comparisons are indexes of a process of political learning. But grade trends do not measure the processes which underlie them; they measure only the effects of such processes. We must turn, therefore, to the underlying interactions themselves for true process explanation.

It is perhaps helpful to divide the latter into two broad categories. First we have the processes of political communication or education that go on between the socializers and the "socializee." Certain cues are passed from the agent of political learning to the young new member within a situational context, which denote the general relationships shared by the two and the resources of communication and reinforcement (or resistance) available to each. A shorthand way of describing these processes is to refer to the effects of the agencies or agents of political socialization—parents, family, teachers, schools, peers, etc.—upon the person being socialized. The standard method of showing such effects is through the degree of correspondence between socializer and socializee—as with percentage agreements or correlations. But to account fully for the similarities and differences we would need to understand the type of child-rearing practices employed, the frequency, warmth, and power of interaction between child and socializing agent, the competition among socializers, and the order of exposure to various socializing influences.

The second major class of process phenomena in need of explanation is the changes that take place within the individual as he receives the stimuli of political communication and adapts his orientations accordingly. These processes are illustrated by the individual's growing capacities of assimilation, his changing needs for certain kinds of information, his building of expectations and values to orient himself in a heterogeneous and changing environment, and his psychological reactions to the bearers of stimuli. Our own data shed little light on such processes of internal adaptation, although in one sense, IQ serves as a measure of the capacity to respond to new political information and thus is an indicator of relevance here. We shall deal with IQ in Chapter 17.

No one has really probed deeply into these processes in a political context, so that it is especially difficult to know precisely what explanations of them would be like. A number of existing models might be adopted, however, as analogs for the description of internal political cue processing: for example, Piaget's stages of intellectual development and the attitudinal maturation processes that he postulates,[7] balance or dissonance theory of attitude change,[8] Freudian concepts of identification,[9] imitation, imprinting, role-learning theory, and a variety of other possibilities.[10] To the present, the internalization aspects of political orientations and behaviors still need to be investigated. As perhaps the most difficult feature of the total problem, internal phenomena have seemingly been left for the last. We have obtained virtually no data on this dimension.

We detect, therefore, two major areas in the explanation of political socialization through its processes. One relies upon the context and content of interactions between the individual and his social environment from the standpoint of who interacts with him, under what psychological conditions, with what kinds of messages, and with which types of reinforcement resources. The other process category contains the internal processes of adaptation: how the person responds to the stimuli presented to him—by understanding them, being converted by them, resisting them, adapting them to his own needs, etc. Our own data tell us relatively little about these two aspects of political socialization. Yet we are not totally without suggestive evidence; and this will be presented shortly.

Generational influences

Another explanatory strategy thus far little pursued in research on political socialization concerns the effects of generational phenomena. There are a number of ways to define generation, but the one we have used, in Chapter 14, emphasized common experiences of a set of people who mature and live through the same historical era and whose behavior reflects the impact of their experiences. Normally, the common experiences that a generation shares and that separate it from other generations result from broad changes in society and its institutions or from the dominant problems of the system in a given epoch, as is reflected in the way we speak of the "Depression generation," the "World War II generation," the "silent generation" (of college students who were educated prior to the student activism and protest of the 1960s), and the like. In one sense, generational variables reflect the individual's interaction with the society at large rather than forces of change within himself or the processes of interaction with people in his immediate social environment. It becomes important, therefore, to distinguish between generational factors and those associated with aging (social and biological) or which concern experiences in such face-to-face groups as family or classroom.

A case in which these several types of variables impinge upon the child's political consciousness so that they are difficult to untangle is in "teen-age rebellion,"[11] or less pejoratively, teen-age differentiation from adults. As the child loosens his bonds with his family as part of growing up, he shows aging or developmental effects. Family ties are loosened as a function of maturing physically, socially, and intellectually. At the same time, it is not simple capacity to be independent that is involved. There are a number of frictions that the child experiences with his family simply because he begins to look elsewhere for cues and values— especially to his peers. Thus a new pattern of interaction with his own family develops that becomes manifested in various forms of differentiation: an opposing style of dress, manners, morality, and even politics in some cases.[12] In addition, however, there is the generational effect of growing up in a period where a set of values, problems, and concerns rather different from those typical of his parents' period of development is central. As a result, response patterns of people from two generations will differ.

Our data, confined as they are to a single point in time and covering a restricted number of years (relative to the twenty to twenty-five years usually thought necessary to the idea of the generation), are simply not very helpful in ferreting out the effects of generations. Indeed we have, for all practical purposes, controlled for the effects of generations in our study. This does not relieve us from the responsibility of suggesting that a special, generational cast to political learning may be given, even in these early years, by pervasive social changes.

Social structure

Although our explanatory matrix is already very complicated, there is one further general category of variables that we wish to include in a study of political socialization within a given system.[13] This class of variables concerns the effects of the individual's membership in various subunits and categories of society. The explanatory value of such categorization of individuals lies mainly in the differentiating effects of social memberships, such as sex, social class, religious affiliation, and geographical area.

Greatest attention in past research has been placed upon sex and social class. General findings have been that the young member of the political system is affected at least marginally in his pattern of political learning by these two variables.[14] We shall give special attention to them below because subgroup differentiation by sex or social status may portend considerable political impact for the child in his later years. We might hypothesize that subgroups that maintain or represent significant subcultural variations, such as social classes or regions in the United States, are the ones most likely to impress their differences in childhood. Sex distinctions and other variables that may be becoming increasingly marginal politically in the United States should show less marked differentiation. Sex, like grade in school, is a summary variable, however, so that whatever differences are found between males and females may include not only certain cultural patterns but also psychological differences that bear upon a few realms of political behavior—such as regard for political authorities.

A number of differentiating effects might be postulated for social-structural variables. Differences that we might expect between the social classes, for example, could include:

1 A difference in perception that appears fairly early and is constant throughout childhood—suggesting that the child is quickly brought to an awareness akin to that of the people of his social milieu—which then persists into later life.

2 A lead-lag effect wherein all children move, over the grades, toward certain common orientations, but those of higher

social standing move more rapidly. Assuming that the period of learning is long enough, the lower-status child may catch up eventually, and if so the social differences in political images will be erased.

3 An increasingly divergent perception which starts early and becomes continually reinforced in the disparate social experiences of the classes as their new members mature.

Any one of these three models of age-related class differences may have political consequences. The first suggests that a distinctive pattern of behavior is set for each stratum in the earliest years. This model is, in a sense, the "medium-impact" case. The second pattern of development may result in a more ambiguous adult response; the classes will see things in roughly the same way, with two exceptions:

1 The higher-status child will have learned his lessons earlier, and thus such lessons may well have taken root more firmly.

2 If the lag for the lower-status child postpones some political learning beyond the most plastic periods of childhood, many political orientations may be unlikely to strike deep roots.

These sorts of effects may apply to other categories also, such as geographical area. One of the strategies of the present project has been to investigate constant, increasing, or decreasing differences of these kinds among sex, social class, and geographical categories over the grades. We undertake these analyses in the next chapter. There we shall describe some of the differences for several types of socializing processes within the general realm of supportive response to political authority. As we will later pursue this range of questions in detail, we need not describe it further here.

In sum, we propose that several key levels of explanation are called for in the investigation of childhood political socialization. We have become increasingly aware of these possibilities in the course of our research. At this juncture, given that our research purpose was to describe more accurately than heretofore the nature and course of childhood support for political authorities, we are not able to give a fully satisfactory account of these possibilities. Our purposes were exploratory, and we were not fully aware of what causal data to collect when we began.

Nonetheless, we have offered certain explanations already — particularly those related to maturational factors and what they portend — and some of the political structural determinants of the child's response that we find. In addition, we shall be able to say something about the effects of subgroup memberships.

We are least able to deal, however, with process and generational influences except in a generally speculative way. Our data do not readily lend themselves to clear connections between patterns of political learning and the internal processes of assimilation by individuals. Neither can they really be used to assess the relative contributions of family, school, peers, and media — where we have some data they are usually very unreliable and highly tentative — nor, indeed, to say much about the effects of the communication patterns that obtain in these social-interaction processes. We are weakest of all in trying to indicate what generational forces are at work; our data in effect cancel such causes from the analysis.

Thus, since we ourselves have not had especially high hopes for our treatment of determinants, we do not expect the reader to be disappointed when he finds we are unable to give good explanations of these phenomena. Our work has been carried on at too early a stage for such hopes to be realistic. Yet we do have some limited explanatory power in our findings.

We turn then to our explanatory data. We shall proceed in two stages. The first part, Chapter 16, is concerned with a few key subgroup differentiations for several of our central developmental hypotheses, especially for politicization, personalization, and institutionalization. These will emphasize the more cognitive aspects of the child's images, particularly of government as a focus of political authority. In the second part, Chapter 17, the analysis will move to the policeman and the President, with special attention to the affective response of the child (idealization). In addition, we shall consider simultaneously a broader range of independent variables than was feasible for the less easily indexed government items.

NOTES

1. For discussion of this and related issues, see R. G. Niemi, "Collecting Information about the Family: A Problem in Survey Methodology," in J. Dennis and F. W. Frey (eds.), *Explorations of Political*

Socialization: A Reader of Contemporary Research (New York: Wiley, forthcoming); and R. G. Niemi, "A Methodological Study of Political Socialization in the Family," unpublished doctoral dissertation, University of Michigan, Ann Arbor, 1967.

2. For a discussion of some of the general issues in locating and researching the effects of various independent variables, see J. Dennis, "Major Problems of Political Socialization Research," *Midwest Journal of Political Science,* 12, pp. 85-114, 1968, and the works cited in note 2 therein.

3. See, for example, J. S. Coleman, *The Adolescent Society* (New York: Free Press, 1951), for a discussion of peer influences in socialization.

4. K. P. Langton and M. K. Jennings, "Political Socialization and the High School Civics Curriculum in the United States," *American Political Science Review,* 62, pp. 852-867, 1968.

5. See D. Easton and R. D. Hess, "The Child's Political World," in S. M. Lipset and L. Lowenthal (eds.), *Culture and Social Character* (New York: Free Press, 1961), pp. 226-251.

6. See, for example, O. G. Brim, Jr., and S. Wheeler, *Socialization After Childhood: Two Essays* (New York: Wiley, 1966), for a discussion of the mechanisms of reinforcement in such learning.

7. J. Piaget, *Judgment and Reasoning in the Child* (New York: Free Press, 1948) and *Language and Thought of the Child* (Paterson, N.J.: Littlefield, Adams, 1959). See also D. E. Berlyne, "Recent Developments in Piaget's Work," *British Journal of Educational Psychology,* 12, pp. 1-12, 1957.

8. See the references cited in R. E. Lane and D. O. Sears, *Public Opinion* (Englewood Cliffs, N.J.: Prentice-Hall, 1964), chap. 5.

9. E. H. Erikson, *Childhood and Society* (New York: Norton, 1950).

10. See, for example, E. R. Hilgard, *Theories of Learning* (New York: Appleton-Century-Crofts, 1956); and *Theories of Learning and Instruction,* Sixty-third Yearbook of the National Society for the Study of Education (Chicago: The University of Chicago Press, 1964) part I; J. C. Jones, *Learning* (New York: Harcourt, Brace & World, 1967); F. Elkin, *The Child and Society: The Process of Socialization* (New York: Random House, 1962); S. A. Mednick, *Learning* (Englewood Cliffs, N.J.: Prentice-Hall, 1964); A. Brandura and R. H. Walters, *Social Learning and Personality Development* (New York: Holt, 1963); N. E. Miller and J. Dollard, *Social Learning and Imitation* (New Haven, Conn.: Yale, 1962); and A. L. Baldwin, *Theories of Child Development* (New York: Wiley, 1967).

11. For fuller discussion of this problem, see Dennis, op. cit., pp. 100-102. For further references to the literature on this question and many others of this type, see J. Dennis, "A Survey and Bibliography of Contemporary Research on Political Learning and Socialization," Occasional Paper no. 8, Wisconsin Research and Development Center for Cognitive Learning, April, 1967.

12. See, for example, R. Middleton and S. Putney, "Political Expression of Adolescent Rebellion," *American Journal of Sociology*, 68, pp. 527-535, 1963.

13. Another distinguishable category of independent variables involves cross-cultural variation, which is not applicable to our problem here.

14. See, for example, H. H. Hyman, *Political Socialization* (New York: Free Press, 1959); and F. Greenstein, *Children and Politics* (New Haven, Conn.: Yale, 1965).

16
PREDICTORS OF COGNITIVE RESPONSES TO POLITICAL AUTHORITIES

The various processes through which we have found a child to be socialized to the structure of political authority in the United States need not be uniform in nature. All children in our group do not perceive the representatives of political authority in the same way or extend to them the same measure of warmth. Nor need politicization proceed at the same pace for all. It would be too much to expect that all children, regardless of social categories such as sex, social class, and region, and regardless of subjective characteristics such as intelligence and personality, would move in a solid phalanx and at the same rate in the direction of the average child in our test group.

In the last chapter we suggested that major group differences might be anticipated. In this chapter we shall concern ourselves with the more cognitive side of authority, and in the next with variations relevant for the more affective aspect. In both instances we shall find that differences occur much less frequently than we might have predicted. In describing these differences we shall also be led to some understanding of why they should appear. In addition we shall be able to explore some of their potential consequences for the political system.

VARIATIONS IN THE IMAGES OF AUTHORITY

For the age-related cognitive and attitudinal changes that we have observed, we find that cues flowing to the child pass through several filters, any one of which could conceivably have lasting effects upon the orientations acquired. The filtering influences upon which we shall focus here can be classified either as aspects of the social environment of the child or as factors pertaining to his internal capacities and resources. In acquiring his new role toward the political authorities, the child is likely to do so within certain differentiating social contexts—especially sex, social class, geographically based subcultures, ethnicity, family, race, religion, and party identification. In addition, he is apt to be affected by his ability to receive and assimilate relevant messages—in particular as a function of his personality and general intellectual development.

As can be seen from this simple listing, incomplete as it is, the number of overlapping filters may be considerable, and we shall encounter additional ones in the next chapter. The effect on the socializing "messages" that get through to the child is enormously complex, and we can hope only to begin to shed a little light on a few of the screens. In this chapter we shall concentrate on the impact of the basic social categories of sex, social status, and geocultural region and, as we have indicated, only for cognitive components of the child's image. In the next chapter we shall add a few more possible independent or explanatory variables, but there we shall relate them to affective components.

Empirically it will appear that our data have led us to identify two main screening potentialities for groups of the children differentiated by these social and subjective criteria: lead-lag differences in patterns of political socialization, and persisting substantive variations in the kinds of images children of various subgroups acquire. The first outcome, reflecting our lead-lag intensity hypothesis, suggests either earlier or later learning, but perhaps eventual similarity among all children. The second suggests an ingrained difference that may be continually reinforced into adulthood, which we shall call our reinforcement of substantive differentiation hypothesis. That is, early social or ability differentiation might have a major effect on the *kinds* of images and commitments the individual forms. The young male may become more attuned to the abstract or impersonal properties of political authority early in life, whereas the young female may continue longer to personalize and thus to restrict her image. In early differentiation of this sort, the significant political effect is early reinforcement of the content of orientations that allows persons of one subgroup to see the political world in a way dissimilar to that of persons who belong to the counterpart social and ability groupings.

From the standpoint of both the substantive terms of the response and its intensity or deep-rootedness, therefore, such early differentiation may be of considerable explanatory interest for the input of support. Let us then turn to an investigation of possible differences in social location. We shall return to those substantive areas in the socialization of the children about political authority already explored for the aggregate as a whole. We shall seek to discover those differences in the processes and outcomes of socialization with respect to political authority that can be accounted for by the factors already mentioned, keeping in mind both the lead-lag intensity hypothesis and the reinforcement of substantive differentiation hypothesis.

SEX DIFFERENCES IN POLITICAL SOCIALIZATION

One of the structural social variables of continuing interest to students of political socialization and to students of politics more generally has been that of sex. Scholars in this century have investigated the origins, nature, and consequences of political differentiation between men and women. With the extension of suffrage to women in the Western democracies, a number of important issues concerning sex typing and variation in political behavior has been raised for public discussion and scholarly inquiry. In particular, attention has centered upon possible differences in electoral behavior of men and women. The rates of female participation have been found to be significantly lower than those of men; and the direction of female voting has somewhat less clearly been found to be more conservative.[1]

The electoral consequences of sex differences, for what we have called allocative processes,[2] have been a major stimulus in generating interest in the circumstances of political socialization. Beginning at least with Hyman's inventory of early material, there has been considerable emphasis upon the possibility that male-female variation in political behavior stretches back to childhood. Hyman concludes at one point, after viewing the existing data: "Thus already at early ages, boys are directed toward politics and here lie the seeds of the adult differentiations everywhere found in studies of political participation."[3] The ego ideals of boys are more likely than those of girls to be public figures.[4] Boys are apt to be better informed politically, more interested in public affairs, and more attuned to the politically relevant aspects of the news media and other communications.[5] Many of these differences have a fairly direct connection to electoral phenomena and to the theories of electoral behavior. The areas of attitudinal and conceptual content which were thought most worthy of investigation about early sex differences in political learning are those most intimately associated with later behavior as voters—political interest, information, attentiveness to political communication, participation levels, and the like.

Our own theoretical focus upon systems persistence and the growth of support for political authorities suggests, however, that we need to expand what is known about childhood political sex differentiation to other content areas. We are concerned with such differences neither for their explanatory power about possible effects upon election outcomes and thus upon the nature of political leadership and policy nor for what they show about the continuity of the wider cultural sex typing of political role behavior. It is not our main purpose, that is, to show how sex differences in political learning are still in progress—as a way of suggesting that the mores of an earlier era are still very much alive today. The latter is no doubt relevant to our inquiry, as a partial explanation of why such sex differences occur, if they do. Nor are we primarily interested in the effects upon the individual and upon his relationship to others that are the result of the political manifestations of his sex roles. (Such psychological factors serve more as an explanation of what we are likely to find than as a theoretical rationale for our looking for sex differences.)

We are not totally oblivious to the consequences for the individual of his or her being brought up to expect to play a greater or lesser role in politics. Nevertheless, our main effort is directed toward understanding what possible consquences sex differences might have, not for allocative politics but for system politics, especially for the nature of the child's early response to political authority. Sex enters the analysis for us only as it affects the relative depth of the commitment or the type of response that is made. When we turn to the data, we shall have this in mind.

One of the general features of our data—not simply the portion we analyze in this book—is that relatively small but pervasive sex differences appear throughout. Boys are generally a bit ahead in the direction of aggregate development. In this section we shall emphasize a few of these differences in the area of political authority that are more striking than others. We shall proceed in our discussion of sex differences by selecting from the earlier chapters a few of our most important hypotheses in the cognitive realm and then by looking at the kinds of differences that we find between boys and girls on the items that pertain to these hypotheses. In particular, we shall focus upon the following hypotheses:

1 Politicization: The child becomes increasingly politicized in elementary school, as revealed in his recognition of government. Also as part of his politicization the child distinguishes between public and private authorities and gives much greater weight, at least initially, to the public ones.

2 Personalization versus institutionalization: The early dominance of personalization in the cognitive image of government is gradually superseded by an institutional emphasis.

Given the number of main and subsidiary hypotheses that could be brought forth again for consideration in this context, these two constitute only a minimal set of key points for illuminating sex differences or similarities. But they will serve reasonably well to accomplish our purposes. We shall take each in turn, using some key items as indicators of our findings. Subsequently we shall follow the same procedure in testing for the only other significant differences, which occur among social-status groups and cities.

SEX DIFFERENCES IN COGNITIVE RESPONSES

Politicization

One challenge for the child in coming to grips with the political world is how to differentiate political authority from other aspects of society. Thereby he begins the important process of becoming politicized. In part, this involves attaining some understanding of government as a distinguishable object; in part, it involves recognizing the difference between that which is governmental and that which is not.

Confidence in understanding the idea of government: Let us look first at how readily boys and girls comprehend the idea of government. Table 16-1 provides relevant information about sex differences in understanding the concept of government.

Table 16-1 Sex Differences in Answering "Not sure what government means"*

| | Boys | | Girls | |
Grade	Percent	N†	Percent	N†
2	23	855	32	800
3	14	833	24	845
4	15	895	21	854
5	10	911	12	892
6	10	883	15	866
7	8	853	9	870
8	7	799	12	896

*CA-9, page 12, item 55. "Some of you may not be quite sure what the word *government* means. If you are not sure what *government* means, put an X in the box below."
†N = number of cases responding.

As we observe, there are more girls than boys who say that they are uncertain about what the word government means at every age. The difference is especially apparent for the youngest children, suggesting that differences in political sex-role typing are acquired as early as second grade. The young male has a higher probability of becoming politically sensitized from the beginning of the age span. Although, with the compressed variance that we find on this item by the later grades, there is a lessening of the political difference of the sexes over the age span, one might speculate that the young male, more likely to have been sensitized to government early, is then in a position to develop deeper and more lasting orientations of other kinds toward government.

The public and private sectors: Perhaps a more typical set of effects is shown in Table 16-2 about the child's growing capacity to differentiate between the public and private sectors. On balance boys tend to lead and girls to lag in terms of the direction of aggregate development. The most striking difference occurs in the postman item, where the difference over the grades is around 10 percent, or about a grade and a half on the average.

In identifying the public or private status of the milkman, policeman, and (at the younger ages) the soldier, boys are in the aggregate somewhat ahead in the direction development is proceeding. This is true even on the policeman question, where the direction shifts in the middle grades. Yet, the boys do not dominate entirely; girls lead on judge and teacher. In general, therefore,

Table 16-2   Sex Differences in Development of an Awareness of the Public and Private Sectors* (percent of children responding)

Grade	Sex	Milk-man	Police-man	Soldier	Judge	Post-man	Teacher	N Responding (varies by item)
2	M	28%	88	74	84	62	47%	824-840
	F	30	84	62	89	52	50	774-792
3	M	28	90	85	87	69	53	809-822
	F	33	88	74	89	57	57	818-834
4	M	26	91	86	89	78	57	871-885
	F	30	91	80	89	64	60	831-845
5	M	17	88	90	90	86	57	893-905
	F	24	90	90	91	74	68	882-889
6	M	14	84	93	90	90	58	875-882
	F	19	91	93	93	80	71	855-865
7	M	12	80	96	94	95	61	841-851
	F	14	85	95	95	84	67	856-867
8	M	6	76	98	92	97	55	792-797
	F	11%	86	98	95	90	63%	888-895

*CA-9, pages 11-12, items 49-54: "Here are some people. Which ones work for the government? Does the _____ work for the government?" Entries are percent answering "yes."

the sex differences we find are small, fairly consistent and suggest a slightly faster rate of politicization for boys.

Personalization versus institutional interpretation of government

Image of government: We find a somewhat similar mixed pattern on our question about the two best pictures of our government. A few consistent differences appear, with boys generally ahead compared with the aggregate development (Table 16-3).

The most notable difference is the special but perhaps significant and increasing divergence between girls and boys on the salience of the President as a symbolic representative of government. Whereas there is virtually no difference of this kind at grade 2, by grade 8 roughly twice as many girls as boys still pick the President. In this sense, girls remain political "primitives" (relative to the direction of aggregate development) on the average two or more years longer than do boys, if we can project from our figures. Indeed, the tendency for personalization of authority persists into adolescence (age thirteen or fourteen), for a significant proportion of females, whereas for males the tendency has declined considerably.

Correspondingly, if not as sharply, boys more often pick Congress as the best representation of government, indicating a greater impetus toward a more impersonal, institutional interpretation. This is not to say that females are always the greatest personalizers (see the Uncle Sam option), nor is it to assert that

Table 16-3 Sex Differences in Development of a Cognitive Image of Government: Symbolic Associations* (percent of children responding)

Grade	Sex	Police-man	[George] Wash-ington	Uncle Sam	Voting	Supreme Court	Capitol	Congress	Flag	Statue of Liberty	Pres-ident [Kennedy]	I Don't Know	N Re-spond-ing	N Not Respond-ing
2	M	8%	40	19	4	5	17	7	15	12	47	12%	837	18
	F	8	39	12	5	4	10	5	17	12	46	20	782	18
3	M	4	25	23	8	8	19	15	15	14	43	11	821	12
	F	4	28	15	9	5	14	11	18	15	50	14	841	4
4	M	5	14	23	11	11	16	33	12	13	35	11	885	10
	F	6	15	13	11	9	17	25	15	13	39	16	841	13
5	M	3	7	21	19	21	11	53	10	11	33	4	902	9
	F	3	7	18	19	13	12	45	13	12	44	6	887	5
6	M	3	6	18	28	18	10	52	11	17	26	4	876	7
	F	2	4	16	28	15	10	47	12	17	35	6	864	2
7	M	2	3	21	39	16	9	48	12	17	22	3	850	3
	F	4	4	15	40	11	10	41	14	20	34	3	864	6
8	M	2	2	17	49	18	6	51	12	19	16	1	795	4
	F	2%	1	16	45	14	8	47	11	20	29	2%	894	2

*CA-9, page 4, item 24.

other types of institutionalization may not draw equally well from both sexes (see voting). Yet the difference is most distinctive on the President option. This suggests that the female child typically enters into the aggregate consciousness of political authority and incorporates its more abstract attributes at a slower rate than does the male.

Concerning the recognition of basic governmental functions, two further examples of the greater attraction that the President as a participant in political authority has for young females are significant. These are shown in Tables 16-4 and 16-5.

Table 16-4   Sex Differences in Perception of the Chief Lawmaker* (percent of children responding)

Grade	Sex	Congress	President	Supreme Court	Don't Know	Total	N Responding	N Not Responding
2	Boys	5%	75	14	6	100%	837	18
	Girls	5	76	8	11	100	790	10
3	Boys	14	62	19	5	100	816	17
	Girls	9	70	15	6	100	832	13
4	Boys	32	36	26	6	100	880	15
	Girls	23	53	16	9	101	843	11
5	Boys	60	15	22	3	100	904	7
	Girls	54	24	18	4	100	889	3
6	Boys	66	10	20	3	99	880	3
	Girls	64	16	16	4	100	863	3
7	Boys	76	6	16	1	99	847	6
	Girls	68	11	17	4	100	865	5
8	Boys	86	5	8	1	100	796	3
	Girls	85%	6	8	1	100%	894	2

*CA-9, page 7, item 33.

Table 16-5   Sex Differences in Perception of "Who does the most to run the country"* (percent of children responding)

Grade	Sex	Congress	President	Supreme Court	Don't Know	Total	N Responding	N Not Responding
2	Boys	4%	88	3	4	99%	844	11
	Girls	3	84	3	9	99	783	17
3	Boys	7	86	3	4	100	824	9
	Girls	6	85	3	6	100	838	7
4	Boys	15	77	4	5	101	880	15
	Girls	11	77	3	8	99	845	9
5	Boys	23	70	4	3	100	905	6
	Girls	17	73	4	6	100	891	1
6	Boys	31	62	4	3	100	880	3
	Girls	18	70	5	6	99	864	2
7	Boys	34	57	7	2	100	845	8
	Girls	22	71	3	4	100	866	4
8	Boys	39	56	3	2	100	793	6
	Girls	32%	61	4	4	101%	890	6

*CA-9, page 9, item 41.

On the chief-lawmaker item, the President is chosen by a larger proportion of girls than of boys at every grade. In the later grades on the item "Who does the most to run the country?" a similar effect obtains. Thus in the instances where a difference is found, the President is more prominent for girls than for boys.

Salience: These findings lead naturally to a further question. How do boys and girls compare on questions that tap more directly the relative salience of various individual authorities? An item that we have used for this purpose puts this question: "Who helps you and your family the most?" The options provided are: policeman, soldier, father, teacher, and President.

From Table 16-6 we see that the President again draws disproportionately from the female respondents for his support. In this respect our previous hypothesis about the child's early differentiation of family from political authority needs to be slightly modified to take into account the greater tendency of girls to prefer the President as an authority figure.

Table 16-6   Sex Differences in Salience of Authority Figures* (percent of children responding)

Grade	Sex	Police-man	Soldier	Father	Teacher	President	Total	N Re-sponding
2	Boys	51%	30	36	26	47	190%	855
	Girls	52	13	40	34	51	190	800
3	Boys	46	24	48	30	40	188	833
	Girls	48	14	47	35	45	189	845
4	Boys	38	19	59	33	32	181	895
	Girls	37	13	59	37	38	184	854
5	Boys	38	18	65	32	28	181	911
	Girls	36	16	63	36	34	185	892
6	Boys	34	15	71	34	26	180	883
	Girls	33	14	66	37	34	184	866
7	Boys	27	17	77	38	22	181	853
	Girls	28	17	71	37	33	186	870
8	Boys	30	13	75	39	21	178	799
	Girls	29%	16	73	41	26	185%	896

*CA-9, page 13, item 58: "Who helps you and your family the most? Put an X by the *two* who help you and your family the most." Percentages do not add to 200% because not all children gave two responses; every child did respond at least once.

Summary

The sex differences that we find are small, and, as can be seen from the above analysis, they do not present a simple pattern. A few are striking, such as the greater response of girls to the President. This may presage a greater personalized interpretation of authority in later years. Most, however, are differences too small to be of great consequence for the operation of the system.

The differentiation may however suggest possible marginal effects, particularly since the politicization of boys starts on the average a little earlier than that of girls; thus the political realm is apt to become a better-rooted part of the young male's conceptual and attitudinal framework. We would certainly expect a continuation of the differentiation already observed in adult political behavior. But such minor differences may reflect as much a long-term lessening of politicocultural sexual differentiation as its continuation. That is to say, sex typing is transmitted from adults to children less than we might have expected, at least for the area of system politics. A difference is still present; but our data do not show it as likely to be more than a minor factor in determining the future level of the child's supportive response to political authority.

SOCIOECONOMIC STATUS DIFFERENCES IN COGNITIVE RESPONSES

Like sex, social class or socioeconomic status (SES) has long occupied a prominent place in political analysis. Students of political socialization have reflected this concern in attempting to describe the differences that appear in childhood and adolescence. Just as for sex, one of the major sources for stimulating an interest in SES differences has been the studies of adult voting.[6] This has led perhaps to an overconcentration upon areas of political learning most related to voting, particularly upon rate of participation and direction of partisanship. These and other differences, including varying levels of political information, have been widely noted.[7] Using the same socialization hypotheses as we used for sex, let us consider whether SES differences appear in childhood.

Politicization

Confidence in understanding the idea of government: If we use the same items again as the occasion for testing SES differences in early cognitive response to political authority, we find a situation somewhat analogous to that for sex differences. There are a number of consistent SES differences—but again, they are not especially large or completely consistent. Table 16-7 presents one of the cases of clear and persistent status differences.

Those not certain about what government means constitute 31 percent of the lower-status second-graders but only 25 percent of the upper-status second-graders. These proportions decline to 13 percent by grade 8 for the lower-status children and to 5 percent for the upper-status group. Thus a noteworthy difference of the lead-lag variety exists.

Public and private sectors: When we turn to the items about whether different roles are governmental or not, however, the

Table 16-7 SES Differences in Answering "not sure what *government* means"*

Grade	Low SES Percent	N	Middle SES Percent	N	High SES Percent	N
2	31	339	27	922	25	394
3	26	398	16	915	18	365
4	22	396	18	838	14	515
5	14	431	11	834	9	538
6	18	405	12	802	8	542
7	8	425	10	772	6	526
8	13	401	11	781	5	513

*CA-9, page 12, item 55: "Some of you may not be quite sure what the word government means. If you are not sure what *government* means, put an X in the box below." SES is measured by father's (or guardians') occupation. Entries are percent of total SES stratum at each grade who answer that they are not sure what government means.

patterns are less clear. As shown in Table 16-8 the lower-status child is more apt to include the milkman among government workers but a little less likely to exclude the teacher. The most striking difference is on the milkman item, and the response pattern for it alone suggests a lead-lag progression. But the lead or lag is by no means uniform across all the items.

Table 16-8 SES Differences in Development of an Awareness of the Public and Private Sectors* (percent of children responding)

Grade	SES	Milk-man	Police-man	Soldier	Judge	Post-man	Teacher	N Responding (varies by item)
2	Upper	25%	85	69	85	54	43%	381-390
	Middle	27	86	69	87	55	48	892-909
	Lower	40	88	65	86	66	53	327-331
3	Upper	26	89	81	91	64	49	355-360
	Middle	30	89	78	89	61	55	883-905
	Lower	37	89	79	84	65	61	389-394
4	Upper	27	90	82	90	72	52	495-510
	Middle	26	91	85	88	72	60	816-829
	Lower	33	92	80	89	68	63	387-393
5	Upper	16	88	93	89	81	58	529-535
	Middle	22	90	90	91	81	65	821-827
	Lower	24	88	87	91	78	64	428-431
6	Upper	11	88	95	93	89	62	537-542
	Middle	17	88	93	91	85	66	790-800
	Lower	21	88	91	92	81	64	402-405
7	Upper	8	82	96	95	89	60	521-526
	Middle	13	84	96	94	89	65	759-769
	Lower	17	81	95	93	89	67	417-423
8	Upper	4	82	99	94	95	56	509-512
	Middle	8	80	98	93	94	59	773-780
	Lower	13%	81	97	94	90	64%	396-400

*CA-9, pages 11-12, items 49-54: "Here are some people. Which ones work for the government? Does the____work for the government?" Entries are percent answering "yes."

Personalization, versus *institutionalization:* A somewhat similar picture obtains for the SES differences shown in Table 16-9 about the "two best pictures of our government." These data would indicate that there is some tendency for the lower-status child to lag, compared with the aggregate development. Such an effect is most prominent on the voting and Congress options and is present to some extent on the President option. Only voting shows very marked differences, however.

Voting—representative as it is of the child's tendency to depersonalize political authority—is of special interest because the difference is not simply a lead-lag phenomenon but more nearly a matter of increasing differentiation with age between the lower- and middle-status children on the one hand and the upper-status children on the other. This difference is presented graphically in Figure 16-1.

The shape of these curves might suggest that the capacity of the child to interpret government as popular participation is

Figure 16-1. SES Differences in Choosing *Voting* as One of the Two Best Pictures of Our Government.

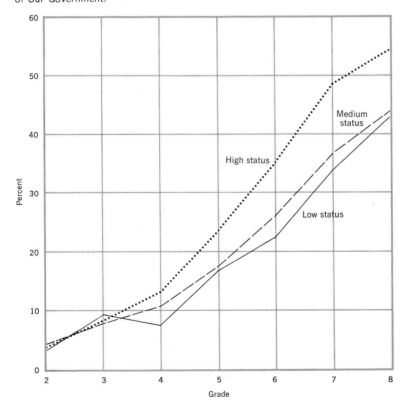

Table 16-9   SES Differences in the Development of a Cognitive Image of Government: Symbolic Associations* (percent of children responding)

Grade	SES	Police- man	[George] Wash- ington	Uncle Sam	Voting	Supreme Court	Capitol	Con- gress	Flag	Statue of Liberty	Pres- ident [Kennedy]	I Don't Know	N Re- spond- ing	N Not Respond- ing
2	Upper	6%	35	15	4	5	17	8	17	11	45	18%	389	5
	Middle	8	39	15	5	5	14	6	15	13	47	15	904	18
	Lower	11	47	19	3	2	8	2	15	12	47	14	326	13
3	Upper	2	15	17	8	6	21	18	18	13	47	16	364	1
	Middle	4	27	20	8	8	15	14	16	14	46	13	909	6
	Lower	6	36	20	10	3	13	6	16	15	49	11	389	9
4	Upper	6	11	19	13	13	18	35	13	13	34	10	504	11
	Middle	6	14	18	11	9	15	29	14	13	37	14	833	5
	Lower	6	18	17	8	8	18	20	13	13	42	16	389	7
5	Upper	1	4	22	24	17	11	51	12	10	36	6	536	2
	Middle	3	7	20	18	16	10	49	12	12	41	4	827	7
	Lower	4	11	15	17	18	15	46	11	10	38	6	426	5
6	Upper	1	2	14	35	16	10	51	12	21	26	4	537	5
	Middle	3	6	18	26	17	9	50	11	16	31	4	799	3
	Lower	3	7	17	22	17	11	47	11	13	35	6	404	1
7	Upper	2	2	17	49	12	10	46	13	18	26	1	523	3
	Middle	4	5	19	36	15	9	44	13	19	26	4	767	5
	Lower	3	3	19	34	13	9	42	13	20	33	3	424	1
8	Upper	1	1	16	54	16	6	51	12	20	17	1	513	0
	Middle	2	2	17	44	14	8	48	13	19	26	1	778	3
	Lower	3%	2	15	43	19	7	49	10	19	24	3%	398	3

*CA-9, page 4, item 24. Percentages do not add to 200% because not all children gave two responses.

more likely to be continually reinforced if he comes from an economically better off home. This would tend to complement general findings on the relative levels of political participation of adult members of different social classes.[8] It also corresponds to the Almond and Verba findings on differences in adult levels of participant orientation relative to the degree of educational attainment,[9] and agrees with other research on pre-adult political socialization.[10]

That such a difference in the institutional interpretation of government appears so sharply in childhood argues strongly for special attention to this matter in future research. Our own data are very limited on this question. Yet it is of special interest that, in this one case at least, there is an increase in substantive differentiation. If social class were more potent in shaping American politics, we might have expected a wide range of such effects in the early reproduction of subcultures based on social strata. As it is, we find this for a very limited type of orientation, albeit a most interesting and suggestive one.

On the Congress and President options, the finding is not so clear as for voting; but differences are present for SES, even though they are minimal. This suggests that SES differences may have little bearing upon the future inputs of support for the organizational aspects of the authority structure.

We obtain a clearer picture of the impact of status differences when we examine related items about who does most to "make the laws" and to "run the country." Table 16-10 shows a marked lead-lag effect for the Congress option. The lower-status child becomes able to relate meaningfully to the impersonal, more abstract objects of governmental authority somewhat later than does the upper-status child. In this case the lead is from a half to more than a whole grade at every stage.

Table 16-11 presents a somewhat similar effect. The aggregate development is toward Congress, and the upper-status child moves there on the average more quickly. The President, or personalized option, might appear to adults to be more appropriate on this question, but nonetheless the Congress choice becomes increasingly important. In this movement, the lower-status child tends to lag.

Thus, on all three of these items the rate of depersonalization of government is slowest for the child whom we suspect would have fewest resources in political communication. But again, these differences are so slight, and the trends are so similar, that we would not expect great differentiation in response to politi-

Table 16-10 SES Differences in Development of an Awareness of the Chief Lawmaker* (percent of children responding)

Grade	SES	Congress	Pres- ident	Supreme Court	I Don't Know	Total	N Re- sponding	N Not Re- sponding
2	Upper	7%	71	15	7	100%	387	7
	Middle	4	75	11	10	100	910	12
	Lower	4	82	9	5	100	330	9
3	Upper	18	56	21	6	101	359	6
	Middle	10	68	16	5	99	901	14
	Lower	9	70	15	6	100	388	10
4	Upper	35	35	24	6	100	507	8
	Middle	28	43	21	8	100	828	10
	Lower	18	58	17	7	100	388	8
5	Upper	68	14	16	2	100	536	2
	Middle	54	22	21	4	101	831	3
	Lower	51	22	23	4	100	426	5
6	Upper	69	12	16	3	100	541	1
	Middle	65	13	18	4	100	799	3
	Lower	60	15	22	3	100	403	2
7	Upper	81	6	11	2	100	524	2
	Middle	70	8	19	3	100	767	5
	Lower	66	13	19	2	100	421	4
8	Upper	90	4	5	1	100	513	0
	Middle	85	6	8	1	100	777	4
	Lower	80%	6	11	2	99%	400	1

*CA-9, page 7, item 33: "Who makes the laws? Put an X next to the one who does the most to make laws."

Table 16-11 SES Differences in Perception of "Who does most to run the country?"* (percent of children responding)

Grade	SES	Congress	Pres- ident	Supreme Court	I Don't Know	Total	N Re- sponding	N Not Re- sponding
2	Upper	7%	85	3	5	100%	390	4
	Middle	2	87	3	8	100	907	15
	Lower	6	85	4	6	101	330	9
3	Upper	7	88	3	2	100	362	3
	Middle	6	85	3	5	99	909	6
	Lower	7	85	3	5	100	391	7
4	Upper	16	76	3	5	100	509	6
	Middle	12	77	3	7	99	828	10
	Lower	11	78	4	6	99	388	8
5	Upper	24	71	3	3	101	536	2
	Middle	19	72	4	6	101	832	2
	Lower	18	74	4	4	100	428	3
6	Upper	33	59	4	4	100	539	3
	Middle	22	69	4	4	99	801	1
	Lower	20	70	6	4	100	404	1
7	Upper	34	58	5	3	100	524	2
	Middle	24	67	6	2	99	766	6
	Lower	27	65	5	4	101	421	4
8	Upper	41	52	4	3	100	509	4
	Middle	34	60	4	3	101	775	6
	Lower	30%	64	3	3	100%	399	2

*CA-9, page 9, item 41.

cal authority in adulthood based upon these early leads (or lags) in rate of development. They do not seem to lead toward social-class-based subcultures. Rather there is a substantial blanketing effect that erases social-status differences in these terms.

Salience: In Table 16-12, for the item "Who helps you and your family the most?" we do see minor lead-lag effects, but once again none is very strong. Thus, we are not apt to project any far-reaching consequences of SES differences derived from early learning of this kind. This finding is perhaps typical of the many SES differences that appear in our data in that it is of relatively low magnitude, if generally fairly consistent.

Table 16-12   SES Differences in Salience of Authority Figures* (percent of children responding)

Grade	SES	Police-man	Soldier	Father	Teacher	Pres-ident	Total	N Re-sponding
2	Upper	48%	22	44	32	46	192%	394
	Middle	52	21	37	28	50	188	922
	Lower	54	24	35	30	49	192	339
3	Upper	41	17	54	39	37	188	365
	Middle	47	19	48	30	45	189	915
	Lower	53	20	40	33	44	190	398
4	Upper	32	17	63	38	32	182	515
	Middle	40	16	60	34	33	183	838
	Lower	41	16	52	32	41	182	396
5	Upper	36	15	70	35	28	184	538
	Middle	38	17	64	33	31	183	834
	Lower	36	19	57	34	34	180	431
6	Upper	30	14	73	34	30	181	542
	Middle	35	14	68	36	30	183	802
	Lower	37	17	64	36	28	182	405
7	Upper	27	15	79	40	26	187	526
	Middle	28	17	73	36	29	183	772
	Lower	28	19	69	38	25	179	425
8	Upper	26	14	80	43	25	188	513
	Middle	31	15	70	39	24	179	781
	Lower	31%	15	73	36	22	177%	401

*CA-9, page 13, item 58.

Summary

Social status, like sex, shows several modest yet suggestive differences in how children relate to political authorities. None of them is so great that we are able to project fundamentally variant perspectives by the social classes when these children reach maturity. That we fail to find substantial differentiation in these terms—especially when borne out in our further analysis in the following chapter—is significant in that it sets some very definite limits upon how we would foresee the child's social status to affect his system-political behavior as an adult.

The effects are likely to be of such relative unimportance, moreover, that we might usefully question some part of the discussion in the literature, which has given special focus to social-class differences in political socialization. The few effects that we have discovered thus far suggest only a different rate of development rather than substantive differentiation in political interpretation among the various SES groups.

We would, however, make two caveats to this generalization: First, these findings pertain only to system politics, and to that part of it having to do with politicization and personalization. Second, we did find a case in which SES differences became sharper with age (for voting on the "two best pictures" item). From either point of view we might project some lasting political consequences. Yet, our overall conclusion would be that none of our substantive propositions needs serious modification in the area of SES. In the next chapter we shall consider SES for the affective items, together with a number of other important independent variables.

CITY DIFFERENCES IN COGNITIVE RESPONSES

The third major subcultural variable that we have attempted to give an account of in our research design is city or region. One large- and one medium-sized city in each region were included in order to test a hypothesis concerning the possibility of marked differences among the various regions, and especially between the two Southern and the six non-Southern cities. Our findings include many moderate city differences, but none fits our major hypothesis in any systematic fashion. We are generally impressed more by the similarities than by the differences among the cities. Indeed, over any fairly substantial number of items, the differences that do appear seem random.

Let us then take initially an approach opposite from our procedure to this point and look at our data from the standpoint of similarities rather than of differences. First, let us consider as representative, the "two best pictures of our government" item, as shown in Table 16-13.

Geographical differences on this key item are not especially noteworthy. By ranking the ten options in each city and grade according to the proportions choosing each option, and correlating the rankings, we find indeed high average correlations among sets of ranks. Thus there is substantial similarity among the cities. The magnitude of these correlations would suggest that this set of symbolic associations becomes sorted out in approximately the same fashion and at the same time in all eight cities of the study. Clearly the political subcultures of these metropolitan areas exhibit considerable uniformity.

Table 16-13 Geographical Similarity in Development Patterns on "The two best pictures of our government" Item

Grade	Average Correlation Among Sets of Ranks (over the 8 cities)
2	.87
3	.87
4	.71
5	.91
6	.91
7	.91
8	.90

To show this similarity (and the attendant random variations) more graphically, let us consider Figure 16-2, which takes the proportion choosing Congress on this item at every grade in each city.

In grades 2 to 7 there is remarkable similarity in the proportions choosing Congress as one of the best pictures of government in all eight cities. Whatever sharper differentiation occurs does so only at grade 8. Our expectation of South-North differences is not upheld.

We should emphasize that this lack of systematic city difference is usual in our data. We shall have more to say in the next chapter about other possible city differences, but our general conclusion for this portion of our data is clear. The uniformities are again far more impressive than the variations. Indeed, the variations that we do find are essentially random. Thus, the child is likely to begin orientating himself to objects of political authority in about the same way and at roughly the same time in all these areas.[11]

CONCLUSION

We have reviewed our major independent variables that concern subgroup or subcultural variations in patterns of early orientation to the political authorities. The analysis has been confined to what we regard as the most strategic of these differences. From these it is clear that on the social-structural variables that we would have expected to yield greatest subcultural divergences—

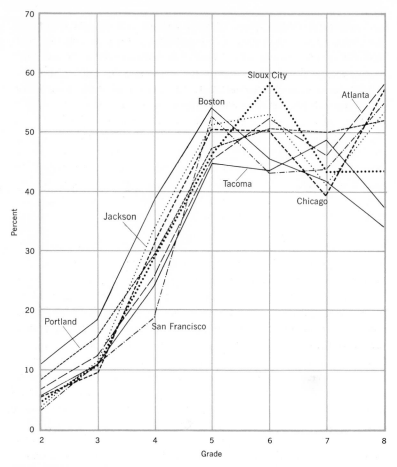

Figure 16-2. City Differences in Choosing *Congress* as One of the Two Best Pictures of Our Government.

sex, SES, and region — we find only scattered instances of differentiated subgroups, at least in the cognitive orientations about phenomena in the general area of system politics.[12]

This is not to say that we have uncovered no noteworthy variations among subgroups. Indeed we believe that the purposes of political analysis in general and of future political-socialization research in particular are best served if we can give more reliable estimates than had previously existed of how much difference these memberships make, in what contexts, and over what periods of development. It is not enough to say that the differences are very small. Our responsibilities go beyond, to show in which respects and to what degree such differences obtain.

We have found some systematic variations for sex and social status. City or region, on the other hand, reveals almost exclusively nonsystematic differences. One searches in vain for some underlying stable pattern of difference among the cities. The political meaning of such nonsystematic differentiation may be considerable, for it foreshadows, we shall see, generally positive support in this realm of basic political orientations. Such similarity among areas may serve as an important source of support which contrasts with the more divisive urges of regionalism in certain policy areas, such as race relations, foreign policy, and civil rights. From our test group the young child in North and South and in large and smaller city areas comes to interpret the political authorities in much the same way as he grows up in the system and becomes politicized at much the same rate.

Social status finds its political meaning in these data in the lead-lag phenomenon, wherein the upper-status child is usually a step or two ahead of the less advantaged child in what he learns about government. This may mean, if earlier learning takes deeper root, *ceteris paribus*, that the upper-status child will have a firmer cognitive base for future political behavior and thus be able to begin developing supportive relationships at an earlier age. In addition, in one instance, a substantive difference in interpretation of government also makes its appearance in these years. Were this kind of effect more frequent in these data, we would postulate the maintenance in the next generation of a social-class-based subculture.

Sex differences, though small, are fairly consistent, particularly in the relative prominence of the President as a focus of political authority. We would think that a variety of possibilities could follow from such a marked and increasing difference between girls and boys. One obvious implication would be that few males but a noteworthy bloc of females might continue to interpret the authorities in a personalized way even as adults. One might suppose, therefore, that the female political temperament would in many cases be susceptible to charismatic (rather than, say, legal-rational) appeals for legitimacy by a given set of incumbent authorities or by a candidate for office. This would certainly be a factor affecting the persistence of a set of authorities and of a political order based more on one than on the other grounds of legitimacy. Furthermore, that boys also move more readily toward the group norms of aggregate choice on these items would suggest much the same kind of political effect as the lead-lag phenomenon associated with status differences.

All these possibilities need further inquiry, both to verify the kinds of effects we have found in other contexts and to trace their consequences into adult political life. For the moment we shall have to be content only with a modest effort at further verfication. To this we turn in the next chapter.

NOTES

1. Summaries of the findings on sex differences in voting can be found in R. Lane, *Political Life* (New York: Free Press, 1959); and L. W. Milbrath, *Political Participation* (Chicago: Rand McNally, 1965).
2. See Chapter 2.
3. H. Hyman, *Political Socialization* (New York: Free Press, 1959), p. 31.
4. Ibid., pp. 30-31.
5. Ibid.; and F. I. Greenstein, *Children and Politics* (New Haven, Conn.: Yale, 1965), pp. 111-118.
6. See Hyman, op. cit., as an example.
7. Greenstein, op. cit., p. 89.
8. Lane, op. cit.; and Milbrath, op. cit.
9. G. A. Almond and S. Verba, *The Civic Culture* (Princeton, N.J.: Princeton, 1963).
10. E. Litt, "Civic Education, Community Norms, and Political Indoctrination," *American Sociological Review,* 28, pp. 69-75, 1963.
11. A number of other variables might also be considered at this point — for example, IQ, religion, and perhaps political-party identification. These and others will be considered in the next chapter as part of a multivariate analysis of predictors of basic affective orientations toward the policeman and the President. We omit any analysis of them here for several reasons. First, the differences found are scattered and not very large in the area of basic orientations toward political authority. Second, other analyses of these same data cover many of the findings that we might present. Clues about the effectiveness of IQ as a predictor, using some of our data, can be found in E. White, "Intelligence and Political Behavior: A Case Study in Political Socialization," unpublished doctoral dissertation. University of Chicago, 1966. In general, IQ shows approximately the same kind of lead-lag effects as does SES, with which it overlaps in considerable part. In a doctoral dissertation still in progress, entitled "Religion as a Factor in the Political Socialization of Pre-adolescents: A Comparative Study of Catholics and Protestants" (University of Chicago), D. Leatherman analyzes the effects of religious preferences and extent of religious attendance upon images of political authority as well as upon other orientations from our data. By adding comparable data from children in parochial schools, Leather-

man finds that slight religious differences between Catholics and others, apparent in our public school children, become magnified. Catholics from parochial schools display more idealized images of authority than do the Catholic children in our test group.

In addition, we have analyzed but will not report here the effects of race and nationality. (For the latter, we separated children whose parents were born in the U.S. from those whose parents were not.) These data are very limited. Our nonwhite sample comprises only a handful of respondents (274). This is largely due to our having sampled exclusively in white public schools. Our "children of immigrants" sample constitutes only 5 percent of the total, moreover. Using these data, we find only a few, very small, and nonsystematic differences between such children and our white or native-born children. Thus, uniformity of socialization in these terms is again the apparent pattern.

12. Had we used a broader range of subcultural variability in our sampling design—especially small-town children. Black ghetto children, parochial children, or rural children—we might have seen much greater divergence. Some work has been done on the last of these types of children in relation to the findings for the kinds of children we have studied. See D. Jaros, H. Hirsch and F. J. Fleron, Jr., "The Malevolent Leader: Political Socialization in an American Sub-Culture," *American Political Science Review,* 62, pp. 564-575, 1968.

17

PREDICTORS OF AFFECTIVE RESPONSES TO POLITICAL AUTHORITIES

In our inquiry into some strategic potential sources of variability in the child's cognitive responses to political authorities (relevant for the processes of politicization in particular), we have found little systematic variation for sex, social status, or region. We may justifiably ask, however, whether in restricting our attention to these variables and to the hypotheses in Chapter 16 we have narrowed the range of possibilities too severely. We should perhaps consider the effects of these and other independent variables for at least our additional major hypothesis about idealization. In this chapter we shall broaden our inquiry in this way.

ALTERNATIVE EXPLANATIONS OF IDEALIZATION

One of our major findings has been that the younger the child the more likely is he to idealize authority; even the older child retains on the average a high regard for most political figures and institutions. In idealization we have identified a crucial socializing process through which diffuse support is generated and sustained. But we have yet to explain how the children happen to view the various authorities in such a glowing light.

Numerous plausible reasons may be advanced, and on a few of these our data can shed some light, though not as much as we had wished. In the first place, as we have already mentioned in Chapter 7, idealization may arise from the feelings of vulnerability children probably have about their environment. Figures such as the policeman and the President may serve as objects of psychological compensation, if they are viewed as powerful and in a commanding position between the child and the unknown dangers of the world. Furthermore, seeing a person so powerful may induce the child, in an intuitive act of appeasement, to construe this person as also helpful, benign, and likable. Fear would seem to cast a longer shadow than love.

To be sure, some children have little if any sense of insecurity and thus little need to idealize personal figures of external authority. In addition there will be some children who visualize these figures as weak, hostile, or malevolent. The child's recognition of them would only add to his sense of potential deprivation.[1] In the main, however, we would think that some of the variance in positive perceptions of the President and the policeman can be connected to the child's state of high dependence.

In the second place, the child's favorable response to the political authorities may simply reflect a "rational" judgment on his part from what he knows about them, whatever the source of his knowledge. He may feel that if parents and other adults in his environment are in general positively disposed to these figures, they must be worthy of a high degree of respect. His evaluation would be nothing more complex than an outcome of his own reality testing about an area of existence that is in most instances remote from him.

There is a third possibility. If we adopt the normal assumption that adults tend to be critical of government in the United States and really do consider it a necessary evil—and in earlier chapters we have already shown our doubt about the validity of this premise—we might well wonder where the child gets his benign image. We might then speculate that however the agents of socialization may themselves feel about political authority, they would instinctively tend to shelter the child from exposure to unfavorable or disparaging comments. Whatever the child's experiences with the proximate authorities at the tail end of the system and whatever his understanding of the nature of the regime, he would be most likely to absorb positive attitudes directly from adults. It is upon them after all that in his earliest years he must mainly rely for an understanding of the broader world. They might consider it appropriate to instruct him only in the conventional ideals about political authority rather than about known or suspected grimmer realities.

Finally, the child may approve so highly because he generalizes from his relationship with more familiar figures of authorities, especially parents, to the external political authorities. In Freudian vein, it could be argued that the child's first and basic orientations toward authority are molded within the family, particularly from experiences with his parents or their surrogates. It has indeed seemed plausible to succeeding generations of students that as the child learns about the presence of authority figures outside the family, he projects his feelings about father authority onto these more remote figures. According to this projection or generalization hypothesis, we should therefore find some relationship between orientations to father and to other, not too dissimilar extrafamilial authorities.

Our own data do not allow us to assign empirical weights to every one of these several lines of explanation to help understand why the child regards political authorities so favorably in the early school years. As we noted earlier, we have little reliable information in our project materials that bears upon the relative influence of various agents of socialization, for this and other areas. The theme we can deal with best perhaps is the generalization hypothesis, wherein the child relates and expands his perceptions of proximate (parental) authorities to political ones. However, our capacity to assess the hypothesis of "rational" inferences from the nature of prevalent adult sentiments about the regime or to assess the vulnerability hypothesis is much less direct. Thus, in what follows below, our main attention will be upon generalization as a mechanism of early political-attitude formation.

Our operational measures of the attitudes generalized from father (if they are) depend upon the child's various ratings of the policeman and President and upon the same ratings for father. We will compare how the child rates his father and how he rates the two political figures. Our discussion will focus on why children do or do not see these authorities in a highly positive spirit, especially to the extent to which we can explain this in terms of the child's tendency to generalize from father to political authorities.

Furthermore, in the analysis we shall include as independent variables a number of other modifying influences, both of the social-structural variety discussed in the last chapter—grade, sex, SES, and city—and others that have seemed more relevant to the idealization variable, as IQ, religious preference and extent of attendance at religious services, membership and officership in school and non-school clubs or teams, political-party preference, assessment of which parent is more nearly "the boss" in the family, and the ratings of father on the same attributes used for the political authorities.[2] In part the latter independent variables may help to identify group differences in the way children evaluate President and policeman. In part they may offer explanations of these differences that compete with the generalization hypothesis.

INDEXES OF POWER AND AFFECT

In order to relate all these independent variables to idealization in a reasonably parsimonious manner, we first reduced the child's variety of perceptions of political authorities to a few basic indexes. In this way we could represent the core of the affective aspects of the child's image. This permitted us to assess the influence of each independent variable, even though in such an analysis we would have to leave out of account other meaningful aspects of the child's orientations. We hypothesized, based on earlier factor analyses of our pretest data, that in this early period at least two dimensions would become stabilized for each authority, one a purely affective response (or simple liking) and the other an evaluation of the role-performance attributes of each authority, especially in relation to his power, leadership, knowledge, and the like. It will be recalled that we have interpreted assessments of these culturally approved qualities also as reflecting the affective orientation of respect for authority.

The procedure we used to devise indexes was as follows. We selected the child's ratings of the policeman and the President as most representative of his early response to political authority. We realize, of course, that other contact points would be worthy of consideration in any subsequent analysis. We then intercorrelated the ratings at each grade, from 4 to 8, for policeman, President, and father. We included the father ratings so that we could use them later as an indexed independent variable. We proceeded next to factor analyze the matrices of intercorrelations among the ratings for each of the three authorities at each grade, giving a total of fifteen separate factor analyses.[3] This series of computations permitted us to describe as simply as possible the basic attitudinal dimensions that our questions evoked for each of the three figures of authority at each grade. We were then able—given that a reasonable degree of stability of these solutions existed across the grades—to score each child on each attitudinal dimension for the three authority figures. With such scores, analysis of the relationship between the child's basic images of the policeman and President on the one hand, and a variety of independent variables on the other, became possible. We included in the analysis the similarly derived scores of the child's image of his father.

In Tables 17-1 to 17-3 we present an abbreviated summary of the fifteen factor analyses of the child's ratings of each figure of authority at each grade. The tables present the factor loadings of the rotated factor matrices at each grade.

These summaries show two highly stable general orientations that appear for each figure at every grade. These we call simply affect and power.

Table 17-1   President Ratings: Rotated Factor Matrix Loadings, by Grade

AFFECT

| Item: | GRADE | | | | |
	4	5	6	7	8
11. I like him	.74	.80	.80	.85	.78
6. He is my favorite	.74	.70	.73	.74	.77
12. He protects me	.63	.69	.71	.68	.62
1. He would want to help me if I needed it	.56	.58	.52	.48	.60
4. He keeps his promises	.49	.36	.35	.22	.43

POWER

Item:

	4	5	6	7	8
5. He can make others do what he wants	.77	.80	.78	.79	.82
9. He can punish others	.68	.81	.81	.83	.78
3. He knows a lot	.42	.32	.18	.19	.44

ROLE PERFORMANCE

Item:

	4	5	6	7	8
8. He is a leader	.61	.57	.66	.54	.68
13. He never gives up	.69	.57	.52	.51	.59
2. He makes important decisions	.19	.53	.58	.58	.53
7. He almost never makes mistakes	.53	.59	.52	.46	.51
10. He works hard	.51	.47	.54	.48	.45
3. He knows a lot	.32	.47	.56	.58	.33
4. He keeps his promises	.13	.46	.48	.62	.24

The affect dimension is best defined by the two ratings "I like him" and "He is my favorite." Given the fact that the two benevolence items ("He protects me" and "He would want to help me if I needed it") also generally load high on this dimension, we could perhaps call the dimension benevolence, attachment, or evaluation. And we could use several different combinations of items to index this dimension, including simply the single phrase "I like him," the two items "protects" and "would want to help me," or "like" plus "favorite." Our general procedure has been to use the latter two (the most directly affective items), indexed straightforwardly as a cluster, or scale, score. We simply added the numerical ratings the child gave on these two items to form the index score with a range of 1 to 11.[4]

A similar procedure was used for the power index, where we employed "He can make others do what he wants" and "He can punish others" with an identical range in the score. These

Table 17-2   Policeman Ratings: Rotated Factor Matrix Loadings, by Grade

AFFECT		GRADE			
Item:	4	5	6	7	8
11. I like him	.74	.80	.84	.81	.73
12. He protects me	.70	.75	.70	.66	.72
10. He works hard	.65	.61	.53	.58	.68
7. He almost never makes mistakes	.42	.27	.36	.45	.55
8. He is a leader	.46	.20	.24	.41	.53
6. He is my favorite	.41	.43	.66	.65	.48
POWER					
Item:					
9. He can punish others	.70	.76	.78	.78	.73
5. He can make others do what he wants	.73	.59	.56	.61	.68
8. He is a leader	.32	.66	.65	.53	.41
7. He almost never makes mistakes	.17	.47	.43	.44	.39
10. He works hard	.11	.32	.41	.31	.25
ROLE PERFORMANCE					
Item:					
1. He would want to help me if I needed it	.52	.43	.68	.62	.68
2. He makes important decisions	.63	.62	.69	.68	.66
4. He keeps his promises	.61	.59	.61	.62	.62
3. He knows a lot	.51	.64	.59	.65	.57
6. He is my favorite	.48	.53	.33	.36	.43

two items even more sharply and uniquely define the nature of the power dimension than do the two affect items for their dimension.[5]

We proceed, therefore, with four basic dependent variables — power and affect for President and the same two for policeman — with two corresponding independent variables, power and affect for father. To use the child's orientations toward his father as the basis for assessing the extent of generalization to political authorities, we assume that these attitudes toward the father become established prior to the development of orientations toward the political authorities. Indeed we found earlier[6] — as partial confirmation of this assumption — that attitudes toward father have already been established by grade 2 or 3 and remain stable thereafter through the elementary school years, whereas the images of the policeman and President shift considerably after the early grades. Our next task, therefore, is to see how our dependent variables — power and affect orientations toward President and policeman as indicators of idealization — are influenced by (or associated

Table 17-3 Father Ratings: Rotated Factor Matrix Loadings, by Grade

AFFECT

Item:	GRADE				
	4	5	6	7	8
11. I like him	.77	.81	.77	.83	.85
6. He is my favorite	.74	.82	.81	.82	.84
1. He would want to help me if I needed it	.56	.75	.75	.75	.78
12. He protects me	.70	.72	.73	.74	.75
4. He keeps his promises	.49	.60	.64	.66	.67
2. He makes important decisions	.22	.38	.46	.49	.51
3. He knows a lot	.21	.24	.44	.38	.38
7. He almost never makes mistakes	.35	.34	.41	.38	.38
10. He works hard	.32	.29	.44	.29	.31

POWER

Item:					
5. He can make others do what he wants	.73	.70	.73	.75	.72
9. He can punish others	.70	.69	.72	.71	.72
8. He is a leader	.49	.52	.64	.60	.59
3. He knows a lot	.55	.59	.50	.51	.58
7. He almost never makes mistakes	.49	.44	.46	.48	.55
10. He works hard	.52	.54	.42	.52	.50
2. He makes important decisions	.53	.48	.39	.44	.42

with) the father variables and with other potentially relevant independent variables.

PREDICTORS OF AFFECT FOR PRESIDENT

To show the relative explanatory power of so large a number of variables as sex, IQ, SES (father's occupation), city, religion, religious attendance, "boss in the family" (child's perception), membership in clubs or teams, grade, party preference, and, especially, orientations toward father, we conducted a series of automatic interaction detection (A.I.D.), or "tree analysis," computations. This variety of multivariate analysis attempts, within certain limits, to determine an optimal set of predictors by using a nonlinear statistical model.[7] The computer program that we used for this series of computations produces, among other things, an ordering of independent variables by relative capacity to account for variance in the dependent variable, an assessment of how much variance each independent variable accounts for, and a summary of the total variance accounted for by all the independent variables together. These computational products are extremely voluminous, so that we can provide only the barest sketch of our results here. We will present a few of the more important and representative of our "trees" that show which "splits" were made with what degrees of success in accounting for the variance in each of the dependent variables.[8]

Figure 17-1 presents the tree of predictors for the President Affect index using the subsample for five cities, grades 4 to 8 (note 8). City is the first predictor, splitting Chicago and Jackson from Atlanta, Portland, and Sioux City. The mean rating (symbolized by $\overline{X}$) in the latter three cities is 5.02, whereas $\overline{X}=5.75$ in Chicago and Jackson. We must bear in mind that the *higher* the numerical value of the mean (the closer it is to 11), the *lower* the rating given by the child on the two President Affect items that constitute our index. Thus the children in Chicago and Jackson regard the President less highly in these terms than do their counterparts in the other three cities.

This is not, we should point out, the precise difference that we had expected. We had assumed rather that the children from the two Southern cities, following the presumed opinion of their parents, would be less approving of the Chief Federal Executive than would the children in the Northern cities, even though the dominant partisan pattern was more Democratic in the South, thus matching the partisan identification of the incumbent. But the actual pattern is simply not explainable in such terms. Nor is the split

Figure 17-1. Predictors of President Affect.[a]

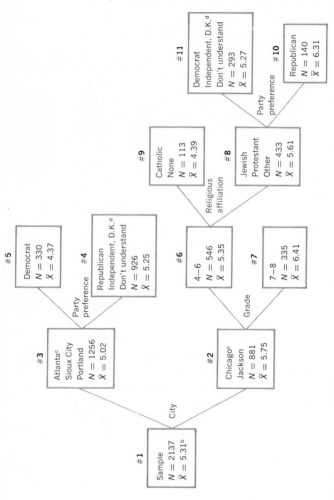

[a] BSS/TSS = 0.07 This number refers to the quantity between the sum of squares divided by the total sum of squares and provides a measure of the total variance accounted for in the given interaction detection analysis.

[b] $\bar{X}$ represents the mean observation for a given group on the dependent variable. On this and subsequent tree diagrams, the lower the numerical value of the mean, the higher is the child's evaluation of the authority figure in question.

[c] Information in the top part of these and all other boxes (aside from box #1) in all figures defines the dichotomization in the independent variable made in order to maximize the variance accounted for in the dependent variable.

[d] For abbreviations about party preferences, see note 2 in this chapter.

a large-city-small-city phenomenon. We had supposed that some effect of size of place might enter the picture; but it does not do so in this case. Neither hypothesis was borne out by the data.

From Figure 17-1 we also find grade, party preference, and religion to be of some value in accounting for variance in affect for President. At least in Chicago and Jackson the older children (Group #7) are somewhat less apt to like the President a great deal ($\overline{X} = 6.41$) than are the grade 4 to 6 children ($\overline{X} = 5.35$). Disenchantment is more acute for the older Chicago or Jackson child than for the younger child from these cities.

Religion comes into the picture for the younger Chicago and Jackson children, splitting the Catholics and those without religious preference away from Jews, Protestants, and adherents of other faiths. The former rate the President more highly on the affect dimension (Group #9). We could have anticipated higher Catholic regard for President Kennedy. The greater affect mean of nonbelievers may be attributed to their having perceived Kennedy to be more liberal politically, thus matching their own probably less conservative outlook.

Party preference also has some predictive value, with Democrats scoring higher (Groups #5 and #11) and Republicans lower [and with the other party-preference options being put in one case with the Democrats (Group #11) and in the other case with the Republicans (Group #4)]. Here again, we could expect that the mean rating of Democrats would be higher than that of Republicans, and such is indeed the case.

With all these predictors together we still account for only 7 percent of the variance (Figure 17-1, note a)—which is fairly low. Thus our effort to explain idealization of the President in terms of our best predictors results in low success, although not in total failure. The child is somewhat influenced in how he responds affectively to the President by the general impact of the community in which he resides and by his religion, age, and party preference. Mostly, however, he is influenced by factors of other, as yet unspecified, kinds.

We should point out, moreover, that, of the things which we include in the interaction detection analysis but which fail to appear in the tree as relevant, the variable we might have thought most related to the generalization hypothesis is notable by its absence. We would have expected affect for President to be associated with affect for father, but this association does not occur. Indeed none of the father evaluations is related to the child's image of the President in these terms, to any significant degree.

Another way to make the same point more sharply is to consider the simple correlations of the children's ratings of their fathers on the Father Affect index with their rating of the President on President Affect. Table 17-4 presents these data. Freudian intimations notwithstanding, once again we do not observe a close association between the child's liking for his father and his liking for the President. On this general evaluative dimension, there appears to be little significant generalization of sentiments for the parent to the President. We must therefore use other ways to account for this aspect of the child's image of political authority.

Table 17-4 Relationship of President Affect Index to Father Affect Index, by Grade* (Pearson r)

	Grade			
4	5	6	7	8
.11	.10	.10	.06	.06

*We used the total samples at each grade for these computations.

Returning to our tree analysis we find (Figure 17-1) that the child who rates the President highest on the affect dimension is either the Atlanta-Sioux City-Portland Democrat ($\overline{X}=4.37$) or the younger Catholic or nonbeliever from Jackson or Chicago ($\overline{X}=4.39$); and the child who is most apt to rate the President low is a seventh- or eighth-grader from Jackson or Chicago ($\overline{X}=6.41$) or a younger Republican non-Catholic (and nonagnostic) from Jackson or Chicago ($\overline{X}=6.31$). These differences are not large; but they do serve to show us the limits of our explanatory power in this case. They are suggestive, if perhaps in a negative way, of where we need to go in future investigation of this kind.

CITY DIFFERENCES IN PATTERNS OF PRESIDENT AFFECT PREDICTORS

In order to probe these patterns of interrelation more deeply before giving up the generalization hypothesis completely, we used the total (grades 4 to 8) samples in each city for separate A.I.D. analyses. Before we present individual city trees, it might be helpful first to get a more comprehensive perspective by comparing the variance accounted for by each of our independent variables in each of the eight cities. The figures shown in Table 17-5 make such a comparison, using the separate city computations.

In six of the cities (Chicago, Sioux City, Boston, Portland, Atlanta, and Tacoma) party preference is the best predictor of any on the list, whereas in the other two cities (Jackson and San

Table 17-5 Predictors of President Affect in Eight Cities* (percent variance between sum of squares divided by total sum of squares)

Predictor	Chi-cago.	Atlanta	Sioux City	San Fran-cisco	Tacoma	Jack-son	Boston	Port-land
Grade	1.8	.1	.5	2.7	1.3	3.4	.5	1.1
I.Q	1.0	.2	.5	.2	.1	.4	1.4	1.2
Sex	.1	.4	1.0	.0	.7	.0	.6	.0
Religious attendance	.5	.1	.8	1.4	.2	.3	1.6	.5
Religious affiliation	4.2	.2	.3	.1	.0	.2	†	3.0
Boss in family	.6	.1	.5	.7	.3	1.0	.2	.2
Party preference	5.0	1.4	3.9	.8	1.8	.1	3.7	3.4
Member of school club	.5	.0	.1	.0	.7	.6	.2	.0
Member of team	.8	.0	.0	.0	.2	.0	.1	.3
Officer of team or club	.7	.3	.0	.2	.5	.3	.0	.0
SES	2.2	.8	.4	.3	.2	.2	2.0	1.2
Father affect	1.8	.4	1.5	1.2	‡	.1	2.9	1.1
Father power	1.3	.8	1.0	.7	‡	.7	.8	.6
Total Mean	5.6	5.1	5.2	4.9	4.6	5.9	4.9	4.8
Sum of squares	7484	6443	6156	7263	5849	7885	5326	6577

*The cell entries are the A.I.D. estimates of the percent of variance in "President Affect" accounted for by each independent variable based on the quantity "between sum of squares divided by total sum of squares" for each independent variable.

†The children were not asked their religious affiliation in the Boston area.

‡No father ratings were administered in Tacoma.

Francisco) grade is the best predictor. The third variable with modest influence in some of these cities is religious affiliation. It is particularly important in Chicago and Portland. SES shows up somewhat in Chicago and Boston; and Father Affect appears to have some weight in Boston.

In only one case does any one of these predictors account for even a modest 5 percent of the variance on its own, so that none is likely to be a major factor in shifting the course of the child's development of these feelings for the President one way or the other. The fact that the child identifies himself with the party of the President adds a small increment to a perception of benevolence; but this effect is not found in all the cities. Equally, a religious preference that corresponds to that of the President (as for Catholics and Kennedy) may add a bit of cement to the bond the child establishes with the President; but again it is of minor consequence and appears only in certain geographical areas.

Figures 17-2 and 17-3 display some of these city differences in patterns of association with President Affect more sharply. Figure 17-2 shows the tree for the Chicago sample. What we find, from the standpoint of a typology of those highest and lowest, is as follows.

   1 For groups with substantial numbers of cases, the child highest in level of President Affect is either a Democrat or one who chooses "I don't know what *Democrat* and *Republican* mean" (Don't understand), and who is in the earlier grades (Group #12, $\bar{X} = 4.39$).

   2 Taking into account groups with relatively small numbers of cases, we find that in Chicago the child highest in President Affect (Group #3) is a Republican or Independent or is undecided in party preference (D.K.), who is also either a Catholic or a nonbeliever (Group #5), and who sees his father as relatively powerful (Group #14, $\bar{X} = 3.32$). In the latter therefore we observe a rather special interaction effect of either Catholicism or religious nonbelief together with a perception of high Father Power. This combination of factors accounts for the deviation of this small group of children from the pattern typical of other Republicans or those with no party preference, as indicated in Groups #3, 4, 6, and 7.

   3 The child scoring lowest on President Affect is a Protestant, Jew, or member of some other non-Catholic faith (Group #4), and a Republican (Group #6), who sees his father to be less powerful (Group #9), and who is high in SES, being in the family of an owner or professional (Group #10; $\bar{X} = 8.02$).

The gap between the last two groups in the above typology, (2) and (3), expressed in their respective means, is a considerable one. Thus our predictors for Chicago separate various types of children more successfully in that we account for 14 percent of the total variance in the dependent variable.

By contrast, our tree for Jackson (Figure 17-3) shows a much different and less complex pattern of predictor variables. Whereas grade had been of only secondary importance in Chicago as a predictor, it is best in Jackson. Furthermore, only one of the

Figure 17-2. Predictors of President Affect, Chicago, Illinois. [a]

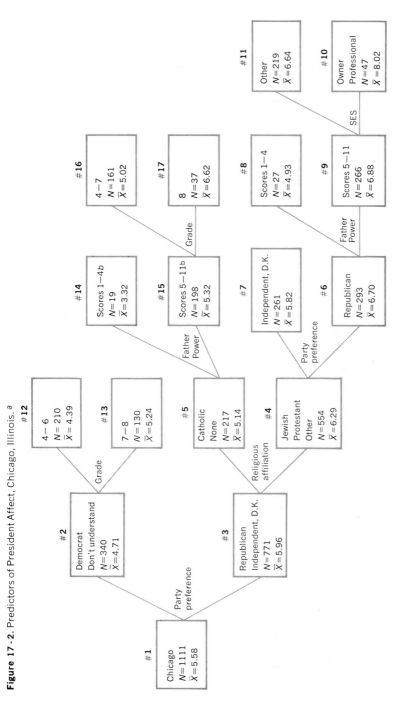

[a] BSS/TSS = 0.14.

[b] In this and subsequent tree diagrams, the word "scores" refers to index score values included for a given dichotomization of the independent variables to which the box refers. In each case, such scores range from 1 to 11. The lower the numerical value of the score, the higher the child's evaluation of the authority figure in question.

other Chicago predictors enters (Father Power) and another secondary predictor appears in Jackson—"boss in the family." In comparison with our predictive capacities in Chicago, we are relatively unsuccessful in differentiating among the children of Jackson about how they relate affectively to the President. We account for only 5 percent of the total variance; and we are able to get very few of our predictors to enter. Several of the variables, which, however slightly, begin to show their differentiating effects in Chicago, are absent in Jackson. This suggests either a more uniform political subculture in Jackson (in these terms) or else a later development of differentiated feelings about the President among relevant subgroups.

The little differentiation that we do get in Jackson shows that the most favorable response is given by younger children who perceive the boss in their family to be either father or both parents (Group #5, $\overline{X}= 5.37$), as against those who perceive mother to be the boss or who say they cannot answer. The children in Jackson who are lowest in affect for the President are the older children who perceive their own father not to be especially powerful (Group #7, $\overline{X}= 7.02$). Thus the patterns of association that

Figure 17 - 3. Predictors of President Affect, Jackson, Mississippi.*

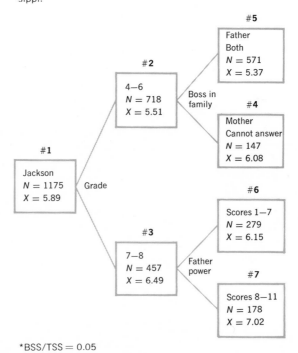

*BSS/TSS = 0.05

appear on President Affect in Jackson and Chicago are somewhat different, with Chicago showing the more varied and extensive set of relationships with our independent variables.

In the other six cities—the tree diagrams for which are not reproduced here—we find other combinations of predictors that form the intermediate cases between Jackson and Chicago. A few other independent variables enter the trees in the other six cities. IQ is a predictor in Portland, with those higher in IQ showing less affection for the President. IQ also appears in Tacoma. In Sioux City, children who have been an officer of a club (among Republicans and those without preference or knowledge of the parties, who rate their father low on power) typically have lower President Affect scores ($\overline{X} = 7.17$ for club officers, $\overline{X} = 5.97$ for nonofficers). Sex enters as a predictor in Tacoma, with Democratic girls showing higher average affect ($\overline{X} = 3.74$) than Democratic boys ($\overline{X} = 4.23$). All these special effects are relatively low in magnitude, so that the practical impact of any one of them is slight. Some variables appear with greater regularity in the eight trees (for the eight cities) than others, especially party preference, grade, SES, and certain feelings about father. Insofar as we have predictors of measurable consequence for affective orientation toward the President under various geocultural conditions, they are these.

Taken as a whole, these variables could suggest that family influences of one kind or another best explain variations in sentiments about President—particularly the SES of the family, and thus possibly its internal communication patterns,[9] or other relationships existing between the child and his parents. One senses that we have perhaps caught only the outer edges of these variables and that more intensive analysis of family variables in this context would yield considerably more explanatory power. That our explanatory power is so slight is perhaps a reflection of the crudity of our measures in relation to the complex and varied environment of the family. Because these variables allow us to explain this orientation so slightly, one could be pessimistic about success in prediction using them; or one could be optimistic, given the fact that a few family variables tend to indicate some underlying pattern of causation amenable to future inquiry.

PRESIDENT POWER

When we turn to our second index of feelings concerning the President—which we have labeled President Power—we find something a little different, however, with greater relevance this time for the generalization hypothesis. In this case, we again are not notably successful in using our range of predictors to account for a substantial portion of the total variance. But among our predictors, Father Power is fairly prominent. Figure 17-4 presents the tree for President Power using the subsample taken from seven of our cities.

What we find is that the Father Power index is the best predictor of scores on the President Power index, followed by city and grade. The child highest in his evaluation of the President's power (Group #5) also rates his father high on power, and the child is from the cities other than Chicago and Atlanta (excluding Tacoma, which had been eliminated from the analysis). The child who is lowest in his rating of the President's power is very low in his rating of his own father's power, he is from the higher grades, and he comes from Jackson, Boston, San Francisco, and Portland (Group #11).

Perhaps our key finding here is that the "best" explanatory variable—and one which does better relative to its analog for President Affect—is how the child rates his father's power. From this perspective we may want to revive the generalization hypothesis, even though its area of application may be much narrower than we had originally supposed. The difference here is possibly between generalizing direct affection from one known individual person (father) to the personality connected with the Presidential role (which generalizing, apparently, does not operate at all) and perceiving and evaluating an external authority's performance characteristics, such as his relative power. One could argue that the latter case of such analogizing behavior by the child is more understandable than the former, given that authority is more likely to be seen as residing in the performance characteristics of the role than in the personal qualities. Thus the child, ignoring Freud, may make a not unreasonable connection in the one case but not in the other.

In Chapters 8, 10, and 13 we have already had occasion to comment on this reluctance of the child to rank external authority figures very high on our most directly affective ratings. There we saw that in comparison with both President and policeman, father was consistently ranked higher on the direct attachment items ("I like him" and "He is my favorite"). Even where the rating of the political authority figures may begin at a fairly high level on these items in the lower grades, unlike the ratings for father they drop precipitously as the child grows older. The data in these

Figure 17-4. Predictors of President Power.*

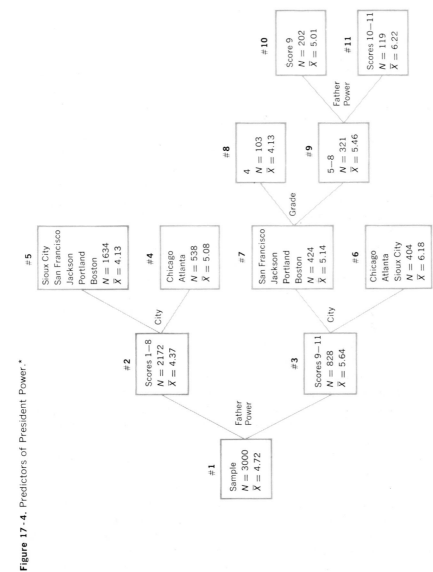

*BSS/TSS = 0.10

earlier chapters gave us the first clue that this kind of direct affect may be reserved only for those authority roles particularly close and familiar to the child, as opposed to those more distant from the nuclear family. If this is true, we would expect to find that feelings for other authorities with whom the child comes into more personal, direct contact might also be influenced by the more intimate feelings of affection the child reserves for father.

Before we leave the subject, therefore, we can take a further test case, using the policeman indexes. This should clarify this more differentiated hypothesis about the generalization of affect from father to external authority figures.

POLICEMAN AFFECT AND POWER

When we turn to the child's basic feelings about the policeman, we see somewhat the same patterns of association as for the President, although with a minor but notable difference about affect. These are shown in Figures 17-5 and 17-6.

Affect

Figure 17-5 shows that grade, sex, Father Helpfulness (an alternative measure of Father Affect), and city are related to some extent to the level of affect for the policeman. Thus, relative to the last of these (although the effect is somewhat marginal), there is a degree of generalization possible on this more affective side of the policeman's image.

We have already hinted at why we might find this relationship for policeman, marginal though it is, but not for President. Although in the aggregate, the children see the President as more likable and more benevolent than the policeman (Table 13-1), as we noted long ago there are good reasons for this, independent of the possible projection of their feelings about father. The President is after all a far more prestigious figure than the policeman, and we would expect children to express somewhat greater affection for the President if they can do it for any external authorities at all.

However, for the very reason that the policeman is less prestigious we would have to account for the child's affect for him in other terms. Undoubtedly there are a number of factors at work, as we noted in Chapters 10 and 11. Among them, however, some generalization from the image of father seems to occur, at least during the middle grades (Figure 17-5, Group #6). The proximity

Figure 17-5. Predictors of Policeman Affect.*

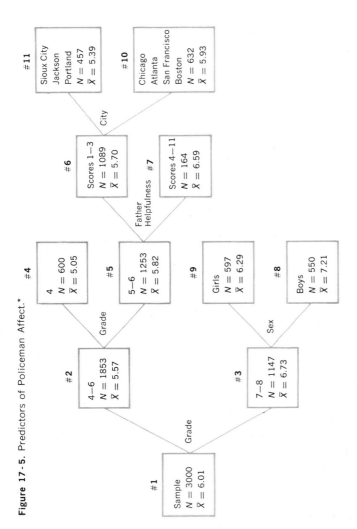

*BSS/TSS = 0.11

of the policeman and the frequency of the child's contact with him — at school crossings, etc.— might enable some children to see him much more in the way they do another proximate authority figure, father, at least on the protective, helpful side of general affect. In this very limited sense then, our data here may lend some weight to the Freudian theme that the child's attitude toward political authority may be somewhat shaped by his feelings about parental authority.

In this same area of Policeman Affect, it is interesting that we find a sex difference, at least for the older children. Girls rate the policeman more highly. If this does not prove the vulnerability hypothesis, at least it adds some greater plausibility to it as an explanation for the tendency to idealize external authority. The sexes are undifferentiated for the earlier grades. Thus one might surmise that the youngest children of both sexes feel an equal regard for the policeman's protective attributes; regardless of sex most young children may feel sufficiently exposed to the dangers of the world to value the policeman. But as they grow older the boys take a relatively less favorable view. Possibly at an earlier age than girls they begin to feel less dependent on such external authority, more confident of their own strength as boys. They may even become a little restless with the constraints on their behavior represented by the police. We have already discussed how the curve of general respect for the police, declining by grade 8, probably continues to drop to a low point in early adulthood (Chapter 14). For boys it no doubt drops at an earlier point in the life cycle.

Power

When we consider Figure 17-6, we again find some confirmation for the generalization hypothesis, this time with regard to the index of evaluation of Policeman Power. Those higher in their evaluation of their own father's power are also more apt to rate the policeman high in power. Thus the effect, in this case, is much like that for the President.

In Figure 17-6 we also have data that might be considered significant for the vulnerability hypothesis. We find a sex difference (Groups #10 and 11) similar to that in Figure 17-5. Girls who see father as not too powerful are more likely than boys in the same category to rate policeman as fairly powerful. These girls seem to be a little more prone than the boys to search for a substitute father protector.

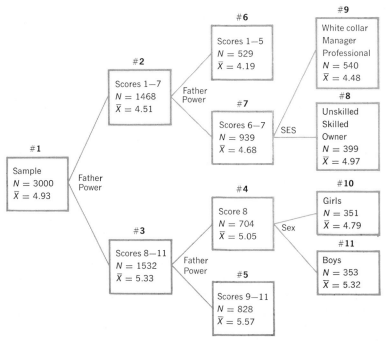

Figure 17-6. Predictors of Policeman Power.*
*BSS/TSS = 0.065

CONCLUSION

Our multivariate analysis yields a complex and inelegant solution to the question of which of our predictors are of value in accounting for how the child responds to the President and policeman on our affect and power indexes. The proportion of variance any one of them accounts for is relatively small, as is the percent of variance explained by all together. There is some consistency across indexes and cities; but it is not high. Using power and affect indexes as general indicators of the child's regard for political authority—his idealization of it—we have not been too successful therefore in explaining variations in it.

The main hypothesis upon which our data have been able to shed some light, however, concerns the tendency of the child to project his images of parental authority to key figures of authority in the political realm. Our general conclusion is that, although the effect is nowhere very strong, there are several instances in which it would appear to have some potential explanatory value. Possibly the most interesting case however—that of the level of child's affective response to the President—does not come under this hypothesis. Nevertheless, how the child perceives his own father on affect and power appears to have at least a selected impact in this area as a whole. The clearest connection comes on the performance dimension, power, both for policeman and President.

Other basic attributes of the child enter marginally as predictors of idealization. Sex, IQ, SES, party, and religious affiliation differentiate to a small degree in a few instances. None of these groupings shows a marked influence, however, nor do they pertain in every one of the eight locales. Several of the differences most expected therefore do not materialize. The period of childhood socialization we must conclude is—on these measures—not generally one of increasing divergency; it is instead a period of striking similarity of response among children of various basic social categories, just as we found from the cognitive analysis in the preceding chapter.

The terms we have used do of course limit the scope of such differentiation, so that students might do well to continue their search by using a broader range of responses relevant to political authority images and reconsidering at least those social categories for which such differences might be most expected. In the one or two cases where we found evidence not inconsistent with the vulnerability hypothesis, for example, we might well have achieved greater success with more incisive measures. Thus future research might usefully begin with the questions that we have raised but have been unable to answer to our own satisfaction.

In general, therefore, we have not been able to find large, consistent differences in our data among various salient subcategories of respondents. The differences we observe are scattered, unsystematic, and more impressive for their absence than for their presence. Even though we are thus restricted in our ability to account for the child's highly positive evaluation of political authority, we can suggest that the lack of any far-reaching differences of these kinds may well provide an important, almost monolithic base of diffuse support for the structure of political authority in the American system. In other words, even the lowest input does not seem to be concentrated in any single identifiable group.

Can we account in any general way for this apparent crossgroup uniformity, both in cognitive and affective respects, at the system-politics level? Here we must turn to more speculative judgments. Regardless of where the children may be acquiring their orientations, there is evidently a strong consensual element. Adult socializing agents and agencies may conflict sharply about issues and candidates and may even differ strongly in their general feelings about the importance of politics, but their children acquire a relatively high degree of consensus about the legitimacy of the authorities.

In part, this may be a product of the special character of our sample. It included only children from white, urban areas not severely depressed economically.[10] However even if a more diversified sample had produced the same homogeneous outlook, we would not expect this situation to last. By the late 1960's this consensus may have begun to dissolve under the impact of the urban and racial crisis and the student revolution. This is especially likely to be the case for black children. Thus future scholarship may need to qualify the finding of uniformity that we have made by recognizing that subcultural forces other than the ones on which we have focused may be modifying the preexisting homogeneity of basic political orientations.

But even if this uniformity is breaking up, in the past it might also have been traceable to another peculiarly American phenomenon. Adults in the United States may themselves have had some special feelings about the area of system politics, regardless of subgroup; they have managed to get this message across to children with a minimum of ambiguity. In fact, in Chapter 18 we shall be led to speculate on the possibility that this whole area of system politics may have been the subject of particularly severe efforts in socialization; hence the tendency toward considerable similarity in supportive outlook among children.

NOTES

1. See D. Jaros, H. Hirsch, and F. J. Fleron, Jr., "The Malevolent Leader: Political Socialization in an American Sub-Culture," *American Political Science Review,* 62, pp. 564-575, 1968.

2. Our measures of these various independent variables were derived as follows:

   a   IQ: IQ scores were available from school records for about 85 percent of our respondents. We used the most recent score available, and we converted various measures of IQ to a common "stanines" scale using a procedure developed by J. C. Flanagan and P. A. Schwarz. See their tables in *Development of Procedures for Converting Intelligence Test Scores to a Common Scale* (Pittsburgh, Pa.: American Institute of Research, 1958) [mimeographed].

b Religious affiliation: CA-9, p. 3, item 19. "Your family is (Choose one): (1) Catholic, (2) Jewish, (3) Protestant, (4) Other, (5) None."

c Religious attendance: CA-9, p. 2, item 18. "How often do you go to Mass, Church, Temple, or Sunday School? (Choose one): (1) Every week, (2) Almost every week, (3) Only once in a while, (4) Almost never."

d Member or officer of clubs or teams: CA-9, p. 23, items 47 to 50.

47. "Do you belong to a school club, organization, or committee (such as student council, musical organization, or service committee)? (1) Yes, (2) No."

48. "Put an X beside each of the clubs or organizations below which you belong to now, or which you have belonged to for at least a year. (1) Boy Scouts (or Cub Scouts), (2) Girl Scouts (or Brownies), (3) Camp Fire Girls, (4) YMCA, YWCA, YMHA, Hi-Y, (5) CYO, (6) Boys' Club, (7) 4-H Club, (8) I do not belong to any club or organization outside of school."

49. "In this school year I belong to some team (which meets after school hours) which plays baseball, volleyball, or some other sport. (1) Yes, (2) No."

50. "I have held some office in my class or in one of the clubs or organizations mentioned. (1) Yes, (2) No."

e Political-party preference: CA-9, p. 9, item 42. For the wording of this see Chapter 9, note 3. On the tree diagrams the options on this question are abbreviated as follows: "Sometimes a Democrat and sometimes a Republican" = Independent; "I don't know which I would be" = D.K.; "I don't know what Democrat and Republican mean" = "Don't understand."

f Boss in the family: CA-9, p. 3, item 20. "Who is the boss in your family? (Choose one): (1) Both fairly equal but *father* more, (2) Both fairly equal but *mother* more, (3) *Both* fairly equal, (4) I can not answer."

g Ratings of father: See Chapter 12.

3. We used for these computations a principal component analysis of Pearson *r* matrices, with varimax rotation.

4. As each rating ranges from 1 to 6, both ratings in the index combine to give an index score of 2 to 12, from which we have subtracted 1 for each score to give a resulting range of 1 to 11.

5. In addition, we find a further dimension or two, depending on how we set the eigenvalue necessary for rotation. We present in Tables 17-1 to 17-3 the three-factor rotation solution at each grade. Given the fact that the third dimension does not appear for father and that it has a somewhat unsteady composition for President and policeman, we have chosen to eliminate it from the present analysis, and we confine our attention to the two stable image dimensions common to all three figures. We should add that, by lower-

ing the eigenvalue necessary for rotation to .90, we were able to obtain at some grades a fourth component on President and policeman that had an eigenvalue almost equal to 1. The instability of these fourth components prevented us from using them to score children's responses to authorities, however.

6. See Chapter 12.

7. The computer program that we used for our "tree," or A.I.D., analysis and its underlying statistical model are described in J. A. Sonquist and J. N. Morgan, *The Detection of Interaction Effects: A Report on a Computer Program for the Selection of Optimal Combinations of Explanatory Variables,* Survey Research Center, Institute for Social Research, Monograph no. 35 (Ann Arbor, Mich.: The University of Michigan Press, 1964).

8. The computational routine that we had available places limits on the number of observations and variables that can be used at any one time. In order to use the number of variables that we thought desirable it was necessary for us to take a random sample of 3,000 from our total set of respondents. The sample was taken from grades 4 to 8 in seven of the cities. (We excluded from the population: the children from Tacoma, where we lacked father ratings; grades 2 and 3, where, owing to testing restrictions imposed on us, we lacked about half of all the ratings used to devise the indexes; and in Figure 17-1 only, Boston and San Francisco, where for similar reason we lacked religious data.) We will present all four of the analyses using this sample. We also carried out the same four basic analyses for each of the eight cities. We will present individual city trees for Presidential Affect only.

9. For a suggestive treatment of the influence of the family environment on the child's early political learning, see J. M. McCleod, S. H. Chaffee, and D. B. Wackman, "Family Communication and Political Socialization," presented at the 1966 convention of the Association for Education in Journalism, Iowa City, Iowa; and "Family Communication: An Updated Report," presented in 1967 to the Theory and Methodology Division, Association for Education in Journalism, Boulder, Colorado. Both papers may be obtained from the Mass Communications Research Center, 425 Henry Mall, University of Wisconsin, Madison, Wisconsin.

10. For unexpected indications of possible Negro and white similarities in orientation to political authority, see D. Jaros, "Children's Orientations towards the President: Some Additional Theoretical Considerations," *Journal of Politics,* 29, pp. 368-387, 1967.

CROSS-SYSTEM
IMPLICATIONS

18

THE MEMBERSHIP ROLE IN THE POLITICAL SYSTEM

Many inferences may be drawn from our findings. If we interpret the American political system as representative of democracy in a mass industrialized society, our findings may help us to understand how this type of system socializes its young politically. If we identify the American system as one of a class of stable political systems, our findings will shed some light on the sources of stability in this kind of system. If we are interested in the factors that shape the political attitudes of adults and wish to designate childhood experiences as a major determinant, we undoubtedly have much to offer.

Yet none of these implications of our research touches on our major purposes. They may be considered welcome but only incidental benefits. The real origins of our purposes lie in theory.

Now that we have covered so much ground, it may be even more helpful than at the outset to clarify just what it is we have *not* been trying to do. Especially because the current assumptions about objectives in the study of political socialization are so seldom questioned, the greatest danger in the interpretation of our conclusions is that our own intent will be obscured or seriously misconstrued.

At least one thing should be transparent. As we established from the beginning, we have not been searching simply for the roots of those patterns of political behavior that contemporary research has found to prevail among adults. That political science happens to have certain kinds of political knowledge about adults is no sound reason in itself for pursuing their sources into childhood. To have done so without adequate prior justification would simply have led to adopting the perspectives of adult research with all the theoretical shortcomings they might possess. As we have observed, these shortcomings are by no means irrelevant for the study of primary socialization. Research about adults has been confined largely to one sector of behavior in political systems — allocative, or partisan, politics. It is an important area. But for children, concentration on orientations relevant to allocative politics would have forced us to conclude that little significant socialization occurs during so early a phase in the life cycle.

We have carefully refrained from implying that in childhood ideological positions begin to take shape, modes of participation first appear (aside perhaps from party identification), political interest arises, or aspirations for political office have their roots. Nor would we contend that even if some slight beginnings in these matters could be discovered, they would be likely to continue into adulthood undeflected by adolescent or later experiences. It would be a very risky business to argue, without far more evidence than a study of children could possibly provide, that adult political orientations and patterns of behavior in areas such as these can be traced directly back to childhood.

We have found, however, that if we adopt a substantially different theoretical point of departure, one associated with systems analysis, we automatically open up a whole new area of political experience to which children may indeed be exposed. This is the area of system politics. This new approach has invited us to explore the consequences of primary socialization for the input of diffuse support to that part of the political system we have identified as the regime, and within the regime, to that element we have described as the structure of political authority.

THEORETICAL PURPOSES

It is time to refresh our minds about the theoretical under-pinnings of our inquiry and, therefore, about the reasons for choos-ing the growth of diffuse support for political authority as our primary focus. There are many types of social systems: groups, such as societies, families, or tribes, and analytically separable aspects of behavior, such as cultural, religious, or personality systems. Among these we have been interested in understand-ing the operations of one special type, political systems, a kind that we have described as consisting of all those social interactions through which authoritative allocations are effected for a soci-ety. Initially, at the most general level of theory, we have considered it important to ask how any and all kinds of political systems manage to persist in a world of both stability and change. This is the central puzzle for a systems-analytic interpretation of poli-tics.

Every political system is subject to various kinds of stress that threaten to prevent a society from continuing to allocate values authoritatively. One type of stress has concerned us—the possi-bility that the members may be unwilling or unable to offer suf-ficient support for some kind of structure of political authority. We have postulated that the regime is a fundamental element in all political systems. Among other things it includes the struc-ture, both formal and operative, through which political authority is organized and exercised. Empirically men have nowhere been able to resolve all their differences without the intervention, however infrequently or intermittently, of special persons speaking in the name of society. To these we gave the designation political authori-ties. If there is to be any operative political system, if a society is to be able to allocate valued things authoritatively, members of the society will have to accept the decisions of one or another set of au-thorities as binding in some areas of social interaction. Otherwise the Hobbesian state of nature would indeed be likely to prevail. Without some structure of political authority (as part of the regime), no political system could endure for long.

Not that a particular kind of structure need be inescapable; indeed, prevention of the total disappearance of political life may entail deep changes in the structure of political authority, as from a totalitarian to a democratic system, or from a tribal to a secu-lar, representative one.

Transformation of structural type may carry very serious consequences for many human values. But we are concerned here only with the possibility that a society may be prevented from sustaining some kind of processes and structures for the authoritative allocation of values. As hypothesized in Chapter 3, socialization is interpreted as one kind of response through which political systems may be able to ward off certain kinds of stress on the structure of political authority (as well as on other elements of the regime, such as its norms, with which we do not deal here).

This theoretical starting point has led us to diverge radically from customary interests in political socialization. It has introduced a very different set of central questions: How does it come about that members of a political system accept (or reject) the decisions of the authorities as binding? Does the system manage to build up a reservoir of support upon which the authorities may rely even in periods when the members may not be able to discern any specific benefits or rewards from belonging to the system, or when the members may be called upon to make extraordinary personal sacrifices for advantages too remote to be perceived clearly?

Speculatively there are many possible sources of support. Among these, we have argued, primary political socialization is one important type. Taking the American political system as a case study, we have sought to explore the way in which socializing processes could be expected to draw support from its members during the earliest phases of the life cycle. Thus, far from simply searching for the roots of adult behavior intuitively selected as interesting, we have laid down some theoretical criteria to guide us in our exploration of primary socialization.

THE EARLIEST POLITICAL ROLE

Where have these theoretical guidelines now led us? They have brought us to recognize the political void in which past research has unwittingly placed children. This past neglect virtually defies rational explanation. From almost time immemorial the great philosophers have reflected on the importance of early experiences for the political sphere. Men have always thought that attitudes toward political authority probably get their start in the home; repeatedly the family has been considered the political system in microcosm.

Strangely, however, this has put modern research workers if not on a false scent at least on one that followed along a secondary trail. It led to the conviction that if childhood has any meaning for later political life, this meaning could derive only from the projection of psychological predispositions gained within the bosom of the family. It was assumed that somehow or other personality traits instilled at an early age would later manifest themselves in adult political behavior and thereby affect the operation of political institutions. This assumption was reinforced, as we noted in Chapter 4, by the belief that specifically political learning is nonexistent during childhood, or if present, trivial in consequence for adult behavior. Upon reviewing the literature, however, we were driven to the surprising discovery that childhood has been thought of as a political vacuum probably only because to this day so little attention has been given to the *specifically political aspects* of the socializing processes during that period.

This conclusion need not impel us to deny that personality, the underlying structure of learned predispositions, imposes a set of durable constraints on an individual's later political actions. But neither is there anything in this assumption that need discourage us from recognizing, as a fundamental fact for political research and analysis, that as a person matures he also begins to acquire basic political orientations and behavior patterns. In the area of diffuse support for the structure of authority these political acquisitions are by no means random. By grade 8 the child has evolved a complex yet predictable pattern of basic political orientations, and these may have significant consequences for the American political system.

The membership role

How are we now to formulate what happens to the individual by the end of his childhood? We might simply accept our findings as manifestations of a variety of political orientations adding up to a miscellaneous aggregate of attitudes and bits of knowledge, and leave it at that. But we might also see in these orientations something more. Through them the maturing individual is introduced to the political system. For the first time he begins to acquire at least a foretaste of a political role in society. Through the process of being recruited as a general supporter (or opponent) of political authority, the child is learning an important ingredient of the meaning of what it is to be a member in a political system.

The role attitudes and behavior patterns about support that he acquires may conform to the expectations among adults about what a person should know and how he should behave. Thereby his political awakening would contribute to the stability of the system. The acquired patterns may however strike out in new directions, a kind which, if carried into adulthood, might produce fundamental transformations in the system. Thereby the newly acquired role might add to the potentialities for change in the system. But regardless of the consequences for the system, in childhood a person begins to absorb a way of looking at the political world, seeing some parts first and others only later, and he even displays distinctive sentiments about the things he sees. In short, he is taking a few firm steps toward becoming a "member" of a political system. The child begins learning what it means to belong to a political system.

If our findings are characteristic, a child is likely to absorb, if only in latent form, some of the most profound feelings human beings are capable of developing toward political systems, what we have called diffuse support. Perceptual patterns impress themselves on him so that he has some idea of the nature of his political world, especially about a characteristic part, political authority. Only later in life does this first step lead to a variety of differentiated roles. Depending upon the kind of system in which the child grows up, he will gradually learn such separable roles as voter, party member, administrator, headman, political innovator, and the like.

However, most of the specific roles do not and probably cannot evolve very far, if at all, in childhood. Most children are capable of adopting only the simplest attitudinal and behavioral patterns, those that sum up to the undifferentiated role of being a beginning member of a system. This is but a more precise way of confirming a process known in other areas of socialization, as we noted in Chapter 4: The acquisition of general motives, values, and cognitions precedes the learning of specific skills. The child develops attitudes about support for the regime before he learns those minimal participant skills in politics that membership in a particular system may require.

The kind of role the child assumes may be shaped in part by generalized personality characteristics, as we have observed. About this we have no data. But our research does demonstrate that specifically political experiences are inescapable determinants from the very earliest stages of childhood. We might even turn the tables here and suggest that political orientations might themselves help to form the basic personality.

Research has managed to overlook the existence of a generalized membership role and its early roots. We have tried to explain this neglect in part as a product of an excessively narrow conception of the nature of politics. As long as politics is interpreted in largely controversial or partisan terms, there is good reason for feeling that the acquisition of major political roles would not occur at least until late adolescence. But once we uncover a deeper level of political experiences, in system politics, we can immediately identify a broad area in which childhood learning not only is rich and varied but also has potentially profound consequences for the functioning, indeed for the very persistence, of political systems.

Ingredients of the membership role

In the American political system part of the major outlines of the general membership role is unmistakable; it is best defined by the specific processes that appear to shape it. We have described these processes in the following terms: politicization, personalization, idealization, and institutionalization. These concepts merely sum up what we have already found about some of the ways in which the maturing member is introduced to the American system by being induced to lend his support to a set of political authorities. Now, however, we may look at these processes and outcomes in a new and more general light, as contributing to the development of the introductory membership role in the political system.

Politicization is critical for the kind of system we find in the United States. In general, the most distinctive feature of the membership role is the knowledge and understanding that the child quickly acquires about the presence of a political sphere external to the family, even though he may be initially unable to give it a name. Without this recognition it would be difficult to understand how in a mass society such as the United States the child could be brought to the point of extending a minimal level of diffuse support for the structure of authority. In the next chapter, we shall return to this point for its implications about diffuse support for other types of systems. But it is clear here that becoming a member of the system in the United States entails a basic acceptance of the presence, power, and legitimacy of an authority external and superior to the family.

Processes are at work, as we have seen, that begin to pry the child away from exclusive bonds to the family and make it possible for him to reach out to the structure of political authority. He is able to sort out the public from the private sphere, to recognize the superior authority of the policeman, and to accept the higher power and performance qualities of political institutions when compared with father. In short, by the time we leave the child in grade 8 he has been thoroughly politicized; he has become aware of the presence of an authority outside of and more powerful than the family.

Personalization of political authority through the head-and-tail effect has seemed to play a vital part in bringing the child to this level of political awareness. The President and policeman at the beginning, and other figures and some institutions at a later stage, represent the exact points of contact. Some figures, such as the senator, who we would have thought play some part, are less significant. We have here specifically political doors through which children are first able to move out of the family and into the political sphere, although we must bear in mind that there are other points of access that we have not yet explored.[1] Membership in the American system involves, as one of its role characteristics, moving through these doors and becoming available for direct mobilization on behalf of (or in opposition to) the structure of political authority.

Personalization in the American system makes possible at a very early stage the virtual *idealization* of political authority. We have already pondered the question of whether this process applies to other systems as well, a point we shall consider further in the following chapter. But at least for the American system the child finds it easy and natural initially to idealize certain objects of political authority if only because they are like the palpable personal beings already familiar to him in the nuclear family. In the American system the authorities draw high positive feelings; hence we have characterized the process as idealization. But in systems where hostility might represent the first feelings about political authority, we might have had to describe the direction of the sentiments as hostile and called the process "hostilization." The important consideration is that through personalization the child is able initially to extend diffuse support, whether positive or negative, to political authority, and in this process lies the means through which he is linked in some way to the structure of political authority.

Furthermore, for at least those systems in which the authorities are organizations which overshadow their constituent individuals, somehow or other the maturing member needs to learn to be able to relate himself to depersonalized objects as well. *Institutionalization* describes the processes in the American system through which the beginning member shifts his early feelings about personalized objects to political institutions. The older the child, the more likely is he to offer a higher evaluation of such institutions of authority as government or the Supreme Court on our measures of role performance, as against such personal qualities as likability or benevolence. In this way it would appear that as part of the beginning membership role the child learns to shift his diffuse support to the less personalized elements of the structure of political authority.

Through these four processes, therefore, the child comes to a minimal knowledge of what it means to be a member of the American political system, at least as it involves the structure of political authority. His membership role will include political orientations of many other kinds as well—about regime goals and norms and about the political community, for example. But the process underlying acquisition of orientations to these is sufficiently different and complex to merit separate examination. Here we have delineated only those processes relevant to the images of political authority.

THE COHERENCE OF THE AUTHORITY IMAGE

To learn the general values and orientations accompanying early membership in the political system, however, seems to involve more than just being able to identify and relate emotionally to selected objects of authority. Does it appear that the child is also on the way to constructing a more comprehensive and cohesive image of political authority, even though he probably could not articulate it for us under the most subtle interrogation?

In effect we are now questioning the validity of speaking not only about the child's orientation to specific authority figures and institutions, separately and discretely, but also about the structure of authority as a set of related roles. Has the child some comprehensive if latent image of political authority to which, as he matures, he may add new components? Here we need to clarify the relationship, as the child becomes a young member of the system, between the links from system to member, which we have necessarily examined in their particularity, and the acquisition of the idea of an overall structure of authority through which binding decisions are in fact made in a system.

Beyond "egocentricity" in the political system

The discovery that during the early grades the child acquires the capacity to orient himself to objects far beyond the family, in the national sector of society, is a finding of decisive significance to our understanding of the socialization of children. Piaget, for example, has maintained that "egocentricity," or an awareness of self and immediate surroundings — such as family, neighborhood, and town — characterizes the child until about ten or eleven years of age.[2] Children, he has contended, lack the capacity to give either intellectual content (meaning) or emotional response to large units beyond the self and objects in the immediate environment.

If, however, there were no way to overcome this limitation described by Piaget, clearly it would be difficult if not impossible for children to relate themselves to so remote a set of objects as the regime or its authority roles. It is surprising to discover that in the American political system processes have arisen that have succeeded in circumventing these apparent limitations. Not that the child is in the least capable of formally articulating a conception of the regime or of the structure of authority. Nevertheless, as we have discovered, there are specific and well-defined points of contact which do fit in with his capabilities. He is not required to orient himself initially to some impersonal and vague set of institutions, even though in fact he does so in some limited degree in his conception of government. Through the personalization of the regime, in the President and policeman, the child is able to find congenial and meaningful content for what he may only later in life, if ever, learn to speak of as political authority. If the authorities presented only an impersonal front to the child, it is difficult to imagine how he would orient himself to them, given the known intellectual and emotional limitations of all children.

Indeed even by ages ten or eleven, the outer limit of Piaget's period of egocentricity, we have found that the child has already become fairly well politicized, using this term, as we have, to indicate not political interest and participation but only a growing awareness of the political sector. The children come to recognize the potency of some political authorities outside the family. In thus distinguishing political from familial authority, the children reveal that they have learned an important lesson, at least in a system in which the political structure is differentiated from other social structures. However inaccurate their image may be from the point of view of the informed adult, the important thing in the political socialization of children is that through the mechanism of personalization they manage to obtain some awareness of and ideas and feelings about the external agents and agencies of political authority. If our study reveals little else, it does establish firmly that, in spite of findings about egocentricity in other areas, the average child in our group has a firm cognitive base on which to affix feelings, at least about selected political authorities.

The probability of a cohesive image

It is now time, however, to rephrase our findings more meticulously. Although we have repeatedly suggested that we considered the child to be orienting himself to the structure of political authority, this conclusion was somewhat premature. In a strictly nominalistic sense our findings permit us to go no further than to conclude that children are able to grasp specific points in the regime. Aside from the special significance of the child's concept of government, we have determined only that children are able to identify and characterize certain discrete objects in what we have called the structure of authority. We have not tested the children for their ability to conceptualize this structure as an undifferentiated or cohesive entity, and for obvious reasons. We could not expect children to be able to formulate so abstract and generalized an idea.

Nonetheless we shall now propose that all these specific linkages probably do add up to a fairly broad and general idea about the presence of some overarching set of political authorities. The child is able only to see and identify limited parts of this set, but he has some inchoate idea about the existence of a whole.

On the face of it, this inference may not appear too reasonable. Can we really think of the child as conceiving anything more than a number of isolated objects of authority floating around in his cognitive space? And if in fact this is all children in our test group are aware of, can we contend that they are learning to relate to political authority in its general sense or to the whole structure of political authority? Certainly it is not self-evident that just because they are able to establish contact with individual political authorities at some points, the children must necessarily absorb a more comprehensive image of political authority and profess feelings about it.

On an a priori basis we might well draw an opposite conclusion. For children—as indeed for many adults—politics in the United States cannot help but present a complex and confusing face, and it would even if they had much more information than in fact they do possess. The American system contains close to one hundred thousand governmental units in all, with wide variations in organization and rules. In them we find approximately five hundred thousand elected officials and over eleven million civilian governmental employees.[3] These are potential ingredients of any image of the political authorities. There are in addition untold numbers of institutions and agencies through which governmental units are organized for action. Moreover all this constitutes only a fraction of the political world. It is also populated by an untallied number of aspirants to political office, party officials, and other political and opinion leaders who participate in public affairs at well above the average level of visibility.

For all practical purposes, everyone, adult and child alike, must enter this vast political world selectively. We have indeed seen this to be true of children. They have preferred points of contact with the structure of authority. Although with age these linkage points grow in quantity, they are easily numerable, so limited are they. Vast regions even of the formal political structure lie hidden well beyond the child's widest horizons. Although we have not elicited points of contact at the state and local levels, our interviews indicated that these are less likely to be visible to the child except under special local circumstances. The child has scarcely any knowledge of the many administrative offices and agencies at all levels. Just how a maturing person ultimately threads his way through the vast complex of figures and political institutions as he moves well into adulthood we cannot even pretend to guess from our research.

The latency of the overall image of political authority

Because of this complex structure, however, can there be no awareness of or idea about some general political authority of which the figures and institutions known to the child are only symbolic or representative? A few things are clear about this. Even though we can isolate the objects of authority most salient for the child, we need not conclude that he has a totally fragmentary image of the structure of political authority. Our evidence indicates just the contrary. It would seem that he has perhaps begun to discern some coherence in the world of political authority; his very ability to speak about and characterize discrete objects of political authority implies this.

There are several reasons for this inference. In the first place, from an early age there is an overarching quality to the child's image of political authority. Even as he grasps the notion of some power beyond the family, he is able to associate it with an amorphous, ill-defined, but nevertheless embracing entity recognized by him as the government. Even though as he grows older he changes his mind about what might be included in this concept —

moving from the President or George Washington and the like to Congress and voting—its very significance is to serve as a container into which he can pour this changing content. The idea of government helps to hold together the discrete elements that go into it.[4]

In the second place, this latent coherence is reinforced by the child's initial hierarchical image of the authorities. When during his early years the child sees the President and policeman and then adds other objects, he attributes to the President the power to order others about and the full responsibility to care for the country, in much the same way as he might conceive of his parents' power over and obligation to the family. Our interviews revealed that as other objects of authority, such as Congress or senators, float into range of the younger child, they are likely to be interpreted as subordinate to the President, his helpers.

As the children grow a little older, however, the potency of the President recedes, although he always remains a prestigious and powerful figure. But now they consider that this power is shared with Congress, with the Supreme Court, and even with the people at large.[5] Nonetheless, the children see little conflict among the political authorities even though the President continues to occupy a position of high status.

The early threads of hierarchy would seem to help to draw together the child's image of authority into some coherent whole. But even when with age the sense of hierarchy is modified, the varied authorities do not become totally unconnected in the child's mind. If they were, he would not conceive of any power sharing (much less subordination) among the various elements. Thus even though each figure and institution of authority is a discrete unit, the very familiarity of the concept government, the perception of hierarchical structure, and the later idea of cooperation or power sharing encourage us to infer that the child is not construing the structure of authority in a totally fragmented or piecemeal fashion. Something larger than any single object of authority seems to permeate his thinking, even though he is unlikely to be able to express this latent concept in discussion.

Finally, if the above is not enough to persuade us fully, we can find additional support for such an interpretation in what we now know about the nature of the learning process itself. It is a peculiar characteristic of the way children learn that they are often able to grasp an idea well enough to deal with its parts before they can clearly articulate the whole idea itself. An appreciation of the whole may be latent and implicit in the very capacity to handle the parts. This seems to be integral to the way the child comes to comprehend broad and abstract concepts in all spheres of knowledge. Thus:

> In the intuitive phase of concrete operations (approximately ages four to eight) [the child] is capable of grasping many of the basic ideas of mathematics, the sciences, the humanities, and the social sciences . . . The apparent mistake of past generations was to assume that the child had to be able to present a formal structure of thought (for example, the formulation of a proof for a geometric theorem) in order to demonstrate his grasp of the concept. The child in the stage of concrete operations cannot give a formal organization of complex theoretical ideas, but he *can* solve many problems depending upon such ideas. [6]

We may speculate that the same mode of thought applies to the acquisition of political knowledge. Although the young child, especially, is able to discern only discrete parts in the structure of political authority (those that for one reason or another are salient for him), even by grade 2 he seems to assume some larger entity. Through it the individual figures and institutions are somehow interconnected. Even though the child is as yet incapable of formally presenting so complex a theoretical idea as the structure of political authority or the political authorities in toto, he is nonetheless able to react to specific objects of authority as though they are part of the large entity. It is his way of expressing a latent concept. The discreteness of his orientations simply reflects his way of grappling with the complexity of his cognitive political space.

This conclusion has an important bearing on our understanding of the way diffuse support emerges. As we now know so well, the children in our test group display a uniformly high respect for the individual components of political authority. We have on occasion proposed that this may be a product of spillover from their early high regard for the President and the policeman. We may now go somewhat further to consider whether the level of approval for all authorities does not represent, rather, a concrete manifestation of positive feelings that the child is acquiring toward political authority in general. If this is so, we have laid bare the very beginnings of the taproot of respect for political authority. In the child's respect for the individual objects of authority what we have probably been observing are the lesser shoots of respect that must presuppose this deeper and richer source of nourishment. This conclusion is certainly as plausible an explanation for the uniformity of regard for all objects of political authority as any hypothesis about spillover or "halo" effect from early personal figures to later impersonal objects. Both types of processes are probably at work and help to account for the high input of support for political authority.

This conclusion—that the child is learning to orient himself to the structure of authority—is critical for our analysis. It means that in the evolution of the child's general membership role, we need not conceive of the child simply as being linked to the regime in a piecemeal way. He is learning that the idea of political authority goes beyond any particular objects he may happen to know of. As additional figures or institutions come into view, we can expect that these will elicit a similar response by virtue of the child interpreting them as part of the same set of objects. In other words, in becoming simply a member of a political system one of the first things a child learns is to extend support to (or reject in varying degrees) whatever he considers to represent the political authorities. Theoretically we have already identified this as a condition for the persistence of any and all political systems.

It is clear that an understanding of the origins and development of diffuse support does more than illuminate one of the sources of regime persistence. It enables us to see this support as part and parcel of the more generalized political role, that of a new member, into which the child steps. Membership involves acquiring both an early awareness of political authorities in some generalized sense and a set of support responses (positive or negative) to these authorities.

NOTES

1. See the implications about these other points in D. Easton and J. Dennis, "The Child's Acquisition of Regime Norms: Political Efficacy," *American Political Science Review,* 61, pp. 25-38, 1967.
2. J. Piaget (assisted by A. M. Weil), "The Development in Children of the Idea of the Homeland and of Relations with Other Countries," *International Social Science Bulletin,* 3, pp. 561-578, 1951.
3. *Statistical Abstracts of the United States—1967* (Washington, D.C.: GPO, 1967), tables 578 and 606.
4. For an elaboration of this point, see once again the introduction and conclusion to Chapter 6.
5. It will be recalled, from Chapter 6, that by grade 8 many children shift from President to voting as the best representative of government.
6. J. J. Gallagher, "Productive Thinking," in M. L. Hoffman and L. W. Hoffman (eds.), *Review of Child Development Research* (New York: Russell Sage, 1964), vol. I, p. 356.

19

BEYOND THE
AMERICAN SYSTEM

Now that we have conceptualized our findings more broadly and have interpreted them as contributing to the delineation of an introductory membership role, the base of much subsequent behavior in the American political system, we may ask whether our findings transcend the particularity of this single case. For our theoretical purposes it would be rewarding if we could argue without fear of contradiction that politicization, personalization, institutionalization, and idealization are the fundamental means through which all political systems strengthen their capacity to persist.

Unfortunately this would be putting our inferences in too strong a form, ascribing to them a greater generality than they permit. Our sample of children severely limits the validity of any generalizations. Yet there is good reason for maintaining that we have obtained some significant clues about the primary socialization of support which may be applicable to instances over and beyond the American political system.

THE LIMITATIONS OF THE SAMPLE

There is little question that our sample imposes narrow limits on any universal generalizations we might hope to obtain. For one thing, we have after all only one case study—a single political system at one moment in time. Our test children represent not a probability sample but a group that was selected to bring out divergent patterns of orientation in the United States toward the political authorities.[1] Furthermore our test group includes only white children at schools in metropolitan areas, no significant numbers of children from the most depressed economic sectors of these cities, and no blacks. Accordingly we have no data on some groups in which political socialization might be proceeding at a very different pace and in which less awareness of and less positive affect for the political authorities might be present.

Nor have we engaged in a real-time longitudinal study, one in which we take a set of children and trace their political development as they actually move through the elementary grades. We have only what we have called a synthetic longitudinal design. We assume that because all our test children fall into one generational group, responses of our seven-year-olds, for examples, are probably not very different from the kinds of responses our thirteen-year-olds would have given if we had tested them when they were only seven.

Furthermore, as we pointed out in Chapters 14 and 15, our techniques prevent us from sorting out the differential effects of social maturation, biological growth, and generational experiences. It could possibly be that our findings are valid only for the particular generations adjacent to the one we have tested. Perhaps the salience of the authorities and their initial idealization are largely products of the modern epoch. In the United States the negative attitudes toward government of the 1920s have yielded, under the impetus of the new role adopted by government during the 1930s, to a more relaxed acceptance of governmental responsibility for sustaining some minimal level of social welfare and economic activity. The children of those adults who lived through the Depression could therefore be expected to look more favorably than their predecessors on the actions of the authorities, as limited evidence seems to indicate.[2]

It is conceivable too that idealization of the political authorities can be time-bound in another way. It may be representative only of the generations of the immediate past and need not describe those of the immediate future. If critical issues of the 1960s are transforming the attitudes of young people, a residue of their experiences may carry over to later periods. The politically active youth of today—those whites and blacks who man the picket lines protesting against the war in Vietnam and against the draft and who actively challenge the disparity between prosperity and poverty and between democratic promise and fulfillment—together with those who stand by quietly but not unsympathetically, will undoubtedly not be able to shake off the memories of these experiences for a long time. If their bitterness toward political authority remains, it could be transmitted to their children. Affect for the authorities among the children of the future might be less enthusiastic, not nearly so idealizing, as it is among the children we have tested.

Hence, our ability to establish with a reasonable degree of confidence whether our test children, in their idealization of authority, are probably representative of the primary socializing process may depend on the time constraints we introduce even within the single system we have examined. For all generations the degree of attachment to the system achieved through personalization need not be so high as we have found, nor need affect always move in a positive direction. The intensity and direction (positive or negative) of affect is likely to depend upon generational influences.

Furthermore, when we move beyond the United States to other systems, there may even be some question about the universality not only of idealization but of personalization as a vital perceptual and cathecting device in relationship to the most inclusive (national) authorities. The linkage between children and the political system may be contingent on the nature of the regime structure, as we have suggested in Chapter 14. It could be that at the most inclusive system level personalization flows only from the prominence of the chief executive under conditions peculiar to the present epoch.

As an integral part of the new responsibilities assumed by political authority in modern mass society during the 1930s, the executive arm of government has moved to the forefront of the political stage. It is conceivable that, as in the more distant past, perhaps in the future, chief executives may recede into a more cooperative, egalitarian structure of authority without nearly the contemporary degree of prominence. If so, for future generations of children the political chief executive may become less significant in the processes through which linkage to the political system occurs. In those systems where the chief executive plays a more limited role today, as Uruguay or Switzerland, perhaps even now other figures or organizations come to the fore. In short, the political structure itself may be a critical variable in shaping the nature of the connecting points.

The universality of early politicization is even more questionable than that of personalization. From our one case study it is not at all clear that politicization may not be limited by the particular characteristics of the American type of system. This is an important point, and shortly we shall explore it more fully, as well as the probable universality of personalizing processes.

But let us accept the plausibility of drawing only the least interesting kind of implications from our findings. Suppose that our study has indeed described only the profile of one generation and in the United States alone. Would this destroy its utility? Not necessarily. At the very least our study would provide a base line against which other generations might be compared. An analysis of trends would become possible, and for the first time we would be able to sort out significant generational shifts. At the same time it would raise intriguing questions about how identification of and attachment to the structure occurs in other generations and in other systems (if not through politicization, idealization, and personalization), about the effects of alternative connective processes, and about the reasons for the differences.

However, the likelihood of one aspect of the early membership role — personalization — being generational, as against age-determined, is not too high. Biological as well as social maturational factors, rather than the fact that we are testing children of a certain generation, would seem to account for early personalization of authority. Regardless of the nature of the structure of political authority, we have suggested more than once, it is difficult to conceive of how a young child especially might apprehend political authority. His emotional and intellectual equipment is too limited to make any other means plausible for his perceiving and cathecting authority. Regardless of generation or system, maturing members probably reach out to the political structure through its most readily personalized aspect, a point that we shall reemphasize shortly in relationship to types of societies other than the American. Furthermore, our conclusions are consistent with what we know about socialization in other areas of behavior, as we have indicated from time to time. But we would not deny that the acid test will come as new generations with new experiences move across the political stage and as replicative research is mounted in the United States as well as in other, dissimilar types of systems.

THE UNIQUENESS OF THE AMERICAN EXPERIENCE

Even if we had a representative sample, however, and could validly extend our findings to all children in the United States, and even if we could assume these findings apply to all recent generations, the question could still be raised of whether our conclusions are not in the end peculiar to the American political system. It is arguable, for example, that adults in the United States have been shown repeatedly to have little interest in politics, and although the level of political concern may slowly be changing under the impact of continuing international and domestic crises, at least during our test period low political interest was still a dominant characteristic. Politics as an area of great salience and concern for adults has been easily preempted by family, job, and leisure.

On these grounds it could be argued plausibly that children might readily construe the lack of adult involvement and concern as consensus, trust, and faith in the political authorities. With no deep and conflicting feelings about political issues, adults might transmit to their children an apparently benign and tolerant political air. The children could interpret this as evidence of the essential benevolence of everything connected with the political sphere. In other systems, however, where politics may play a more meaningful role for adults, primary socialization might be different. Among adults in France, for example, the political cleavages and the attendant disillusionment with, if not cynicism about, politics seem to be transferred readily to the maturing children with some dampening effect perhaps on their perception of politics and even on their attachment to the regime. [3]

The severity of socialization about system politics

Perhaps it is true that the American political system embodies certain special characteristics relevant to primary socialization, but if so, this is probably not for the reasons just discussed. The fact would seem to be that not all forms of politics are low in salience for the members. To be sure, in comparison with partisan politics other interests have commanded a higher priority. We might expect adults to transmit the same ordering of concerns to children. But for system politics—those matters that relate to identification with and support for the basic aspects of the system and often referred to as Americanism, patriotism, loyalty, allegiance, and the like—we may appropriately doubt whether adults do display the same apathy or indifference.

Rather, the idealization of political authority among our group of children may spring from deep historical roots. In a society such as the United States, in which at the turn of the century a vast variety of nationalities came together in a historically brief period, the emphasis on system politics may mirror a deep anxiety about the difficulties of integrating the population and creating a strong sense of political identification. It may represent a typical response to fears of cultural, ethnic, and linguistic cleavages.

In the past the influx of immigrants into the United States was accompanied by widespread, conscious policies seeking to blend them into a culturally homogeneous whole in the image of the prior Anglo-Saxon society. This was the dynamic behind the subtle but dominant underlying ideology about America as a melting pot of nationalities, and it constituted a potent belief system. Immigrants were expected to give up their languages and to modify drastically their national identities for the bountiful rewards of admission to America. Immigrants arrived anticipating that they would abandon these particularistic identifications. They positively sought to melt into the common pot.

In the schools there was little question that it was the task of education to provide what was considered to be an appropriate kind of civic or citizenship training. "Civic pride," "patriotism," or Americanism was to be specifically and directly inculcated. If school curricula have any significance in the socializing processes, these deliberate policies helped to assimilate or blend the offspring of immigrants to the second and third generations. The social sciences curriculum was in some ways seriously crippled by the use of educational institutions in this way, and only in recent years have the elementary and secondary schools begun to escape the consequences and return to professionally dictated subject matters.

Outside the schools the pressures for conformity and homogeneity in underlying political sentiments were equally intense. Patriotic societies abounded, patriotic oratory rang true to the popular ear even when it rose to hyperbolic heights. The suspicion of disloyalty or un-Americanism, defined in monolithic terms, appeared to be the most heinous of crimes. McCarthyism in the 1950s revealed these forces in a garish light.

It is not true, therefore, to conclude that in the United States politics has been a matter of low salience and interest. At most this description can apply only to partisan, or allocative, politics. System attitudes have not been left to chance. Socialization in this sphere has had a great deal of meaning for a system whose ethnic mixture and potential for divisiveness might lead it to doubt the strength of its own unity and the unity of its own purposes.

It would appear that system politics is an area of severe socialization. The American system may be exemplary for the low level of political involvement among its members; it may be equally unique however in placing an extraordinary emphasis on civic or political education for the young, at least through the schools. For example, in the Soviet Union, where political education has been thought to weigh heavily in the school curriculum, surprisingly less time seems to be devoted to political matters in the elementary and secondary schools than in those of the United States. Political education, Bereday and Stretch estimate, ". . . did not find an unusual amount of political exposure on the Soviet side; we found, in fact, that the Americans demand greater exposure in spite of the American school year being shorter . . . In the United States in grades 5 to 12 almost 46 percent of school time was devoted to some form of political and social education. In the Soviet Union the relevant percentage for grades 5 to 11 was only just short of 38 percent."[4]

It could be that in the United States this concentration on citizenship education has provided a powerful impetus toward the idealization of political authorities by children and accounts for both the little cynicism or distrust evident and the surprising consensus among the children regardless of sex, geographical region, and social class. Children seem to be blended into a common mold with respect to system attitudes, as we observed in Chapters 16 and 17. No glimmering of a critical awareness of the political authorities is apparent.

We know that in other areas of behavior such as toilet training, sex behavior, and the handling of aggressions, cultures will differ in the severity of childhood training.[5] We might also suspect that this is equally true in the political sphere. It may be that the American system is uncommon among mass industrialized societies in the intensity of primary socialization about system politics. If so, generalization from the American to other systems, especially to those older systems where ethnic integration has not in the past been of such moment (as Britain or France[6]), would need to be handled with extreme care.

Generalization to multi-ethnic societies

It would appear however that the hypothesis about the severity of system-political socialization in the United States might with some justification be extended to other types of multi-ethnic societies, especially those still struggling with the development of their political systems. We say "to other types" because it does seem that the United States is and has been a multi-ethnic society, however unwilling it has been to conceptualize itself in these terms. For certain historical reasons, perhaps because the major minority racial group rose out of legal slavery and then has remained in social bondage for almost a century, American society has been able to deny the reality.

The racial crisis of the 1960s has vividly revealed that even though the prevalent white and Anglo-Saxon ideology has been built around melting-pot aspirations, and even though this has militated against alternative ways of conceptualizing the American social context, the United States has been unable to escape the strife and turbulence of many other multi-ethnic societies. American ideology has failed to constrain American reality. This may ultimately force the United States to alter its political self-image radically so that it may begin to reinterpret itself for what it really is, a society composed of several large and residentially concentrated ethnic groups—black, Puerto Rican, Mexican-American, American Indian, and others—in tense juxtaposition to the dominant white, English-speaking population.

The same severity of primary socialization at the system-politics level found in the United States may therefore turn out to be characteristic of other multi-ethnic societies in which assimilation is the prevalent norm. It could be that in other systems like the American, where interethnic tensions have been muted by the unchallenged dominance of the majority group and its assimilative norm, the authorities will also tend to be perceived by children in more personal and idealized terms.

SOCIALIZATION OF DIRECT VERSUS MEDIATED SUPPORT

Severity of political socialization in the area of system politics would, therefore, not appear to be necessarily unique to the

American system, even though there are probably few other systems in which a melting-pot ideology has prevailed so easily for so many decades. We might also surmise that other aspects of the socializing processes might be found even more generally. As we have already proposed, the burden of our analysis presses us toward the conclusion that without some means for politicizing children and for coupling them through personalization to the structure of authority, it would be difficult to bring maturing members in most systems to accept the legitimacy of the regime. The emotional and cognitive limitations of children would seem to require some high degree of personalization in their younger years, and in one way or another, if a system is to persist, the children must become aware of the presence and power of the relevant political authorities. It is highly unlikely that in any political system childhood political socialization would be largely neglected or that most of the burden of apprizing members of the political authorities and of generating responses about them would be left to adolescence and beyond. Personalization and politicization during childhood are likely universal cathecting processes.

But the location of these processes need not necessarily be the same in other systems as they are in the American. In the latter the child is withdrawn from the family, as it were, and brought out into the broader society. The political authorities have direct access to him. Intermediaries do not bar the child from the authorities. He sees the structure of authority through his own eyes, and he responds to it directly in his own terms. The capacity to do this is closely related to the whole personalizing and politicizing processes. In short the input of support in the American system is directly from the child to the authorities.

Need we infer from this that we should expect to find an equally direct input of support in all other systems? We shall conclude that this is not a necessary generalization.

Direct support for the authorities

A peculiarity of the American political system (and probably of others of the same type) is that the adult member can and does put in support for the various major political objects (authorities, regime, and political community) directly. The authorities in turn can and do appeal directly to the members rather than through intermediaries alone. The authorities expect that the outputs they create will frequently have a direct impact on the individual or can be made to do so if they, the authorities, so choose. The system's rules do not provide for a necessary go-between in all cases, nor does the nature of the social structure compel such mediation. This is not to say that frequently the authorities and the members may not be related through mediating interest groups, vocational associations, regional organizations, or even other formal political units such as states or municipalities. But the national authorities do have regular means for direct access to the membership without having to filter communications or administrative actions through others.

Important kinds of consequences for the relationship of the ordinary individual to government and for his exposure to the influence of political authority flow from such direct access. The philosophy of pluralism, from Duguit, Krabbe, Cole, the early Laski, and others, sought to devise an ideology and structural arrangement precisely for the purposes of sheltering the individual from the hazards of this direct exposure to the power and persuasion of the authorities. But aside from the dangers or advantages (and the ameliorating circumstance that the individual in return may have direct access to the authorities, if only nominally, through the vote and informal means), the political fact is that in the type of system we find in the United States, under conditions of large-scale, mass industrialized society, such direct access between the authorities and the members of the system does exist. Does it begin in childhood? If so, ought we to expect that it will occur with equal prominence in the primary socialization of all political systems?

Our research suggests that fundamentally in the American system direct access derives from the success with which the socializing processes are able to disengage the child from some of his primordial ties to the nuclear family and to bring him under the broader canopy of the political structure. This appears to be the critical starting point in the evolution of direct support for the system.

If the child's initial and exclusive bonds to the family could not be loosened, as we indicated in Chapter 13, this would seriously embarrass the authorities in their efforts to reach out to him directly, especially during the early and presumably formative period of childhood. But we do know that in the American system the child at an early stage has become fairly well politicized: He is able to distinguish the public from the private sphere, he accepts the higher authority of the policeman, and he recognizes the greater power of political as against parental authority. This is strong testimony that before the end of grade school the child has moved beyond the narrow confines of the family to the broader society and has begun to accept the validity at least of his own availability to the authorities.

This has many consequences for the system, as we have noted. But we have now to recognize that for the persistence of the system or for the input of support for the structure of authority, even though personalization and politicization may indeed be universal processes, the generation of direct support need not be. This may be a function rather of the peculiar conditions of the class of systems of which the United States represents one instance.

The generation of direct support may be critical for the United States, for example, because the kinds of efforts in which a modernized society is engaged require a fairly high level of popular commitment and performance—through personal services, payment of taxes, and conformance to a vast number of legal rules and norms. Without the system's direct access to the members, goal-directed collective action would be enormously complicated, indeed even impossible. In a mass industrialized society, no authorities could afford to bargain and negotiate for compliance through intermediaries representing a vast network of small units, such as heads of nuclear families. The role-specific, stratified social structure probably makes direct access unavoidable, at least in comparison with a lineage structure in which heads of large kinship segments act as intermediate-level authorities.

Plural groups do of course exist, and these may serve either to enhance or to diminish the input of support for the authorities, depending on the political circumstances. To the extent that the group leaderships are conceived to have the backing of their members, these leaderships may act as intermediaries between the political authorities and the individual. But over and above these groups, the members of the system at times act simply in their unmediated roles as members of a system, responding directly to the political authorities. It is the beginning of this capacity of the authorities to bypass plural groups that we have detected during primary socialization. Socialization about the input of mediated support transparently belongs to another phase of the life cycle.

Mediation of support for the authorities

However, regardless of the function of direct support in American-type systems, we cannot generalize and assert that socialization must produce a similar pattern of direct input of support for all systems. In other systems the authorities may have far less opportunity for direct access to the members. Where subsystems exist, such as lineage segments in tribal societies, or cohesive ethnic, linguistic, or religious groups in modern and developing societies, or even corporate regional entities (as in a confederal system), these may all present narrow filters or even barriers impermeable to the political authorities. Schools, mass media, and other cultural means may have little penetrative effect. There would thus be little opportunity for the children in these subsystems to perceive distant figures or institutions of authority, much less to acquire sentiments about them, either positive or negative. The accompanying residential and cultural localism and regionalism ("communalism" so called in India, for example, or *la société globale* in French Canada) would tend to disconnect the members from the national symbols and representatives of authorities.

Cohesive subsystems like these, however, may but do not necessarily impose stress on the regime of a political system. At times these arrangements may be the only conditions under which a regime may be able to endure and a political system persist. But we would expect that in these systems children grow up to look to the lineage, ethnic, linguistic, or regional leaders as their authorities. What is of particular significance is that at this level, if our conclusions about socialization of support are correct, children would still go through the personalizing, politicizing, idealizing (or "hostilizing"), and institutionalizing processes, except that the relevant authorities would be at the subsystem level. The subsystem authorities would represent gatekeepers who could regulate the flow of support to the authorities of the more inclusive political system.[7] In French Canada, for example, a French child might be aware of the Premier of Quebec sooner than he would be of the Prime Minister of Canada. In much the same way the members of peasant societies, even of the ethnolinguistic homogeneous type, because of lack of comprehensive and penetrative communications, might rely on the village and regional chiefs, headmen, notables, and the like to serve as bridges to some distant and unknown authorities.[8] To some extent there are mediators of support as part of the infrastructure in all modern societies as well.

System persistence and indirect support

It is clear that having found early socialization of direct support for the structure of political authority in the United States, we need not postulate that system persistence is consistent only with this kind of early learning about support. We are proposing only that no system will be possible unless it can support some kind of structure of political authority at the most inclusive system level. In the American system, if our data are not atypical, this seems to be achieved through the initial socialization of direct support for the national authorities as well as for a local symbol of political authority. The process of socialization focuses the attention of the maturing members on political objects at the polar extremes of the system. These become system symbols, and thereby they lend a degree of integration and coherence to the political community that other systems may lack.

Yet we do not suggest that other kinds of systems have no alternative means for breeding this kind of diffuse support for the authorities, even though the process may be an indirect one. In systems where local, regional, or communal ties are strong, we would expect the maturing child to be far less aware of the overall system authorities than he is in the United States. But persistence of the system need not be undermined. The strength of the bond between the members of a subsystem and their immediate authorities on the one hand, and between the latter (now conceived of as gatekeepers or mediators) and the inclusive (national) system authorities on the other, will establish the level of diffuse support for the regime. Today we would expect to find Switzerland or India somewhat closer to an indirect-support-input model of socialization than, say, France, Great Britain, or the United States.

At the very least, it is clear that our data have given us some understanding of how a stable system goes about providing diffuse support for the structure of political authority from early childhood. Our analysis leads us to believe that similar kinds of processes may be found in other types of systems, even though where localism of various kinds may prevail, the authorities at the most inclusive level of the system may play a lesser role in primary socialization than they do in the United States. Yet we would suspect that the personalizing and politicizing dynamics of the process through which maturing members are brought to accept the legitimacy even of the intermediate authorities is probably akin to what we have found for the most inclusive authorities in the American system. This is at least a useful working hypothesis in approaching other types of political systems.

CHANGE, STABILITY, AND PERSISTENCE

In spite of our arguments to the contrary, it is still possible that our inferences about the characteristics of socialization with respect to the structure of political authority are less universal than we may think but for reasons other than those we have advanced. It could be that however valid our conclusions about the socializing processes, at best they apply only to stable political systems. Perhaps at most we have discovered only the way in which new members learn to adapt or conform to existing political patterns. Could we with justification expect that our findings would have been essentially the same if we had examined a clearly unstable system?

It is readily understandable why our research might be construed as having implications only for stability. For one thing, until the end of the 1950s at least, the United States had shown all the earmarks of a relatively stable system. It would have been very surprising indeed if the test children had not reflected this, that is, if we had found that the children were not positively supportive in their earliest sentiments. At the same time the theoretical objectives of our inquiry could be easily misunderstood as involving us heavily in a search only for the conditions of stability.

Misconstruction of this sort represents such a great danger that we might profitably reexamine our theoretical foundations for a moment in order to clear away any lingering ambiguities about the relationship of system-stability to our basic purposes. With a substantial body of data and analysis now behind us we shall be able to reassert, at a new level of understanding, the point we made at the outset of the book. There we sought to establish that our theoretical guidelines would lead us toward an understanding of the relationship of socialization to system persistence and not to system maintenance, or stability, however much attention the latter subject would of necessity receive in a study of the American system.

Structural legitimacy and stability

On theoretical grounds we had pointed to the need to look for the beginnings of diffuse support in the early growth of a belief in the legitimacy of the authority structure, what we called structural legitimacy. We had contended that over time every system will probably accumulate a large repertoire of responses for coping with stress on the input of support. In this repertoire are typically efforts to increase the quantity and nature of specific rewards for the members, the use of rational persuasion to arouse favorable sentiments, and the application of coercion in varying degrees. But few systems manage to sustain sufficient diffuse support by these means alone. Efforts are also usually made to cultivate a deep-rooted belief in the legitimacy of the authorities and the regime, including the structure of authority. In most systems the members are encouraged to believe that the structure through which the authorities operate is legitimate and valid, that the arrangements for distributing authority in the system are right and proper and as such ought to be accepted.

Promotion of a belief in the structural legitimacy of the regime may be described therefore as a characteristic system response to stimulate the input of support. This response goes beyond seeking the mere approval of a system; it requires a deeper conviction, that the system is ethically acceptable. A belief like this may even constitute a more stable base of support for a regime than a rational calculus of self-interest; in childhood, we may suspect from our findings, it is virtually the only foundation that is laid.

On theoretical grounds, therefore, we were deeply sensitive to the desirability of testing whether support, in the form of a sense of legitimacy, itself makes a start in childhood. But the continuing dialogue over the whole history of political philosophy cautions us that legitimacy is no simple idea, that it may include many elements difficult to break down for empirical research. The limited maturational level of our subjects made it virtually impossible to examine directly any feelings they might have of this complex sort.

Nevertheless in one instance we did come close to the general idea of legitimacy. We asked our test children, it will be recalled, whom it is most wrong to disobey—mother, teacher, father, or policeman. The policeman was the dominant choice.[9] This encouraged us to believe that the child was beginning to acquire some sense of the legitimacy of this symbol of authority external to the family.

We may now go even further. This question about obedience, we suspect, really reflects the overall implications of our findings about the high level of respect for all authorities and not for the policeman alone. To be sure, esteem and regard for the various figures and institutions of political authority are not identical with a belief in their legitimacy. But it is highly unlikely that children will display such feelings about these authorities without at the same time considering that it is ethically right for them to care for the country. Drawing on Piaget for support, we have already suggested that this is implicit in the child's specific conceptions of the President and the policeman.[10] Here we may broaden this to infer that it is also undoubtedly implicit in the very positive images of all the authorities.

This strongly suggests therefore that we have pinned down one of the earliest sources of that elusive and complex sentiment that we call the belief in legitimacy. It seems reasonable to conclude that if primary socialization can make any contribution to the durability of a system, it must do so at least through sentiments about legitimacy. With this implication so prominent in our findings, any reader would be justified in feeling that perhaps after all, despite our early protests to the contrary, the major emphasis (even if unintended) of our research has indeed been upon the determinants of stability, and our major findings may be relevant only in this context.

Stability and persistence

It should be evident by this time, however, that in fact our interest in the childhood beginnings of feelings of legitimacy derives only from the light these feelings throw on the way in which a maturing member is brought to accept (or reject) the structure of political authority. Our concern with legitimacy helps us to understand how at least a class of political systems, those we call stable, such as the American has been, manages to persist through obtaining support for some structure of political authority. Legitimacy is therefore a kind of sentiment that is relevant for both stability and persistence.

It may appear to be but a quibble thus to attempt to differentiate between stability and persistence. But there is a vital theoretical distinction between them. Recognition of this distinction permits us to lift the study of political socialization out of a realm of interpretation in which it is seen largely as a device to perpetuate the status quo.

Persistence refers to the capacity of a society to provide for the making and implementing of binding decisions. Without some kind of regime, including as this concept does the structure of political authority, such allocations would be impossible.[11] In some systems the preference is for stable regimes. But in other systems dissatisfaction with (or open opposition to) the regime or the particular way of organizing political authority may be sufficient to force changes in its structure. On occasion, a system may undergo a succession of transformations in the regime. Historically this has been true of France in its shifts through five republics and an equal number of intermediary regimes. In other instances, as in many developing systems in Africa today, the regime may totter on the brink for long periods of time, giving all the appearances of instability but never quite collapsing.

Even though a regime may reveal itself as very unstable, however, the members of the system may be able to continue to make and implement binding decisions, even if not with the orderliness or effectiveness implicit in most ideals of good government. But general theory does not seek to measure a system's ethical adequacy; it simply hopes to understand and account for variations in a system's operations. In short, the stability or instability of a system as a whole each represents a condition consistent with the persistence of the system. There are other important relationships between persistence and stability or instability, but these do not concern us at the moment. All we need note is that instability does not preclude the persistence of some kind of political system. On occasion it may be a central mechanism for achieving a desired transformation in a regime considered to have outlived its usefulness. Thereby it may contribute to the persistence, in some form, of a system for the authoritative allocation of values.

From the point of view of our theoretical objectives it is only a matter of incidental interest that the American system had been stable in the years prior to and coincident with our research. We selected this system not because of its stability but for other reasons already stated. However, the fact that it is stable does limit the scope of our findings. Strictly speaking, if from our study we do learn anything about the input of diffuse support for the structure of political authority, our knowledge should apply only to stable systems. Whether similar modes of contact between children and the structure would occur under conditions of rapid or disorderly change in the United States would require research under different conditions or in other types of systems that typically experience unstable regimes.

For theoretical purposes, however, our conclusions would not have been different if in the American system we had discovered that primary socialization conduced to political instability. This might have been the expected outcome, for example, if we had found that children first learned to distrust or hate the President and the policeman and, in later grades, ignored or rejected them together with such institutional representatives as the Supreme Court or the government. It may well be that some segments of the children in the United States, as in the most poverty-stricken urban and rural slums, do in fact have feelings closer to these than to the feeling of our test children.[12] Not even children in the lowest socioeconomic status of our group, however, are so impoverished as to fall into these depressed sections of the population.

But even with these findings, and assuming for the moment that children such as those not tested grow up to fight for changes in their regime, our inferences about the socializing processes for the persistence of some kind of regime need not have been different. It could be that for the children to develop hostility toward the authorities, it is also necessary that they become politicized enough to differentiate parental from political authority, that they make personalized contact with figures of authority so as to learn whom to hate (rather than idealize), and that they go through a process of depersonalizing authority so that they may transfer their negative affect to institutions. Indeed, as we have observed before, we find it difficult to visualize some alternative set of socializing processes.

It should be clear by this time that we are concerned only with the underlying processes through which maturing members in a system acquire supportive orientations about the regime. We have repeatedly cautioned that this support may move in a negative as well as a positive direction. To the present we have been compelled to confine our remarks to positive support only because this is the kind we have consistently found to dominate in our group of children. But if we had discovered widespread negative support (hostility), however interesting this might have been for those concerned with sustaining something called stability, for us it would simply have indicated that a structural shift might be under way in the regime. Instability need not necessarily be interpreted as contributing to the destruction of the system, although this is always a possible outcome. Instability might represent the beginning of a shift in support to some new kind of regime, under which the members of the system could continue to make authoritative allocations. In this event the change would contribute to the persistence of the system.

Briefly, then, in seeking an understanding of the sources of diffuse support, such as legitimacy, for a regime, we need to realize that negative sentiments need not destroy a system. The change implicit in the input of negative support may well be a major condition for the persistence of a capacity to make authoritative allocations. We would expect that the presence of negative support among most of our test children would not have changed by very much our inferences about the basic processes through which they become aware of the structure of authority and learn to relate to it. We have some reasons for believing therefore that the empirically verified processes of politicization, personalization, institutionalization, and idealization (or "hostilization") in the American system may represent socializing processes in childhood with regard to the structure of political authority in many other systems as well.

NOTES

1. See Appendix.
2. See M. Janowitz, *Public Administration and the Public; Perspectives toward Government in a Metropolitan Community* (Ann Arbor: Bureau of Government, University of Michigan, 1968), pp. 3-7, 11-12, and 102-103. This study shows that in the Detroit area negativism and suspiciousness of administrative authority are less concentrated among young people, the offspring of the Depression generation.
3. L. Wylie, *Village in the Vaucluse* (Cambridge, Mass.: Harvard, 1957); P. E. Converse and G. Dupeux, "Politicization of the Electorate in France and the United States," *Public Opinion Quarterly,* 26, pp. 1-23, 1962; P. Auerbach, "The French Child and Interest in Municipal Elections," unpublished master's thesis, University of Chicago, 1967; and R. Inglehart, "The Socialization of 'Europeans'—Nation Building in Western Europe," unpublished doctoral thesis, University of Chicago, 1967.
4. G. Z. F. Bereday and B. B. Stretch, "Political Education in the U.S.A. and the U.S.S.R.," *Comparative Education Review,* 7, pp. 9-16, 1963.
5. I. L. Child, "Socialization," in G. Lindzey (ed.), *Handbook of Social Psychology* (Cambridge, Mass.: Addison-Wesley, 1954), vol. II, especially p. 662; J. W. M. Whiting, "Socialization Process and Personality," in F. L. K. Hsu (ed.), *Psychological Anthropology: Approaches to Culture and Personality* (Homewood, Ill.: Dorsey, 1961), pp. 355-380.
6. For Britain it has been said that "there is little emphasis in English schools on overt civic training . . . compared with the United States there is relatively little effort made to instill feelings of patriotism." P. Abramson, "The Differential Political Socialization of English Secondary School Students," *Sociology of Education,* 40, p. 255,

1967. Some data that possibly bear on this concern the relatively lower awareness by British children of the concept democracy as compared with American, Italian, and German children. See also J. Dennis, L. Lindberg, D. McCrone, and R. Stiefbold, "Political Socialization to Democratic Orientations in Four Western Systems," *Comparative Political Studies,* 1, pp. 71 - 101, 1968.

7. For the idea of gatekeepers, see D. Easton, *A Systems Analysis of Political Life* (New York: Wiley, 1965), pp. 424 - 426.

8. See D. Lerner, *The Passing of Traditional Society* (New York: Free Press, 1958).

9. See Chapter 10.

10. See Chapters 8 and 11.

11. On the need for a regime, see D. Easton, op. cit., pp. 190 - 211.

12. See D. Jaros, H. Hirsch, and F. J. Fleron, Jr., "The Malevolent Leader: Political Socialization in an American Sub-Culture," *American Political Science Review,* 62, pp. 564 - 575, 1968.

APPENDIX

METHODS
AND PROCEDURES

DESIGN

This study was undertaken when extremely few guidelines existed for identifying relevant variables or for forming working hypotheses. Indeed, scholarship had advanced very little in the centuries since Plato and Aristotle first raised the problem of the role of political education in the political system. Essentially no firm evidence was available concerning when new members of a political society typically learn their basic lessons. What little empirical data had come to light seemed to assume that adolescence or early adulthood is politically the most formative period.

To test this assumption, a pilot study with high school students in the Chicago area was carried out in 1959. The finding on this point was that few if any developmental trends in orientation were detected during these years; our attention then turned naturally to the years before the child reaches high school. In the series of studies that has culminated in this book, investigation moved to consideration of those aspects of fundamental political consciousness that come into being as the child makes his way through elementary school.

Given this purpose, the ideal research design would have been to identify a number of representative children who could be questioned and observed over a broad span of years in order to record the moments of origination of political orientations and their subsequent development. With the primitive state of knowledge in this area at that time, however, a large investment in longitudinal studies did not seem to be warranted. Rather, we felt that such an ideal study design could best be executed only after a more modest series of exploratory studies had been carried out in which new concepts, methods, and hypotheses might be generated. With this necessity in mind plus the usual situation of scarce economic resources for research, it was thought more appropriate to undertake a less ambitious, exploratory program, using modal and purposively selected rather than broadly representative children of elementary school age and a cross-sectional design.

The basic design of the study was developmental. We sought to obtain children at relatively close age intervals in order to observe the year-by-year shifts in political orientations. We also wished to begin as early in the grade span as possible in order to be able to observe the earliest developments, if these began close to the time when the child first enters school.

Limitations, of course, were imposed by the nature of the research instruments that we were able to devise, so that in fact we had to begin with grade-2 children. As we found in pretesting, only at grade 2 were children able to read well enough to follow simple questionnaire items as they were read out to them. First-grade and kindergarten children appeared almost universally in our pretests to lack this capacity. In the end therefore we made a practical compromise by beginning with grade-2 children and obtaining respondents at each successive grade level through grade 8.

Besides grade, three other variables were of sufficient theoretical interest to require relatively even distributions on them. These were sex, socioeconomic status (SES), and geographical region.

Sex was a relatively straightforward matter in that almost no systematic separation of boys and girls either by schools or classrooms existed in the schools in which we were apt to obtain respondents. Thus we were able to rely upon the normal rates of incidence of males and females without further attention in our selection procedures.

SES was less simple in that public schools tend to be somewhat diverse in terms of the social origins of their pupils; but, by taking equal numbers of what were considered by the local school authorities to be "middle-class" and "working-class" schools, we were able to insure no great preponderance of either social class in any given metropolitan area.

For region, our procedure was to divide the country into four major areas—Northeast, North Central, South, and West—and then to select a large and medium-sized city in each region. In a few cases school officials refused to allow us to test in their schools. As a result of their decision, alternative cities had to be chosen.

For reasons both of economy and feasibility, we limited our test population to urban children. Testing of children from the black or other major distinctive ethnic groups, such as the Spanish-American, would have required special instruments and different testers. Economy and feasibility therefore also dictated that we restrict our study to white and English-speaking school children. The target population was conceived therefore as consisting of modal children in elementary schools whose processes of individual political development could serve as a bench mark for future studies. The latter might include especially those types of children deliberately excluded: non-English speaking children, nonwhites, pupils at private and parochial institutions, and those living outside major metropolitan areas. The rationales of exploratory scientific strategy, economy, and feasibility of access therefore suggested a purposely drawn set of subjects (12,052 in the main group) that could serve to identify when (and thus, potentially, under what circumstances) the child begins to acquire political orientations (see Table A-1).

Prior to the selection of this main sample, we carried out a sizable series of pilot and pretest investigations with other respondents in Illinois and Indiana. Both the distribution of respondents in the final test group and that for the pilot and pretest groups are reported in this appendix.

Pilots, pretests, and other data

In addition to the main questionnaire, we developed a series of prior instruments, some of which have been referred to in the text. Two pilot studies preceded the project reported in this book,

Table A-1 Number of Respondents in Final Sample (CA-9) by Region, City Size, SES of the Neighborhood of the School, and Grade in School

			Grade in School						
Region	City Size	SES	2	3	4	5	6	7	8
North-east	Boston (Large)	middle	114	113	107	97	85	104	83
		lower	102	87	106	120	98	125	106
	Portland, Me. (Small)	middle	105	119	109	119	119	103	117
		lower	89	113	120	132	97	119	124
North Central	Chicago (Large)	middle	92	105	110	112	128	107	110
		lower	122	121	120	142	115	125	109
	Sioux City (Small)	middle	91	90	105	98	114	107	115
		lower	96	107	104	111	106	50	44
South	Atlanta (Large)	middle	111	122	120	127	130	112	78
		lower	109	112	108	92	100	102	101
	Jackson (Small)	middle	128	129	134	128	112	121	114
		lower	129	81	111	117	121	101	121
West	San Francisco (Large)	middle	97	91	109	116	120	100	119
		lower	115	116	121	109	121	116	123
	Tacoma (Small)	middle	81	116	110	101	108	94	105
		lower	125	91	100	103	102	122	132

both of which were carried out in 1959. One consisted of a questionnaire administered to approximately eighteen hundred students in grades 9 to 12, and the second a questionnaire filled out by 366 students in grades 2 to 8—both in the Chicago area.

In the project proper the first series of data-collection activities centered in nearly a hundred semistructured individual interviews with children in grades 1 to 8 in the Chicago area. Secondly, children in other schools were asked to draw pictures concerning such subjects as government and citizenship. Thirdly, a dozen different pencil-and-paper questionnaires were developed using a variety of content areas and item formats, including a number of picture-option items found to be relatively successful in engaging younger children. Finally, two supplementary questionnaires were used—one for teachers of the classrooms where our main instrument was administered, and the second a subsequently developed questionnaire mailed to many teachers and concerning the relative amount of attention given to various political subjects in the social studies curriculum.

A list of the pretest and other questionnaires used is as follows:

Table A - 2   (a) Pretest Instruments

Name of Questionnaire	Where Used	Grades	Number of Respondents
Citizen Attitudes no. 3	Arlington Heights, Ill.; East Chicago, Ind.	2 - 8	788
Citizen Attitudes no. 4	Homewood, Ill.; Whiting, Ind.	2, 3, 5, 7	345
Citizen Attitudes no. 5	Gary and Mishawaka, Ind.; Winnetka and Homewood, Ill.	3 - 8	338
Citizen Attitudes no. 6	Hammond, Ind.; Winnetka and Glencoe, Ill.	4, 6, 7, 8	242
Citizen Attitudes no. 7	Park Forest, Ill.; East Chicago, Ind.	3 - 5, 8	314
Citizen Attitudes no. 8 (non CA - 9 portion)	Winnetka, Ill.; Gary, Ind.; Atlanta, Ga.	2 - 8	1297
In My Opinion no. I	Homewood, Ill.; Whiting, Ind.	4, 6, 8	252
In My Opinion no. II	Gary, Mishawaka, and Ham- Ind.; Winnetka and Glencoe, Ill.	4, 6 - 8	471
In My Opinion no. IIIa In My Opinion no. IIIb	Waukegan, Bensonville, Matteson, and Wilmette, Ill.	3 - 8	807
G2 - NR	Park Forest, Ill.; East Chicago, Ind.	2, 3, 6, 7	235
G2 - R		2, 4, 6, 7	235
Rate the Man no. 1	Hammond and Mishawaka, Ind.; Glencoe, Ill.	3 - 5, 7	333
Rate the Man no. 2		3, 5, 7	247
(b) Teacher Instruments			
Teacher Questionnaire (shortened version of CA - 9)	Eight cities	2 - 8	390
Curriculum Questionnaire	Six cities (excluding Jackson and Tacoma)	2 - 8	139

Administration

Questionnaire administration was in general carried out in regular classrooms under the direction of a member of the project staff. Although a single form of the questionnaire was used, not all items were administered to all grades. The items in the questionnaire were arranged in order of appropriateness and difficulty so that children in grade 2 completed only the first sixteen pages of the forty-page instrument and children in grade

3 progressed through the first twenty-four pages. From grade 4 on, all children were asked to answer the whole questionnaire.

For all grades except 7 and 8, the complete questionnaire administered at the given grade was normally read out by the staff member while the children marked their answers. In most cases the teacher remained present and marked his or her own questionnaire. For grades 2 and 3, two former grade school teachers were employed to administer the questionnaire.

At the beginning of the session, the staff member would announce the name of the study, the fact that the questionnaire was an opinion survey rather than examination, and that all respondents would remain anonymous and all answers would be kept confidential. These remarks, of course, were all phrased in language the child could readily understand.

Dates of administration

The dates of administration of the pretests and interviews included most of 1961 and early 1962. The main instrument was administered in late 1961 and early 1962.

Final test questionnaire — Citizen Attitudes no. 9 (CA-9)

A copy of the forty-page questionnaire used for testing the attitudes of our sample of children is on deposit with the ADI Auxiliary Publications Project, Photoduplication Service, Library of Congress, Washington, D.C. 20540. A copy may be obtained by requesting Document no. 9365 and upon payment of a nominal fee. This final questionnaire is identified in our text as Citizen Attitudes no. 9, abbreviated to CA-9.

INDEX

INDEX

This book was set in Vladimir by University Graphics, Inc., printed on permanent paper and bound by The Maple Press Company. The designer was Jack Ellis; the drawings were done by James Harvin. The editors were R. D. Kissack and Helen Greenberg. Robert R. Laffler supervised the production.

988 3476